T0220801

Communications
in Computer and Information Science 1459

More information about this series at http://www.springer.com/series/7899

Boris Villazón-Terrazas ·
Fernando Ortiz-Rodríguez ·
Sanju Tiwari · Ayush Goyal ·
MA Jabbar (Eds.)

Knowledge Graphs and Semantic Web

Third Iberoamerican Conference and
Second Indo-American Conference, KGSWC 2021
Kingsville, Texas, USA, November 22–24, 2021
Proceedings

 Springer

Editors
Boris Villazón-Terrazas ⓘ
Tinamica/Universidad Internacional
de la Rioja
Madrid, Spain

Sanju Tiwari ⓘ
Tamaulipas Autonomous University
Ciudad Victoria, Mexico

MA Jabbar ⓘ
Vardhaman College of Engineering
Hyderabad, Telangana, India

Fernando Ortiz-Rodríguez ⓘ
Tamaulipas Autonomous University
Ciudad Victoria, Mexico

Ayush Goyal ⓘ
Texas A&M University – Kingsville
Kingsville, TX, USA

ISSN 1865-0929 ISSN 1865-0937 (electronic)
Communications in Computer and Information Science
ISBN 978-3-030-91304-5 ISBN 978-3-030-91305-2 (eBook)
https://doi.org/10.1007/978-3-030-91305-2

This Springer imprint is published by the registered company Springer Nature Switzerland AG
The registered company address is: Gewerbestrasse 11, 6330 Cham, Switzerland

Preface

This volume contains the main proceedings of the Third Iberoamerican Knowledge Graph and Semantic Web Conference and the Second Indo-American Knowledge Graphs and Semantic Web Conference (KGSWC 2021), which were held jointly during November 22–24, 2021. KGSWC is established as a yearly venue for discussing the latest scientific results and technology innovations related to knowledge graphs and the Semantic Web. At KGSWC, international scientists, industry specialists, and practitioners meet to discuss knowledge representation, natural language processing/text mining, and machine/deep learning research. The conference's goals are (a) to provide a forum for the AI community, bringing together researchers and practitioners in the industry to share ideas about research and development projects, and (b) to increase the adoption of AI technologies in these regions.

KGSWC 2021 took place virtually from Kingsville, Texas, USA, building on the success of past events in 2019 and 2020. It was also a venue for broadening the focus of the Semantic Web community to span other relevant research areas in which semantics and web technology play an important role and for experimenting with innovative practices and topics that deliver extra value to the community.

The main scientific program of the conference comprised 24 papers: 22 full research papers and two short research papers selected out of 85 reviewed submissions, which corresponds to an acceptance rate of 28.2%. The conference was completed with four workshops, a hackathon, and a winter school where researchers could present their latest results and advances and learn from experts. The program also included five exciting invited keynotes (James Hendler, Amit Sheth, Soren Auer, Pascal Hitzler, and Paco Nathan), with novel Semantic Web topics.

The General and Program Committee chairs would like to thank the many people involved in making KGSWC 2021 a success. First, our thanks go to the local chairs of the main event and to the Program Committee for ensuring a rigorous review process that led to an excellent scientific program with an average of three reviews per paper.

We also had a great selection of workshops and tutors from the winter school. Thanks to our Cuban peers for the continued support of this event and for organizing IWSW 2021: the 4th International Workshop on Semantic Web. We had the opportunity to initiate two workshops in Europe with the support of our colleagues in ENGIE-France (PGMOnto2021: the First International Workshop on Joint Use of Probabilistic Graphical Models and Ontology and IWDLQ2021: the First International Workshop on Deep Learning for Question Answering). Thanks to Patience Usoro Usip for the organization of IWMSW-2021: the First International Workshop on Multilingual Semantic Web. We are also grateful to Amit Sheth's team at the Artificial Intelligence Institute of the University of South Carolina, USA, for the work and commitment involved in organizing the hackathon for the second year in a row.

Further, we thank the kind support of Springer. We also thank Antonio Cardona and Gerardo Haces, who administered the website. We finally thank our sponsors and our community for their vital support of this edition of KGSWC. The editors would like to close the preface with warm thanks to our supporting keynote speakers and our enthusiastic authors who made this event truly international.

November 2021

Boris Villazón-Terrazas
Fernando Ortiz-Rodríguez
Sanju Tiwari
Ayush Goyal
MA Jabbar

Organization

Chairs

Boris Villazón-Terrazas   Tinámica/Universidad Internacional de La Rioja, Spain
Fernando Ortiz-Rodriguez   Universidad Autonoma de Tamaulipas, Mexico
Sanju Tiwari   Universidad Autónoma de Tamaulipas, Mexico

Local Chairs

Ayush Goyal   Texas A&M University – Kingsville, USA
MA Jabbar   Vardhaman College of Engineering, India

Workshops

Shishir Shandilya   VIT Bhopal University, India

Winter School

Sanju Tiwari   Universidad Autónoma de Tamaulipas, Mexico
Fernando Ortiz-Rodriguez   Universidad Autonoma de Tamaulipas, Mexico
Boris Villazón-Terrazas   Tinámica/Universidad Internacional de La Rioja, Spain

Hackathon

Kaushik Roy   University of South Carolina, USA
Manas Gaur   University of South Carolina, USA

Program Committee Chairs

Sanju Tiwari   Universidad Autónoma de Tamaulipas, Mexico
Fernando Ortiz-Rodriguez   Universidad Autonoma de Tamaulipas, Mexico
Boris Villazón-Terrazas   Tinámica/Universidad Internacional de La Rioja, Spain

Program Committee

Aidan Hogan   Universidad de Chile, Chile
Alberto Fernandez   University Rey Juan Carlos, Spain
Alejandro Rodriguez   Universidad Politécnica de Madrid
Amed Abel Leiva Mederos   Universidad Central de las Villas, Cuba
Ana B. Rios-Alvarado   Universidad Autónoma de Tamaulipas, Mexico
Anastasija Ņikiforova   University of Latvia, Latvia
Anna Fensel   University of Innsbruck, Austria

Nandana Mihindukulasooriya	IBM Research, USA
Nelson Piedra	Universidad Técnica Particular de Loja, Ecuador
Nicholas Beliz-Osorio	Universidad Tecnológica de Panamá, Panama
Panos Alexopoulos	Textkernel B.V., The Netherlands
Patience Usoro Usip	University of Uyo, Nigeria
Regina Motz	Universidad de la República, Uruguay
Rim Hantach	ENGIE, France
Roberto Navigli	Sapienza University of Rome, Italy
Rosa M. Rodríguez	University of Jaén, Spain
Russa Biswas	FIZ Karlsruhe, Germany
Samir Sellami	ENSET-Skikda, Algeria
Sanju Tiwari	Universidad Autónoma de Tamaulipas, Mexico
Shikha Mehta	Jaypee Institute, India
Takanori Ugai	Fujitsu Laboratories Ltd., Japan
Tassilo Pellegrini	St. Pölten University of Applied Sciences, Austria
Terunobu Kume	Fujitsu Laboratories Ltd., Japan
Tommaso Soru	University of Leipzig, Germany
Victor Saquicela	Universidad de Cuenca, Ecuador
Yusniel Hidalgo Delgado	Universidad de las Ciencias Informáticas, Cuba
Zarour Nacer Eddine	University of Constantine 2, Algeria

Keynote Abstracts

Knowledge Graph Semantics

James Hendler

Institute for Data Exploration and Applications, Rensselaer Polytechnic Institute

Oh dear, there's that word again – "semantics!" Isn't that what doomed that Semantic Web thing and led to knowledge graphs instead? In fact, many of the same problems, and particularly problems with interoperability, arise again for KGs, and thus we must explore the old problem in this new area. This is even more important when we start to explore the "personal knowledge graph (PKG)," that is, the ability to have private and public information combined in KG technology. In this talk, I discuss how knowledge graphs, PJGs, linked data and, yes, semantics are all critically linked and why the latter is still relevant to the growth and scaling of knowledge graphs into the future - and specifically to the ability to extract better data from them.

Don't Handicap AI without Explicit Knowledge

Amit Sheth

AI Institute at the University of South Carolina

Knowledge representation as expert system rules or using frames and variety of logics, played a key role in capturing explicit knowledge during the hay days of AI in the past century. Such knowledge, aligned with planning and reasoning are part of what we refer to as Symbolic AI. The resurgent AI of this century in the form of Statistical AI has benefitted from massive data and computing. On some tasks, deep learning methods have even exceeded human performance levels. This gave the false sense that data alone is enough, and explicit knowledge is not needed. But as we start chasing machine intelligence that is comparable with human intelligence, there is an increasing realization that we cannot do without explicit knowledge. Neuroscience (role of long-term memory, strong interactions between different specialized regions of data on tasks such as multimodal sensing), cognitive science (bottom brain versus top brain, perception versus cognition), brain-inspired computing, behavioral economics (system 1 versus system 2), and other disciplines point to need for furthering AI to neuro-symbolic AI (i.e., hybrid of Statistical AI and Symbolic AI, also referred to as the third wave of AI). As we make this progress, the role of explicit knowledge becomes more evident. I will specifically look at our endeavor to support higher-level intelligence than what current AI systems support, our desire for AI systems to interact with humans naturally, and our need to explain the path and reasons for AI systems' workings. Nevertheless, the variety of knowledge needed to support understanding and intelligence is varied and complex. Using the example of progressing from NLP to NLU, I will demonstrate varieties of explicit knowledge (represented as knowledge graphs), which may include, linguistic, language syntax, common sense, general (world model), specialized (e.g., geographic), and domain-specific (e.g., mental health) knowledge. I will also argue that despite this complexity, such knowledge can be scalability created and maintained (even dynamically or continually). Finally, I will describe our work on knowledge-infused learning as an example strategy for fusing statistical and symbolic AI in a variety of ways.

Graph Thinking

Paco Nathan

Managing Partner at Derwen, Inc.

In an effort to bridge between current research and industry practices for graph technologies, a few observations help. First, recent innovations such as graph neural networks provide immediate solutions in business use cases for inference which have perplexed the semantic web community for decades. Second, given more stringent reproducibility requirements for researchers to publish source code and datasets alongside peer-reviewed papers, a skills gap emerges in the crucial area of open source integration. Third, while currently there are more than 30 vendors in the graph database space, and data management is of course quite important, lessons from the arc of Big Data circa 2006–2015 indicate that demands for scalable graph computation outpace the supply focused on database-centric approaches – as industry use cases confirm. These factors are disruptive for current industry narratives, as we shall explore in the talk. They also represent substantial opportunities for the research community.

Since the late–2010s, business use cases for graph technologies have become more widespread. Along with that, a practice of graph data science has emerged, blending graph capabilities into existing data science teams and industry training curricula. However, these nascent practices tend to face common hurdles: (1) enterprise IT staff who are familiar with relational databases yet unfamiliar with graph use cases, so they tend to discourage the latter (turf wars); (2) the fact that graph practices in industry at generally must cut across company divisions and lines of executive responsibility – e.g., where an enterprise knowledge graph integrates data from logistics, research, and market analysis to provide a "business 360" for top execs – so this tends to alarm mid-level executives (more turf wars); and (3) graph database vendors tenaciously concerned with database features and corresponding lock-in for licensing strategies that don't scale effectively, while generally less concerned with horizontal scale-out for graph computing (the turf wars to come).

Taking inventory of these observations and hurdles commonly encountered, enterprise graph practices are being pushed toward open source integration to obtain effective technology solutions. That said, other challenges remain for graph technologies which can be described in terms of behavioral economics. The academic community should become more fully aware about these points in particular. This talk explores current solutions and near-term outlook including: (1) graph thinking as a cognitive framework for approaching complex problem spaces; (2) open source integration as the key both for viable industry practices as well as an essential pathway for validation of academic research; and (3) a survey of industry use cases aside from the "usual suspects" of advertising, e-commerce, social networks, and financialization.

One overall theme emerges from these arguments: whereas data science use cases from a decade ago tended to focus on extractive business models and "low-hanging fruit" such as online marketing or financialization, the graph data science uses have veered away from the tech giants, focusing instead on more complex industry problems: waste mining and circular economy in the manufacturing, network medicine and personalized drug discovery in pharma, identifying obfuscated cyber attacks in security, tracking carbon footprint across thousands of vendors in global supply chain, and so on. This talk will explore the inherent connections between graph technologies and complexity, along with what learnings can be applied to AI from more established work in pedagogy, behavioral economics, and leadership. NB: core parts of this material were prepared during a 2021 independent assessment of the graph technologies space, conducted on behalf of a large EU-based manufacturing firm, and the approaches described here have been developed working with business units in the context of their production practices.

Building Knowledge Graphs Leveraging Expert, Crowd and Machine Intelligence

Soren Auer and Allard Oelen

Director TIB, Head of Research Group Data Science and Digital Libraries

The Need for a Scholarly Knowledge Graph. The amount of published scholarly articles remains to grow steadily every year. Therefore, new methods are needed to organize this growing number of publications. Traditionally, scholarly communication is largely document-based, hindering machine-actionability of the presented knowledge. If scholarly knowledge is provided in a structured format, via knowledge graphs, the knowledge becomes readable for machines. This addresses, and largely resolves, the issues scholarly communication currently faces. However, creating such a knowledge graph is a complicated endeavor. Automated techniques, possibly powered by machine learning, are currently not sufficiently accurate to autonomously create a high-quality knowledge graph. The quality aspect of the graph is crucial for it to become a valuable tool for researchers. On the other hand, a fully manual approach, in which humans create structured paper descriptions, does not scale well to large quantities of papers. A hybrid approach can solve the quality issues of the automated approach while also addressing the scalability issues of the manual approach. In this hybrid approach, human intelligence is supported by machine intelligence to create a scalable high-quality knowledge graph.

Open Research Knowledge Graph. The Open Research Knowledge Graph (ORKG) is a scholarly knowledge graph that contains high-quality manually curated scholarly knowledge. In contrast to other scholarly knowledge graphs, the data in the ORKG represents the actual knowledge presented in the paper, instead of merely metadata. This includes knowledge related to research problems, materials, methods, and results. This structured data is used to semi-automatically create overviews of the state-of-the-art. These overviews are called "comparisons" in the ORKG. Comparisons can be used for different purposes, for example, to compare results of different approaches to the same research problem (i.e., leader boards), to show an overview of the transformation of research results over time, or to provide comprehensive summaries of related work.

The ORKG leverages crowdsourcing to populate the graph. At the core, users (who are generally researchers) enter data related to their work and publications. They collaborate with knowledge engineers, which includes subject librarians, to determine what to describe and how to describe this. This includes the generation of "Graph templates", a construct to unify different contribution descriptions for papers addressing the same research problem. Research can be organized in ORKG observatories which address a specific set of research problems maintained by researchers and domain experts for the respective research field.

Human and Machine Intelligence. Within the ORKG, multiple approaches are used to populate the graph. As previously mentioned, the ORKG does not use manual or automated approaches in isolation but leverages hybrid forms instead. This includes machine-in-the-loop and human-in-the-loop approaches. In the former approach, the machine assists the user, while in the latter approach the human assists the machine. For the machine-in-the-loop approach, the human initiates the process of adding new content to the graph and intelligent machine components assist the user while doing so. The ORKG leverages this approach at several locations, including the "Abstract annotator", which extracts scientific concepts from a user-provided abstract. The user can decide which concepts to add and which to remove. This approach is also used in the "Sentence annotator" in which the user is assisted by an intelligent user interface to annotate key sentences within a scholarly article. The intelligent components include key sentence highlighting and annotation class suggestions.

Finally, a human-in-the-loop approach is used in a novel ORKG feature that is currently under development. This feature autonomously processes scholarly article abstracts at scale using a set of different Natural Language Processing (NLP) tools. The resulting data from the NLP processing will be validated by humans in the form of microtasks. Each task presents an easy to answer, for example asking the user whether a displayed statement is correct or not. User votes are stored as provenance data on the statements, allowing others to evaluate the credibility and correctness of a statement based on the user votes. We envision that any ORKG user, whether it is an incidental visitor or a researcher, can vote on statements and that aggregating all votes provides a scalable and high-quality method for validating scholarly NLP data.

Modular Schema Development for Wikibase

Pascal Hitzler

Endowed Lloyd T. Smith Creativity in Engineering Chair and Director of the
Center for Artificial Intelligence and Data Science at Kansas State University

Wikibase - the software that underlies Wikidata - provides excellent support for knowledge graph construction. Key features include an intuitive MediaWiki interface, native support for context (qualifiers) and provenance (references), and compatibility with W3C standards, in particular RDF. Originally developed for the open crowd-sourced setting of Wikidata, it can also be used for knowledge graph development in more controlled use cases. However, if the use case calls for a tightly defined graph schema in the form of a traditional ontology, it is not immediately clear how to do traditional ontology development such that it is compatible with the modeling and graph structuring choices of Wikibase. In this talk, we will report on our recent efforts to close the gap between traditional ontology engineering and Wikibase. Drawing from our experiences in the Enslaved project which uses both ontology modeling and Wikibase to realize a database on the history of the slave trade, we present a solution based on ontology design patterns that closes the gap between the two approaches and thus enables ontology design that can then be used directly with Wikibase.

Contents

InDO: the Institute Demographic Ontology

Neha Keshan[(✉)], Kathleen Fontaine, and James A. Hendler

Rensselaer Polytechnic Institute, New York, USA
{keshan,fontak}@rpi.edu, hendler@cs.rpi.edu

Abstract. Graduate education institutes in the United States (US) have been working on programs to increase the number of students and faculty from marginalized communities. When choosing to pursue a doctoral degree, the common question is 'where is the best fit for me?' Aspiring graduate students may feel the need for a reference point - someone with a similar background who has experienced or is currently experiencing the doctoral process, whether that be a student or a faculty member. Currently, there is no single location where that question can be answered for those in marginal communities, however answering that question also has an impact on the student's post-graduation career path. In lieu of a single person, and to help provide information critical to answering the question, we built the Institute Demographic Ontology (InDO). InDO integrates US graduate institute's doctoral recipient demographic data with data describing broad field of study, fine field of study, and the pursued career path to produce a knowledge graph for each prospective student's query. The terminology is structured in five levels of hierarchy providing room for the most abstract top level (basic components used to describe an institute's demographics), to the most concrete bottom levels (particular graduate program offered by the institute, along with corresponding provenance). Our resource (InDO) could be used by students within a marginalized community in the US to infer whether a given institute has the resources to support a given program, based on demographic information such as number of doctorates awarded in a given field. We design a use case where an InDO-based knowledge graph is created incorporating some of the National Science Foundation (NSF) Doctoral Recipient Survey 2019 data. Our use case demonstrates the usage of InDO in the real world while providing a way to access NSF data in a machine readable format. Evaluation of our ontology is done with a set of competency questions created from the perspective of an aspirant marginalized graduate student who would be willing to use our system to gather information for making an informed decision. InDO provides an ontological foundation towards building a social machine as an aid to higher education and graduate mobility in the US.
Resource Website:
https://tetherless-world.github.io/institute-demographic-ontology

Keywords: Ontology · Knowledge graph · Institute demographics · Graduate mobility · NSF doctoral recipients survey data

© Springer Nature Switzerland AG 2021
B. Villazón-Terrazas et al. (Eds.): KGSWC 2021, CCIS 1459, pp. 1–15, 2021.
https://doi.org/10.1007/978-3-030-91305-2_1

1   Introduction

Doctoral programs are challenging for all students, but can be more challenging for students from marginalized communities - groups of students excluded based on ethnicity, race, linguistic, gender identity, age, physical ability, and/or immigration status [1,2]. It is seen that marginalized students might have to go an extra mile to prove their worth [1,2]. A study run under Rensselaer Polytechnic Institute's IRB #1924 demonstrated that the lack of a reference - someone who has had a similar experience - was one of the major challenges impacting the student's graduate experience [3] (for this study graduate experience refers to the experience during doctoral study). The survey analysis also suggested that lack of a reference contributed to graduate mobility as well (for this study graduate mobility refers to transition from being a student towards their chosen career path). For example, students stated they felt lost as to available career paths after graduation. They also indicated having difficulties with getting proper guidance due to their demographic. From these survey responses, we can infer that the preparation of graduate mobility doesn't start when one is approaching graduation, but rather much earlier, perhaps even during the time of program selection. We anticipate that to help students have a smooth transition, it is important for the students to have an adequate amount of program information. The information should include past doctoral recipient demographics and the career paths they chose. Students can then use the provided information along with the general program ranking to make an informed decision. The literature survey (Sect. 2) suggests most of the issues can be mitigated by providing required resources catered towards marginalized groups.

Potential mitigating solutions fall into three main areas - 1) understanding the demographics of an institute's doctoral students; 2) understanding the career paths these doctoral students take; and 3) understanding the social and communication habits of the students within and outside of their communities. The statistics would produce demographic information for marginalized groups. Further information could be gleaned on whether the institute has created programs supporting those groups, including those associated with career planning and social networking. Creating a resource to realize a system that satisfies all the above stated components would require a knowledge system that is able to pull and integrate information from different places. Information about a given institute can be accessed through their website, through articles on the web and via multiple surveys conducted by the National Science Foundation (NSF) and the Council of Graduate Schools (CGS). Because the information is so distributed and heterogeneous, though, a semantic solution should be applied.

We built the Institute Demographic Ontology (InDO) consisting of 99 classes across 5 levels. InDO is modelled around the institute's doctoral recipient demographics in both broad and fine fields of studies, all while incorporating the provenance of the shared information. The hierarchy allows an aspiring graduate student to understand how many of the past doctoral student recipients from a program were from their community (suggesting that the program and its resources may be structured to incorporate their needs), and the career paths those doctoral students chose (providing them with knowledge of career training options). Five levels of hierarchy in the ontology allow the users to get both abstract/generic and concrete/specific information of the institute's demographic. We used Protégé-5.5.0 to create our ontology and knowledge graph. We used Hermit and Pellet reasoners on our built ontology and knowledge graph for logical consistencies. We used Blazegraph Workbench to run the SPARQL queries on our built knowledge graph. To test the feasibility of the ontology we decided to integrate a part of the published NSF 2019 Doctoral Recipients Survey data (henceforth referred to as NSF results) [4]. The NSF results consists of hundreds of data points across 95 tables. Currently, we have added 538 of those data points as a test to create our knowledge graph. These 538 instances comprises of the entire NSF results Table 1 - Doctorate Recipients from U.S. Universities:2019 (total doctoral recipients from 1958 to 2019), entire NSF results Table 3 - Top 50 doctorate-granting institutions ranked by total number of doctorate recipients, by sex: 2019 and, a part of NSF results Table 4 - Top 20 doctorate-granting institutions ranked by total number of doctorate recipients, by broad field of study and sex: 2019 (currently contains data points for Life Sciences and MathemeticsAndComputerSciences). The current instance would help a student to understand the overall demographic for the top 50 US doctoral granting institute and the top 20 doctoral granting institute in Science domain in a binary gender form, along with seeing a trend of the total number of doctoral recipient from a US institute from the year 1958 to 2019.

1.1 Contributions

We make the following contributions in this paper as an aid to marginalized graduate students:

1. A consolidated Institute Demographic Ontology to allow users to extract both general and specific information.
2. A knowledge graph integrating data points from NSF 2019 Doctoral Survey and web.
3. A resource website[1] for more information on our ontology, its creation, and usage. The resource website also hosts the created ontology and knowledge graph for our users to download and use for various purposes based on the provided guidelines. In addition, the website provides links to the tools used and the detailed SPARQL queries to acquire data presented in Sect. 5.

2 Background and Related Works

A plethora of work [5–7] has been done on the experiences of marginalized students from a social science perspective. These works provide insight into how

---

[1] https://tetherless-world.github.io/institute-demographic-ontology.

a challenging graduate journey becomes even more challenging for students from the marginalized communities [8]. For example, students from minority groups experience less access to mentors and role-models and more isolation than their non-minority peers [8]. The level of challenge increases for those falling under multiple marginalized communities [1,9]. The authors in [9] discuss issues and support strategies for African-American women in higher education. Issues include the lack of critical mass of African-American women in higher education, the impact of a gender gap, and the lack of black faculty. Support strategies include providing more resources for programs to help the female African-American community. Research suggests that there is a clear need for a single, comprehensive resource to help members of marginalized communities navigate challenging graduate experiences. Creating such a resource becomes vital, especially today when the required information from which to extract knowledge is spread across the web in structured, semi-structured, and unstructured data formats. This single, comprehensive resource would need to access demographic information regarding doctoral students by institute, as well as the chosen career paths.

The University Ontology[2], an ontology which can be considered as the closest work form to our research, consists of university concepts including faculty, student and staff information, affiliation, and department. The University Ontology doesn't define the demographic of an individual, however, nor does it include a mechanism to store the number of doctoral recipients of an institute in a given year. Two of the most prominent ontologies incorporating demographics are NCI Thesaurus (NCIT) OBO Edition [10] and the Children's Health Exposure Analysis Resource (CHEAR) ontology [11]. The NCIT ontology is catered towards the cancer domain while the CHEAR ontology is catered towards childrens' health with respect to environmental exposure. The Job Description Ontology (JDO) [12] relates to our section of career paths. JDO is inspired from job position schema and segregates the job description from the job position concepts. Even though there are multiple resources that could help store and present a section of the data for marginalized community students, we could not find one existing ontology that could either directly, or by extension, fulfill the requirement of a comprehensive resource. The missing comprehensive ontology inspired us to create one by leveraging already existing ontologies. Even when an ontology provides us with the taxonomy and is helpful, it is important to create a knowledge graph by adding instances to the ontology for maximizing the ontologies usage. The knowledge graphs survey articles [13–15] discuss the applications, problems, challenges, refinement, and evaluation of knowledge graphs while stating how they can be created using unstructured, semi-structured or structured data. These surveys provide information on some already-used methods of creating and evaluating knowledge graphs from tables.

---

[2] http://swat.cse.lehigh.edu/onto/univ-bench.owl.

3   Institute Demographics Ontology Modeling

Web resources exist describing doctoral programs offered by a given institute, be it on the institute's web page, other social media platforms, or through survey results published by various organizations. It is challenging to infer knowledge from the available heterogeneous scattered data, especially if the data are sparse and not machine readable. These challenges highlight the need for a semantic representation of an institute's doctoral student demographics and post-graduate plans. In designing our "Institute Demographic Ontology" (InDO), we have used both a bottom-up and top-down modeling approach [16]. We undertook the bottom-up approach to primarily identify by institute the various demographic groups, study fields and their definitions in the literature. We utilize the literature review and NSF results [4] as a base for our ontology modeling. The top-down approach was used to refine the modeling by analyzing the usage of different statistical information that would be of help to aspiring graduate student users.

Table 1. List of ontology prefixes used in the paper.

Ontology prefix	Ontology	URI
sio	SemanticScience Integrated Ontology	http://semanticscience.org/resource
indo	Institute Demographic Ontology	http://www.semanticweb.org/neha/ontologies/2021/5/indo#

3.1   Ontology Composition

Our ontology is designed around the central institute class (indo:Institute). We include the entities and attributes based on the factors affecting graduate mobility. These factors were based on the information gathered through the literature survey and the available heterogeneous resources. As discussed earlier, we modeled our ontology in a five-level hierarchy system to allow our users to get as general as the institute's overall doctoral recipients statistics or as specific as the fine field of study statistics. Figure 1 represents the top-level conceptual diagram of our ontology depicting the major classes. Table 1 lists ontology prefixes used in our ontology to refer to classes and properties. Currently the system is modeled to store the statistical values for each class (sio:hasValue) but can be expanded to incorporate any other information related to an institute.

3.1.1   Class Institute Modeling

As discussed earlier, our ontology is designed around the main Institute class. Each class and attribute is introduced as necessary to construct a model of the institute's doctoral recipient information. We note that all the required institute statistics are based on its demographics (indo:DoctoralRecipients) and the graduate programs (indo:FieldOfStudy) it offers. Figure 2 provides the conceptual diagram of our Institute class modeling.

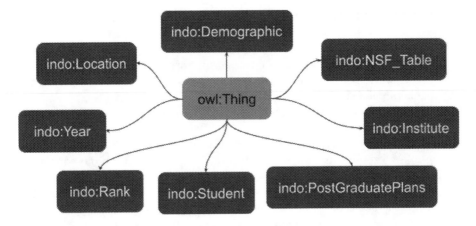

Fig. 1. A conceptual diagram depicting the top-level classes of our Institute Demographic Ontology.

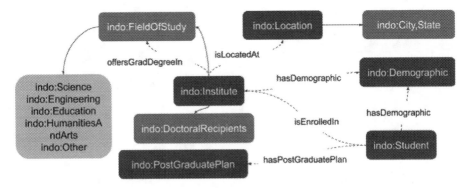

Fig. 2. A conceptual overview of our Institute Demographic Ontology's institute class. The arrows depict the subclass relationship between classes while the dashed arrows depict the property association between two classes.

3.1.2 Class Demographics Modeling

Since InDO is a part of the ongoing project of incorporating the concept of a social machine in decision making support tools to assist marginalized students in graduate education and mobility [3], we based our demographic class (indo:Demographics) modeling on our definition of the term 'marginalized' and on the terminology used in the published NSF results. For this study, the term 'marginalized' is defined as a group of students excluded based on ethnicity, race, linguistics, gender identity, age, physical ability, and/or immigration status. Figure 3 represents the three levels of component hierarchies of demographics included in the ontology.

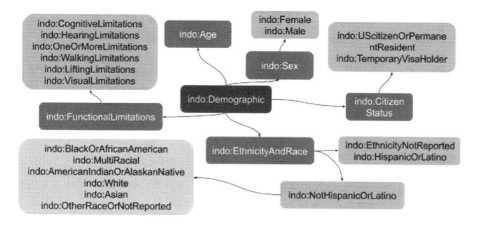

Fig. 3. A conceptual overview of the class Demographic depicting the subclass hierarchies. The different colors represent the classes in the same hierarchy.

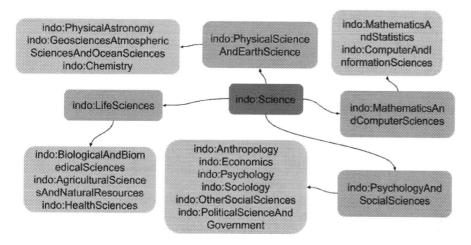

Fig. 4. A conceptual overview of class Science (part of the third-level hierarchy of our ontology) representing the subclass relationship. Colors represents classes of the same hierarchy level.

3.1.3   Class Fine Field of Study Modeling

To help a student from a marginalized community find specific information regarding a particular program, it is important for our ontology to be as specific as possible. We therefore divide the entire field of study (indo:FieldOfStudy) into the major domains inspired by the terminology used in the published NSF results - Science, Engineering, Humanities and Arts, Education and Others. Each of these is then divided into broad field of study which is further sorted based on fine field of study. The created structure provides a three-level hierarchy to accommodate the maximum possible number of graduate programs offered by an institute. For example, Life Science (indo:LifeSciences), a broad field of study, becomes a part of the science domain (indo:Science), and can have biological and biomedical sciences (indo:BiologicalAndBiomedicalSciences) or agricultural sciences (indo:AgriculturalSciences) as its fine fields. A conceptual overview for Science domain is represented in Fig. 4.

3.1.4   Provenance

With all kinds of information available all over the web, it is vital to know the source of the information. Ontologies and knowledge graphs provide a mechanism to maintain provenance, hence we leverage this feature for our ontology InDO. For example, every data point taken from the NSF 2019 Doctoral Recipient Survey results has the corresponding table number and the year added to it, providing the source point for the provided demographic and post-doctorate mobility statistics.

4   NSF Doctoral Recipients Survey 2019 Use Case

We demonstrate the use of InDO by designing and ingesting NSF 2019 Doctoral Survey Recipients data (henceforth referred to as NSF results) [4]. We assume that this information could be beneficial for an aspiring graduate student to find US institutes that have prior experience in training and graduating doctoral students from their marginalized community. Figure 5 illustrates the general process of converting the semi-structured NSF Tables to machine readable form as our knowledge graph instances. As a proof of concept, we have integrated 538 data points from NSF results Table 1, NSF results Table 3 and a part of NSF results Table 4 with some additional information about the institute's location from the web.

Table 1 of the NSF results includes the US graduate institutes' total number of doctoral recipients for the years 1958 to 2019. Each of these years becomes an instance of the class year (indo:Year) and the corresponding values become an instance of the class doctoral recipients (indo:DoctoralRecipients). These two instances are connected through the indo:hadDoctoralRecipients relation. One could easily plot an overview of the trend of number of doctoral recipients from US institutes.

NSF results Table 3 provides the information for the top 50 doctorate granting institutes in the US ranked by total number of doctorate recipients and some overall gender demographics. The table includes the institute's name (indo:Institute), its rank (indo:Rank), total doctoral recipients (indo:DoctoralRecipients) in 2019 (indo:Year), how many of them were male (indo:Male) and how many of them were female (indo:Female). The knowledge graph is built to incorporate various scenarios, such as displaying the information of institutes with the same rank but a different male-female ratio, so that the users can have accurate information to make an informed decision. The knowledge graph also stores the institute's location in the form of the state and the city to help students gather information of all the institutes by location of interest.

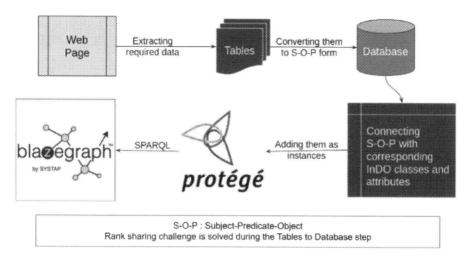

Fig. 5. An overview of the process of adding data to a knowledge graph using InDO.

NSF results Table 4 provides information for the top 20 doctorate-granting institutes in the US ranked by total number of doctoral recipients by broad field of study and sex. From this we get the demographic information for an institute program in the broad field of study. For example, suppose a female user Y who is a Life Science doctoral aspirant and is looking to get into a program in Institute X. Since Institute X is a part of both NSF Table 3 and NSF Table 4, our user Y will be able to see the overall doctoral recipients for Institute X in 2019, as well as how many of those were female. If this number is high then user Y can infer that Institute X's resources are in some way geared towards her needs. The user could also get the total number of doctoral recipients for 2019 from NSF results Table 1 and calculate the percentage of doctorate recipients for Institute X based on overall recipients. Now since our user Y is a Life Science doctoral aspirant, she could receive the information about the total number of doctoral recipients from Institute X from Life Science program. She could also query how many of those were females, indicating how well Institute X might meet the needs of her marginalized group in her field of interest.

We ran SPARQL queries on Blazegraph Workbench for the provided competency questions (Sect. 5) against our created knowledge graph with above discussed NSF results to demonstrate a way to use the provided resources.

5   Evaluation

We evaluate our ontology through a set of competency questions created from the perspective of an aspiring graduate student from a marginal community who may need to gather required information to make an informed decision of where to enroll. Some of these competency questions are also based on the questions asked over multiple social platforms and through discussions with graduate students.

In our example, a female student wants to understand the demographic of the doctoral recipients for University of California, Berkeley to make a decision on whether to enroll in their Mathematics and Computer Science doctoral program.

Please refer to our resource website[3] for detailed SPARQL queries and corresponding responses. The following are a set of competency questions with references to the candidate responses produced by our ontology:

1. A given year's total doctoral recipients from US institutes between 1958 and 2019. For example, how many total doctoral recipients were there from 1960–62 and 2016–19 from US institutes? (candidate response shown in Fig. 6).
2. US institute that graduated the most doctorates in a given year and the binary gender representation of those students. For example, what is the US Institute with the maximum doctoral recipients in 2019 and how many of them were females? (candidate response shown in Fig. 7)
3. Number of <marginalized community> doctoral recipients from institutes at a given location. For example, provide the number of female doctoral recipients from institutes in California. (candidate response shown in Fig. 8)
4. Institute with the most doctoral students in a given field of study. How many of those were from their marginalized community? For example, how many female doctoral recipients in 2019 were from University of California Berkeley, in Mathematics and Computer Science graduate program?(candidate response shown in Fig. 9).
5. The percentage of <marginalized group> doctoral recipients in a particular institute or its program in a given year? (response provided rounded off to nearest integer). This could also be used to compare the <marginalized community> percentages among programs or institutes. For example, what was the percentage of female doctoral recipients from University of California, Berkeley and Walden University in 2019? (candidate response shown in Fig. 10).

Year	DoctoralRecipients	NSFTable
1960	9733	NSF Table 1 Doctoral Recipients US Universities 2019
1961	10413	NSF Table 1 Doctoral Recipients US Universities 2019
1962	11500	NSF Table 1 Doctoral Recipients US Universities 2019
2016	54809	NSF Table 1 Doctoral Recipients US Universities 2019
2017	54554	NSF Table 1 Doctoral Recipients US Universities 2019
2018	55103	NSF Table 1 Doctoral Recipients US Universities 2019
2019	55703	NSF Table 1 Doctoral Recipients US Universities 2019

Fig. 6. Competency question 1 example SPARQL query output obtained on Blazegraph Workbench.

[3] https://tetherless-world.github.io/institute-demographic-ontology.

The first competency question extracts the knowledge regarding the total number of doctoral recipients from US institutes for year range 1958–2019. The question resolves into a simple query if we want to get the entire data, or the data points can be filtered out using the FILTER command in our Query for specific years as used for the example in Fig. 6.

Institute	Rank	TotalDoctoralRecipients	Female
UniversityOfCaliforniaBerkeley	1	864	218

Fig. 7. Competency question 2 example SPARQL query output obtained on Blazegraph Workbench.

Institute	TotalDoctoralRecipients	Female
UniversityOfCaliforniaBerkeley	864	372
UniversityOfCaliforniaLosAngeles	701	311
UniversityOfCaliforniaDavis	521	240
UniversityOfCaliforniaSanDiego	492	118
UniversityOfCaliforniaIrvine	407	163
StanfordUniversity	770	279

Fig. 8. Competency question 3 example SPARQL query output obtained on Blazegraph Workbench.

Institute	TotDocRec	OfferedDegree	TotalInDegree	FemaleInDegree
UniversityOfCaliforniaBerkeley	864	MathematicsAndComputerScience	181	21

Fig. 9. Competency question 4 example SPARQL query output obtained on Blazegraph Workbench.

The second competency question allows to find the US institute with most doctoral recipients and their demographics. This requires data points from NSF results Table 3. The provided example (Fig. 7) provides 2019's maximum doctoral recipient US institute, the total number of doctoral recipients from University of California, Berkeley and how many of those were females.

The third competency question allows a user to find the doctoral institutes at a particular US location (state or city), the total doctorates from those institutes in a given year, and how many of them were from their community. The provided

Institute	TotDocRec	FemaleInDegree	PerFemaleDR
UniversityOfCaliforniaBerkeley	864	372	43
WaldenUniversity	820	557	67

Fig. 10. Competency question 5 example SPARQL query output obtained on Blazegraph Workbench.

example (Fig. 8) tells us the number of female doctorates from institutes in California (institutes who are a part of top 50 institutes based on the total number of doctoral recipients in 2019), along with the total number of doctorates from those institutes. This information comes from NSF results Table 3 and the integrated location information from the web.

The fourth competency question allows a student to get information regarding the demographic of a broad field of study offered by the US institute. In our example, (Fig. 9) the query combines data points from NSF results Table 3 and NSF results Table 4 to provide the total doctorates from University of California, Berkeley, total doctorates in their Mathematics and Computer Science program and how many of them were females.

The fifth competency question provides the percentage of the doctoral recipients from their marginalized group from a given institute. The student could either get this percentage for a specific field of study or for the institute itself. The student can also find the percentage of total doctoral recipients at an institute with respect to the overall doctoral recipients from the US in a given year. This provides a better comparison between the two programs. In our example, we see that Walden University had 820 doctoral recipients in 2019 in comparison to the University of California, Berkeley which had 864 doctoral recipients. The percentage of female graduates shows that even when WU is ranked below UCB in terms of total doctoral recipients, 67% of the WU recipients were females compared to UCB's 43%. The percentage in the example query result provided (Fig. 10) is rounded off to the nearest integer. This utilizes a complex SPARQL query and can be found in our resource website[4].

6   Discussion

To address the gap in the availability of an institute's graduate student demographic information in a machine readable format, we designed an OWL ontology, the Institute Demographic Ontology (InDO), that could be used by students from marginalized community to gather relevant information towards making an informed decision. We demonstrate the use of InDO by creating a knowledge graph using the NSF 2019 Doctoral Recipient Survey data currently available in table format. We create our ontology by leveraging the widely-used general

---

[4] https://tetherless-world.github.io/institute-demographic-ontology.

purpose ontology - SIO. The modeling is inspired by the available ontologies - University (for institutes) and CHEAR ontology (for demographics) - and our knowledge of the use of demographics based on its applications. The classes and properties are introduced as necessary for the system to provide both generic and specific information regarding the institutes demographics.

We understand that gender identity is a sensitive issue and needs to be very carefully addressed to respect and make our system inclusive. The biggest challenge was to gather data that represents the entire gender family. In our research we understood that most of the information to date has been gathered using the binary Male/Female options and its evolving to incorporate individual gender identity. We addressed the issue by creating an extensible ontology. InDO currently represents the binary gender based on the NSF results, but can be extended to incorporate the entire gender family. We are also constantly looking for a much more robust dataset that correctly represents the gender identities of doctoral recipients from US institutes.

The second biggest challenge was to convert the NSF results into a machine readable form. The NSF results provided institute rankings based on the number of doctoral recipients (if two or more institutes had the same number of total doctoral students then they were ranked the same). Having the same rank did not mean that they had the same demographics, however. Let us take examples from the NSF results Table 3 data points. We see that both the University of Michigan, Ann Arbor (UMAA) and the University of Texas, Austin (UTA) share rank 3 as a doctorate-granting institute in US with 801 total doctoral recipients. Even though they share the same rank, UMAA's 801 doctoral recipients is comprised of 465 Males and 336 Females while UTA has 473 Males and 327 Females. We addressed this issue by connecting all the institutes sharing the same rank with the same rank instance while creating a separate demographic instance for each of the institutes. We also recognize that providing information based on just the total doctoral recipients rank could be deceptive for our aspiring graduate student users. For example, the University of California, Berkeley (UCB), ranked 1 with 864 doctoral recipients in 2019, had 492 males and 372 females, whereas Walden University (WU) ranked 2 with 820 doctoral recipients had 263 males and 557 females. Investigating the resources at WU would be more helpful for our female aspirant if the choice is between UCB and WU since the number of WU female recipients is higher. Currently, we add instances through Protégé-5.5.0 to our ontology to create the knowledge graph and test the logical consistencies using Pellet reasoner.

7   Conclusion

In this paper, we discussed the challenges marginalized graduate students face when trying to gather sufficient information to make their graduate experience a productive one. Currently, such information is distributed across heterogeneous resources and needs integration to be useful. In this case, using semantics tools, especially an ontology and knowledge graph, is the best solution. We demonstrated the use of our resource using NSF results and shared the SPARQL query outputs for the competency question examples.

In particular, we provide a comprehensive and flexible ontology which could help in converting available NSF Doctoral Recipient survey data into a machine readable form making it more useful for the community to work with. Our ontology also provides a way to gather and display all of the available data from an institute in one place, from graduate student or program specific demographics to post-graduate career paths. The Institute Demographic Ontology is designed to be easily extended to accommodate other factors and resources required for graduate education and mobility focusing on marginalized communities. Though the focus of this work is on students in marginalized communities, the application of InDO is more inclusive and could be used by anyone who would want to get the same information.

Future work includes building a semi-automated process to populate our knowledge graph with all the available NSF doctoral recipients survey data along with data from other available sources. The created knowledge graph would then be used as a basis for the tool assisting marginalized graduate students [3]. The initial focus of our work is with institutes within the United States. We hope to demonstrate in future how users in other countries can use InDO. Along with this, we hope to more fully address maintainability of InDO as well as the dynamic nature of the survey data, perhaps through a controlled versioning process. In addition, we will explore increasing the representation of other marginalized communities by bringing in more sources that extend the ontology to handle the needs of students dealing with gender bias, physical disabilities, and other issues.

Acknowledgement. This work is part of the "Building a Social Machine for Graduate Mobility" project and is supported in part by the Rensselaer-IBM Artificial Intelligence Research Collaboration. We would like to thank all the participants of the RPI IRB study #1924 that provided more insights into the graduate mobility gap. We would also like to thank Dean Stanley Dunn, Dean of Graduate Education, who provided expert insights into this issue. We would also like to thank the members of the Tetherless World Constellation at RPI who provided insights into this research.

References

1. Gay, G.: Navigating marginality enroute to the professoriate: graduate students of color learning and living in academia. Int. J. Qual. Stud. Educ. **17**(2), 265–288 (2004)
2. Sevelius, J.M., et al.: Research with marginalized communities: challenges to continuity during the Covid-19 pandemic. AIDS Behav. **24**(7), 2009–2012 (2020)
3. Keshan, N.: Building a social machine for graduate mobility. In: 13th ACM Web Science Conference 2021, pp. 156–157 (2021)
4. Foley, D.: Survey of Doctorate Recipients, 2019. NSF 21–230. National Center for Science and Engineering Statistics (NCSES), National Science Foundation, Alexandria (2021). https://ncses.nsf.gov/pubs/nsf21320/

5. Thomas, K.N., Willis, L.A., Davis, J.: Mentoring minority graduate students: issues and strategies for institutions, faculty, and students. Equ. Oppor. Int. **26**, 178–192 (2007)
6. McGee Jr., R.: Saran, S., Krulwich. T.A.: Diversity in the biomedical research workforce: developing talent. Mt. Sinai. J. Med. **79**(3), 397–411 (2012)
7. Ullrich, L.E., Ogawa, J.R., Jones-London, M.D.: Factors that influence career choice among different populations of neuroscience trainees. bioRxiv (2021)
8. Girves, J.E., Zepeda, Y., Gwathmey, J.K.: Mentoring in a post-affirmative action world. J. Soc. Iss. **61**(3), 449–479 (2005)
9. Bartman, C.C.: African American women in higher education: issues and support strategies (2015)
10. Balhoff, J.P., et al.: Tailoring the NCI thesaurus for use in the obo library. In: ICBO (2017)
11. Balshaw, D.M., Collman, G.W., Gray, K.A., Thompson, C.L.: The children's health exposure analysis resource (chear): enabling research into the environmental influences on children's health outcomes. Curr. Opin. Pediatr. **29**(3), 385 (2017)
12. Ahmed, N., Khan, S., Latif, K.: Job description ontology. In: 2016 International Conference on Frontiers of Information Technology (FIT), pp. 217–222. IEEE (2016)
13. Tiwari, S., Al-Aswadi, F.N., Gaurav, D.: Recent trends in knowledge graphs: theory and practice. Soft Comput. **25**(13), 8337–8355 (2021)
14. Paulheim, Heiko: Knowledge graph refinement: a survey of approaches and evaluation methods. Seman. Web **8**(3), 489–508 (2017)
15. Guo, O., et al.: A survey on knowledge graph-based recommender systems. IEEE Trans. Knowl. Data Eng. (2020)
16. Kendall, E.F., McGuinness, D.L.: Ontology engineering. Synthesis lectures on the semantic web. Theory Technol. **9**(1), i–102 (2019)

Bridging Upper Ontology and Modular Ontology Modeling: a Tool and Evaluation

Abhilekha Dalal$^{(\boxtimes)}$, Cogan Shimizu, and Pascal Hitzler

Data Semantics Laboratory, Kansas State University, Manhattan, USA
{adalal,coganmshimizu,hitzler}@ksu.edu

Abstract. Ontologies are increasingly used as schema for knowledge graphs in many application areas. As such, there are a variety of different approaches for their development. In this paper, we describe and evaluate UAO (for Upper Ontology Alignment Tool), which is an extension to CoModIDE, a graphical Protégé plugin for modular ontology modeling. UAO enables ontology engineers to combine modular ontology modeling with a more traditional ontology modeling approach based on upper ontologies. We posit – and our evaluation supports this claim – that the tool does indeed makes it easier to combine both approaches. Thus, UAO enables a best-of-both-worlds approach. The evaluation consists of a user study, and the results show that performing typical manual alignment modeling tasks is relatively easier with UAO than doing it with Protégé alone, in terms of the time required to complete the task and improving the correctness of the output. Additionally, our test subjects provided significantly higher ratings on the System Utilization Scale for UOA.

1 Introduction

In many application areas, ontology modeling has become a primary approach to schema generation for data integration and knowledge graphs [11,14,32]. Lately, the policies of Findability, Accessibility, Interoperability, and Reusability (FAIR) have been formulated as essential goals that data receptacles should meet to enhance their data holdings' usefulness [33]. The quest for efficient approaches to model useful and reusable ontologies has, over the years, led to different proposals for ontology creation processes and tooling.

One classic approach is based on so-called upper or foundational ontologies [1,21,31]. Central to this paradigm is the utilizing of ontologies that are generic and large, and as such cover a wide swath of domains, such as BFO [1], DOLCE [10], SUMO [18]. In this approach to modeling, a new (domain) ontology is created in accordance with the mindset or structure conveyed by these upper or foundational ontologies. Technically, alignment of the domain ontology classes and relations to the upper/foundational ontology entities – meaning creating appropriate sub-class and sub-property relationships so that relevant structure or axioms are inherited – play a prominent role.

A more recent approach to ontology modeling is based on a different mindset; modular ontology modeling [27] is based on the idea that an ontology may best

© Springer Nature Switzerland AG 2021
B. Villazón-Terrazas et al. (Eds.): KGSWC 2021, CCIS 1459, pp. 16–30, 2021.
https://doi.org/10.1007/978-3-030-91305-2_2

be viewed as a collection of interconnected *modules*, each of which correspond to a key notion according to the terminology used by a domain expert. The approach is related to other recent proposals to approach ontology modeling in a *divide and conquer* fashion [22,30] and is a refinement of the eXtreme Ontology Design methodology [24] based on Ontology Design Patterns [15]. In its original conception, and the corresponding tooling, in particular the CoModIDE Protégé plugin [27], the approach de-emphasizes sub-class and sub-property relationships when reusing patterns, and in particular does not account for upper or foundational ontologies.

Different ontology modeling paradigms have different emphases and as such the resulting ontologies have different strengths and weaknesses. Approaches based on foundational ontologies lead to ontologies that are based on a singular philosophical paradigm to ontology building, and thus are internally coherent and deeply thought-out. On the flip side, they are large and monolithic, with little immediately discernible internal structure, and modeling choices are sometimes hard to understand for those who are not ontology engineering specialists. The modular approach, on the other hand, puts less emphasis on overall philosophical coherence, but results in a highly structured ontology that natively aims to reflect conceptualizations by domain experts. Which approach is chosen may also sometimes be subjective, based on perceived advantages or disadvantages, or on particulars of the use case.

In this paper, we provide a case in point that the two just mentioned approaches to ontology engineering are in fact not mutually exclusive, but that it is possible to use a combination of modular and upper ontology modeling. Combining the best of both worlds can help ensure consistent development of ontologies across multiple domains, and to accomodate a team with differing preferences and perspectives. It will increase the flexibility of training; it will allow more effective governance and quality assurance of ontology development, and it will promote the degree to which multiple different groups of ontology developers and users can inspect and critique.

We thus extend CoModIDE, a graphical paradigm based on Protégé for modeling modular ontologies, with additional functionality, namely the Upper Alignment Tool (UOA) that supports the manual alignment of the currently modeled ontology to a chosen upper ontology, and thus makes it possible to follow both or either of the approaches, as desired.

As CoModIDE did previously not have such alignment capabilities, a user would have needed to use the default Protégé experience to load, identify, and align classes and properties. Thus, we hypothesize (and substantiate in our evaluation) that manual upper ontology alignment with any modular ontology using the plugin developed is comparatively easier than doing it with Protégé alone.

The rest of this paper is organized as follows. Section 2 introduces the UOA. Section 3 discusses relevant work on graphic modeling and ontology development methods and tools. Sections 4 and 5 present our study design for evaluating the tool and the results of our experiment. Section 6 discusses these findings and their implications. Finally, Sect. 7 sums up the paper and proposes some possibilities for future research. A preliminary demonstration of the Upper Ontology Alignment tool, without evaluation, was already provided in [8].

2   UOA: the Upper Ontology Alignment Tool

Motivation. The Upper Ontology Alignment plugin is intended to simplify ontology development for users who want to combine a modular development approach with an upper ontology based one. The UOA thus provides a straightforward interface that gives the user the ability to manually align parts of the currently modeled ontology to a chosen upper ontology. The tool is based on manual alignment, because this is how it is usually done and discussed during modeling with upper ontologies. In principle, algorithms for mapping recommendations could be added, but this is not part of the current functionality.

The UOA is provided as part of CoModIDE [27], which is a versatile and established Protégé plugin that supports intuitive and agile visual modeling, reusing ODPs as templates to create modules but does not account for alignment with upper or foundational ontologies [27]. Therefore, we used the following as our design criteria:

1. full integration with Protégé and CoModIDE along with leveraging the graphical user interface of CoModIDE and the creation of pattern-based modules,
2. easy loading of any ontology as an upper ontology and extraction of its concepts and relations, and
3. simple selection of checkboxes to define subClass and subproperty relationships between the currently modeled ontology and the loaded upper ontology.

Implementation. The Upper Ontology Alignment (UOA) tool extends CoModIDE, which provides three views: schema editor, pattern library, and the configuration view. UOA is an additional, fourth view, labeled as (1) in Fig. 1. Classes are diagrammatically represented as cells, and properties are represented as edges between them. The highlighted red box in the schema editor shows a diagrammatic rendering of an alignment with the loaded upper ontology, UOA user interface displays the list of classes when a cell is selected from the schema editor and likewise, it will switch to list of properties from upper ontology when edges are selected.

Since UOA provides additional functionality to CoModIDE, one of the leading design criteria is that it must be compatible and support the graphical representation of an ontology created with CoModIDE, and should be consistent across all reboots, instruments, and operating systems or versions of Protégé.

The UOA view allows a user to load an ontology file using a load button – which may be an upper or foundational ontology – directly into the view (which is kept isolated from the ontology active in Protégé). The view extracts all of the classes and properties (excluding annotation properties) from the loaded ontology. The user then selects classes (cells) or object/data properties (edges) on the graphical canvas. The UOA tool then displays the pertinent entities depending on which glyph is selected on the graphical canvas. The view will automatically

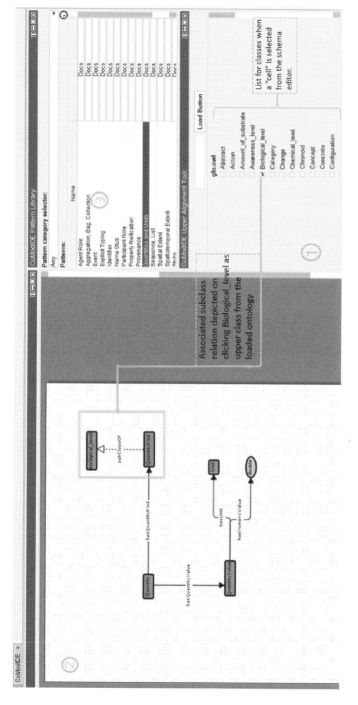

Fig. 1. CoModIDE plugin views – 1) UOA, 2) schema editor, 3) pattern library.

construct and add – or remove – the pertinent subClass or subproperty axioms to the ontology when the user selects or deselects checkboxes next to these entities. CoModIDE detects these additions and will also diagrammatically display the added relationships.

The view also provides some supporting functionality for ease and clarity of use: the view will display the currently selected entity, automatically select checkboxes for axioms that are already present in the ontology (e.g., if some entity is already a subClass of the Perdurant class, that particular checkbox will be selected), will display the currently loaded ontology file name, allows for different ontologies to be loaded (i.e., a user is not limited to a single upper ontology), and provides descriptive logging in the case of failure.

3   Related Work

The intention behind having a tool like UOA that supports the interactive visual alignment of ontologies within the modular ontology methodology is to enhance ontology engineers' experience by merging modular ontology modeling with foundational ontologies based modeling. We briefly discuss some other tools that support the same or related goals.

eXtreme Design (XD) [4] was initially proposed to emphasize waterfall methodologies in ontological engineering to introduce a new, more flexible thinking in ontological engineering. It was originally inspired by software engineering methods such as eXtreme Programming (XP) [29] and the experience factory approaches [2]. With the growth of the ontology, instead of a one-time process, an emphasis is placed on the iterative delivery approach to success. The methodology can be divided into three parts. (1) a project initiation and definition phase that is executed only once at the beginning of the project. It is about collecting realistic requirements based on stories that come directly from customers. It is equally necessary to involve domain experts as customers in the development process to confirm the correctness of domain functionality and coverage and the adequacy of terminology and other non-functional requirements.

(2) XD emphasizes the divide and conquer paradigm, takes requirements piece by piece to create modules for each requirement by reusing ODP building blocks, adapting and integrating into the ontology module under development, and like this, all requirements are covered through a development loop that iteratively produces new modules. The module is tested against the selected requirements to ensure that it covers them adequately.

(3) The methodology provides a tangible result in the initial phase and then extends this result with each iteration. As soon as all requirements have been met, the module is released and integrated into the overall solution. XD has been classified as a requirement-driven, inherently modular methodology which focuses on creating reusable modules and reduces failures in ontologies [3,5]. However, the findings also indicate that pitfalls are associated with the possibility of over-reliance on ODPs, as discussed in [12].

Ontology Design Patterns Gangemi [9], and Blomqvist and Sandkuhl [6] introduced Ontology Design Patterns (ODPs) in 2005 to simplify ontology development. ODPs are designed to guide unskilled users by consolidating best practices into reusable building blocks that these users accommodate and specialize in individual ontology development projects. Presutti et al. [25] define a typology of ODPs, including reasoning patterns, naming, transformation, etc. The eXtreme Design methodology [4] describes how ontological engineering projects can be broken down into discrete sub-tasks to be solved using ODPs. Previous studies have shown that using ODPs can reduce the number of modeling errors and inconsistencies in ontologies and that they are found to be useful and helpful by users [3,5].

CoModIDE [26] has been developed as a plugin for the versatile and conventional Protégé environment. The plugin presents three Protégé views and a tab that stores these views. The Schema Editor view provides a graphical overview of the structure of the ontology, including ontology classes, their subClass relationships, and the object type and data type properties of the ontology that associate these classes with data types. All of these objects can be graphically edited by dragging and dropping. The pattern library view offers a number of integrated ontology design patterns from various projects and from the ODP portal.[1] The user can drag and drop design models from the library to the drawing area in order to display these models as modules in their ontology. In the configuration view, the user can set the behavior of other CoModIDE views and their components.

When a pattern is dragged over to the canvas, the constructs of that pattern are copied into the ontology. In addition, they are annotated using the Ontology Pattern Language OPLa [16] to indicate that they belong to a specific module, and are based on a particular pattern. In this way, origin information of the modules is recorded, and the modules can be controlled (folded, unfolded, deleted, commented) as required.

However, the approach de-emphasizes sub-class and sub-property relationships, and in particular does not account for alignment with upper or foundational ontologies.

Prompt-Viz [23] is a visualization tool for the Protégé Prompt [19] plugin that extends PROMPTDiff [20] with information visualization techniques to provide advanced cognitive support for understanding the differences between versions of ontologies. It provides one single visual representation of ontologies within a treemap layout [28]. This visualization aims to provide users the ability to determine the Location, Impact, Type, and Extent (LITE questions) of the changes that have occurred to the ontology. Histogram bars represent the percentage of descendants classified as unchanged, appended, removed, moved-from, moved-to, and directly edited, respectively. It is divided into four linked frames [17]: (1) An expandable horizontal tree layout of the ontology showing the differences; it contains a search tool to locate specific concepts quickly. (2) A treemap layout of

---

[1] http://ontologydesignpatterns.org/.

the ontology installed in a zoomable user interface; (3) A path window showing the location of currently selected concepts in the ontology within the is-a hierarchy and serving as a navigation aid for the treemap component. The treemap view can be zoomed in to show all of the boundaries for each route's level. (4) A comprehensive list of changes that have happened to the currently chosen concept, for instance, the classification of the change, the change procedure, and the reference frame in the previous and new versions of the ontology.

Prompt-Viz offers a sophisticated visualization, but it loses some intuitive aspects of a graphical visualization (e.g., hierarchical relationships between concepts). Using a single visualization to represent the two ontologies, the properties of the source ontologies lose their clarity, which can be sufficient to merge, but makes is less suitable for alignment.

4   Research Method

We conducted a user study to assess the added value of the UOA. The user study consists of four parts: a questionnaire survey to collect necessary data on the subject (e.g., familiarity with ontologies and corresponding tools), two modeling tasks, and a follow-up questionnaire survey to collect information on the usability of Protégé and UOA. The tasks were designed to imitate a standard ontology modeling process in which a conceptual design is developed and approved through whiteboard prototyping. A developer is then to perform a simple alignment task with an upper ontology.

During each modeling task, participants are asked to create an appropriate and correct OWL file for the proposed tasks. To avoid a learning effect, the two tasks use two different schematic diagrams; one is an instance of a pattern, and the other is a small ontology. The specific order in which the user used which tool first and next was randomized among participants (some used Protégé first for the first activity and others used UOA) to avoid bias differences in the activity's complexity. The precision of the developed OWL files and the time required to complete each task were recorded (the latter being limited to 20 minutes per task). Each step of the study has been explained below.

Introductory Tutorial. We provided participants with a brief tutorial on the basics required to understand and perform the required tasks. As such, we did not have to impose any prerequisites for participants. The 10-min tutorial established a common basic understanding of the basic concepts of ontology modeling and Protégé, including ontologies, top-level ontologies, classes, properties, domains, ranges, sub-class relations.

Prior-Questionnaire Survey. The idea of a prior questionnaire survey was to collect information relating to the participant's prior knowledge and experience with topics related to ontology modeling or alignment of ontologies, to be used as control variables in the evaluation. We also asked the participants if they have a Computer Science Background. The questions are listed in Table 1. We used a 5-point Likert scale[2] for the rating.

We also asked the participants to describe their relationship to the test leader, (like student, colleague, same research lab, not familiar).

We had two tasks A and B, with two parts to each task. In task A, participants were asked to develop an ontology to model an Event module and then align the entities or properties with an identified upperlevel ontology, specifically GFO [13]. For the first part, participants were asked to perform the modeling task using UOA, and for the second they were asked to do it using Protégé alone. Figure 2 (top) shows the expected result.

Similarly, for task B, participants were to develop an ontology to capture information about dog sales, in particular

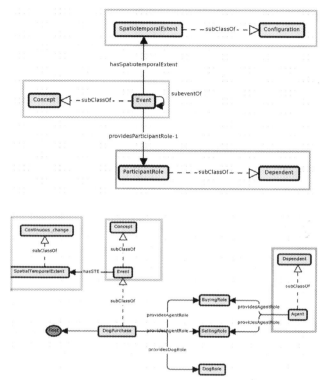

Fig. 2. Tasks A (top) and B (bottom) schema diagrams

information about pertinent events and roles, and to later align the model with GFO. For the first part, participants were asked to perform the modeling task using the Upper Ontology Alignment Tool, and for the second, they were asked to do it using Protégé alone. Figure 2 (bottom) shows the expected result.

Follow-up Questionnaire Survey. The follow-up survey included the SUS evaluations for both Protégé and UOA. The SUS is a ubiquitous "quick and dirty" yet reliable tool for measuring a system's usability. It consists of 10 questions, the responses of which are used to calculate an overall usability score from 0 to 100. The purpose of the selected questions was to capture the tool's learnability, effectiveness, and efficiency which are the main components of the usability goals. Additional information on the SUS and its included items can be found

---

[2] https://www.simplypsychology.org/likert-scale.html.

Table 1. Mean, median, standard deviation and relative standard deviation responses to a priori questionnaire

	Mean	Median	σ	Relative σ
CV1: I have done ontology modelling before	2.14	1	1.46	68%
CV2: I am familiar with ontology design patterns	2.14	2	1.35	63%
CV3: I am familiar with manchester syntax	1.52	1	1.03	68%
CV4: I am familiar with top-level ontology	1.76	1	1.04	59%
CV5: I am familiar with Protégé	2.24	1	1.58	71%
CV6: I am familiar with CoModIDE pattern library	2.10	1	1.41	67%

online.[3] Additionally, we inquire about UOA-specific features. These statements are also scored using a Likert scale. However, this data has not been used in our evaluation, except to inform our future work, as described in Sect. 7. At the end of the survey, participants could provide free comments on UOA's features or their experience with the tool. Our hypothesis underlying the experiment design described above was that UOA improves the approachability of knowledge graph development in such a way that users require less time to produce correct and reasonable output in comparison to using Protégé alone; we also hypothesized that UOA will have a higher SUS score.

5   Results

Participant Distribution. The total number of subjects who participated in the user study evaluation was 21, out of which 13 stated that they knew the test leader (the first author); the rest did not report any such relationship. The user study was not limited to subjects having a computer science (CS) background in order to have diversity and capture usability goals across different backgrounds, and we had a small number of participants from fields such as entomology, agriculture engineering, and biochemistry. For self-reported ontological engineering knowledge, the answers are shown in Table 1. The responses differ significantly, with a relative standard deviation (σ/mean) of 59–71%.

Metric Evaluation. The metrics that we considered for the result calculation are

1. Time Taken: number of minutes for each modeling task to run were recorded and rounded to the nearest full minute and limited to 20 min for a task to run due to practical limitations;
2. Correctness: structural accuracy of the output generated. The complete structurally correct file received 2 points on examining URIs, axioms generated, alignments, 1 point was awarded for a partially correct file (e.g., one or two incorrect linkages, incorrect axiom creation, labels); and 0 points for incorrect files (e.g., absence of axioms, alignment).

---

[3] https://www.usability.gov/how-to-and-tools/methods/system-usability-scale.html.

Table 2. Summary of statistics comparing Protégé and UOA.

	mean	median	σ
Protégé	17.29	18	4.11
UOA	13.81	15	4.76

(a) Mean, median and standard deviation of *total time-taken* to complete both modeling task.

	mean	median	σ
Protégé (task A)	0.71	1	0.78
Protégé (task B)	0.52	0	0.74
UOA (task A)	1.38	2	0.86
UOA (task B)	1.05	1	0.86

(b) Mean, median and standard deviation of *the output's correctness*.

	CV1	CV2	CV3	CV4	CV5	CV6
T_P	-0.26	-0.07	-0.36	-0.47	-0.23	-0.16
C_P	0.05	-0.02	0.12	0.22	0.05	-0.03
T_U	0.05	0.18	-0.13	-0.15	0.10	0.18
C_U	0.08	-0.03	-0.02	0.03	0.19	0.12

(c) Correlations of control variables (CV) on the Time Taken (T) and Correctness of Output (C) for both Protégé (P) and UOA (U).

	CV1	CV2	CV3	CV4	CV5	CV6
SUS (P)	0.28	0.27	0.28	0.28	0.24	0.26
SUS (U)	0.00	0.02	0.01	0.10	0.13	0.01

(d) Correlations with control variables (CV) on the SUS scores for both tools Protégé (P) and UOA.

	mean	median	σ
Protégé	44.05	42.5	21.04
UOA	71.79	72.5	13.06

(e) Mean, median and standard deviation for SUS score of each tool. The maximum score is 100.

Result	Significance (p)
Time-taken	$p \approx 0.010 < 0.05$
Corr. (Task-A)	$p \approx 0.004 < 0.05$
Corr. (Task-B)	$p \approx 0.012 < 0.05$
SUS Evaluation	$p \approx 0.0000015 < 0.001$

(f) Significance of results.

For the metrics defined, we calculated simple statistics through which data of each modeling task is described. Table 2a and 2b each show the mean, median, and standard deviation of time-taken, and the output's accuracy for each modeling activity through Protégé as well as UOA.

Also, we examined the effects of our control variables (CVs). This analysis is vital because it provides the context for the representation or bias of our dataset. Results can be found in Table 2c, where CV1–CV6 correspond precisely to the questions asked during the prior questionnaire survey (see Table 1). We calculated each CV's bivariate correlation between the sample data and the self-reported data in the survey. We believe calculating correlation has a reasonable measure of impact on the effect, as our sample's limited size is not suitable for partitioning. The partitions (based on the prior questionnaire survey responses) could have been tested in pairs for statistical significance, but the partitions would have been too small to perform the proper statistical tests. However, we emphasize that the sample size strongly influences the correlation effects. SUS scores are analyzed in the same way. Table 2d shows our observed correlations of the SUS score for both tools with our control variables, and Table 2e shows the mean, median, and standard deviation of the data set.

Finally, we compared each metric (time taken and accuracy of output) for one tool against the other, assessing statistical significance; results are given in Table 2f. We see that UOA performs better on both metrics and SUS, with at least $p < 0.05$ in each case, i.e., the results are indeed statistically significant at the 0.05 level. To make the comparison, we calculatee the probability for the null hypothesis that the samples in each dataset come from different underlying distributions, using the paired (two-tail) T-Test, which is a standard tool for this type of analysis and suitable for limited sample size if it is reasonable to assume that values follow a Gaussian distribution, as in our case.

Additional Free-Text Responses. Of the 21 participants, 11 decided to leave free-text comments at the end of the questionnaire. We applied qualitative coding and analysis based on the fragments of these comments. That is, we divided the comments based on the line breaks, read the details, and created basic categories. We then allocated the fragments into the categories (with a maximum of one category per segment) [7]. Participants left between 2–5 fragments each to analyze for a total of 35 fragments, 25 of which were encoded, as shown in Table 3.

6 Discussion

Participant Distribution. The data show no correlation (bivariate correlation $\leq \pm 0.1$) between the reported familiarity of the subjects and the reported SUS values; for example, this would have happened if the subjects who knew the author were biased. The

Table 3. Free text comment fragments per category

Category	Fragments no.
User-interface	5
Tree structure layout	2
Bugs	5
Additional features	4
Valuable statements	9

high relative standard deviation of knowledge level responses from the prior questionnaire survey shows that our subjects are very diverse in skills. In other words, they are not entirely made up of a limited-experience class or from a particular background of users that UOA will hopefully support at some point. This variation and diversity of education help us evaluate and compare the user's performance and the tool's usability more impartially.

Metric Evaluation. To analyze the correlations coefficient between our results and the control variables score collected in the prior survey, we have used threshold values for a correlation $|r|$: 0–0.19 very weak, 0.20–0.39 weak, 0.40–0.59 moderate, 0.60–0.79 strong, 0.80–1.00 very strong.

As depicted in the Table 2c, the metric time-taken used to complete tasks using Protégé correlates negatively with each of the control variables (taken from the prior survey), and the strength of the relationship varies from very weak to moderate. In contrast, the accuracy metric correlates weakly positively as the absolute value ranges from 0 to 0.22 except CV2 and CV6. Analysis for Protégé indicates that familiarity with ontology modeling, top-level ontology, related concepts, and the tool decreases the time required to finish the task and, to any degree, improves the output's accuracy.

However, for the metrics (time-taken and output's correctness) concerning UOA, the relationship's strength and direction are dubious since there are only very weak correlations with control variables varying from 0–0.19. We may interpret that familiarity with ontology modeling does not have much influence and that performance when using UOA is mostly skeptical of the study's control variables. UOA reports having better scores when considering the mean and median for the metric time-taken as described in Table 2a. When examining the underlying data (2f), the significance of the p-value is approx. $0.010 < 0.05$. Subsequent, consider Table 2b for the correctness of both the tasks, UOA performs better for both mean and median score than Protégé. Comparing underlying data for correctness, the statistical significance of the p-value is approx. $0.004 < 0.05$ and $0.012 < 0.05$. Considering both the comparisons, we reject the null hypothesis and confirm that *a user produces correct and reasonable output in less time when using UOA than when using Protégé alone.*

From the above analysis of the correlation coefficient where we observe a very weak correlation between the familiarity of ontology modeling and UOA performance results and the confirmation that the user performs better in terms of time required and output's accuracy when using UOA rather than Protégé, it indicates that UOA has delivered increased accessibility and learnability.

Further, Table 2e illustrates that the SUS scores for UOA have a greater mean, greater median, and smaller σ, attaining a substantial statistical significance of approx. $0.0000015 < 0.001$. Hence, we confirm that the *user finds UOA to have a higher SUS score than when using Protégé alone* from the evaluation. On examining SUS scores (Table 2d), we find that Protégé correlates strongly positively with control variables. The absolute values indicate that subjects do not find the tool very useful in terms of usability goals, including adequate to use, easy to learn, and suitable. In contrast, the SUS correlation coefficient for UOA suggests that there is either a very weak or weak correlation with the CVs. By showing that in less time, users produce accurate output when using UOA and users find UOA to have higher scores, we can say that UOA improves usability and approachability for knowledge graph development, especially for those unfamiliar with ontological modeling.

Additional Free-Text Responses. The fragments summarized in Table 3 show the advantages and disadvantages of UOA recognized by subjects as follows:

– *User Interface*: UOA's design format is confusing and less-informative; the button used for loading files into the tool does not serve the purpose much and reduces approachability.
– *Tree Structure Layout*: The users find the view crowded and uncomfortable, not easy to find the classes or properties down in the list.
– *Bugs*: Graphical display on canvas is faulty; checking boxes stopped adding alignments to the model.
– *Additional Features*: There should be a search box to find the classes resp. properties from the list; there should be prompts for the user in case of error; zooming is requested.
– *Valuable Statements*: Users appreciate graphical modeling with the additional feature of alignment with upper ontologies. E.g. *"The Upper Ontology Alignment tool made it much easier to add classes with specific sub-class axiom*

relations," "This system is very useful and easier to use," "The tool effi-ciently reduces the manual steps and easy to use. I loved the concept and would highly rate it."

Some users opted to only leave comments about their performance in the experiment or knowledge about the tool, hence containing no codable fragments. We find that there is an agreement among participants that UOA adds value to graphical modeling and is intuitive and useful. Criticism is aimed at specific, simple bugs or UI functionality.

7   Conclusion and Future Work

Our experiments indicates that UOA allows users to develop ontologies with the option of combining modular ontology modeling with modeling approaches based on upper/foundational ontologies, more correctly and faster than Protégé, irrespective of their previous knowledge level. Our experiments indicates that UOA is more user-friendly and has improved usability goals (SUS score) than the standard Protégé and that UOA concerns affecting users, as opposed to methodological or modeling problems, mainly derive from simple faults in the tool. Overall, this means that modular graphical ontological engineering with alignment to upper ontology using the tool is a practical way to improve ontological engineering accessibility.

Possible extensions of this work, as indicated by feedback from the user study, include: automation or semi-automation of the alignment, provision of more complex alignment capabilities beyond sub-classes or sub-properties, namespace prefix and label presentation, search functionality, and improving the display of the tree structure of classes and properties [8].

Acknowledgement. This work was supported by the U.S. Department of Commerce, National Institute of Standards and Technology, under award number 70NANB19H094.

References

1. Arp, R., Smith, B., Spear, A.D.: Building Ontologies With Basic Formal Ontology, MIT Press, Cambridge (2015)
2. Basili, V.R., Caldiera, G., Rombach, H.D.: Experience factory. Encycl. Softw. Eng. (2002)
3. Blomqvist, E., Gangemi, A., Presutti, V.: Experiments on pattern-based ontology design. In: Proceedings of the Fifth International Conference on Knowledge Capture, pp. 41–48 (2009)
4. Blomqvist, E., Hammar, K., Presutti, V.: Engineering ontologies with patterns-the extreme design methodology. Ontol. Eng. Ontol. Des. Patt. **25**, 23–50 (2016)
5. Blomqvist, E., Presutti, V., Daga, E., Gangemi, A.: Experimenting with eXtreme design. In: Cimiano, P., Pinto, H.S. (eds.) EKAW 2010. LNCS (LNAI), vol. 6317, pp. 120–134. Springer, Heidelberg (2010). https://doi.org/10.1007/978-3-642-16438-5_9

6. Blomqvist, E., Sandkuhl, K.: Patterns in ontology engineering: classification of ontology patterns. In: ICEIS, vol. 3, pp. 413–416 (2005)
7. Burnard, P.: A method of analysing interview transcripts in qualitative research. Nurse Educ. Today **11**(6), 461–466 (1991)
8. Dalal, A., Shimizu, C., Hitzler, P.: Modular ontology modeling meets upper ontologies: the upper ontology alignment tool. In: The 19th International Semantic Web Conference, vol. 2721, pp. 119–124, October 2020
9. Gangemi, A.: Ontology design patterns for semantic web content. In: Gil, Y., Motta, E., Benjamins, V.R., Musen, M.A. (eds.) ISWC 2005. LNCS, vol. 3729, pp. 262–276. Springer, Heidelberg (2005). https://doi.org/10.1007/11574620_21
10. Gangemi, A., Guarino, N., Masolo, C., Oltramari, A., Schneider, L.: Sweetening ontologies with DOLCE. In: Gómez-Pérez, A., Benjamins, V.R. (eds.) EKAW 2002. LNCS (LNAI), vol. 2473, pp. 166–181. Springer, Heidelberg (2002). https://doi.org/10.1007/3-540-45810-7_18
11. Gutiérrez, C., Sequeda, J.F.: Knowledge graphs. Commun. ACM **64**(3), 96–104 (2021)
12. Hammar, K.: Ontology design patterns in use: lessons learnt from an ontology engineering case. In: Workshop on Ontology Patterns in Conjunction with the 11th International Semantic Web Conference 2012 (ISWC 2012) (2012)
13. Herre, H.: General formal ontology (GFO): a foundational ontology for conceptual modelling. In: Poli, R., Healy, M., Kameas, A. (eds.) Theory and Applications of Ontology: Computer Applications, pp. 297–345. Springer, Dordrecht (2010). https://doi.org/10.1007/978-90-481-8847-5_14
14. Hitzler, P.: A review of the semantic web field. Commun. ACM **64**(2), 76–83 (2021)
15. Hitzler, P., Gangemi, A., Janowicz, K., Krisnadhi, A., Presutti, V. (eds): Ontology Engineering with Ontology Design Patterns - Foundations and Applications, Volume 25 of Studies on the Semantic Web. IOS Press, Amsterdam (2016)
16. Hitzler, P., Gangemi, A., Janowicz, K., Krisnadhi, A.A., Presutti, V.: Towards a simple but useful ontology design pattern representation language. In: Blomqvist, E., Corcho, Ó.. Horridge, M., Carral, D., Hoekstra, R. (eds.) Proceedings of the 8th Workshop on Ontology Design and Patterns (WOP 2017) Co-located with the 16th International Semantic Web Conference (ISWC 2017), Vienna, Austria, 21 October 2017, volume 2043 of CEUR Workshop Proceedings. CEUR-WS.org (2017)
17. Lanzenberger, M., Sampson, J.: Alviz - a tool for visual ontology alignment. In: Tenth International Conference on Information Visualisation (IV 2006), pp. 430–440. IEEE (2006)
18. Niles, I., Pease. A.: Towards a standard upper ontology. In: Proceedings of the 2nd International Conference on Formal Ontology in Information Systems, FOIS 2001, Ogunquit, Maine, USA, 17–19 October 2001, pp. 2–9. ACM (2001)
19. Noy, N.F., Musen, M.A.: The PROMPT suite: interactive tools for ontology merging and mapping. Int. J. Hum-Comput. Stud. **59**(6), 983–1024 (2003)
20. Noy, N.F., Musen, M.A., et al.: Promptdiff: a fixed-point algorithm for comparing ontology versions. In: AAAI/IAAI, pp. 744–750 (2002)
21. Oberle, D., et al.: DOLCE ergo SUMO: on foundational and domain models in the SmartWeb Integrated Ontology (SWIntO). J. Web Semant. **5**(3), 156–174 (2007)
22. Osumi-Sutherland, D., Courtot, M., Balhoff, J.P., Mungall, C.J.: Dead simple OWL design patterns. J. Biomed. Seman. **8**(1), 18:1–18:7 (2017)
23. Perrin, D.S.J.: Prompt-viz: ontology version comparison visualizations with treemaps (2004)

24. Presutti, V., Daga, E., Gangemi, A., Blomqvist, E.: eXtreme design with content ontology design patterns. In: Blomqvist, E., Sandkuhl, K., Scharffe, F., Svátek, V. (eds.) Proceedings of the Workshop on Ontology Patterns (WOP 2009), Collocated with the 8th International Semantic Web Conference (ISWC-2009), Washington D.C., USA, 25 October, 2009, Volume 516 of CEUR Workshop Proceedings. CEUR-WS.org (2009)
25. Presutti, V., et al.: NeOn deliverable D2.5.1. a library of ontology design patterns: reusable solutions for collaborative design of networked ontologies. NeOn Project (2008). http://www.neon-project.org
26. Shimizu, C., Hammar, K.: Comodide - the comprehensive modular ontology engineering IDE. In: ISWC 2019 Satellite Tracks (Posters & Demonstrations, Industry, and Outrageous Ideas) co-located with 18th International Semantic Web Conference (ISWC 2019) Auckland, New Zealand, 26–30 October 2019, vol. 2456, pp. 249–252. CEUR-WS (2019)
27. Shimizu, C., Hammar, K., Hitzler, P., et al.: Modular graphical ontology engineering evaluated. In: Harth, A., et al. (ed.) ESWC 2020. LNCS, vol. 12123, pp. 20–35. Springer, Cham (2020). https://doi.org/10.1007/978-3-030-49461-2_2
28. Shneiderman, B.: Tree visualization with tree-maps: 2-D space-filling approach. ACM Trans. Graph. 11(1), 92–99 (1992)
29. Shore et al., J. : The Art of Agile Development: Pragmatic Guide to Agile Software Development. O'Reilly Media Inc (2007)
30. Skjæveland, M.G., Lupp, D.P., Karlsen, L.H., Forssell, H.: Practical ontology pattern instantiation, discovery, and maintenance with reasonable ontology templates. In: Vrandečić, D., et al. (eds.) ISWC 2018. LNCS, vol. 11136, pp. 477–494. Springer, Cham (2018). https://doi.org/10.1007/978-3-030-00671-6_28
31. Smith, B.: Classifying processes: an essay in applied ontology. Ratio 25(4), 463–488 (2012)
32. Vita, R., Overton, J.A., Mungall, C.J., Sette, A., Peters. B.: FAIR principles and the IEDB: short-term improvements and a long-term vision of OBO-Foundry mediated machine-actionable interoperability. Database 2018:bax105 (2018)
33. Wilkinson, M.D., et al.: The FAIR guiding principles for scientific data management and stewardship. Sci. Data 3 (2016)

Empirical Evaluation of a Cloud-Based Graph Database: the Case of Neptune

Ghislain Auguste Atemezing[(⊠)]

Mondeca, 18 rue de Londres, 75009 Paris, France
`ghislain.atemezing@mondeca.com`

Abstract. Since the announcement by Amazon of its own graph database service Neptune in November 2017, there have been many expectations on how to compare Neptune with other state-of-the-art enterprise graph databases. Neptune is defined as a high-performance graph database engine supporting popular graph models: RDF and Property Graph Model (PGM). This paper aims at giving an empirical evaluation of AWS Neptune on real-world RDF datasets. We use three different versions of Neptune (Preview, Neptune 1.0, and Neptune 1.0.1) to evaluate how fast and reliable the engine is with real-world SPARQL queries. Additionally, we compare some of the results with our previous benchmark with other enterprise RDF database graphs, even though one should be careful with such comparison since the hardware settings are not completely equivalent. The results of this evaluation give some preliminary insights about AWS Neptune in the RDF benchmark task. The results demonstrate that Neptune is the fastest in loading 2 Billion triples, performs better on analytical queries, and outperforms on updates queries. However, Neptune performs poorly on SELECT queries with the shortest response time (60 s).

Keywords: AWS Neptune · RDF · SPARQL · Benchmark

1 Introduction

The adoption of semantic technologies for data integration is continuing to gain attention and adoption in industry, after the first impact in the research community. Knowledge Graphs (KGs) have proven to be an efficient way to structure, connect and share knowledge within organizations by bridging data silos. SPARQL [6] is the W3C *lingua franca* recommendation to access to the KGs encoded in RDF stored in graph database management systems. Since the announcement by Amazon of its own graph database service Neptune in November 2017 [2], there have been many expectations on how to compare Neptune with other state-of-the-art enterprise graph Database Management Systems (DBMS). According to 2020 DB-Engines ranking of Graph DBMS[1], Amazon Neptune is

---

[1] https://db-engines.com/en/ranking/graph+dbms, accessed 2020-12-17.

Permanent URL: https://doi.org/10.6084/m9.figshare.13414817.

B. Villazón-Terrazas et al. (Eds.): KGSWC 2021, CCIS 1459, pp. 31–46, 2021.
https://doi.org/10.1007/978-3-030-91305-2_3

the second after Virtuoso for RDF Graph DBMS. Neptune is defined as a high-performance graph database engine supporting popular graph models: RDF and Property Graph Model (PGM). This paper aims at giving an empirical evaluation of AWS Neptune on real-world RDF datasets, hence dealing with its RDF support.

In industry, many business requirements dealing with data management are shifting to use cloud-based services. This benchmark is motivated by following our previous assessment [3] using real-world datasets from the Publications Office (PO)[2] using Neptune. We were also able to assess on three different versions of Neptune corresponding to three different periods in time. This paper contributes to an empirical evaluation of Neptune across the evolved versions (Preview, 1.0 and 1.0.1) and to give an insight with our previous benchmark without entering in the "fairness" debate with the reader. We argue that the resource has an impact in assessing RDF stores in general, hence supports the adoption of Semantic Web technologies in industry.

The remainder of the paper is structured as follows: Sect. 2 presents a brief review of some related works on benchmarking enterprise RDF stores, although none of them are cloud-based Graph DBMS. Section 3 describes the selected queries and datasets used for the experiments. Section 4 describes the settings. The report of the loading process is described in Sect. 5. Then, we provide with the results of the benchmark in Sect. 6, followed by a discussion in Sect. 7. Section 8 concludes the paper and highlights future work.

2   Related Work

In the literature, several general purpose RDF benchmarks were developed on both artificial data and real datasets. We briefly summarize them in this section. FEASIBLE [10] which is a cluster-based SPARQL benchmark generator, which is able to synthesize customized benchmarks from the query logs of SPARQL endpoints.

The Lehigh University Benchmark (LUBM) [7] uses a dataset generated for the university domain. In the publication domain, the SP2Bench [11] benchmark uses a both a synthetic test data and artificial queries.

The Berlin SPARQL Benchmark (BSBM) [4] applies a use case on e-commerce in various triple stores. BSBM data and queries are artificial.

The DBpedia SPARQL Benchmark (DBPSB) [8] is another more recent benchmark for RDF stores. It uses DBPedia with up to 239M triples, starting with 14M to compare the scalability. The Waterloo SPARQL Diversity Test Suite (WatDiv) [1] addresses the stress testing of five RDF stores for diverse queries and varied workloads.

Iguana framework [5] provides with a configurable and integrated environment for executing SPARQL benchmarks. It also allows a uniform comparison of results across different benchmarks. However, we use for this benchmark a

---

[2] https://publications.europa.eu.

different tool and plan to use Iguana for a more systematic benchmark with cloud-based RDF stores.

All the above-mentioned benchmarks are not in the cloud environment as it is the case of this work. We aim at pushing the benchmark comparison into the cloud since many stakeholders are transitioning to adopt the Software-as-a-Service (SaaS) paradigm.

However, our work is similar to the report by TigerGraph [12] where the authors make a comparison of Amazon with other four property graph (PG) databases: TigerGraph, Neo4J, JanusGraph and ArangoDB. The main difference with our work is the focus of the study. While in [12] they examine the data loading and query performance of Neptune supporting PG model, we explore in this work the support of RDF by Neptune.

3   Dataset and Queries

3.1   Datasets

Two datasets are used for the loading experiment, a dump dataset used in production with 2,195 nquads files [9] and an augmented version based on the previous dataset of 2B triples. The dataset is available in Zenodo.[3]. For comparison in the loading process, we use a dump version of Wikidata[4] with 9.43B triples. Table 1 summarizes the statistics of the datasets.

Table 1. Datasets statistics and RDF serializations.

Dataset	#Files	#Triples	RDF Format
PO Dataset	2195	727 959 570	NQUADS
PO Augmented Dataset	6585	2 183 878 710	NQUADS
Wikidata Dump	1	9.43B	Turtle

3.2   SPARQL Queries

We use three different types of SPARQL queries according to their usage at Pulications Office. Each time has a different goal with respect to the required time to complete.

- *Instantaneous queries*: These queries are generally used to dynamically generate dynamic visualizations on the website. Thus, they should be faster for user experience. In this group, we have a total of 20 queries, divided into 3 types of SPARQL queries: SELECT with 16 queries, DESCRIBE with 3 queries and CONSTRUCT with one query.

---

[3] https://doi.org/10.5281/zenodo.1036738.
[4] https://dumps.wikimedia.org/wikidatawiki/entities/20190729/wikidata-20190729-all.ttl.gz.

– *Analytical queries*: These queries are used for validation and mapping purposes at PO, where the most important feature is the quality of the results, not only the time to answer the query. In a total of 24 validation and mappings queries, all of them are SELECT SPARQL queries.
– *Update queries*: This set is composed of 5 SPARQL queries with 1 CONSTRUCT; 1 DELETE/INSERT and 3 INSERT with a limit time to get the results in 10s.

4   Neptune Benchmark Settings

We now cover the settings for configuring AWS Neptune instance, and the benchmark settings.

4.1   AWS Neptune Configuration

Neptune is a service in the Amazon Web services (AWS). This means you need to first have an account. Once logged into the profile, the following steps are the ones required specifically for creating an instance of Neptune:

– Configure an Amazon Virtual Private Cloud (VPC), which is important to secure the access to your endpoint.
– Configure an Amazon Elastic Compute Cloud (EC2) instance. This is an important step because it is the location of the scripts to access the Neptune instances. Additional information is also useful for security reason, such as a private key (.pem) and a public DNS.
– Configure a S3 bucket. It is the container to host the data to be loaded in Neptune, with the corresponding Identity and Access Management (IAM) role.
– Create an instance DB Neptune: This is where we actually create an endpoint in the same VPC as the Bucket S3. In our case, we choose the EAST-1 region. We use a db.r4.4xlarge (16 vCPU, 122 GB RAM)[5], which is somewhat close to the settings on the previous benchmark[6]. However, for the purpose of comparing the effects of varying the size of the instances during the loading time, we use other types of instances, respectively db.r4.8xlarge and db.r5.12xlarge.

4.2   Benchmark Settings

The benchmark starts once the datasets are loaded into the AWS Neptune. We do not take into account the time of loading the source files in an S3 bucket. The benchmark comprises the following steps:

---

[5] https://docs.aws.amazon.com/AmazonRDS/latest/UserGuide/Concepts.DBInstanceClass.html.
[6] Hardware configuration: Intel(R) Xeon(R) CPU E5-2620 v3 @ 2.40 GHz, 6C/12T,128 GB RAM with SATA disk.

1. **Configuration step**: We set in the corresponding configuration file the time-out value for the queries. This forces the store to abort or kill the process running the query.
2. **Warm-up step**: To measure the performance of a triple store under operational conditions, a warm-up phase is used. In the warm-up phase, queries are executed on the triple store. We used a warm-up set to 20, meaning that we run 20 times the set of queries in each category before starting the run phase.
3. **Hot-run step**: During this phase, the benchmark query mixes were sent to the tested store. We keep track of each run and output the results in a CSV file containing the statistics. We perform 5 runs in this stage and also set the max delay between query is set to 1000s.

5   Results Bulk Loading

We go through the results obtained during the loading process, querying both sets of SPARQL queries and a stress test.

The loading in Neptune is possible once the dataset is already available in a S3 Bucket. In our case, we had to first transfer it into the bucket, without reporting the time taken for this task. Hence, we assume the dataset is ready to be loaded into Neptune.

```
1  curl -X POST \
2      -H 'Content-Type: application/json' \
3      http://opocegen2bio.c1hdbvigzcza.us-east-1.neptune.amazonaws.com
          :8182/loader -d '
4      {
5        "source" : "s3://mdk-neptune-gen2bio",
6        "format" : "nquads",
7        "iamRoleArn" : "arn:aws:iam::672418254241:role/
            neptuneFroms3LoaderRole",
8        "region" : "us-east-1",
9        "failOnError" : "FALSE"
10     }'
```

Listing 1.1. Loading call process with AWS Neptune

In the Listing 1.1, line 3 specifies the endpoint for the loader, and lines 4–8 the source S3 bucket, format, IAMRole and the location of the endpoint.

Loading on Db.r4.4xlarge Instance. Table 2 summarizes the time to load different sizes of datasets. Wikidata Dump is used to estimate the time for almost 10 Billion. The results show an increase of 1 hour compared to Neptune Preview for loading 727.95 Million triples. Overall, the order of magnitude (less than 5 h) is like Virtuoso (3.8 h) and Stardog (4.59 h). However, when it comes to load 2.18 Billion triples, Neptune is faster than Virtuoso (13.01 h) and Stardog (13.30 h)

This result is useful in an emergency case of a database corruption with the need to reload the dataset from scratch within a reasonable exploitation time frame maintenance.

Table 2. Loading time per dataset in Neptune 1.0.1.

Dataset	Size	Time(h)
PO Dataset	727.95 Million	4.2
PO Augmented Dataset	2.183 Billion	12.9
Wikidata Dump	9.43 Billion	72

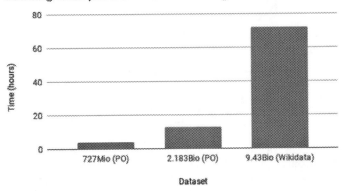

Fig. 1. Loading time in hours with Neptune. Mio=Million ; Bio=Billion

Figure 1 depicts the performance time in hours taken by Neptune 1.0.1 on a db.r4.xlarge instance.

Loading on Other EC2 Instances. We evaluate the loading with bigger instances of Neptune to evaluate the impact of the loader with respect to the hardware. We observe a high correlation (0.999) between the times on loading the above-mentioned datasets in both 4xlarge and 8xlarge. Table 3 shows the corresponding values obtained during this sub task.

Table 3. Loading on a db.r4.4xlarge vs r4.8xlarge

Dataset size	Time 4xlarge (h)	Time 8xlarge (h)
727 Million	4.2	2.7
2.18 Billion	12.95	7.29
9.43 Billion	72	42.63

We even decide to load Wikidata Dump on a r5.12xlarge[7] (vCPU: 48 RAM: 384 GiB), and the task completed in $75,932s$, that is $21.09h$. Thus, reducing to almost one day compared to its predecessor, r4.8xlarge (Fig. 2).

---

[7] https://aws.amazon.com/ec2/instance-types/r5/.

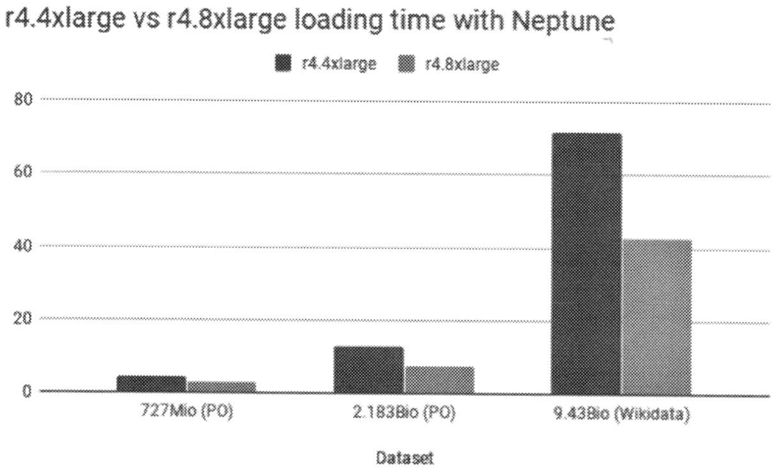

r4.4xlarge vs r4.8xlarge loading time with Neptune

Fig. 2. Overview of the completion time on different EC2 instances.

6   Benchmarking AWS Neptune

We use the SPARQL Query Benchmarker tool[8], an open-source tool based on Jena to run our experiment. We set 20 runs of mix queries per category to warm up the server. Furthermore, we make 5 additional runs to compute the average of the time taken for each query. Each group of queries has different time out which was decided based on functional requirements by experts at Publications Office. The timeout settings are 60s for instantaneous queries and 600s for analytical queries.

The script in Listing 1.2 shows the setup of the benchmark with a timeout value of 600s on a set of queries in a TSV file, and the results gathered in a CSV file.

```
1 ./benchmark -s 0 -t 600 -q \ http://mdk.cluster-cai4oe44teuh.us-east-1-
       beta.rds.amazonaws.com:8182/sparql -m mixqueries_cat2_neptune.tsv \
2 -r 5 -w 20 -c results/results_neptune_group2.csv
```

Listing 1.2. sample command used to run an instance of AWS Neptune with analytical queries

6.1   Evaluating Instantaneous Queries

We proceed to compare the results of querying the RDF stores using the benchmarker tool. We gathered the output of each run in CSV files as explained in the previous section. We use set two substasks: (i) first by using a single thread and (ii) by emulating multiple clients with the same set of queries.

Single Thread. Table 4 shows the results obtained by the 3 versions of Neptune. Neptune 1.0.1 timed out with 8 queries, which an improvement over the preview version

---

[8] https://github.com/rvesse/sparql-query-bm.

(9 timed out), but not with Neptune 1.0 (7 timed out). While query IQ10 was under 60s, the same query with Neptune 1.0.1 timed out.

Comparing the results obtained with other enterprise RDF stores, such are Virtuoso, Oracle 12c, Stardog and GraphDB, we conclude that Neptune performs poorly with respect to this set of queries. Table 5 summarizes the number of queries with timeout obtained by all five RDF stores. Neptune is at the bottom of the ranking with Virtuoso the clear winner.

Table 4. Average response time in second per queries over different versions of Neptune. Neptune P. = preview version.

Query	Neptune P.	Neptune 1.0	Neptune 1.0.1
IQ1	.04	.07	.08
IQ2	.05	.07	.08
IQ3	.09	.07	.09
IQ4	.12	.05	.07
IQ5	60	60	60
IQ6	60	20.47	59.96
IQ7	60	60	60
IQ8	60	60	60
IQ9	60	60	60
IQ10	60	55.99	60
IQ11	.12	.05	.06
IQ12	60	60	60
IQ13	.09	.07	.11
IQ14	60	60	60
IQ15	.08	.04	.04
IQ16	.09	.05	.04
IQ17	60	60	60
IQ18	.21	.15	.21
IQ19	.14	.11	.14
IQ20	.09	.04	.05

It indicates that Neptune 1.0.0 solved the problem with IQ10, but it appeared in version 1.0.1. We observe also in general that Neptune 1.0 performed better than the other two versions.

Table 5. Number of timeouts per RDF stores

RDF Stores	nbTimeOut	Rank
Virtuoso	0	1
Oracle	2	2
Stardog	2	2
GraphDB	4	3
Neptune 1.0.1	8	4

Next, we manually rewrite seven queries (IQ5, IQ6, IQ7, IQ8, IQ12, IQ14 and IQ17) using the `EXPLAIN`[9] feature of Neptune. The main strategy is to incorporate `hint:Group hint:joinOrder"Ordered"`. Interestingly, Neptune is 4x faster (QMpH[10] = 6.65 w.r.t. 26.59), and with a reduced number of queries reaching the limits. Table 6 shows the differences using optimized queries.

Table 6. Average response time in second per queries with optimized queries in Neptune 1.0.1

Query	Avg. time (s)	Previous bench (s)
IQ5r	.04	**60**
IQ6r	.68	59.96
IQ7r	.057	**60**
IQ8r	.03	**60**
IQ12r	.14	**60**
IQ14r	.03	**60**
IQ17r	.05	**60**

Multi-Thread. In real-world settings, a SPARQL endpoint usually receives concurrent queries. We test this feature in the benchmark by emulating multi-threading to AWS Neptune 1.0.1 with respectively 5 clients, 20 clients, 50 clients, 70 clients and 100 clients. We observe a constant value of QMPH of **6.65**. Moreover, it places Neptune in second position after Virtuoso, and before Oracle, GraphDB and Stardog. Table 7 presents the results of QMpH values in case of multi-thread benchmark for instantaneous queries.

Table 7. QMpH values in multi-threading bench for instantaneous queries

RDF Store	5clients	20clients	50clients	70clients	100clients
Neptune 1.0.1	6.653	6.654	6.655	6.654	6.654
Virtuoso 7.2.4.2	367.22	358.27	371.76	354.60	341.02
GraphDB EE 8.2	2.13	2.12	2.13	2.12	2.13
Stardog 4.3	1.973	1.94	1.97	1.96	1.95
Oracle 12c	2.10	1.99	2.01	2.01	2.02

---

[9] https://docs.aws.amazon.com/neptune/latest/userguide/sparql-explain-operators.html.
[10] QMpH = Query Mixed per Hour.

6.2 Evaluating Analytical Queries

We set 600 s for timeout because the queries in this category are more analytical-based queries, and so need more time to complete. This value is based on the business requirement at PO. Table 8 presents the results of Neptune throughout the different versions. Surprisingly, there is no time out with these set of queries, and the latest version of Neptune is 4x faster than the two previous versions. Regarding the comparison with related triple stores, Table 9 reports the 3rd position for Neptune, compared to Virtuoso, GraphDB, Oracle and Stardog.

Table 8. Average response time in second per analytical SPARQL queries with Neptune versions.

Query	Neptune Preview	Neptune 1.0	Neptune 1.0.1
AQ1	15.94	13.69	12.98
AQ2	36.12	30.10	20.98
AQ3	56.62	43.71	28.81
AQ4	1.08	2.89	1.12
AQ5	63.71	102.75	19.70
AQ6	1.12	3.56	1.14
AQ7	.04	.14	.05
AQ8	.84	2.20	.62
AQ9	.06	.24	.05
AQ10	25.80	102.71	62.71
AQ11	.97	3.74	1.37
AQ12	28.16	594.60	87.79
AQ13	.24	.91	.74
AQ14	120.36	300.85	120.60
AQ15	14.01	28.39	15.42
AQ16	5.24	6.89	2.69
AQ17	2.63	17.16	1.56
AQ18	12.89	21.58	14.35
AQ19	5.23	8.09	2.72
AQ20	2.60	1.37	1.50
AQ21	17.78	25.42	19.71
AQ22	5.36	12.71	2.96
AQ23	2.77	5.14	1.78
AQ24	3.04	7.34	2.21

Table 9. Ranking of Neptune with other RDF stores using analytical queries

RDF Store	QMpH	Rank
Virtuoso 7.2.4.2	80.23	1
GraphDB EE 8.2	19.94	2
Neptune 1.0.1	8.4	3
Oracle 12c	2.41	4
Stardog 4.3	.89	5

6.3 Evaluating Updates Queries

Single Thread. We set the queries in this group of queries to finish in 10s. Table 10, with a total of **14,694** QMpH. This result is almost 2K more than the results obtained with Virtuoso under the same queries. This is the first scenario where Neptune outperforms any other RDF store in this benchmark, with all the precaution with the comparison as we stated in the previous section. Table 11 summarizes the ranking for this set of queries.

Table 10. Average time in seconds with update queries

Query	Avg time (s)
UQ1	0.05
UQ2	0.07
UQ3	0.01
UQ4	0.01
UQ5	0.01

It also shows that the winner for this task is Neptune. Additionally, Neptune shares more or less the same order of magnitude with regards to numbers of QMpH. However, there is a huge gap with the three other RDF stores.

Table 11. Ranking of Neptune

RDF Stores	Avg time (s)	QMpH	Rank
Neptune	.24	14,594.81	1
Virtuoso	.29	12,372.49	2
GraphDB EE	.87	4,133.53	3
Stardog	11.83	304.14	4
Oracle	50	71.99	5

Multi-thread. In this scenario, we observe a non constant values when varying the number of clients. Figure 3 presents the evolution of QMpH, which starts with QMpH = 5225 on 5 clients to reach the value of 461 with 100 simultaneous clients.

Table 12 presents an overview values with other RDF stores. Neptune follows Oracle in the highest numbers of QMpH. Surprisingly, this is the only situation where Oracle performs better than the rest of the RDF stores.

6.4 Stability Test

We perform a stress test on the triple stores to have a quantitative indication related to stability. For this purpose, all the set of instantaneous queries are run continuously under a progressively increasing load to see how the engine reacts to high load. We use this test to empirically evaluate how stable is the RDF store.

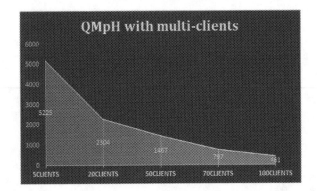

Fig. 3. Evolution of QMpH for different clients on updates queries

Table 12. QMpH values in multi-threading bench for updates queries

RDF Store	5clients	20clients	50clients	70clients	100clients
Neptune 1.0.1	5225	2304	1467	797	461
Virtuoso 7.2.4.2	71.32	48.34	48.51	48.32	48.26
GraphDB EE 8.2	273.18	146.87	79.52	52.18	56.24
Stardog 4.3	35.47	36.65	35.18	32.42	26.17
Oracle 12c	8382.21	8358.48	6980.34	7771.74	8718.96

The test starts by specifying the number of parallel clients within the script. Each client completes the run of the mix queries in parallel. The number of parallel clients is then multiplied by the ramp up factor and the process is repeated. This is repeated until either the maximum runtime or the maximum number of threads are reached. We set the maximum runtime to 180 minutes and set the maximum parallel threads to 128.

Listing 1.3 displays a sample command used to run the stress test on a given triple store.

```
1  ./stress -q <https://my/neptune.location.amazonaws.com:8182/sparql> -m
       mixqueries_cat1.tsv --max-runtime 180 --max-threads 128 --ramp-up 2.
```

Listing 1.3. Sample command used to run the stress test

Neptune finishes with the limit of the parallel threads, unlike Virtuoso and GraphDB that completed the test after 180 min, reaching 256 parallel threads. The results in Table 13 suggest that Neptune is less stable than GraphDB and Virtuoso based on the total mix runs, the parallel threads and the total errors.

Table 13. Results of the stress test on triple stores using instantaneous queries.

RDF Store	#mix runs	#op. run	Max.//.threads	# HTTP 5xx Errors
GraphDB	255	5,100	256	139
Virtuoso	255	5,100	256	4,732
Neptune 1.0.1	127	2,540	256	1,136
Stardog	92	1,840	128	576
Oracle	63	1,260	128	1,009

7   Discussion

We proceed to compare the results across the versions of Neptune, as well as with non cloud-based solutions of our previous work. We also briefly highlight some arguments for the potential impact of the resource.

7.1   Comparison Across Neptune Versions

The loader of Neptune 1.0.1 is less faster compared to Neptune Preview, at least with the experiment on 727 Million datasets, with almost the same behaviour with the previous version of 1.0. We observe a regression in terms of engine optimization when upgrading the minor version of Neptune 1.0. in the case of querying instantaneous queries. We agree on a faster engine after the preview release on the same set of queries.

7.2   Comparison with Non-cloud-based RDF Stores

We use Neptune 1.0.1 to proceed with some of our previous results with non-cloud RDF stores. Table 14 presents the results when querying those 8 queries with at least 6 Basic Graph Patterns (BGPs) in instantaneous queries. Neptune falls in 80% of the total queries.

Table 14. Comparison results time execution (in second) of the seven instantaneous queries with at least seven six BGPs.

Query	Neptune	Virtuoso	GraphDB	Stardog	Oracle	#BGP
IQ5	**60**	.09	.01	.82	31.35	7
IQ6	59.96	.28	.01	.10	39.35	6
IQ7	**60**	.06	.01	.01	34.82	7
IQ8	**60**	.10	.01	1.35	31.88	7
IQ9	**60**	.05	.01	.20	**60**	7
IQ10	**60**	.12	**60**	**60**	3.64	7
IQ19	.04	.11	**60**	**60**	.04	11

Table 15. Comparison results time in seconds of querying analytical queries with a mix of SPARQL features.

Query	Neptune	Virtuoso	GraphDB	Stardog	Oracle
AQ13	.74	.06	.01	26.28	85.19
AQ14	120.60	.06	.01	.10	206.308
AQ15	15.42	.72	.06	**60**	3.74
AQ18	14.35	.06	.01	292.24	2.93

Now, we consider in the analytical queries, those queries containing a combination of at least three of the SPARQL features REGEX, DISTINCT, FILTER, OPTIONAL and GROUP BY. Table 15 shows the results by comparing Neptune with other RDF stores. While AQ14 hits a highest time reported by Neptune, it is rather surprising the huge difference with GraphDB, Virtuoso and Stardog.

7.3 Potential Impact

The main dataset used in production by the Publications Office for this benchmark has been granted usage to three persons from different organizations and RDF vendors (Allegrograph, RDFox) with the goal of replicating this benchmark. The recent justification of usage last September was by someone who wanted to:

- Perform more benchmarks against Neptune
- See how Neptune Query Plans hints can influence the response of complex SPARQL queries

We imagine that the person is either using Neptune or works closely with Amazon. Therefore, we argue that the resource has an impact in assessing RDF stores in general, hence supports the adoption of Semantic Web technologies in industry.

In summary, this benchmark shows the following insights:

- Neptune loader has been slower since the Preview version, probably a design choice while gaining new features.
- Neptune 1.0 is faster than the upgraded minor version with instantaneous queries.
- Neptune 1.0.1 engine is 4x faster than the previous versions when it comes to analytical queries.
- In general, Neptune performs well in multi threading scenario, and outperforms in updates queries.
- The stability test reveals that Neptune is less stable than GraphDB and Virtuoso, which are the most stables in this task.
- Benchmarking a cloud-based solution comes with a financial cost, that has be taken into consideration when planning such task.

8 Conclusion

We have presented in this paper an empirical evaluation of AWS Neptune on real-world RDF datasets. We have described the steps to do such a benchmark with the goal to ease reproducibility. To this end, we used the same resource across three different versions of Neptune, which span for almost two years.

We compare the results obtained with our previous work on benchmarking enterprise RDF stores. This comparison is used to put in perspective, knowing the limitations of a strict comparison. For example, the settings of the hardware used in that work (SATA disk and 128 GB RAM) are not *stricto sensu* comparable with Amazon instance (db.r4.4xlarge), or that Neptune is a multi-modal data graph on the cloud.

The resource for this benchmark and the results are accessible online on Zenodo[11] with a CC-BY-4.0[12] license attached to it. We hope this work will show a growing interest in a more rigorous assessment of AWS Neptune with existing latest versions of RDF Graph Databases on the cloud.

Acknowledgments. We would like to thank the AWS team based in Paris, in particular Jean-Philippe Pinte and Alice Temem for granting us credits to perform our test on Neptune.

References

1. Aluç, G., Hartig, O., Özsu, M.T., Daudjee, K., et al.: Diversified stress testing of RDF data management systems. In: Mika, P. (ed.) ISWC 2014. LNCS, vol. 8796, pp. 197–212. Springer, Cham (2014). https://doi.org/10.1007/978-3-319-11964-9_13

2. Amazon: Amazon neptune: Fast, reliable graph database built for the cloud (11 2017). https://aws.amazon.com/about-aws/whats-new/2017/11/amazon-neptune-fast-reliable-graph-database-built-for-the-cloud/

3. Atemezing, G.A., Amardeilh, F., et al.: Benchmarking commercial RDF stores with publications office dataset. In: Gangemi, A. (ed.) ESWC 2018. LNCS, vol. 11155, pp. 379–394. Springer, Cham (2018). https://doi.org/10.1007/978-3-319-98192-5_54

4. Bizer, C., Schultz, A.: Benchmarking the performance of storage systems that expose SPARQL endpoints. World Wide Web Internet And Web Information Systems (2008)

5. Conrads, F., Lehmann, J., Saleem, M., Morsey, M., Ngonga Ngomo, A.C.: IGUANA: A generic framework for benchmarking the read-write performance of triple stores. In: International Semantic Web Conference (ISWC) (2017), https://svn.aksw.org/papers/2017/ISWC_Iguana/public.pdf

6. Consortium, W.W.W., et al.: SPARQL 1.1 overview (2013)

7. Guo, Y., Pan, Z., Heflin, J.: LUBM: a benchmark for owl knowledge base systems. Web Semant. Sci. Serv. Agents World Wide Web **3**(2), 158–182 (2005)

8. Morsey, M., Lehmann, J., Auer, S., Ngonga Ngomo, A.C.: DBpedia SPARQL benchmark-performance assessment with real queries on real data. In: ISWC 2011 (2011). http://jens-lehmann.org/files/2011/dbpsb.pdf

9. Publications, O., Mondeca: dump of RDF dataset used for RDF benchmark (2017). http://doi.org/10.5281/zenodo.1036739

---

[11] https://doi.org/10.6084/m9.figshare.13414817.
[12] https://creativecommons.org/licenses/by/4.0.

10. Saleem, M., Mehmood, Q., Ngonga Ngomo, A.-C., et al.: FEASIBLE: a feature-based SPARQL benchmark generation framework. In: Arenas, M. (ed.) ISWC 2015. LNCS, vol. 9366, pp. 52–69. Springer, Cham (2015). https://doi.org/10.1007/978-3-319-25007-6_4
11. Schmidt, M., Hornung, T., Lausen, G., Pinkel, C.: Sp^2Bench: a SPARQL performance benchmark. In: IEEE 25th International Conference on Data Engineering, 2009. ICDE 2009, pp. 222–233. IEEE (2009)
12. TigerGraph: Benchmarking graph analytic systems. Technical report, TigerGraph (2018). https://cdn2.hubspot.net/hubfs/4114546/Collateral/TigerGraph%20Benchmar%20Report.pdf

Towards Knowledge Graphs Validation Through Weighted Knowledge Sources

Elwin Huaman[1]([✉])[iD], Amar Tauqeer[1][iD], and Anna Fensel[1,2][iD]

[1] Semantic Technology Institute (STI) Innsbruck, Department of Computer Science, University of Innsbruck, Innsbruck, Austria
{elwin.huaman,amar.tauqeer}@sti2.at
[2] Wageningen Data Competence Center and Consumption and Healthy Lifestyles Chair Group, Wageningen University & Research, Wageningen, The Netherlands
anna.fensel@wur.nl

Abstract. The performance of applications, such as personal assistants and search engines, relies on high-quality knowledge bases, a.k.a. Knowledge Graphs (KGs). To ensure their quality one important task is knowledge validation, which measures the degree to which statements or triples of KGs are semantically correct. KGs inevitably contain incorrect and incomplete statements, which may hinder their adoption in business applications as they are not trustworthy. In this paper, we propose and implement a Validator that computes a confidence score for every triple and instance in KGs. The computed score is based on finding the same instances across different weighted knowledge sources and comparing their features. We evaluate our approach by comparing its results against a baseline validation. Our results suggest that we can validate KGs with an f-measure of at least 75%. Time-wise, the Validator, performed a validation of 2530 instances in 15 min approximately. Furthermore, we give insights and directions toward a better architecture to tackle KG validation.

Keywords: Knowledge graph validation · Knowledge graph curation · Knowledge graph assessment

1 Introduction

Over the last decade, creating and especially maintaining knowledge bases have gained attention, and therefore large knowledge bases, also known as knowledge graphs (KGs) [12], have been created, either automatically (e.g. NELL [4]), semi-automatically (e.g. DBpedia [2]), or through crowdsourcing (e.g. Freebase [3]). Today, open (e.g. Wikidata) and proprietary (e.g. Knowledge Vault) KGs provide information about entities like hotels, places, restaurants, and statements about them, e.g. address, phone number, and website. With the increasing use of KGs in personal assistant and search engine applications, the need to ensure that statements or triples in KGs are correct arises [9,13,19]. For example, Google shows the fact (*Gartenhotel Maria Theresia GmbH, phone, 05223*

B. Villazón-Terrazas et al. (Eds.): KGSWC 2021, CCIS 1459, pp. 47–60, 2021.
https://doi.org/10.1007/978-3-030-91305-2_4

563130), which might be wrong because the *phone* number of the *Gartenhotel* is *05223 56313*, moreover, there will be cases where the *phone* number is not up-to-date or is missing [14].

To face this challenge, we developed an approach to validate a KG against different knowledge sources. Our approach involves (1) mapping the different knowledge sources to a common schema (e.g. Schema.org[1]), (2) instance matching that ensures that we are comparing the same entity across the different knowledge sources, (3) confidence measurement, which computes a confidence score for each triple and instance in the KG, and (4) visualization that offers an interface to interact with. Furthermore, we describe use cases where our approach can be used.

There have been a few approaches proposed to validate KGs. In this paper, we review methods, tools, and benchmarks for knowledge validation. We found out that most of them focus on validating knowledge against the Web or Wikipedia. For example, the approaches measure the degree to which a statement (e.g. *Paris is the capital of France*) is true based on the number of occurrences of the statement in sources such as Wikipedia, websites, and/or textual corpora. In addition, to the best of our knowledge, no studies have investigated how to validate KGs by collecting matched instances from other weighted structured knowledge sources.

In this paper, we propose a weighted approach that validates a KG against a set of weighted knowledge sources, which have different weight (or degree of importance) for different application scenarios. For example, users can define the degree of importance of a knowledge source according to the task at hand. We validate a KG by finding the same instances across different knowledge sources, comparing their features, and scoring them. The score ranges from 0 to 1, which indicates the degree to which an instance is semantically correct for the task at hand.

This paper is structured as follows. Section 2 presents related state-of-the-art methods, tools, and benchmarks. Section 3 describes our validation approach. We evaluate our approach and show its results in Sect. 4. Furthermore, in Sect. 5 we list use cases where our approach may be needed. Finally, we conclude with Sect. 6, providing some remarks and future work plans.

2   Literature Review

Knowledge Validation (KV), a.k.a. fact checking, is the task of assessing how likely a given fact or statement is true or semantically correct [10,15,20]. There are currently several state-of-the-art methods and tools available that are suitable for KV. One of the prior works on automating this task focuses on analysing trustworthiness factors of web search results (e.g. the trustworthiness of web pages based on topic majority, which computes the number of pages related to a query) [17]. Another approach is proposed by Yin et al. [27]. Here, the authors

---

[1] https://schema.org/.

define the trustworthiness of a website based on the confidence of facts provided by the website, for instance, they propose an algorithm called *TruthFinder*. Moreover, [5] present Knowledge Vault, which is a probabilistic knowledge base that combines information extraction and machine learning techniques to compute the probability that a statement is correct. The computed score is based on knowledge extracted from the Web and corroborative paths found on Freebase. However, the Web can yield noisy data and prior knowledge bases may be incomplete. Therefore, we propose an approach that not only takes into account the user's preferences for weighting knowledge sources, but also complements the existing probabilistic approaches.

We surveyed methods for validating statements in KGs and we distinguish them according to the data used by them, as follows: a) *internal* approaches use the knowledge graph itself as input and b) *external* approaches use external data sources (e.g. DBpedia) as input. In the context of this paper, we only consider the approaches that use external knowledge sources for validating statements.

The external approaches use external sources like the DBpedia source to validate a statement. For instance, there are approaches that use websites information [5,11,22], Wikipedia pages [7,18,23], DBpedia knowledge base [16,20], and so on. In contrast to other approaches, [16] present an early stage approach that uses DBpedia to find out *sameAs* links, which are followed for retrieving evidence triples in other knowledge sources and [20] uses DBpedia to retrieve temporal constraints for a fact. However, [16] do not provide an evaluation of the approach to be compared with our approach and [20] focus on validating dynamic data, which we do not tackle in the scope of this paper. Furthermore, there are methods that use topic coherence [1] and information extraction [22] techniques to validate knowledge. Obviously, there is not only one approach or ideal solution to validate KGs. The proposed tools – DeFacto[2], Leopard[3], FactCheck[4], and FacTify[5]– rely on the Web and/or external knowledge sources like Wikipedia.

The current Web-based approaches can effectively validate knowledge that is well disseminated on the Web, e.g. *Albert Einstein's date of birth is March 14, 1879*. Furthermore, the confidence score is based on the number of occurrences of a statement in a corpus (e.g. Wikipedia). Unfortunately these approaches are also prone to spamming [24]. Therefore, a new approach is necessary to further improve KG validation. In this paper, we propose a KG validation approach, which computes a confidence score for each triple and instance of KGs.

Furthermore, an evaluation of validation approaches is really important, therefore, we also surveyed knowledge validation benchmarks that have been proposed, however, the number of them is currently rather limited. [26] and [7] released a benchmark consisting of triples extracted from a KG (e.g. Yago) and textual evidences retrieved from a corpus (e.g., Wikipedia). Furthermore. [25]

---

[2] https://github.com/DeFacto/DeFacto.
[3] https://github.com/dice-group/Leopard.
[4] https://github.com/dice-group/FactCheck.
[5] http://qweb.cs.aau.dk/factify/.

released FEVER[6] that is a dataset containing 185K claims about entities which were verified using Wikipedia articles. Moreover, FactBench[7] (Fact Validation Benchmark) provides a multilingual (i.e. English, German and French) benchmark that describes several relations (e.g. Award, Birth, Death, Foundation Place) of entities.

All benchmarks mentioned above have focused mostly on textual sources, i.e. unstructured information. Therefore, from the best of our knowledge, there is no available benchmark that can be used for validating knowledge graphs via collecting matched instances from other structured knowledge sources.

Last but not least, the reviewed approaches are mostly focused on validating well disseminated knowledge than factual knowledge. Furthermore, benchmarks are built for validating specific tools or to be used during contests like FEVER. Another interesting observation is that Wikipedia is the most frequently used by external approaches (i.e. Wikipedia as textual corpus for finding evidences). Finally, to make future works on knowledge graph validation comparable, it would be useful to have a common selection of benchmarks.

3   Approach

In this section, we present the conceptualization of our KG validation approach. First, we give an overview of the knowledge validation process (see Fig. 1). Second, we state the input needed for our approach in Sect. 3.1. In Sect. 3.2, we describe the need for a common attribute space between knowledge sources. Then, in Sect. 3.3, we explain the instance matching process. Afterwards, confidence measurement of instances is detailed in Sect. 3.4. Finally, in Sect. 3.5, we describe the output of our implemented approach.

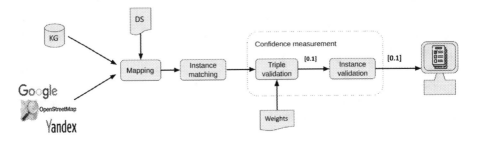

Fig. 1. Knowledge graph validation process overview.

The input to the Validator is a KG, which can be provided via a SPARQL endpoint or an RDF dataset in Turtle[8] format. This input KG is first mapped

---

[6] https://github.com/sheffieldnlp/fever-naacl-2018.

[7] https://github.com/DeFacto/FactBench.

[8] https://www.w3.org/TR/turtle/.

based on a Domain Specification[9] (DS), which basically defines the mapping of the KG to a common format, e.g., this process may be performed by a domain expert, who defines the types and properties that are relevant to the task at hand or the user's need [21]. A DS defines the instance type and properties values to be validated. Internally, the Validator is configured to retrieve data from external sources, which are also mapped to the common format. After the mapping process has been done, the instance matching is used to find the same instances across the KG and the external sources. Then, the confidence measurement process is triggered and the features of same instances are compared with each other. For example, we compare the name value of an instance of the KG against the name value of the same instance in an external source. We repeat this process for every triple of an instance and we compute a triple confidence score, the triple confidence scores are later added to an aggregated confidence score for the instance. The computed scores are normalized according to the weights given to each knowledge source. We consider the quality of the external sources subjective, therefore, we provide a graphical user interface that allows users to weight each knowledge source.

3.1   Input

At first step, a user is required to provide a KG to be validated. For this, the user has two options, a) to provide a SPARQL endpoint where to fetch the data from or b) to load a dataset in a Turtle format. Moreover, the user is required to select, from a list of DSs, a DS that defines an instance type (e.g., Hotel, Person) and their corresponding properties (e.g., name, address). Internally, the Validator has been set up to fetch data from different external sources (e.g. Wikidata, DBpedia), which were selected based on their domain coverage for the task at hand and their widely use [8].

3.2   Mapping

Based on the DS defined in the input, the validator maps the input KG and the external sources to a common format, e.g., a telephone number of a hotel can be stored with different property names across the knowledge sources: *phone*, *telephone*, or *phone_number*. The validator provides a basic mapping feature to map the input KG and external data sources to a common attribute space. This step is not trivial. There is a huge number of knowledge sources and their schemas might be constantly changing [6]. As a result, schema alignment[10] is one of the major bottlenecks in the mapping process. Therefore, new methods and frameworks to tackle the schema heterogeneity are needed.

---

[9] Domain Specification are design patterns for annotating data based on Schema.org. This process implies to remove types and properties from Schema.org, or add types and properties defined in an external extension of Schema.org.

[10] Schema alignment is the task of determining the correspondences between various schemas.

3.3   Instance Matching

So far, we mapped knowledge sources to a common attribute space. However, a major challenge is to match instances across these knowledge sources. For that, the Validator requests to define at least two or more properties (e.g., *name* and *geo coordinates*) that are to be used for the instance matching process, which is constrained to strict matches on the defined property values. The resulting matched instance is returned to the Validator and processed to measure its confidence.

3.4   Confidence Measurement

Computing a confidence value can get complicated as the number of instances and their features can get out of hand quickly. Therefore, a means to automatically validate KGs is desirable. To compute a confidence value for an instance, the confidence value for each of its triples has to be evaluated first.

Triple Validation. calculates a confidence score of whether a property value on various external sources matches the property value in the user's KG. For example, the user's KG contains the *Hotel Alpenhof* instance and statements about it; *Hotel Alpenhof's phone is +4352878550* and *Hotel Alpenhof's address is Hintertux 750*. Furthermore, there are other sources, like Google Places, that also contain the *Hotel Alpenhof* instance and assertions about it.

The confidence score of *(Hotel Alpenhof, phone, +4352878550)* triple is computed by comparing the phone property value *+4352878550* against the same property value of the same instance in Google Places. For that, syntactic similarity matching of the attribute values is used. Then the phone property value is compared against a second knowledge source, and so on. Every similarity comparison returns a confidence value that later is added to an aggregated score for the triple.

We define a set of knowledge sources as S, $S = \{s_1, \ldots, s_m\}$, $s_i \in S$ with $1 \leq i \leq m$. The user's KG g consists of a set of instances that are to be validated against the set of knowledge sources S. A knowledge source s_i consists of a set of instances $E = \{e_1, \ldots, e_n\}$, $e_j \in E$ with $1 \leq j \leq n$ and an instance e_j consists of a set of attribute values $P = \{p_1, \ldots, p_M\}$, $p_k \in P$ for $1 \leq k \leq M$.

Furthermore, *sim* is a similarity function used to compare attribute pair k for two instances. We compute the similarity of an attribute value of two instances a, b. Where a represents an instance in the user's KG g, denoted $g(a)$, and b represents an instance in the knowledge source s_i, denoted $s_i(b)$.

$$triple_{confidence}(a_{p_k}, S, sim) = \sum_{i=1}^{m} sim(g(a_{p_k}), s_i(b_{p_k})) \tag{1}$$

Next, users have to set an external weight for each knowledge source s_i, $W = \{\omega_1, \ldots, \omega_m\}$ is a set of weights over the knowledge sources, such as ω_i defines a weight of importance for s_i, $0 \leq i \leq m$, $\omega_i \in W$ with $\omega_i \in [0, 1]$

where 0 is the minimum degree of importance and a value of 1 is the maximum degree. For the sum of weights $w_{sum} = \sum_{i=1}^{m} w_i = 1$ has to hold. We compute the weighted triple confidence as follows:

$$triple_{confidence}(a_{p_k}, S, sim, W) = \frac{1}{w_{sum}} \sum_{i=1}^{m} sim(g(a_{p_k}), s_i(b_{p_k}))w_i \quad (2)$$

The weighted approach[11] aims to model the different degrees of importance of different knowledge sources. None of the parameters can be taken out of their context, thus a default weight has to be given whenever the user does not set weights for an external source. The Validator assigns an equivalent weight for each source: $w_i = \frac{1}{m}$.

Instance Validation. computes the aggregated score from the attribute space of an instance. Given an instance a that consists of a set of attribute values $P = \{p_1, \ldots, p_M\}$, $p_k \in P$ for $1 \leq k \leq M$:

$$instance_{confidence}(a_{p_k}, S, sim, W) = \frac{1}{M} \sum_{k=1}^{M} triple_{confidence}(a_{p_k}, S, sim, W) \quad (3)$$

The instance confidence measures the degree to which an instance is correct based on the triple confidence of each of its attributes. The instance confidence score is compared against a threshold[12] $t \in [0,1]$. If $instance_{confidence} > t$ indicates its degree of correctness.

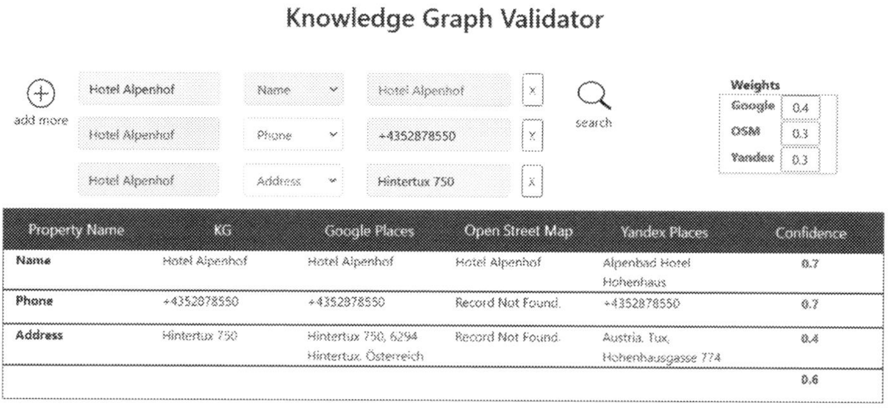

Fig. 2. Screenshot of the Validator Web interface.

---

[11] To define weights, a proper quality analysis of the knowledge sources must be carried out [8]. It may assist users in defining degrees of importance for each knowledge source.

[12] The default threshold is defined to 0.5.

3.5   Output

The computed scores for triples and instances are shown in a graphical user interface, see Fig. 2. The interface provides many features: it allows users to select multiple properties (e.g. address, name) to be validated, users can assign weights to external sources, it shows instance information from user's KG and external sources. For example, the Validator shows information of the *Hotel Alpenhof* instance from all sources. It also shows the triple confidence score for each triple, e.g. the triple confidence for the address property is 0.4, because the address value is confirmed only by Google Places.

Tools and Technologies. We implemented our approach in the Validator tool[13], which has been implemented in JavaScript[14] for retrieving data remotely, and Bootstrap[15] for the user interface.

4   Evaluation

This section describes the evaluation of our approach. The aim of the experiments is to show a qualitative and quantitative analysis of our approach. The setup used for the evaluation is described in Table 1.

Table 1. Evaluation setup

CPU	RAM	OS
AMD Ryzen 7 pro 4750u (16 Cores)	32 GB	Ubuntu 20.04.2 LTS 64-bit

In Sect. 4.1, we compare the Validator's validation result against a baseline. Next, we look into the scalability of the Validator in Sect. 4.2.

4.1   Qualitative Evaluation

The qualitative evaluation measures the effectiveness of the Validator based on a baseline validation. To do so, first, we describe a dataset to be used on the quality evaluation of our approach, later on we define a setup for the Validator and execute it. Then, we stablish a baseline to compare the result of the Validator.

Hotel Dataset. It was fetched from the Tirol Knowledge Graph[16] (TKG), which contains ∼15 Billion statements about hotels, places, and more, of the Tirol region. The data inside the TKG are static (e.g. name, phone number) and dynamic (e.g. availability of rooms, prices) and are based on Schema.org

---

[13] https://github.com/AmarTauqeer/graph-validation.
[14] https://developer.mozilla.org/en-US/docs/Web/JavaScript.
[15] https://getbootstrap.com/.
[16] https://graphdb.sti2.at/sparql.

annotations, which are collected from different sources such as destination management organizations and geographical information systems. We have created a benchmark dataset of 50 hotel instances[17] fetched from the TKG. We randomly selected 50 hotel instances in order to be able to perform a manual validation of their correctness and establish a baseline. The process of creating the Hotel dataset involved manual checking of the correctness of all instances and their attribute values.

Setup and Execution. First, we set up the Hotel dataset on the Validator. Second, we defined external sources, namely: Google Places[18], OpenStreetMap (OSM)[19], and Yandex Places[20]. Third, we defined the *Hotel* type and *address*, *name*, and *phone* properties that are used for mapping place instances from external sources. Then, for the instance matching process, we set up the *name* and *geo-coordinates* values to search for places within a specified area. We use the built-in feature provided by the external sources (e.g. Nearby Search for Google places) to search for an instance with the same name within a specific area. Furthermore, weights for the external sources are equally distributed. Finally, we run the validation task.

Baseline. In order to evaluate the results of the Validator, a baseline must be established. Given that no prior validation tool addresses exactly the task at hand, we made a manual validation of the Hotel dataset. We computed the precision, recall, and f-measure that a manual validation would achieve (See Fig. 3). During this evaluation, the 50 hotel instances are manually searched and compared to the results coming from each of the external knowledge sources: Google Places, OSM, and Yandex Places. The compared attributes are the *address*, *name*, and *phone*.

Result. We analyse the result of running the Validator on the Hotel dataset. These results are shown in Fig. 3. On one hand, it shows that the Validator performs almost equally similar as the manual evaluation when it comes to *name* and *phone* properties, on the other hand, the Validator does not perform well on the validation of the *address* property. Moreover, the results suggest that we can validate hotel instances with an f-measure of at least 75% on *address*, *name*, and *phone* properties. To interpret the results of our validation run, we choose precision, recall, and f-measure. Given the results of the Validator run, every validated triple result was classified as True Positive, False Positive, True Negative, or False Negative based on the baseline results.

---

[17] https://github.com/AmarTauqeer/graph-validation/tree/master/data.

[18] https://developers.google.com/maps/documentation/places/.

[19] https://www.openstreetmap.org/.

[20] https://yandex.com/dev/maps/.

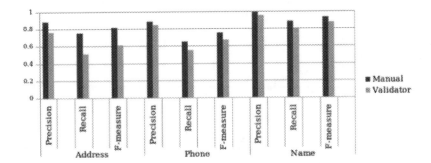

Fig. 3. Comparison of precision, recall, and f-measure scores over the manual and semi-automatic validation.

4.2   Scalability Evaluation

Another challenge of a validation framework is the scalability. In this section, we describe our evaluation approach in terms of scalability of our approach.

Pantheon Dataset. It contains manually validated data with 11341 famous biographies [28]. Pantheon describes information like name, year of birth, place of birth, occupation, and many more. We have selected politician domain and created a dataset of 2530 politician instances. We selected the politician domain because it has the highest number of instances in the Pantheon dataset. Furthermore, we had to convert the Pantheon dataset to Turtle format, for that we used Tarql[21] tool. Last but not least, we selected the politician domain in order to prove the general applicability of our approach in different domains (e.g., Hotel, Person).

Setup and Execution. The setup for validating datasets from different domains changes slightly, for example, defining the external sources where to fetch the data from. First, we set up the Pantheon dataset on the Validator. Then, we defined Wikidata and DBpedia as external sources and we distributed equivalent weights for them. Moreover, we defined the *person* type and *name* and *year of birth* properties for mapping politicians from the external sources. Moreover, we set up the *name* and *year of birth* for the instance matching process. Finally, we execute the validation task.

Result. We validated 2530 politician instances by using the Validator, which compares and computes a confidence score for each triple and instance. To execute this task the Validator required ∼15 min approximately on a CPU described on Table 1. Results are presented in Fig. 4. On one hand, it shows that Wikidata outperforms DBpedia on validated properties, on the other hand, it shows lower

---

[21] https://tarql.github.io/.

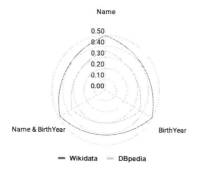

Fig. 4. The recall score results of the validation of politician instances.

recall scores, by the Validator, on both sources, e.g. the overall recall scores are 0.36% (DBpedia) and 0.49% (Wikidata).

Furthermore, the Validator gets lower recall on DBpedia and Wikidata sources due to two reasons. First, DBpedia contains the validated politician instances, however many of them are classified in DBpedia as *agent* type and not as politician (e.g., *Juan Carlos I*[22]). Second, the Wikidata query service raised timeout errors when querying data, so we decided to fetch the maximum allowed number of politician instances from Wikidata and stored them locally. We fetched 45000 out of 670810 politicians.

5   Use Cases

Our approach, as described in Sect. 3, aims to validate KGs by finding the same instances across different knowledge sources and comparing their features. Later on, based on the compared features our approach computes a confidence score for each triple and instance, the confidence score ranges from 0 to 1 and indicates the degree to which an instance is correct. Our approach may be used in a variety of use cases, we list some of the cases where the approach can be used:

- To validate the semantic correctness of a triple, e.g., to validate if the phone number of a hotel is the correct based on different sources.
- To link instances between knowledge sources, e.g. linking an instance of the user's KG with the matched instance in Wikidata.
- To find out incorrect data on different knowledge sources. For instance, suppose that the owner of a hotel wants to validate whether the information of his or her hotel provided by an external source are up-to-date.
- To validate static data, for example, to check whether the addresses of hotels are still valid given a period of time.

There are more possible use cases where our validation approach is applicable. Here, we presented some of them to give an idea about how useful and necessary is to have a validated KG (i.e. a correct and reliable KG).

---

[22] https://dbpedia.org/page/Juan_Carlos_I.

6   Conclusion and Future Work

In this paper, we presented the conceptualization of a new KG validation approach and a first prototypical implementation thereof. Our approach measures the degree to which every instance in a KG is semantically correct. It evaluates the correctness of instances based on external sources. Experiments were conducted on two datasets. The results confirm its effectiveness and are promising great potential. In future work, we will improve our approach and overcome its limitations. Here, we give a short overview of them:

- **Assessment** of knowledge sources. Finding the most suitable knowledge source for validating a KG is challenging [8]. Therefore, it is desirable to implement a quality assessment mechanism for assessing external sources. It may assist users in defining degrees of importance for each knowledge source.
- **Automation** of the setting process. It is desirable to allow users to create a semi-automatic **mapping** (or schema alignment [6]) between their KG and the external sources, e.g. the heterogeneous scheme of OSM has caused low performance of the Validator (see Sect. 4.1).
- **Cost-sensitive methods**. The current version of the Validator relies on proprietary services like Google, which can lead to high costs when validating large KGs. Therefore, it is important to evaluate the cost-effectiveness of knowledge sources.
- **Dynamic data** is fast-changing data that also needs to be validated, e.g. the price of a hotel room. The scope of this paper only comprises the validation of static data.
- **Scalability** is a critical point when we want to validate KGs. KGs are very large semantic networks that can contain billions of statements.

Above, we pointed out some future research directions and improvements that one can implement on the development of future validation tools.

Acknowledgments. This work has been partially funded by the project WordLiftNG within the Eureka, Eurostars Programme of the European Union (grant agreement number 877857 with the Austrian Research Promotion Agency (FFG)) and the industrial research project MindLab (https://mindlab.ai/). We would like to thank Prof. Dr. Dieter Fensel for his insightful comments regarding the definition of the overall validation approach.

References

1. Aletras, N., Stevenson, M.: Evaluating topic coherence using distributional semantics. In: Proceedings of the 10th International Conference on Computational Semantics, (IWCS2013), Potsdam, Germany, 19–22 March 2013, pp. 13–22. The Association for Computer Linguistics (2013)

2. Auer, S., Bizer, C., Kobilarov, G., Lehmann, J., Cyganiak, R., Ives, Z.: DBpedia: a nucleus for a web of open data. In: Aberer, K., et al. (eds.) ASWC/ISWC 2007. LNCS, vol. 4825, pp. 722–735. Springer, Heidelberg (2007). https://doi.org/10.1007/978-3-540-76298-0_52

3. Bollacker, K.D., Evans, C., Paritosh, P., Sturge, T., Taylor, J.: Freebase: a collaboratively created graph database for structuring human knowledge. In: Proceedings of the 2008 ACM International Conference on Management of Data (SIGMOD2008), Vancouver, Canada, 09–12 June 2008, pp. 1247–1250. ACM (2008)

4. Carlson, A., Betteridge, J., Kisiel, B., Settles, B., Hruschka, E.R., Mitchell, T.M.: Toward an architecture for never-ending language learning. In: Proceedings of the 24th Conference on Artificial Intelligence (AAAI2010), Atlanta, Georgia, 11–15 July 2010, pp. 1306–1313. AAAI Press (2010)

5. Dong, X., et al.: Knowledge vault: a web-scale approach to probabilistic knowledge fusion. In: Proceedings of the 20th International Conference on Knowledge Discovery and Data Mining (KDD2014), New York, USA, 24–27 August 2014, pp. 601–610. ACM (2014)

6. Dong, X.L., Srivastava, D.: Big Data Integration. Synthesis Lectures on Data Management, Morgan & Claypool Publishers (2015)

7. Ercan, G., Elbassuoni, S., Hose, K.: Retrieving textual evidence for knowledge graph facts. In: Hitzler, P., et al. (eds.) ESWC 2019. LNCS, vol. 11503, pp. 52–67. Springer, Cham (2019). https://doi.org/10.1007/978-3-030-21348-0_4

8. Färber, M., Bartscherer, F., Menne, C., Rettinger, A.: Linked data quality of DBpedia, Freebase, OpenCyc, Wikidata, and YAGO. Semant. Web 9(1), 77–129 (2018)

9. Fensel, D., et al.: Knowledge Graphs - Methodology, Tools and Selected Use Cases. Springer, Cham (2020). https://doi.org/10.1007/978-3-030-37439-6

10. Gad-Elrab, M.H., Stepanova, D., Urbani, J., Weikum, G.: Tracy: tracing facts over knowledge graphs and text. In: Proceedings of the 19th World Wide Web Conference (WWW2019), San Francisco, USA, 13–17 May 2019, pp. 3516–3520. ACM (2019)

11. Gerber, D., Esteves, D., Lehmann, J., Bühmann, L., Usbeck, R., Ngomo, A.N., Speck, R.: DeFacto - temporal and multilingual deep fact validation. J. Web Semant. 35, 85–101 (2015)

12. Hogan, A., et al.: Knowledge graphs. ACM Comput. Surv. 54(4), 71:1–71:37 (2021)

13. Huaman, E., Kärle, E., Fensel, D.: Knowledge graph validation. CoRR abs/2005.01389 (2020)

14. Kärle, E., Fensel, A., Toma, I., Fensel, D.: Why are there more hotels in Tyrol than in Austria? Analyzing schema.org usage in the hotel domain. In: Inversini, A., Schegg, R. (eds.) Information and Communication Technologies in Tourism 2016, pp. 99–112. Springer, Cham (2016). https://doi.org/10.1007/978-3-319-28231-2_8

15. Lehmann, J., Gerber, D., Morsey, M., Ngonga Ngomo, A.-C.: DeFacto - deep fact validation. In: Cudré-Mauroux, P., et al. (eds.) ISWC 2012. LNCS, vol. 7649, pp. 312–327. Springer, Heidelberg (2012). https://doi.org/10.1007/978-3-642-35176-1_20

16. Liu, S., d'Aquin, M., Motta, E.: Towards linked data fact validation through measuring consensus. In: Proceedings of the 2nd Workshop on Linked Data Quality co-located with 12th Extended Semantic Web Conference (ESWC2015), Portorož, Slovenia, 1 June 2015. CEUR Workshop Proceedings, vol. 1376. CEUR-WS.org (2015)

17. Nakamura, S., et al.: Trustworthiness analysis of web search results. In: Kovács, L., Fuhr, N., Meghini, C. (eds.) ECDL 2007. LNCS, vol. 4675, pp. 38–49. Springer, Heidelberg (2007). https://doi.org/10.1007/978-3-540-74851-9_4

18. Padia, A., Ferraro, F., Finin, T.: SURFACE: semantically rich fact validation with explanations. CoRR abs/1810.13223 (2018)
19. Paulheim, H.: Knowledge graph refinement: a survey of approaches and evaluation methods. Semant. Web **8**(3), 489–508 (2017)
20. Rula, A., et al.: TISCO: temporal scoping of facts. J. Web Semant. **54**, 72–86 (2019)
21. Şimşek, U., Angele, K., Kärle, E., Panasiuk, O., Fensel, D.: Domain-specific customization of schema.org based on SHACL. In: Pan, J.Z., et al. (eds.) ISWC 2020. LNCS, vol. 12507, pp. 585–600. Springer, Cham (2020). https://doi.org/10.1007/978-3-030-62466-8_36
22. Speck, R., Ngomo, A.N.: Leopard - a baseline approach to attribute prediction and validation for knowledge graph population. J. Web Semant. **55**, 102–107 (2019)
23. Syed, Z.H., Röder, M., Ngomo, A.N.: FactCheck: validating RDF triples using textual evidence. In: Proceedings of the 27th ACM International Conference on Information and Knowledge Management, (CIKM2018), Torino, Italy, 22–26 October 2018, pp. 1599–1602. ACM (2018)
24. Tan, C.H., Agichtein, E., Ipeirotis, P., Gabrilovich, E.: Trust, but verify: predicting contribution quality for knowledge base construction and curation. In: Seventh ACM International Conference on Web Search and Data Mining, WSDM 2014, New York, NY, USA, 24–28 February 2014, pp. 553–562. ACM (2014)
25. Thorne, J., Vlachos, A., Christodoulopoulos, C., Mittal, A.: FEVER: a large-scale dataset for fact extraction and verification. In: Proceedings of the 2018 Conference of the North American Chapter of the Association for Computational Linguistics: Human Language Technologies (NAACL-HLT2018), New Orleans, USA, 1–6 June 2018, pp. 809–819. Association for Computational Linguistics (2018)
26. Vlachos, A., Riedel, S.: Fact checking: task definition and dataset construction. In: Proceedings of the Workshop on Language Technologies and Computational Social Science (ACL2014), Baltimore, USA, 26 June 2014, pp. 18–22. Association for Computational Linguistics (2014)
27. Yin, X., Han, J., Yu, P.S.: Truth discovery with multiple conflicting information providers on the web. IEEE Trans. Knowl. Data Eng. **20**(6), 796–808 (2008)
28. Yu, A.Z., Ronen, S., Hu, K., Lu, T., Hidalgo, C.A.: Pantheon 1.0, a manually verified dataset of globally famous biographies. Sci. Data **3**(1), 1–16 (2016)

Design and Analysis of NICS Based Web Attack Detection for Advanced Intrusion Detection System

Shishir Kumar Shandilya[1,2]([envelope])

[1] School of Data Science and Forecasting, Devi Ahilya University, Indore, MP, India
[2] School of Computing Science and Engineering, VIT Bhopal University, Bhopal, India

Abstract. Worldwide Web has been the most prominent data sources since its inception, and several technologies have emerged around it and finally amalgamated with it. With the decades of progression and advancements, web is still structuring and welcoming latest technologies. However, cyber threats are also raising and becoming the concern. Since last decade, the defensive methods in Cyber Security domain have also transformed from conventional pattern/rule-based response systems to more active defensive systems. The active defensive methods are now equipped with Artificial Intelligence and Machine Learning techniques which are capable enough to learn and respond quickly to an entirely new cyber-attack. However, these techniques needs training and sometimes fail to perform in case of incomplete or inaccurate training data. Nature-inspired Cyber Security attempts to deliver robust solution to this problem as they are fundamentally tolerant to the missing, incomplete and inaccurate data. While the development both in Worldwide Web and Cyber Security is still continuing, the researchers are working on advanced security measures to make the worldwide web safe in all respects. This paper focuses on the design and analysis of NICS-based web attack detection system in cooperation with the existing Intrusion Detection System (IDS), by experimenting with the methods and procedures of Nature-inspired Cyber Security to generate adaptive responses against advanced cyber-attacks. The proposed method is tested and validated on multiple attack scenarios and achieved better results in early detection of suspicious activities of web attacks for IDS.

Keywords: Nature-inspired cyber security · Adaptive defense · Intrusion detection system · Firefly algorithm

1 Introduction

With the industrial and technological advancements in last decade, electronic commerce and online transactions became integral part of worldwide web. Though, the web 4.0 is integrated well with AI (Artificial Intelligence), DM (Data Mining), and CS (Cyber Security), but still web data security is a major concern as along with the technological developments, the security breaches are also becoming more advanced and the recent

© Springer Nature Switzerland AG 2021
B. Villazón-Terrazas et al. (Eds.): KGSWC 2021, CCIS 1459, pp. 61–70, 2021.
https://doi.org/10.1007/978-3-030-91305-2_5

research is attempting to resolve this by introducing variety of defense mechanisms for securing the web.

As most of the businesses are now moving towards web, the volume and complexity of dynamic web applications is increasing. One way to provide better security is to test these web applications for possible vulnerabilities through a strong testing mechanism called Dynamic Application Security Testing (DAST), also known as web application vulnerability scanner, which is a black-box security test. It communicates with the web application as a frontend identify the possible vulnerabilities by executing attack scenarios on the web application. However, there is a possibility that the data may lost/overwritten while scanning with a DAST tool. Intrusion Detection Systems (IDS) can be another option to detect the attacks but has its own issues and limitation. First is that they are generally signature-based, and find difficulty in detecting the zero-day attacks. The variety and growth of technologies are also making the situation difficult for IDS. Therefore, due to the weak security testing at the development phase and thereafter (post-deployment), make the overall scenario more vulnerable and unsafe for legitimate processes. Multi legal restrictions, open source development software and variety of data formats are the added issues which are to be take care of.

IDS can be classified as HIDS (Host-Based Intrusion Detection System) and NICS (Network-Based Intrusion Detection System). Network-Based Intrusion Detection System works on traffic patterns for the predicting the potential attacks. It can also be categorized into three types: Anomaly-based IDS that detects the events or observations that do not match with the given group and it is assumed that abnormal behavior of a system can be distinguished from normal behavior; Signature-based IDS that have predefined database rules which were pre-configured by the administrator of the system. It checks all the ongoing activities through these rules; and Hybrid IDS that is the combination of both anomaly and rule-based IDS but it has high computational overhead because it has the capability to detect known as well as unknown attacks. However, the Hybrid IDS can easily be integrated with AI&ML for better performance and accuracy.

A good IDS requires a good amount of time for testing, verification, updation and deployment. A strong defensive mechanism can only be achieved through trustworthy processes, strict compliance and adaptive responses, but unfortunately, the development of such system requires a lot of training and re-configuration. Also, if IDS is unable to adapt and respond to the rapidly changing environments, then such IDS becomes burden due to its resource-constrained poor performance monitoring activities.

Nature-inspired Cyber Security may provide a robust security solution to IDS by implementing well-established nature-inspired optimization techniques to effectively shortening the time take to identify the potential threats. NICS-based method can be deployed as a pre-processing or as an integral part of IDS for better efficient in intrusion detection through strict monitoring on various parameters of suspicious activities. Nature-inspired Cyber Security utilizes the advanced optimization techniques for effectively achieving security in variety of networks, by mimicking the characteristics, behaviors, and processes of nature (insects, plants, animals, human etc.). NICS attempts to achieve the same intelligence and optimization for security and resilience. NICS can be implemented in IDS by implementing the NICS activities at monitoring and response steps, to achieve better security and resilience at the cost of minimum processing overhead. Unlike AI, such integration of NICS to IDS will provide the robustness without the need of training along with several unique features like camouflaging of network architectures, and cyber immunity.

2 NICS-Based Defense Mechanism

With the technological growth in every field of computing, attackers are also gaining advantage of this. They are now more organized and equipped with latest AI-Based techniques to target the individuals or organizations. The payloads are more transparent ever and attacks can have better foot-hold quickly in the network. Such situation can be taken care by NICS methods which are capable to generate intelligence for adaptive defense against metamorphic or polymorphic virus attacks [1, 2]. These adaptive capabilities are difficult to achieve through training on dataset to recognize the attacks. NICS can also be a major step to achieve an active resilience through the ability of self-awareness, and adaption while proactively monitoring activities by IDS. NICS may also boost the other security steps of threat identification, isolation and resolution.

With several benefits, NICS also has few limitations as it is currently a comparatively new concept than AI which is well-explored. NICS rely highly on multi-objective optimization which in turn takes time to converge, so the process that uses it [3–5].

The proposed method employs an efficient method for early identification and analysis of threats to support the existing IDS. The proposed method works well for the dense networks also due to the advanced multi-factor optimization.

3 Related Works

The initial works on IDS was done by Anderson et al. in early 80's to monitor the computer network, detect the anomalies and to generate alerts. This was followed by Denning et al. for monitoring the systems' audit records. Nature-inspired cyber Security is gaining attention by security researchers due to the multiple benefits [6, 7]. For example, firefly meta-heuristic optimization is implemented by conceptualizing the flashing light behavior of fireflies proposed by Yang et al. [8]. It is a nature-inspired swarm-based meta-heuristic optimization algorithm. This stochastic global algorithm works on the principle of attractions towards the luminescence of each firefly. This attraction directs the swarm of fireflies towards the brighter fireflies in search of optimal solutions.

The location of the firefly i at each iteration can be modeled as,

$$X_i^{t+1} = X_i^t + \beta^{\gamma r_{ij}^2} + \left(X_j^t - X_i^t\right) + \alpha_t \varepsilon_t \tag{1}$$

where β is the attractiveness, γ is the absorption coefficient, α_t is the step-size, ε_t is the Gaussian vector and r is the distance between x_i and x_j nodes.

Also, β is the brightness value of the firefly which can be calculated as,

$$\beta = \beta_0 e^{-\gamma r^2} \tag{2}$$

Following is the general algorithm of firefly optimization method,

Algorithm 1: General Firefly Optimization Algorithm
Input: Target Function
Define Objective Function f(x), where x = x₁, x₂, ..., xₘ and m ∈ 1, 2, ...N
Generate initial firefly population with x_i, (i ∈ 1, 2, ..., N)
Define an association of brightness β with objective function f(x)
Define absorption coefficient γ
while t < MaxGen do
    for i ← 1 to N do
        for j ← 1 to N do
            if $\beta_j > \beta_i$ then
                Calculate attraction with distance r via $e^{-\gamma rk}$
                Move x_i towards x_j
                Update β_{new}
            end if
        end for
    end for
end while
Output: Best fireflies (Solution)

There are many works which are based on implementation of IDS using meta-heuristic techniques [9–11]. In year 2018, Ram et al. have proposed a fuzzy-based firefly algorithm for fast learning networks [12]. In year 2019, Dhanarao et al. have proposed a hybrid IDS for mobile adhoc networks [13], which was taken forward by Albadran et al. in year 2020 for more efficient algorithm for fast learning networks [14]. Pakdel et al. have implemented the similar algorithm with some modification in Wireless Sensor Networks [15].

The following table shows the prominent research on IDS using Firefly Optimization (Table 1),

Table 1. Firefly optimization in IDS

Published work	Key concept	Type
FA based feature selection for network IDS [10]	Used FA as wrapper method for feature selection	Machine Learning
A feature selection approach using binary FA for network IDS [11]	Used FA for selecting optimal number of features to reduce false alarms	NICS
An efficient IDS based on Fuzzy FA optimization and fast learning network [12]	Used FA in Fast Learning System on KDD99 dataset	NICS

(continued)

Table 1. (*continued*)

Published work	Key concept	Type
Hybridization of K-Means and FA for IDS [16]	Used FA for better detection on NSL-KDD dataset	Machine Learning and NICS
An IDS using modified-FA in cloud environment [17]	Used the modified FA for better performance on NSL-KDD dataset	Machine Learning

Further, many other research has been carried out recently on utilizing the meta-heuristic optimization methods to facilitates IDS to quickly identify and classify the suspicious activities while closely observing the processes.

4 Proposed Method

In the presented work, we have utilized the general framework of firefly optimization method to modify the IDS system against the common web attacks. There are several modifications possible, but for the presented work, we are only focusing on the categorization of malicious activities at IDS. The proposed method is focused on generating the early alerts for suspicion and thereby provides additional support to IDS for effective monitoring and attentive response. This concept of improving the classification and prediction of IDS is taken by Karatas et al. [18] and Bhattacharya et al. [19].

The proposed algorithm which is a modified version of firefly optimization algorithm categorizes the activities based on the selected features (customized as per the type and work of application). Figure 1 depicts the general working mechanism of the proposed system.

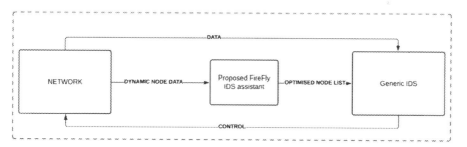

Fig. 1. General working of proposed system

The generic IDS will get benefited by proposed algorithm for early detection of attacks by categorizing them based on the various features. The proposed algorithm can be fine-tuned as per the type of the web application and what type of data/process it caters.

The activities will be analyzed as per their luminescence values which will characterize their behavior. These behaviors of various real-time activities will be recorded and compared continuously by the activity monitor. In case when an activity exceeds the threshold value, the activity monitor notifies the IDS system to give more attention to such activity(s). Thereafter, the IDS closely monitor the activity(s) with an additional surveillance for some more time before blacklisting it. This time is configured to be modified (increased or decreased) based on the trustworthiness of proposed system to categorize the activities. This implies that the reliability of the proposed system is inversely proportional with the additional time allowed by the IDS for further surveillance. Ideally, this time should be zero which implies that the proposed method is completely integrated with IDS for effectively categorizing the suspicious activities. Figure 2 depicts the process of activity monitor of proposed system.

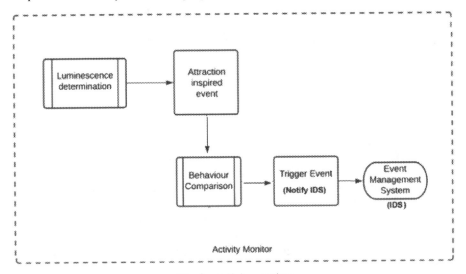

Fig. 2. Activity monitor

The proposed method assist the IDS to observe and identify the suspicious activities in more realistic way which is highly influenced by determining the behavior of activities adaptively based on the previous functions of such activities.

5   Experimental Results

The experimental setup is done on NS-2 (Network Simulator-2) environment and coded in Python 3 programming language. We have used our own network testbed which is having various NICS libraries to setup the experimental model for the proposed method. We have implemented and tested the proposed method under several attack scenarios and observed the dependencies and cause-effect relationships. Specifically, we have implemented low-rate denial of service (LDoS) attack which can degrade the quality of communication. We have considered throughput as the main parameter to compare and establish the effectiveness of proposed method under normal, under attack and with proposed defensive mechanism results. We have examined the proposed method on three customized test cases in which the network data is chosen randomly from the standard datasets (Table 2).

Table 2. Description of Test Cases

Characteristics	Test Case #1	Test Case #2	Test Case #3
Number of Nodes per Cluster (*NpC*)	5	10	50
Key parameter	Average Throughput		
Simulated attack	Low-rate Denial of Service (LDoS)		
Link type	Duplex-link		
Link bandwidth	1000.0 Mb/200 Mb		
Simulation time	60 s		

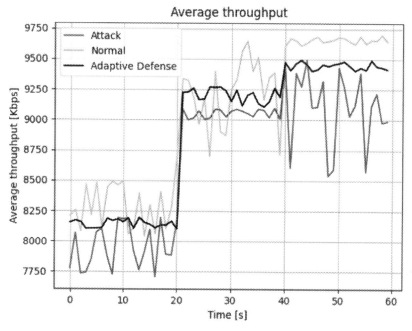

Fig. 3. Test Case #1 results

Figure 3 clearly shows that the adaptive defense is able to consistently maintain the better throughput as compared to the system under attack scenario (depicted by Red Color). Obviously, the improvement in adaptive defense also comes with an overhead, but this can further be refined to achieve the better performance at the cost on minimum possible overhead in terms of time and processing.

In Fig. 4 depicts the results of Test Case #2 which not only shows the improvement in results but also the stability of proposed method from 00:40 to 00:50 s. This stability supports the convergence of proposed method.

By observing Fig. 5, we may conclude that the proposed adaptive defense method performs consistently irrespective to the configuration and type of data or application.

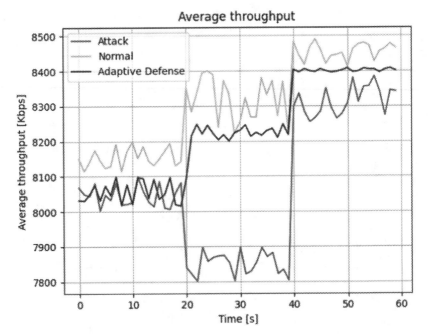

Fig. 4. Test Case #2 results

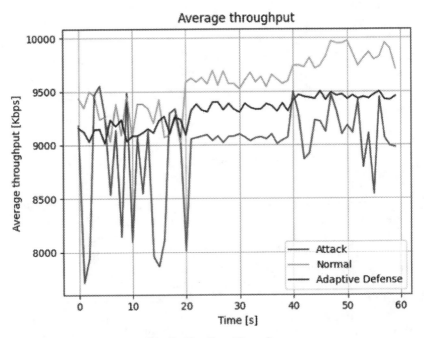

Fig. 5. Test Case #3 results

Table 3. Key observations after simulation

Characteristics	Test Case #1	Test Case #2	Test Case #3
Throughput in presence of attack	93.39%	96.05%	97.12%
Throughput in presence of attack with proposed method	97.31%	98.60%	98.98%
Improvement with the proposed method	+3.92%	+2.55%	+1.86%

As per Table 3, a significant amount of improvement can be observed in the average throughput after implementing the proposed method. Likewise, many simulations can be performed using variety of attack scenarios using this system, which is customizable as per the need of organization/individual for examining the proposed method.

6 Conclusion and Future Works

In this paper, the NICS-based adaptive defense is implemented and analyzed through the proposed method which is a modified version of firefly optimization, to assist the effective monitoring by the existing IDS. The experimental results were verified and evaluated under normal, under attack and under attack with proposed defense mechanism, using various attack scenarios. It is observed by simulation that the proposed method is capable of detecting the suspicious activities early, by categorizing the behavior of activities. In this paper, we have also used a novel testbed for designing and experimenting the NICS-based defense methods and algorithms. We have found the testbed easy to implement and analyze for the proposed method while considering the customization and control parameters.

The immediate extension of the proposed method is to explore more ways to optimize the results with minimum overhead. Another work that can be implemented is to transform the proposed method as a service for the web applications.

Acknowledgements. The author is thankful for all the support from the research team and professors who are extensively working on Nature-inspired Cyber Security at VIT Bhopal University-India (Mr. Saket Upadhyay), Soongsil University-South Korea (Dr. Ajit Kumar & Dr. Bong Jun Choi), Liverpool Hope University-United Kingdom (Prof. Atulya K Nagar) and Devi Ahilya University-India (Prof. VB Gupta).

References

1. Fraley, J.B., Cannady, J.: The promise of machine learning in cybersecurity. In: Southeast Conference, pp. 1–6. IEEE (2017)
2. Ghafir, I., et al.: Detection of advanced persistent threat using machine learning correlation analysis. Future Gener. Comput. Syst. **89**, 349–359 (2018)
3. Breza, M., McCann, J.A.: Lessons in implementing bio-inspired algorithms on wireless sensor networks. In: 2008 NASA/ESA Conference on Adaptive Hardware and Systems, pp. 271–276 (2008)

4. Mthunzi, S., Benkhelifa, E., Bosakowski, T., Hariri, S.: A Bio-inspired Approach to Cyber Security: Principles, Algorithms, and Practices, pp. 75–104 (2019)
5. Mishra, S., Sagban, R., Yakoob, A., Gandhi, N.: Swarm intelligence in anomaly detection systems: an overview. Int. J. Comput. Appl. **43**(2), 109–118 (2021)
6. Rauf, U.: A taxonomy of bio-inspired cyber security approaches: existing techniques and future directions. Arab. J. Sci. Eng. **43**, 6693–6708 (2018)
7. Thakkar, A., Lohiya, R.: Role of swarm and evolutionary algorithms for intrusion detection system: a survey. Swarm Evol. Comput. **53**, 100631 (2020)
8. Yang, X.S.: Nature-Inspired Metaheuristic Algorithms, vol. 12. Luniver Press, Bristol (2008)
9. Pervez, M.S., Farid, D.: Feature selection and intrusion classification in NSL-KDD cup 99 dataset employing SVMs. In: SKIMA 2014 - 8th International Conference on Software, Knowledge, Information Management and Applications (2015)
10. Selvakumar, B., Muneeswaran, K.: Firefly algorithm based feature selection for network intrusion detection. Comput. Secur. **81**, 148–155 (2019)
11. Najeeb, R.F., Dhannoon, B.N.: A feature selection approach using binary firefly algorithm for network intrusion detection system. ARPN J. Eng. Appl. Sci. **13**(6), 2347–2352 (2018)
12. Ram, B.H., Rao, B.V.: An efficient ids based on fuzzy firefly optimization and fast learning network. Int. J. Eng. Technol. (UAE) **7**, 557–561 (2018)
13. Dhanarao, S., Kumar, M.: Efficient IDS for manet using hybrid firefly with a genetic algorithm (2019)
14. Albadran, M.: A new firefly-fast learning network model based intrusion-detection system. Int. J. Innov. Technol. Exploring Eng. (2020)
15. Hossein, P., Reza, F.: A firefly algorithm for power management in wireless sensor networks (WSNs). J. Supercomputing **77**, 1–22 (2021)
16. Kaur, A., Pal, S.K., Singh, A.P.: Hybridization of kmeans and firefly algorithm for intrusion detection system. Int. J. Syst. Assur. Eng. Manag. **9**(4), 901–910 (2018)
17. Ghosh, P., Sarkar, D., Sharma, J., Phadikar, S.: An intrusion detection system using modified-firefly algorithm in cloud environment. Int. J. Digit. Crime Forensics (IJDCF) **13**(2), 77–93 (2021)
18. Karatas, G., Demir, Ö., Sahingoz, O.: Increasing the performance of machine learning-based IDSs on an imbalanced and up-to-date dataset. IEEE Access **8**, 1 (2020)
19. Bhattacharya, S., et al.: A novel PCA-firefly based XGBoost classification model for intrusion detection in networks using GPU. Electronics **9**, 219 (2020)

A System for Traffic Events Detection Using Fuzzy C-Means

Hayder Endo Pérez[1], Amed Leiva Mederos[1], Daniel Galvez Lio[1],
Luis Ernesto Hurtado[1], Doymer García Duarte[1,2],
and Ghislain Auguste Atemezing[2(✉)]

[1] Research Center in Informatics, Semantica Web Group,
Central University "Marta Abreu" of Las Villas, Santa Clara, Cuba
{hendo,amed,dgalvez,luhgonzalez,dgduarte}@uclv.cu
[2] Mondeca, Paris, France
ghislain.atemezing@mondeca.com

Abstract. Systems for traffic events administration are important tools in the prediction of disasters and management of that of the movement flow in diverse contexts. These systems are generally developed on non-fuzzy grouping algorithms and ontologies. However, the results of the implementation do not always give high precision scores due to different factors such as data heterogeneity, the high number of components used in their architecture and to the mixture of highly specialized and diverse domain ontologies. These factors do not ease the implementation of the systems able to predict with higher reliability traffic events. In this work, we design a system for traffic events detection that implements a new ontology called *trafficstore* and leverages the fuzzy c-means algorithm. The indexes evaluated on the fuzzy c-means algorithm demonstrates that the implemented system improves its efficiency in the grouping of traffic events.

Keywords: Semantic web · Fuzzy C-means · IoT · Traffic event detection

1 Introduction

The prediction of traffic events has been one of the most important research fields in smart cities. Sensors are an important source of data available in this field today. While sensor data can be published as mere values, searching, reusing, integrating, and interpreting this data requires a little more than the verification of observation results. Intelligent traffic systems use sensors to correctly interpret the values of humidity, carbon dioxide, etc. The sensors provide information on the observed properties and the sampling strategy used. The Open Geospatial Consortium (OGC) sensor web standards provide a means to annotate sensors and their observations. Nevertheless, these standards are not integrated or aligned with the W3C Semantic Web technologies and Linked Data in particular, which are key mechanisms for creating and maintaining a tightly

© Springer Nature Switzerland AG 2021
B. Villazón-Terrazas et al. (Eds.): KGSWC 2021, CCIS 1459, pp. 71–83, 2021.
https://doi.org/10.1007/978-3-030-91305-2_6

interconnected global data graph. With the rise of the Web of Things (WoT), smart cities and smart buildings in general, actuators and the data produced by the sensors become first-class citizens of the web. One of the most used ontologies in the detection of traffic events is called SSN, which follows a horizontal and vertical modular architecture by including a lightweight but autonomous central ontology called SOSA (Sensor, Observation, Sample and Actuator) [17], which are key mechanisms for creating and maintaining a global and tightly interconnected graph of data. SSN/SOSA are used in several existing work in the literature to semantically annotate and analyze data in the IoT domain.

The development of traffic systems in smart cities goes through various development paradigms, among which is OBDA. These traffic management systems use OBDA (Ontology Based Data Access) that allows access to information stored in heterogeneous data sources through an abstraction layer that mediates between data sources and data consumers. Some of these tools used in OBDA are D2RQ, Mastro, morph-RDB, Ontop, OntoQF, Ultrawarp and others. In the OBDA paradigm, an ontology defines a high-level global schema of (existing) data sources and provides a vocabulary for user queries. An OBDA system rewrites such queries in both the ontologies and the vocabulary of the data sources and then delegates the actual evaluation of the query to a suitable system [8]. The DL-Lite description logic, which underpins OWL 2 QL is the one that represents the ontology in OBDA [15].

Traditional traffic management systems have evolved to Data Stream Management Systems [7,11]. It is a system that is designed to execute continuous queries on a continuous flow of data or data stream. Traffic data is data that is generated from many sources, typically sending data records simultaneously in small-sized sets (several kilobytes).

This data must be processed sequentially and incrementally, record by record or in incremental time windows, and is used for a wide variety of analysis types, such as correlations, aggregations, filtering, and sampling. The information derived from the analysis provides the transport companies with the visibility of numerous aspects of the business and the activities of the clients, such as the use of the traffic service, the server activity, the clicks on the website of the transport company and the geographical location of means of transport, people and goods, and allows them to respond quickly to any situation that arises [6]. This would be great when it comes to detecting and correcting some events that traffic systems may have in advance.

IoT applications for traffic control in smart cities should have the ability to process event broadcasts in real time, extract relevant information and identify values that do not follow current trends. Beyond the identification of relevant events, the extraction of high-level knowledge from heterogeneous and multimodal data flows is an important component in traffic control systems. Existing flow reasoning techniques use prior knowledge and flow queries to reason about data flows. However, they do not meet the needs of IoT due to the lack of adequate treatment of uncertainty (for example, possible reasons for traffic jam) in the IoT environment [7]. Nor are they operable in any traffic environment due to the constant overlaps that generate the results of their services. This article seeks to provide with solutions to detect traffic events with fuzzy algorithms to achieve greater efficiency in transport event detection systems. The paper is organized as follows: Sect. 2 describes related work in the domain of streaming data and traffic events, followed by our proposal in Sect. 3 composed of an ontology, a system architecture. The first validation with results are shown in Sect. 4. Section 5 provides some conclusions remarks.

2   Related Work

Intelligent transport systems are a set of technological solutions used to improve the performance and safety of road, air and land transport. A crucial element for the success of these systems is the exchange of information, not only between vehicles, but also between other components of the road infrastructure through different applications. One of the most important sources of information in this type of system is the sensors. The sensors can be inside vehicles or as part of infrastructure, such as bridges, roads, traffic signs, traffic lights, etc. These sensors can provide information related to weather conditions and the traffic situation, which is useful to improve the driving process. To facilitate the exchange of information between different applications that use sensor data, a common knowledge framework is needed to enable interoperability.

In recent years, there has been a growing interest in ontologies for road transport systems. Gorender and Silva [9] in their work developed an ontology to represent road traffic. Their goal was to build a reliable traffic information system that provides information on roads, traffic, and vehicle-related scenarios on the highways. It also helps the traffic information system to analyze specific critical situations in this environment. For example, an ambulance may need to know the congestion status of a toll plaza. Requesting this information is essential if the ambulance is transferred to the scene of the accident. On the other hand, if a normal vehicle is moving down a highway without rushing, then this requested information is not that critical. Morignot and Nashashibi in [14] proposed a high-level representation of an automated vehicle, other vehicles, and their environment, which can help drivers make 'unorthodox' but practical relaxation decisions (for example, when a damaged car does not allow circulation, make the decision moving to another lane by crossing a solid line and passing the stopped car, if the other lane is clear). This high-level representation includes topological knowledge and rules of inference, in order to calculate the next high-level movement to be made by an automated vehicle, to aid the driver's decision-making. The main weakness of this approach is the lack of rules that represent the previous traffic regulations. They have just defined a set of traffic law infractions, that allow classifying the motion given as "legal" or "illegal". Zhao, IchiseySasakien [11] introduced an ontology-based knowledge base, containing maps and traffic rules. It can be aware of speed situations and make decisions at intersections to comply with traffic regulations, but it does not consider important elements such as traffic signs and weather conditions.

The proposed work in [5] is an approach to creating a generic situation description for advanced driver assistance systems using logical reasoning in a traffic situation knowledge base. It contains multiple objects of different types such as vehicles and infrastructure elements such as roads, lanes, intersections, traffic signals, traffic lights and relationships between them. Logical inference is made to verify and expand the description of the situation and interpret the situation, for example, by reasoning about traffic rules. The capabilities of this ontological description approach are shown in the example of complex intersections with multiple roads, lanes, vehicles, and different combinations of traffic signals and traffic lights. As a restriction, in this work, the destination road that passes over the intersection must be known for each vehicle, so it is not possible to model different possibilities according to the actual situation of the intersection.

From an implementation point of view, there are several services whose practical applications already serve as services in some territories. Londonair is the London Air Quality Network (LAQN) website that shows air pollution in the City of London and South East England. The website provides information for the public, policy users, and scientists. LAQN was formed in 1993 to coordinate and improve air pollution monitoring in London. The network provides independent scientific assessments and measurements. This site does not monitor the entire area [13]. This site arises due to concerns regarding air pollution on the part of the London Department of Public Health. The measurements obtained here are used, in addition to evaluating air pollution, to track its trends over time and to create models that can evaluate how different government policies affect air pollution. These measurements also help to comply with the legal obligations of local authorities regarding air pollution. London air is maintained by the Environmental Research Group at Imperial College London. Monitoring is owned and funded by local authorities, Business Improvement Districts.

Open Data DK, as another solution, which is an association of Danish municipalities and regions that since 2016 have collaborated to open their data, that is, in a common open data portal [5]. Open data is non-personal data that anyone can access and use for free. They can be anything from data on municipal infrastructure to socioeconomic composition. The purpose of open data is: (i) Create transparency in public administration, (ii) Create fertile ground for data-driven growth and innovation and (iii) Ensure a higher degree of utilization of the data already collected. In this way, open data can be used in the development of applications and services or be a starting point for analysis, trend assessments, research, etc. Open Data DK has a data portal from which everyone can use the data for free without registering. The data portal is based on the open source software CKAN (Open Knowledge Foundation). All the datasets in the Open Data DK portal are grouped together to create an overview. They are divided into the same categories as in the European Data Portal. Among some of these datasets that are offered are those related to:

- Population and society, which include: demographic data, migration, employment, socioeconomics, etc.
- Energy, which include: energy consumption, energy sources, etc.

- Health, which include: assisted devices, dental care, drug/alcohol treatment, etc.
- Transport, including: mobility, parking, roads, winter maintenance, public transport, etc. such as agriculture, fishing and rural communities in the UK.

3   System Design

In this section, we describe the ontology for stream annotation, the system architecture, our annotation system and the different formats flowing from different modules of the system.

3.1   Ontology

The development of this system involves the management of a new ontology. As mentioned above regarding the reuse of ontologies, the information system adopts several concepts that are considered core attributes to provide a real-world context to the IoT stream and traffic events.

The ontology relates the spatial attributes of `IotStream`. The W3C geographical ontology provides a set of basic concepts that represent the location of a feature or a traffic event. The main concept of interest is the `geo:Point` that contains geospatial properties (latitude, longitude, and altitude). The IoT-lite ontology [2] expands properties to include relative location and relative altitude. To maintain the historical context of `StreamObservations`, especially in the case of mobility, a `geo:Point` can be linked to each `StreamObservation`. IoTStream is also associated with a defined coverage area where it is also relevant. Regarding the IoT-lite ontology: Coverage concept is used for simple coverage definitions, and GeoSPARQL [1], a well-established ontology for spatial attributes.

The next subset of concepts adopted relates to the IotStream generating source, the phenomena, and the measurement of your observations. As the streams in the real world are generated by sensors, the SOSA ontology has been used [10]. Through the object properties defined by *IoTLite*, the concepts `qu:QuantityKind` and `qu:Unit` of the QU ontology are also linked.

Although it is the sensor that generates the IoT stream, over the Internet, the stream data is usually provided by a TCP/IP application layer service. The IoT-Lite class provides `iot-lite:Service` class that contains fields related to the address of the service endpoint, the interface type, and the link to the interface description, which provides details on how to interact with the service.

Finally, over the lifespan of an IotStream, the quality of stream observations can change over time. For data analysis, knowledge of quality is very important so that adaptation measures can be applied when necessary. The Quality of Information (QoI) ontology provides the `qoi:Quality` concept that has subclasses that focus on a particular aspect of data quality, such as `qoi:Timeliness` and `qoi:Completeness` of observations. Table 1 lists the namespaces of the linked ontologies and their preferred prefixes.

Table 1. Prefixes and namespaces of the linked ontologies.

Prefix	Namespace
iot-lite	http://purl.oclc.org/NET/UNIS/fiware/iot-lite#
iot-stream	http://purl.org/iot/ontology/iot-stream#
owl	http://www.w3.org/2002/07/owl#
qoi	https://w3id.org/iot/qoi#
what	http://purl.oclc.org/NET/ssnx/qu/qu#
rdf	http://www.w3.org/1999/02/22-rdf-syntax-ns#
rdfs	http://www.w3.org/2000/01/rdf-schema#
sosa	http://www.w3.org/ns/sosa/
wgs84_pos	http://www.w3.org/2003/01/geo/wgs84_pos#
xml	http://www.w3.org/XML/1998/namespace
xsd	http://www.w3.org/2001/XMLSchema#
traff	http://sem.uclv.cu/def/trafficstore#

New classes were placed in the ontology with the prefix `traff` combining new conditions for `FeatureOfInterest` which describes the conditions that may affect any means of transport including `Climatologycall` Condition, `EnvironmentalCondition` and `TrafficConditions`. To monitor the traffic conditions, `SeaSection`, `RoadSection`, `LineSection` and `AirSection` classes were created. It is important to describe the Observation class where observations are detailed for plane, ship, train line and motor vehicle.

Likewise, the `TrafficConditions` class and the `EventCauses` class are detailed, in which causes of traffic problems are described, associated with international traffic rules and speed limits for various types of means of transport Fig. 1 and Table 1[1].

3.2   System Architecture

There are many works related to this topic. This paper is dedicated to improving the architecture of the referenced system [6]. It has several components that can be optimized in the implementation process. The proposed architecture is simple and adapts to the conditions of the work environments. Following the work in [6] these components are reused: Producer, Analytics Service, Consumer and the Registry (see Fig. 2).

1. Producer: The producer is responsible for fetching stream observations from the designated source of open data according to the application domain and publishing them to the message broker (4).

---

[1] The online documentation is available at http://linkedvocabs.org/onto/trafficstore/trafficstore.html.

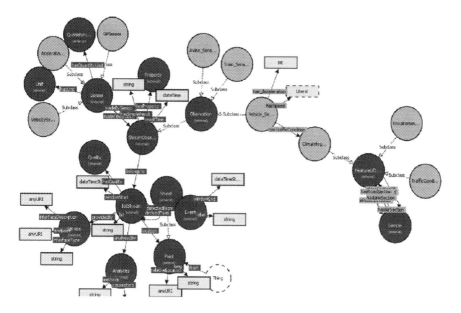

Fig. 1. Trafficstore ontology for semantic annotation.

2. Analytics Service 1: The analytics service 1 is responsible for grouping atomic data points into windows of several sizes which may be consumed by another analytics service.
3. Consumer (Client): The client application, responsible for showing produced stream observations and detected events in a suitable way, decoupled from the data sources.
4. Message Broker: The message broker is responsible for receiving and propagating events (new stream observations generated by a producer or derived events generated by some analytic service).
5. Analytics Service 2: The analytics service 2 is responsible for generating events produced by some labeling algorithm, yet to be defined.
6. Registry: The registry is responsible for storing, generating, and exposing (via SPARQL) sensor and stream metadata.

3.3   Annotation System

The annotation process is shown in Fig. 3. The frequency of the data generated by the sensors is five minutes and is set to represent patterns for each hour. The representation of the hourly pattern, the size of the movement in this case would be 12. For the analysis, the data is divided into windows of 12 data points and LPR is applied [16] in every window. The result is hourly data patterns. Then apply the LPR algorithms [16], the Fuzzy C-means (RI) algorithm [18] is used to apply grouping on the patterns into three different groups. By looking at the centers of the cluster, each group is given a label.

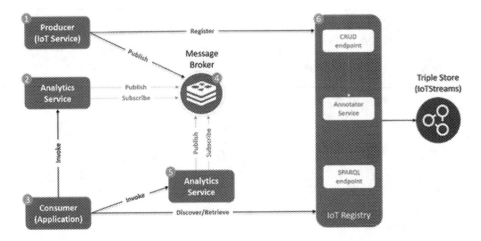

Fig. 2. System architecture scheme.

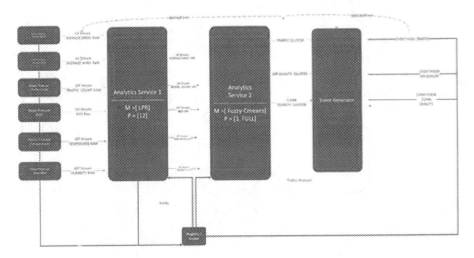

Fig. 3. Annotation system.

In Analytics services, "M" and "P" correspond to the methods and parameters applied to incoming *StreamObservations*. Seven IotStream Producers publish *StreamObservations* to the broker, and two analytics services subscribe to *StreamObservations* notifications from the broker. In the case of Analytic Service 1, the *StreamObservations* is received within one hour and the data is processed using LPR [16], and the output is annotated with an IotStream [6][2] instance which was *derivedFrom* and published in the broker. The Analysis Service 2 is then notified and the Fuzzy C-means [12,18,19] algorithm is applied in the

---

[2] See the ontology online at https://linkedvocabs.org/onto/trafficstore/trafficstore. html.

analyzed flow observations, and then grouped into the predefined groups. The output of the clusters is sent to an Event Generator. Each logged Event has a label and is associated with the IotStream instance from which it was detected. This output is then published in the broker for any consumer.

3.4   Data Flow

A system that consumes IoT data streams needs to employ some type of data analysis to handle the degree of volume, speed, intermittent, irregularity, and dimensionality. Libraries and frameworks for popular programming languages have allowed the creation of tools that handle data according to its nature and the expected knowledge obtained. Depending on the application, the tools involve forms of pre-processing, machine learning, or correlation.

The result of such techniques can be fed to enrich a semantic knowledge graph. As described in [6], the Reception of Knowledge (RC) web service allows the consumer to use remote IoT data sources with different cascades of methods to study which one works best for them. By exposing a RESTful interface, RC queries data streams from an IoT data stream store using a SPARQL query with a predefined format for the output variables. In turn, the service will generate a new data stream based on the selected methods and their corresponding parameters. The new *StreamObservations* are then annotated and linked to a new IotStream, with the Analytical details used, and then sent back to the Consumer. Figure 4 illustrates the process.

4   Validation

For the validation of the system, we have carried out an experiment with two datasets used in the research: London Air [13] and Open DK [5]. To evaluate the system, the results of the grouping were evaluated from the following indices PC [4], XB [19], PE [3] and OS [18].

We found that the two datasets have the three well-defined classes. An optimal number of bunches is obtained for each index. All indices report the correct cluster number. The Open DK dataset has three clusters. Because two clusters overlap and one cluster is separated from the rest, this is also an acceptable result. The correct cluster numbers and indexes are correctly identified by 3, as reported in Table 2.

Table 2. Result of different indices.

Dataset	Nuñ.C	PC	PE	XB	YOU
London Air	3	3	3	3	3
Open DK	3	2	3	3	3

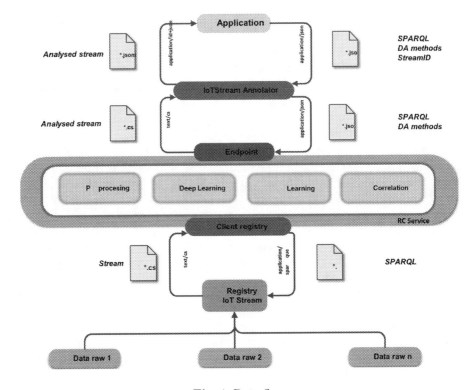

Fig. 4. Data flow.

We carried out two experiments to evaluate the yield of the system. The first one was guided to evaluate the quantity of events of those detected by the humans compared to the events detected by the fuzzy C-means algorithm. The second experiment with the objective to see how many events the system was able to detect in certain time with the algorithm.

In the two tests, the results are satisfactory as reported respectively in figures Fig. 5 and Fig. 6.

Fig. 5. Humans events vs Fuzzy C-means.

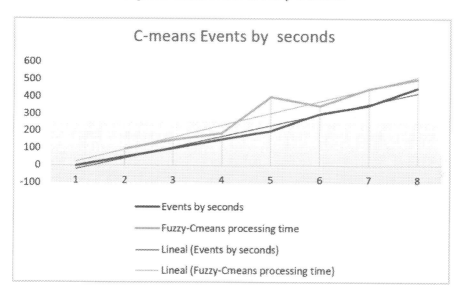

Fig. 6. Events by time.

5 Conclusions

The systems that are currently used for the detection of traffic events are developed with little heterogeneous ontologies. The algorithms used for the detection of events do not allow the evaluation of overlap and sometimes the results that they emit to IoT users have distortions.

The proposed system shows a novelty in the architecture by implementing Open Data schemes and using few components. The evaluation of the results of the use of Fuzzy C-means (FCM) with different indices shows the efficiency of these algorithms in IoT systems when the data even has overlap. It is evident that the use of fuzzy algorithms improves the yield of the IoT system, and it enhances the localization of overlapped data. The ontology developed in this work constitutes a novelty being the first time that a knowledge base is combined with FCM in the transport domain, the ontology improving some pitfalls in previous works.

Although the annotation pattern and the data flow are based on precedent systems. The implementation approach and the novelty in handling the components give validity to precedent investigations in this topic.

Acknowledgments. GA acknowledges grant ANR-19-CE23-0012 from Agence Nationale de la Recherche for project CoSWoT. We thank three anonymous reviewers for their helpful comments.

References

1. Battle, R., Kolas, D.: Enabling the geospatial semantic web with parliament and geosparql. Semantic Web **3**(4), 355–370 (2012)
2. Bermudez-Edo, M., Elsaleh, T., Barnaghi, P., Taylor, K.: IoT-Lite: a lightweight semantic model for the internet of things and its use with dynamic semantics. Pers. Ubiquitous Comput. **21**(3), 475–487 (2017)
3. Bezdek, J.C.: Cluster validity with fuzzy sets (1973)
4. Bezdek, J.C.: Numerical taxonomy with fuzzy sets. J. Math. Biol. **1**(1), 57–71 (1974)
5. Dk, O.D.: What is open data dk, March 2015. https://www.opendata.dk/hvad-er-open-data-dk
6. Elsaleh, T., Enshaeifar, S., Rezvani, R., Acton, S.T., Janeiko, V., Bermudez-Edo, M.: IoT-Stream: a lightweight ontology for internet of things data streams and its use with data analytics and event detection services. Sensors (Basel, Switz.) **20**(4) (2020). https://doi.org/10.3390/s20040953
7. Gao, F., Ali, M.I., Mileo, A.: Semantic discovery and integration of urban data streams. Challenge **7**, 16 (2014)
8. Gómez, S.A., Fillottrani, P.R.: Completitud de los métodos de acceso a datos basado en ontologías: enfoques, propiedades y herramientas. In: XIX Workshop de Investigadores en Ciencias de la Computación (2017)
9. Gorender, S., Silva, Í.: An ontology for a fault tolerant traffic information system. In: 22nd International Congress of Mechanical Engineering (COBEM 2013) (2013)
10. Janowicz, K., Haller, A., Cox, S., Phuoc, D., Lefranois, M.: SOSA: a lightweight ontology for sensors, observations, samples, and actuators. J. Web Semant. **56**, 1–10 (2018). https://doi.org/10.1016/j.websem.2018.06.003
11. Kharlamov, E., et al.: Towards analytics aware ontology based access to static and streaming data. In: Groth, P. (ed.) ISWC 2016. LNCS, vol. 9982, pp. 344–362. Springer, Cham (2016). https://doi.org/10.1007/978-3-319-46547-0_31

12. Kim, D.W., Lee, K.H., Lee, D.: On cluster validity index for estimation of the optimal number of fuzzy clusters. Pattern Recogn. **37**(10), 2009–2025 (2004)
13. London, I.C.: London air quality network (2021). https://www.londonair.org.uk/ LondonAir/General/about.aspx
14. Morignot, P., Nashashibi, F.: An ontology-based approach to relax traffic regulation for autonomous vehicle assistance. arXiv preprint arXiv:1212.0768 (2012)
15. Nikolaou, C., Kostylev, E.V., Konstantinidis, G., Kaminski, M., Grau, B.C., Horrocks, I.: The bag semantics of ontology-based data access. arXiv preprint arXiv:1705.07105 (2017)
16. Rezvani, R., Enshaeifar, S., Barnaghi, P.: Lagrangian-based pattern extraction for edge computing in the Internet of Things. In: 2019 6th IEEE International Conference on Cyber Security and Cloud Computing (CSCloud)/2019 5th IEEE International Conference on Edge Computing and Scalable Cloud (EdgeCom), pp. 177–182. IEEE (2019)
17. Tambassi, T.: From a geographical perspective: spatial turn, taxonomies and geo-ontologies. In: The Philosophy of Geo-Ontologies. SG, pp. 27–36. Springer, Cham (2018). https://doi.org/10.1007/978-3-319-64033-4_3
18. Wu, K.L., Yang, M.S.: A cluster validity index for fuzzy clustering. Pattern Recogn. Lett. **26**(9), 1275–1291 (2005)
19. Xie, X.L., Beni, G.: A validity measure for fuzzy clustering. IEEE Trans. Pattern Anal. Mach. Intell. **13**(8), 841–847 (1991)

Multilingual Short Text Analysis of Twitter Using Random Forest Approach

S. Mehta$^{(\boxtimes)}$, T. Jain, and N. Aggarwal

Computer Science Department, Jaypee Institute of Information Technology, Noida, India

Abstract. In this digital era language recognition of text plays an important role in the fields like information retrieval systems. Language recognition makes such systems capable of handling multilingual queries for which relevant documents are fetched according to their respective language. It also helps in retrieving information from multilingual sites such as Twitter. Existing work in language identification mainly focuses on large text. This works addresses the problem of language recognition of short text. The work employs two machine learning approaches based on n-gram representation of text - Random Forest and Weighted Ensemble learning. The study performed over 4 popular languages (English, Spanish, French, and German) reveals that Random Forest Algorithm outperforms Naive Bayes, Logistic Classifier and Weighted Ensemble approaches by up to 33.

Keywords: Language identification · Weighted Ensemble · Random Forest · Twitter data analytics

1 Introduction

We are living in a digital society which has no boundaries. People across the world with different languages and cultures are part of this society. Social media like facebook, twitter etc. are the key which provide a platforms for the people around to the globe to interact and share their opinions. These platforms have also become a marketplace for the organizations to sell their products and services. Organizations exploit the opinions of people expressed over social media portals in order to understand view of users about their products and services, new expected features, new demands of products etc. In recent years, microblogging sites such as Twitter have gained much of popularity and hence have become an important source of information mining for various fields such as social network analysis, studying human behavior etc. More than a billion users post on twitter and facebook every day. As these microblogging sites are used by people all over the world, it contains multilingual data which makes the task of information retrieval cumbersome. Another important application

© Springer Nature Switzerland AG 2021
B. Villazón-Terrazas et al. (Eds.): KGSWC 2021, CCIS 1459, pp. 84–92, 2021.
https://doi.org/10.1007/978-3-030-91305-2_7

of language detection is query processing by the web browsers. By identifying the language of the query in the preprocessing phase, relevant documents in the respective language can be fetched. Language identification also acts as a pre-filtering step in many other systems such as email interception and text categorization. Most of the existing methodologies focus on language identification for well organized and reasonably long text. But microblogging sites like twitter and facebook mostly contain short text. In fact, the maximum allowed length of a post on Twitter is 280 characters. Therefore in order to facilitate the efficient and reliable working of above-mentioned systems, it is important to focus on a linguistic aspect of the text as well as the length of the text. By taking into consideration these two factors we propose a language recognition system which can identify different languages from the given short text. The proposed methodology is based on the notion that each language has some characteristic n-grams which occur frequently. For example in the English language 'ei' is one of the most frequently occurring 2-gram. With help of different machine learning approaches and the n-gram profiles of different languages, our method is able to learn a language with a monolingual training set in that language. Currently, the proposed system detects four languages - English, French, Spanish, and German. The performance of the proposed system has been compared with different machine learning approaches such as Naive Bayes, Logistic Regression etc. The proposed system also uses two novel approaches to machine learning by implementing an ensemble voting classifier which uses a bucket of different models to predict the outcome and ensemble based Random Forest classifier. Rest of the paper is organized as follows: Sect. 2 presents related work followed by proposed methodology in Sect. 3. Experiments and analysis of results are given in Sect. 4. Section 5 details conclusion and future work.

2   Related Work

Most of the proposed methodologies are based on the assumption that the length of the text is reasonably long and data is monolingual. Some of the available systems also provide quite accurate results for short query-style data. [1] identified the various factors that affect the accuracy of language identification in the multilingual corpus. The research concluded that the accuracy of language recognition depends on several factors - the length of the text, the similarity between the languages which are being identified, the algorithm applied to identify different languages and the features that are used in the algorithm. It was also found that it is more tedious to recognize the difference in languages which were similar in terms of the most frequently used n-grams Authors [2] presented an automatic language detection to extract corpus of a particular language for Twitter. The system identified various confusing languages such as Urdu and Nepali. The system created a feature vector of each of the text and then applied various Natural Language detection such as partial matching to detect the language of the text. [3] presented their work on native languages. [4] compared various approaches to identify language from the spoken queries. The system compared independent language models which were built using unsupervised learning and neural networks. It also proposed Query-by-example method to detect the language of a short spoken text. [5] presented transliteration of Indian language words into their native scripts.

[6] developed a scheme for language detection by analyzing a monolingual dataset of microblogging sites by considering 4 features - languages used by the author in other blogs, languages used by the people tagged in the blog, the content of hyperlink present in the blog and the language of tags present in the blog. Though the proposed methodology outperformed various existing systems but suffered a major drawback. The monolingual dataset was used for analyzing the language but in real-case scenarios, language has to be identified from the multilingual text. [7] evaluated the performance of varied language identification techniques and frameworks over DBpedia. Authors observed that these frameworks perform poorly on rdfs:labels.

[8] presented a system that detects language from the multilingual corpus and the relative proportion of each of the language in the corpus. The model used supervised machine learning approaches based on n-gram frequency to predict the language of the text. One of the major disadvantages of this system is that it is built by considering texts of reasonably long length. It did not take into the consideration short query-style text [1]. [9] performed a complete survey on features and methods used for language identification.

3   Proposed Methodology

In the recent past machine learning algorithms have been widely used for various applications [10,11]. Our system employs machine learning algorithms to recognize four languages - French, English, German and Spanish. Most of the previously proposed models are based on n-gram frequencies in various languages but they suffer a major shortcoming that they are not able to detect ambiguous languages accurately. It is possible that the feature vector of a text built using the above n-gram approach may reflect similarity to multiple languages. To address this problem we introduce another scalar quantity in the feature vector of text - the score of the text in each of the languages according to the importance of generated 2-grams in each language. Also, our system uses novel approaches of ensemble based classifier. First is Weighted Ensemble classifier which is a hybrid of various supervised machine learning algorithms such as Naive Bayes and Logistic Regression. It acts as a voting classifier which gives importance to each of the individual approaches according to their accuracy. Second is Random Forest which uses multiple decision trees to predict the outcome. The language identification system consists of various steps as shown in Fig. 1. Each of them is described below.

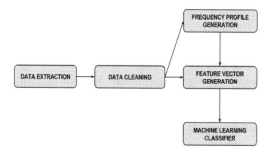

Fig. 1. Architecture of proposed model

3.1 Data Extraction and Cleaning

The preliminary task for language identification is the collection of the multilingual corpus which is required for training the machine learning classifiers as well as testing them. As our work focuses on short text language identification, it uses tweets acquired from Twitter as the corpus.

Data were extracted from Twitter using the Tweepy API. More than 125000 tweets are extracted for training as well as testing.

After data extraction, it is cleaned. Slang words are standardized, punctuation marks are removed, white spaces and extra characters are removed. Spellings are also corrected using the edit distance algorithm.

3.2 Frequency Profile Generation

Frequency profile of a language depicts the frequency of all the possible 2-grams in that language. It helps in identifying the most frequently used grams in a language.

To generate the frequency profile of a language, the frequency of all the possible 2-grams are calculated using the data set of that language. Our algorithm optimizes the frequency profiles by eliminating the 2-grams which occur less frequently in English, French, Spanish as well as German. This further reduces the size of feature generated for each text.

3.3 Feature Generation

To train the machine learning classifiers the multilingual training dataset was converted to a feature vector using the English, French, German and Spanish frequency profiles. The feature vector consisted of the frequency of all possible 2-grams in the text except those which were eliminated during frequency profile generation.

Our methodology introduces another scalar quantity in the feature vector - score of the text in each of the four languages. The score in a language basically represents the overall importance of 2-grams of the text in that language. This parameter solves the problem of identifying similar languages. It is possible that the frequency set of 2-grams of a text may represent multiple languages but the score helps in differentiating between the languages. This is because all the 2-grams generated are less likely to have the same importance in all the languages.

3.4   Machine Learning Classifiers

The proposed system uses several machine learning based models and each one of them is described below.

Naive Bayes Classifier [6] describes Naive Bayes classifier as a simple probabilistic model based on the Bayes rule along with a strong independence assumption. The previously proposed works have mostly used Naive Bayes classification for language identification. Our model further increases the performance of this classifier by introducing the language score as a new parameter in the feature vector of text.

Logistic Regression: Logistic Regression is an approach for modeling the relationship between a scalar dependent variable and one or more explanatory variables (or independent variables) denoted X. To our knowledge, no previous work has been done in this area. In our system, frequency feature vector of the text act as the independent variable while the languages act as the dependent variable.

Random Forest: Random Forests or random decision forests are an ensemble learning method for classification, regression, and other tasks, that operate by constructing a multitude of decision trees at training time and outputting the class that is the mode of the classes (classification) or mean prediction (regression) of the individual trees [1].

Weighted Ensemble: The goal of weighted is to combine a set of regressors in order to improve the predictive accuracy. Traditionally, the weighted average of the outputs is treated as the final prediction. This means each base model plays a constant role in the whole data space [12]. In our work, Weighted Ensemble uses Random Forest, Logistic Regression and Naive Bayes as the base models. The weight of prediction for each of the model is considered according to their individual accuracy.

4   Experiments and Results

This work compares various machine learning approaches on the basis of accuracy of predicting the language of twitter text as French, Spanish, German or English. For experiments more than 125000 tweets were collected for different languages. 80% of the tweets were used for training and rest for testing the performance of algorithms. Results have been depicted through Fig. 2. It can be clearly observed that both Random Forest and Weighted Ensemble provide better accuracy than Logistic Regression and Naive Bayes. From Table 2, it can be observed that percentage difference in accuracy of Naive Bayes and Logistic Regression with respect to Weighted Ensemble is 19.64% and 33.82% respectively. Also, the accuracy of Random Forest exceeds the accuracy of Naive Bayes and Logistic Regression by 19.64% and 12.5% which further proves that Random Forest and Weighted Ensemble are more efficient than Naive Bayes and Logistic Regression (Table 1).

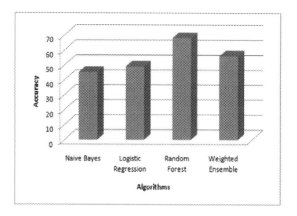

Fig. 2. Accuracy of machine learning techniques

Table 1. Accuracy of respective algorithms

S no	Technique	Accuracy
1	Naive Bayes	45.15
2	Logistic Regression	49
3	Random Forest	68
4	Weighted Ensemble	56

Table 2. Percentage improvement in accuracy

S no	Technique	Random Forest	Weighted Ensemble
1	Naive Bayes	33.82	19.64
2	Logistic Regression	27.94	12.5

However, Random Forest outperforms Weighted Ensemble in terms of accuracy. Random Forests constructs multiple decision trees by splitting the training data into different groups. It takes into account the prediction of each tree in order to produce the final outcome. Hence, it proves to have greater accuracy from the rest. Though Weighted Ensemble also uses a similar approach unlike Random Forest, predictions of different individual machine learning algorithms are used. As both Naive Bayes and Logistic Regression have lower accuracy, thus, bringing down the accuracy of Weighted Ensemble. The accuracy of Weighted Ensemble can be improved by adding more machine learning techniques such as Support Vector Machine to it. Next results depict the accuracy of these approaches for language classification. The accuracy of both Random Forest and Weighted Ensemble were calculated in each of the languages.

Figure 3 shows that Random Forest is able to identify 80% of the total tweets in English accurately while Weighted Ensemble detects approximately 60% of

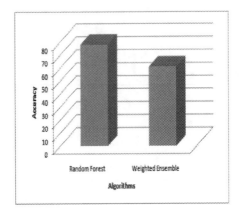

Fig. 3. Accuracy of English language

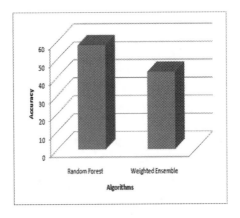

Fig. 4. Accuracy of French language

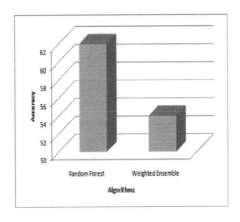

Fig. 5. Accuracy of Spanish language

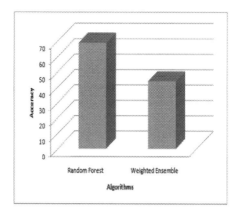

Fig. 6. Accuracy of German language

English tweets correctly. Similarly, from Fig. 4, 5 and 6, it can be concluded that Random Forest provides better accuracy than Weighted Ensemble for French, Spanish, and German languages too.

5   Conclusion, Limitations and Future Scope

Language recognition plays an important role in various data mining systems and hence need to be carried out with immense efficiency and accuracy. Our work recognized short text in four languages - French, English, German and Spanish. For this, we introduced two new ensemble-based approaches - Random Forest and Weighted Ensemble. The model also introduces a new parameter to detect the language of the text - score of text in a language which depicts the importance of n-grams of a text in that language. This will prove to be useful while detecting similar languages. In a nutshell, the model can be used to recognize any number of languages and remains unaffected by the length of the text. One major limitation of the proposed system is that it can detect languages which use the standard alphabet (a–z). Hence, it cannot detect languages like Chinese and Japanese. So, such languages can also be detected in future. Currently, system uses 2-grams for the purpose of language detection. The system can be tested by increasing the size of grams generated. Another improvement that can be applied to the current model is incorporating more machine learning algorithms such as bagging which is another type of ensemble learning can also be used to identify languages. The accuracy of Weighted Ensemble can further be increased by adding appropriate machine learning approaches to it. At present, various automated systems and language detection frameworks like Tika, lanagdetect, openNLP, langTagger and langid are also available. So the next work would be to assess the performance of machine learning models with these frameworks.

Compliance with Ethical Standards
This assessment was not sponsored by any honor. No creatures were included. Neither any of the appraisals are associated with people or creatures nor performed with the assistance of columnists. Trained assent was secured from every single individual part connected with the assessment.

References

1. Botha, G.R., Barnard, E.: Factors that affect the accuracy of text-based language identification. Comput. Speech Lang. **26**(5), 307–320 (2012)
2. Bergsma, S., McNamee, P., Bagdouri, M., Fink, C., Wilson, T.: Language identification for creating language-specific twitter collections. In: Proceedings of the Second Workshop on Language in Social Media, pp. 65–74 (2012)
3. Križ, V., Holub, M., Pecina, P.: Feature extraction for native language identification using language modeling. In: Proceedings of the International Conference Recent Advances in Natural Language Processing, pp. 298–306 (2015)
4. Tejedor, J.E.A.: Comparison of methods for language dependent and language independent query by example spoken term detection. ACM Trans. Inf. Syst. **30**(3), 1–34 (2012)
5. Patel, S., Desai, V.: LIGA and syllabification approach for language identification and back transliteration: a shared task report by DA-IICT. In: Proceedings of the Forum for Information Retrieval Evaluation, pp. 43–47 (2014)
6. Carter, S., Weerkamp, W., Tsagkias, M.: Microblog language identification: overcoming the limitations of short, unedited and idiomatic text. Lang. Res. Eval. **47**(1), 195–215 (2013)
7. Hinguruduwa, L., Marx, E., Soru, T., Riechert, T.: Assessing language identification over DBpedia. In: 2021 IEEE 15th International Conference on Semantic Computing (ICSC), pp. 296–297 (2021). https://doi.org/10.1109/ICSC50631.2021.00084
8. Lui, M., Lau, J.H., Baldwin, T.: Automatic detection and language identification of multilingual documents. Trans. Assoc. Comput. Ling. **2**, 27–40 (2014)
9. Jauhiainen, T., Lui, M., Zampieri, M., Baldwin, T., Lindén, K.: Automatic language identification in texts: a survey. J. Artif. Intell. Res. **65**, 675–782 (2019)
10. Gaurav, D., Rodriguez, F.O., Tiwari, S., Jabbar, M.: Review of machine learning approach for drug development process. In: Deep Learning in Biomedical and Health Informatics. CRC Press, pp. 53–77 (2021)
11. Gaurav, D., Shandilya, S., Tiwari, S., Goyal, A.: A machine learning method for recognizing invasive content in memes. In: Villazón-Terrazas, B., Ortiz-Rodríguez, F., Tiwari, S.M., Shandilya, S.K. (eds.) KGSWC 2020. CCIS, vol. 1232, pp. 195–213. Springer, Cham (2020). https://doi.org/10.1007/978-3-030-65384-2_15
12. Graham, M., Hale, S.A., Gaffney, D.: Where in the world are you? Geolocation and language identification in twitter. Prof. Geogr. **66**(4), 568–578 (2014)

Quality Assessment of Library Linked Data: a Case Study

Yusniel Hidalgo-Delgado[1]([⊠]) [iD], Yoan A. López[1][iD],
Juan Pedro Febles Rodríguez[1][iD], and Amed Leiva Mederos[2][iD]

[1] Departamento de Informática, Universidad de las Ciencias Informáticas,
Havana, Cuba
{yhdelgado,yalopez,febles}@uci.cu
[2] Centro de Investigaciones en Informática, Universidad Central "Marta Abreu" de
Las Villa, Santa Clara, Cuba
amed@uclv.edu.cu

Abstract. The linked data principles provide an efficient way to inter-
link resources across several datasets, improving interoperability and
discoverability. Several digital libraries around the world are publishing
their legacy data from catalogs and authority files following the linked
data principles. However, selecting the most suitable datasets for creating links between them is becoming a complex task due to most of them
not having the proper data quality. In this paper, we evaluate the quality
of data of the LinkedDL dataset. The results are compared to four other
datasets in the state-of-the-art. The evaluation showed promising results
in the accuracy, consistency, and accessibility metrics.

Keywords: Linked data · Digital libraries · Interoperability · Data
quality

1 Introduction

Libraries play an important role in the visibility and access to scientific production. Currently, libraries are classified into conventional, digital, and hybrid. In
the particular case of digital libraries, they collect, store and distribute information on digital media [16]. On the other hand, digital library systems are
information systems that support the management of organized collections of
digital objects (digital resources) that are oriented to users by providing value-
added services [1].

Interoperability and sustainability are keys to realizing the vision of digital
libraries that are able to communicate with each other. Interoperability is the
ability of a system or a product to work with other systems or products without
special effort on the part of the customer. In recent years, several approaches
have been proposed to address the problem of semantic interoperability in digital
libraries. The studies focus on three fundamental approaches, metadata crosswalk [2,6,11], ontology alignment [12], and linked data [3,18]. Linked data refers

© Springer Nature Switzerland AG 2021
B. Villazón-Terrazas et al. (Eds.): KGSWC 2021, CCIS 1459, pp. 93–108, 2021.
https://doi.org/10.1007/978-3-030-91305-2_8

to a set of principles and best practices for publishing and linking structured data on the Web. Data comes from different sources that can be maintained by organizations with different geographic locations [3].

The publication of data following the linked data principles enhances the discovery and reuse of data in the Web space while solving the semantic interoperability problems between information systems through the use of ontologies as a way of representing knowledge. There are several approaches for publishing library data as linked data, most of them are based on transforming legacy metadata to RDF graphs. Recently, a novel semantic interoperability model called LinkedDL for building linked data-based digital libraries was proposed [10]. In this paper, we asset the quality of library linked data generated by LinkedDL. Preliminary results show an improvement in the quality of linked data generated by LinkedDL in comparison with similar models proposed in the literature.

The paper is organised as follows: in the section Related Work, a brief overview of the quality of linked data is presented. Section Quality Metrics presents the scores for each quality metric evaluated in the LinkedDL dataset. Section Results and Discussions presents a qualitative description of the main results and their practical implications. Finally, the section Conclusions and Future Work presents our final remarks and future research lines.

2 Related Work

In recent years, many data publishers have been translating legacy data to linked data without checking the quality of data sources. For this reason, data consumers need to check the quality of linked data to ensure that they are fit for use according to certain quality needs. In this sense, several authors have proposed categories, dimensions, metrics, and tools to measure the quality of the existing linked data on the web of data [4,7–9,14,17,20].

According to Wang et al. [19], a data quality criterion is a particular characteristic of data concerning its quality and can be either subjective or objective. To measure the degree to which a certain data quality criterion is fulfilled for a given linked dataset, each criterion is formalized and expressed in terms of a function with the value range of $[0, 1]$. This function is called the data quality metric. Finally, one or several data quality criteria belongs to a data quality dimension.

A recent survey on quality assessment for linked data found a comprehensive list of 18 quality dimensions and 69 metrics [20]. Additionally, the authors qualitatively analyzed the 30 core approaches and 12 tools using a set of attributes. Most of these quality dimensions were used to evaluate the quality of five large knowledge graphs [9].

In the particular case of quality assessment of linked data in digital libraries, Candela and collaborators adapted existing quality dimensions to the context of digital libraries [4,5]. They carried out an extensive quality assessment study over four digital libraries. This study was taken as a baseline for the quality assessment in this paper. In Table 2, we include results obtained by Candela et al. [4] and compared them with our evaluation results.

3   Quality Metrics

To assess the quality of Library Linked Data, we use the LinkedDL[1] dataset. This dataset exposes bibliographic metadata from several scientific journals from Cuba following the Linked Data principles. It contains metadata about Authors, Articles, and Journals. In the case of Journals, links were generated with two other datasets in the web of data: wikidata and ISSN. In the next sections, we detailed each metrics and its corresponding scores in the LinkedDL dataset.

3.1   Accuracy

According to Wang et al. [19], the accuracy dimension determines the extent to which data are correct, reliable and certified free of error. The accuracy dimension was evaluated by means of the following four metrics:

Syntactic Validity of RDF Documents: syntax errors in RDF can be identified using tools such as the W3C RDF Validator[2]. The metric was originally defined as:

$$m_{synRDF} = \begin{cases} 1 & \text{if all RDF documents are valid} \\ 0 & \text{otherwise} \end{cases} \tag{1}$$

At the time of writing this paper, all RDF graphs were validated using the W3C validator, determining that all graphs are found free of syntactic errors. This check will be carried out periodically, taking into account that the graphs are generated regularly incorporating new information.

Syntactic Validity of Literals: this metric consists of determining if the literals stored in the RDF graph correspond to the syntax defined for each literal. In digital libraries, it is common to find syntactic patterns in the metadata, such as: names of authors, dates of publication, and identifiers (DOI, ISSN, among others). The syntax of these literals can be checked using regular expressions. The RDF graph $\mathcal{G}$ consists of RDF triples (s, p, o) and a set of literals $\mathcal{L}$.

$$m_{synLit} = \frac{|\{\mathcal{G} \wedge \mathcal{L} \wedge o \text{ is valid}\}|}{|\{\mathcal{G} \wedge \mathcal{L}\}|} \tag{2}$$

The syntactic validity of the literals was checked using regular expressions in the SPARQL query language. The names of the authors, dates, titles, and ISSNs of the journals, among other literals, were checked. In all cases, the results were correct. The following SPARQL query checks and returns the ISSNs of all the journals in the repository:

---

[1] https://yhdelgado.github.io/linkeddl/.
[2] https://www.w3.org/RDF/Validator/.

```
prefix bibo: <http://purl.org/ontology/bibo/>
SELECT ?issn WHERE{
?s bibo:issn ?issn.
FILTER(regex(?issn,"^\\S{4}\\-\\S{4}$","i"))
}
```

Semantic Validity of Triples: this metric consists of evaluating the extent to which an RDF graph $\mathcal{G}$ contains the same values as an RDF graph $\mathcal{S}$ that *a priori* is known to have all its valid triples.

$$m_{semTriple} = \frac{|\{\mathcal{G} \wedge \mathcal{S}\}|}{|\{\mathcal{G}\}|} \tag{3}$$

For the evaluation of the semantic validity of the triples, all the triples that semantically describe the journals included in the repository were selected. To establish the semantic comparison, the existing triples in the semantic description in Wikidata were used. In all cases, the results were correct. For example, the title, ISSN, and URL of the entity *Revista Cubana de Información en Ciencias de la Salud* match both in Wikidata[3] and in the repository generated by LinkedDL[4].

Duplicate Entities: this metric consists of calculating the Wikidata link rate with duplicate identifiers, since there can be multiple identifiers in an RDF graph for the same entity. Let n_w^u the number of unique entities linked to Wikidata, and n_w the number of entities linked to Wikidata, then:

$$m_{checkDup} = \frac{n_w^u}{n_w} \tag{4}$$

For the duplicate entities detection, the RDF graph containing links to Wikidata was selected. The existing links are of the type *owl:sameAs*. After executing the following SPARQL query, no duplicate entities were detected in the graph.

```
SELECT ?s (COUNT(?id) AS ?total)
WHERE{?s owl:sameAs ?id}
GROUP BY ?s
HAVING (COUNT(?id)>1)
```

3.2 Trustworthiness

Trustworthiness is defined as the degree to which the information is accepted to be correct, true, real and credible [20]. Trustworthiness is evaluated at the following three levels:

Trustworthiness on the Data Set Level: the metric is originally defined as shown in Table 1.

---

[3] http://www.wikidata.org/entity/Q50816707.
[4] https://data.infocientia.com/resource/journal/2307-2113.

Table 1. Possible scores according to the metric trustworthiness on the data set level.

Description	Score
Manual data curation, manual data insertion in a closed system	1
Manual data curation and insertion, both by a community	0.75
Automated data curation, data insertion by automated knowledge extraction from structured data sources	0.25
Automated data curation, data insertion by automated knowledge extraction from unstructured data sources	0

The LinkedDL model establishes that the insertion and curation of bibliographic data are carried out by implementing specific wrappers for each data source. Some of these wrappers can insert metadata automatically, as is the case with the implemented wrapper for the OAI-PMH protocol. In other cases, the metadata is inserted manually by experts in library and information science. In both cases, the metadata goes through a manual cataloging and review process, with the aim of guaranteeing their veracity and consistency.

Trustworthiness on the Statement Level: this metric assesses whether there is information about the provenance at the instance level. Information about the provenance of the data can be semantically described using a vocabulary or ontology for this purpose, for example, PROV-O. The metric is defined as:

$$
m_{fact} = \begin{cases} 1 & \text{provenance on statement level is used} \\ 0.5 & \text{provenance on resource level is used} \\ 0 & \text{otherwise} \end{cases} \tag{5}
$$

The LinkedDL model does not include information about the provenance of the data at the instance level. Something similar happens with the rest of the digital libraries that are compared in the state of the art.

Using Unknown and Empty Values: trustworthiness can be increased by supporting unknown and empty values. These statements require unknown and empty values to be encoded with a different identifier. The metric was originally defined as:

$$
m_{NoVal} = \begin{cases} 1 & \text{unknown and empty values are used} \\ 0.5 & \text{either unknown or empty values are used} \\ 0 & \text{otherwise} \end{cases} \tag{6}
$$

In the LinkedDL model, an automatic conversion is performed from the relational database to the RDF data model. The conversion only takes into account the data that resides in the database, so no triples with unknown or empty values are generated. Something similar happens with the rest of the digital libraries that are compared in the state of the art.

3.3   Consistency

Consistency is defined as two or more values that do not conflict with each other [13]. Semantic consistency is the extent to which the repositories use the same values and elements for conveying the same concepts and meanings throughout [15]. Three aspects of consistency are measured as follows:

Consistency of Schema Restrictions During Insertion of New Statements: checking the schema restrictions during the insertion of new statements is often done on the user interface in order to avoid inconsistencies. For instance, that the entity to be added has a valid entity type, as expressed by the *rdf:type* property:

$$m_{checkRestr} = \begin{cases} 1 & \text{schema restrictions are checked} \\ 0 & \text{otherwise} \end{cases} \tag{7}$$

For the evaluation of this metric, the first 100 results were selected for each of the entities modeled in the graph. For all instances, it was checked using the *rdf:type* property. As a result, in all cases, the entities used this property properly. The following SPARQL query lists the first 100 triples of scientific articles type:

```
PREFIX fabio: <http://purl.org/spar/fabio/>
SELECT ?s ?p ?o WHERE {
?s ?p ?o.
?s rdf:type fabio:JournalArticle.
}
LIMIT 100
```

Consistency of Statements with Respect to Class Constraints: this metric measures the extent to which the instance data are consistent with regard to the class restrictions. Let C be the set of all class constraints, defined as $C = \{(c_1, c_2)|(c_1, \text{owl:disjointWith}, c_2) \in \mathcal{G}\}$. Then, let $c_{\mathcal{G}}(e)$ be the set of all classes of instance e in $\mathcal{G}$, defined as $c_{\mathcal{G}}(e) = \{c|(e, \text{rdf:type}, c) \in \mathcal{G}\}$. Then, we can state:

$$m_{conClass} = \frac{|\{(c_1, c_2) \in C | \neg \exists e : (c_1 \in c_{\mathcal{G}}(e)) \wedge c_2 \in c_{\mathcal{G}}(e))\}|}{|\{(c_1, c_2) \in C\}|} \tag{8}$$

For the evaluation of this metric, the existing restrictions between the classes used to model the data in the graph are determined. In none of the cases were restrictions of the type *owl:disjointWith* encountered. However, it was found that there is not the same entity modeled with two or more different classes. The following SPARQL query was designed to verify that an entity is not at the same time of type *fabio:Journal* and *fabio:JournalArticle* is shown. No entity with this characteristic was found.

```
PREFIX fabio: <http://purl.org/spar/fabio/>
SELECT COUNT(?entity) as ?total WHERE{
?entity rdf:type fabio:Journal.
?entity rdf:type fabio:JournalArticle.
}
```

Consistency of Statements with Respect to Relation Constraints: this metric measures the extent to which the instance data are consistent with the relation restrictions.

$$m_{conRelat} = \frac{1}{n} \sum_{i=1}^{n} m_{conRelat,i}(\mathcal{G}) \tag{9}$$

For the evaluation of this metric, the relationships between classes (Object-Property) existing in the graph were determined. For each one of them, the range is determined and it is verified that the instances of classes existing in the graph comply with the range restrictions of the corresponding properties. For example, the *dc:creator* property has the class *fabio:JournalArticle* as the range and the class *foaf:Person* as domain, indicating that a person is the author of a scientific article. To verify this restriction, the following SPARQL query was designed, obtaining that all instances are correct.

```
PREFIX dc: <http://purl.org/dc/elements/1.1/>
SELECT (COUNT(?x) as ?total) ?rangeType WHERE{
?x dc:creator ?o.
?o a ?rangeType
}
GROUP BY ?rangeType
```

3.4   Ease of Understanding

The ease of understanding is the degree to which data are understood, readable and clear [19]. In the context of a digital library, this is focused on users and addresses issues such as using textual descriptions and descriptive Uniform Resource Identifiers (URIs). Since most of libraries are local or national, they often provide their content in a single language. The ease of understanding is measured by means of the following four metrics:

Description of Resources: Repositories based on semantic web principles may use basic properties (for instance, *rdfs:label* and *rdfs:comment*) to describe resources. Formally, let $\mathcal{P}_{IDesc}$ be the set of relations that contains a label or description and $U_{\mathcal{G}}^{local}$ be the set of all URIs in $\mathcal{G}$ with local namespace.

$$m_{Descr} = \frac{|\{u|u \in U_{\mathcal{G}}^{local} \wedge \exists(u,p,o) \in \mathcal{G} : p \in \mathcal{P}_{IDesc}\}|}{|\{u|u \in U_{\mathcal{G}}^{local}\}|} \tag{10}$$

In all RDF graphs generated by the LinkedDL model, the *rdfs:label* properties are used to describe all the resources. In the case of authors, the label stores their full name, in the case of journals, the label stores the title of the journal, and in the case of articles, their title is stored.

Labels in Multiple Languages: this metric measures whether labels in additional languages are provided.

$$m_{Lang} = \begin{cases} 1 & \text{labels provided in at least one additional language} \\ 0 & \text{otherwise} \end{cases} \tag{11}$$

The bibliographic metadata published by LinkedDL were harvested from Cuban journals that use the OAI-PMH protocol for the exchange of metadata. Although this protocol supports the export of metadata in several languages, Cuban journals only publish metadata in Spanish, so RDF graphs currently do not have labels in more than one language.

Understandable RDF Serialization: this metric measures the use of alternative encodings that are more understandable for humans than RDF/XML format, such as N-Triples, N3 and Turtle.

$$m_{uSer} = \begin{cases} 1 & \text{other RDF serializations than RDF/XML format available} \\ 0 & \text{otherwise} \end{cases} \tag{12}$$

All the RDF graphs generated by the model are serialized in several formats, such as N3, TTL, HDT, and XML. The graphs and their different serializations can be downloaded from the project website.

Self-describing URIs: self-descriptive URIs contain a readable description of the entity rather than identifiers, and they help users to understand the resource.

$$m_{mURI} = \begin{cases} 1 & \text{self-describing URIs always used} \\ 0.5 & \text{self-describing URIs partly used} \\ 0 & \text{otherwise} \end{cases} \tag{13}$$

During the URI design stage for the construction of the RDF graphs generated by the model, best practices existing in the literature were adopted. It was taken into account that the URIs contain some term or keyword that reflects the type of the entity it describes. For example, the URIs that describe journals have the structure https://data.infocientia.com/resource/journal/2307-2113. In all of them, the term *journal* appears to denote that the URI identifies a journal in the context of the RDF graph. On the other hand, universal identifiers were used, in this case, the ISSN. This ensures that, regardless of whether or not the semantic description of the entity changes, the URI that identifies it never changes, because the ISSN of a journal does not change regularly.

3.5   Interoperability

According to Färber et al. [9], the interoperability is calculated using the following metrics:

Avoiding Blank Nodes and RDF Reification: this metric allows to evaluate if there are blank nodes and triples *rdf:Statement* in the RDF graph. The equation that defines the metric is shown below.

$$m_{reif} = \begin{cases} 1 & \text{no blank nodes and no reification} \\ 0.5 & \text{either no blank nodes or noreification} \\ 0 & \text{otherwise} \end{cases} \tag{14}$$

The generated RDF graph was modeled with ontologies and vocabularies developed by third parties, avoiding the reification of the graph by using *rdf:Statement,* considering that it is a non-recommended practice in these cases. To check the existence or not of blank nodes in the generated RDF graph, the following SPARQL query was designed and executed, obtaining false in all the results. The query uses the *isBlank* function of the SPARQL language, which returns true if there are blank nodes in the RDF graph and false otherwise. Based on the definition of the metric, the resulting value after the evaluation is 1.

```
SELECT ?s ?p ?o ?blankTest
WHERE {
?s ?p ?o.
BIND(isBlank(?o) as ?blankTest)
}
```

Provisioning of Several Serialization Formats: In the interoperability process, the format (s) in which the data is exchanged between information systems play an important role. This metric assesses the support offered by the digital library to serialize the RDF graphs in one or more interchange formats. The equation that defines the metric is shown below.

$$m_{iSerial} = \begin{cases} 1 & \text{RDF/XML and further formats are supported} \\ 0.5 & \text{only RDF/XML is supported} \\ 0 & \text{otherwise} \end{cases} \tag{15}$$

In the proposed approach, the use of the Virtuoso triplestore was adopted. This tool supports the publication of the RDF graphs using a SPARQL Endpoint to perform queries on the stored RDF graphs. Virtuoso supports several RDF graph serialization formats, such as: RDF/XML, Turtle, JSON-LD and N-Triples, all of which are W3C standards. Based on the definition of the metric, the resulting value after the evaluation is 1.

Using External Vocabulary: this metric evaluates the use of ontologies and external vocabularies by dividing the number of triples whose predicate uses an external vocabulary by the total number of triples existing in the RDF graph. The equation that defines the metric is shown below.

$$m_{extVoc} = \frac{|\{(s,p,o)|(s,p,o) \in \mathcal{G} \wedge p \in \mathcal{P}_{\mathcal{G}}\}|}{|\{(s,p,o) \in \mathcal{G}\}|} \tag{16}$$

where $\mathcal{P}_{\mathcal{G}}$ is the set of external properties to the graph $\mathcal{G}$.

To evaluate the metric, two SPARQL queries were designed that obtain the existing classes and properties in the RDF graph. Three classes and 14 relationships were obtained. Both the classes and the properties obtained belong to ontologies and vocabularies designed by third-parties and reused in the solution proposal. Based on the definition of the metric, the resulting value after the evaluation is 1. The corresponding SPARQL queries are shown below.

```
SELECT DISTINCT ?type
WHERE {
?subject a ?type.
}

SELECT DISTINCT ?property
WHERE {
?subject ?property ?object.
}
```

Interoperability of Proprietary Vocabulary: this metric calculates the fraction of classes and properties with at least one equivalence link to classes and properties in external vocabularies. The equivalences can be declared through the properties *owl:sameAs, owl:equivalentClass, rdfs:subPropertyOf* or *rdfs:subClassOf*. Let $\mathcal{P}_{eq} = \{$owl:sameAs; owl:equivalenClass; rdfs:subPropertyOf; rdfs:subClassOf$\}$ and $U_{\mathcal{G}}^{ext}$ consists of all URIs in U_g which are external to the graph $\mathcal{G}$, we can state:

$$m_{propVoc} = \frac{|\{x \in \mathcal{P'}_{\mathcal{G}} \cup C_{\mathcal{G}} | \exists (x, p, o) \in \mathcal{G} : (p \in \mathcal{P}_{eq} \wedge (o \in U \wedge o \in U_{\mathcal{G}}^{ext}))\}|}{|\mathcal{P}_{\mathcal{G}} \cup C_{\mathcal{G}}|} \tag{17}$$

Taking into account the maturity of the existing ontologies in the state-of-the-art and their wide adoption by the producers of linked data in digital libraries, we decided to adopt and reuse existing ontologies and vocabularies in the solution proposal. The reuse of ontologies and vocabularies constitutes one of the recommendations of the scientific community that contributes to increasing interoperability between information systems. Considering that the proposed solution does not use its own ontology, it is decided not to calculate the metric $m_{propVoc}$.

3.6   Accessibility

Accessibility is the extent to which data are available or easily and quickly retrievable [19]. Accessibility requires the data to be available through SPARQL endpoints and RDF dumps. SPARQL endpoints also allow the execution of federated queries across different data sets, enhancing and increasing the visibility of the LOD. The accessibility involves a variety of criteria as follows:

Dereferencing Possibility of Resources: dereferencing of resources is based on URIs that are resolvable by means of HTTP requests, returning useful and valid information. The dereferencing of resources is successful when an RDF document is returned and the HTTP status code is 200. This metric assesses for a set of

URIs whether dereferencing of resources is successful. Let $\mathcal{U}_g$ be a set of URIs, we can state:

$$m_{Deref} = \frac{|Dereferencable(\mathcal{U}_g)|}{|(\mathcal{U}_g)|} \tag{18}$$

To evaluate this metric, the first 500 existing resources were selected in the RDF graph generated by the LinkedDL model. Then, an HTTP request was made to each of the URIs that identify the resources, obtaining the 200 status code in all cases. In this way, it is verified that all resources are dereferenced. The RDF graph is published using the Linked Data Fragments server[5], a tool that guarantees the dereferencing process of all existing resources in the graph. This run this metric evaluation, we designed a python script available at Google Colab[6].

Availability of the Digital Library: This metric assesses the availability of the digital library in terms of uptime. It can be measured using a URI and a monitoring service over a period of time. Let S_r be the number of successful requests and T_r be the total number of requests, then:

$$m_{Avai} = \frac{S_r}{T_r} \tag{19}$$

To evaluate this metric, the Linked Data Fragments server that publishes the RDF graph was monitored for a period of seven days. Every five minutes an HTTP request was made to the server, storing the status code obtained. In all cases, the status code was 200, evidencing the high availability of the service.

Availability of a Public SPARQL Endpoint: This metric indicates the existence of a publicly available SPARQL endpoint.

$$m_{SPARQL} = \begin{cases} 1 & \text{SPARQL endpoint publicly available} \\ 0 & \text{otherwise} \end{cases} \tag{20}$$

For storing the RDF graph generated by the LinkedDL model, the Virtuoso Open Source server is used. This server provides a public SPARQL endpoint, which can be consulted at https://data.infocientia.com/sparql.

Provisioning of an RDF Export: In addition to the SPARQL endpoint, an RDF data export can be provided to download the whole data set.

$$m_{Export} = \begin{cases} 1 & \text{RDF export available} \\ 0 & \text{otherwise} \end{cases} \tag{21}$$

A web page has been designed and published in order to guarantee the reuse of the RDF graphs. The RDF graphs generated by the project can be downloaded

---

[5] https://linkeddatafragments.org/.
[6] Google Colab.

from https://yhdelgado.github.io/linkeddl/. This page contains an overview of the dataset, as well as links to files in several formats, such as N-Triples, Turtle, HDT, and RDF/XML.

Support of Content Negotiation: This metric assesses the consistency between the RDF serialization format requested (RDF/XML, N3, Turtle and N-Triples) and that which is returned.

$$m_{Negot} = \begin{cases} 1 & \text{content negotiation supported and correct content types returned} \\ 0.5 & \text{content negotiation supported but wrong content types returned} \\ 0 & \text{otherwise} \end{cases}$$
(22)

Content negotiation is provided by Linked Data Fragments server, however only HTML and RDF/XML formats are supported.

Linking HTML Sites to RDF Serializations: HTML pages can be linked to RDF serializations by adding a tag to the HTML header with the pattern $<link\ rel = $ *'alternate' type = 'content type' href = 'URL'>*.

$$m_{HTMLRDF} = \begin{cases} 1 & \text{autodiscovery pattern used at least once} \\ 0 & \text{otherwise} \end{cases}$$
(23)

This feature is not currently supported on the Linked Data Fragments server used for publishing RDF graphs.

Provisioning of Repository Metadata: The repository can be described using VoID. This metric indicates whether a machine-readable metadata about the data set is available.

$$m_{Meta} = \begin{cases} 1 & \text{machine-readable metadata available} \\ 0 & \text{otherwise} \end{cases}$$
(24)

The repository generated by LinkedDL supports the description of it using the VoID vocabulary. The metadata describing the repository can be downloaded at https://data.infocientia.com/void.ttl#linkeddl. This feature is essential for the discovery and reuse of published RDF graphs.

3.7 Interlinking

Interlinking is the extent to which entities that represent the same concept are linked to each other, be it within or between two or more data sources. The interlinking dimension measures the number and validity of external links as follows:

Interlinking via owl:sameAs: This score is obtained as the rate of instances having at least one owl:sameAs triple pointing to an external resource. Let $\mathcal{I}_\mathcal{G}$ be the set of instances in $\mathcal{G}$ we can state:

$$m_{Inst} = \frac{|\{x \in \mathcal{I}_\mathcal{G} | \exists \{x, sameAs, y\} \in g \wedge y \in U_\mathcal{G}^{ext}\}|}{|\mathcal{I}_g|} \tag{25}$$

To evaluate this metric, the total number of existing instances in the RDF graph is first calculated. For this, the following SPARQL query was used:

```
SELECT (COUNT(*) as ?Instances) WHERE { ?s rdf:type ?o}
```

After executing the query, a total of 25657 instances was obtained at the time of the evaluation. Then, the total number of instances that have links to external data sources was calculated, in all cases the instances have the property *owl:sameAs.* To determine the number of instances, the following SPARQL query was executed:

```
SELECT (COUNT(*) as ?Instances) WHERE { ?s owl:sameAs ?o}
```

After executing the query, 27 instances were obtained, so the metric m_{Inst} gets a value of 0.001. The value of the metric is low, so that in successive iterations the graph will be enriched with links to other existing data sources on the data web.

Validity of External URIs: Linking to external resources can lead to invalid links. Given a list of URIs, this criterion checks if there is a timeout or error. Let $\mathcal{A}$ be the set of external URIs, then:

$$m_{URIs} = \frac{|\{x \in \mathcal{A} \wedge x \text{ is resolvable}\}|}{|\mathcal{A}|} \tag{26}$$

To calculate the value of the metric, an HTTP request was executed on the 27 links to external data sources existing in the graph. In all cases, the status code 200 was obtained.

4   Results and Discussion

The Accuracy dimension achieves a high score in all the repositories evaluated. In the particular case of the duplicate entities metric, the LinkedDL dataset achieves the highest score, which means that no duplicate entities were detected in the repository concerning existing entities in Wikidata.

The Trustworthiness dimension is not very high in any of the repositories evaluated. However, the LinkedDL dataset scores higher in the library level trustworthiness metric. This is because the existing repositories in the state-of-the-art perform the automatic conversion to linked data from the legacy data sources without previously being reviewed. In the case of the LinkedDL dataset, the metadata is reviewed before and after conversion.

The Consistency dimension obtains the highest score in all the metrics evaluated in the LinkedDL dataset. In the particular case of the consistency metric of the schema restrictions during the insertion of new instances, a higher value is obtained than the rest of the repositories. This is because a check of the schema restrictions is performed during the insertion of new instances into the repository.

The Interoperability dimension obtained the same scores as the evaluated repositories, except for the interoperability of the proprietary vocabulary metric. Similar scores were obtained in the Accessibility dimension, where values similar to those existing in the state-of-the-art were obtained, except the availability of the repository metric. In the case of the linking HTML sites to RDF serializations metric, the only repository that implements this functionality is the British National Bibliography (BNB).

Assessing the quality of linked data is becoming very hard, due to the size of the knowledge base and the lack of automatic tools to measure some dimensions and metrics, among other factors. Also, the majority of the used dimensions and metrics are focused on evaluating the syntaxis and semantic of the linked data generated. However, the research community must define new metrics for assessing the usability of the linked data in real-world scenarios.

Table 2. Comparative table of five datasets. BNE: Biblioteca Nacional de España; BNF: Bibliothèque nationale de France; BNB: British National Bibliography; BVMC: Biblioteca Virtual Miguel de Cervantes. Partial results from [4]

Dimension	Metric	BNE	BNF	BNB	BVMC	LinkedDL
Accuracy	Syntactic validity of RDF documents	1	1	1	1	1
	Syntactic validity of literals	1	1	0.99	1	1
	Semantic validity of triples	1	1	1	1	1
	Check of duplicate entities	0.99	0.99	0	0.96	**1**
Trustworthiness	On library level	0.25	0.25	0.25	0.25	**0.75**
	On statement level	0	0	0	0	0
	Using unknown and empty values	0	0	0	0	0
Consistency	Consistency of schema restrictions during insertion of new statements	0	0	0	0	1
	Consistency of statements with respect to class constraints	1	1	1	1	1
	Consistency of statements with respect to relation constraints	0.98	1	1	1	1
Ease of understanding	Description of resources	0.93	0.91	0.89	0.92	1
	Labels in multiple languages	0	1	0	0	0
	Understandable RDF serialization	1	1	1	1	1
	Self-describing URIs	1	1	0	1	1
Interoperability	Avoiding blank nodes and RDF reification	1	1	1	1	1
	Provisioning of several serialization formats	1	1	1	1	1
	Using external vocabulary	0.53	0.69	0.90	1	1
	Interoperability of proprietary vocabulary	0.81	0.85	0.35	1	0
Accessibility	Dereferencing possibility of resources	1	1	1	1	1
	Availability of the repository	0.86	0.99	1	0.99	1
	Availability of a public SPARQL endpoint	1	1	1	1	1
	Provisioning of an RDF export	1	1	1	0	1
	Support of content negotiation	0.5	0.5	0.5	0.5	0.5
	Linking HTML sites to RDF serializations	0	0	1	0	0
	Provisioning of metadata	0	0	1	1	1
Interlinking	Interlinking via $owl{:}sameAs$	0.07	0.39	0.17	0.04	0.001
	Validity of external URIs	1	1	1	1	1

5   Conclusions and Future Work

Assessing the quality of linked data is becoming very hard, due to the size of the knowledge base and the lack of automatic tools to measure some dimensions and metrics, among other factors. In this paper, we evaluated the quality of data of the LinkedDL dataset. The comparison with similar approaches in the literature shows that the LinkedDL dataset improves those reported in the state-of-the-art in terms of accuracy, consistency, and accessibility metrics. This assessment is useful for data consumers that need to enrich their collections based on accuracy, consistency, and accessibility metrics. Future work includes the improvement of the LinkedDL dataset, taking into account the quality metrics evaluated with low scores, and the formalization of new quality metrics for assessing the usability of the linked data generated in real-world scenarios.

Acknowledgments. We thank the anonymous reviewers for their careful reading of our manuscript and their many insightful comments and suggestions.

References

1. Agosti, M., Ferro, N., Silvello, G.: Digital library interoperability at high level of abstraction. Future Gener. Comput. Syst. **55**, 129–146 (2016). https://doi.org/10.1016/j.future.2015.09.020. http://www.sciencedirect.com/science/article/pii/S0167739X15003003

2. Barroso, I., Hartmann, N., Ribeiro, C.: Metadata crosswalk for a museum collection in a thematic digital library. J. Libr. Metadata **15**(1), 36–49 (2015). https://doi.org/10.1080/19386389.2015.1011025

3. Berners-Lee, T.: Linked Data - Design Issues (2006). https://www.w3.org/DesignIssues/LinkedData.html

4. Candela, G., Escobar, P., Carrasco, R.C., Marco-Such, M.: Evaluating the quality of linked open data in digital libraries. J. Inf. Sci., 0165551520930951 (2020). https://doi.org/10.1177/0165551520930951

5. Candela, G., Escobar, P., Sáez, M.D., Marco-Such, M.: A shape expression approach for assessing the quality of linked open data in libraries. In: Semantic Web Preprint(Preprint), pp. 1–21. IOS Press, January 2021. https://doi.org/10.3233/SW-210441. https://content.iospress.com/articles/semantic-web/sw210441

6. Chen, Y.N.: A RDF-based approach to metadata crosswalk for semantic interoperability at the data element level. Library Hi Tech **33**(2), 175–194 (2015). https://doi.org/10.1108/LHT-08-2014-0078

7. Debattista, J., Auer, S., Lange, C.: Luzzu-A methodology and framework for linked data quality assessment. J. Data Inf. Qual. **8**(1), 4:1–4:32 (2016). https://doi.org/10.1145/2992786

8. Debattista, J., Lange, C., Auer, S., Cortis, D.: Evaluating the quality of the LOD cloud: an empirical investigation. Semant. Web **9**(6), 859–901 (2018). https://doi.org/10.3233/SW-180306. https://content.iospress.com/articles/semantic-web/sw306

9. Färber, M., Bartscherer, F., Menne, C., Rettinger, A.: Linked data quality of DBpedia, freebase, OpenCyc, Wikidata, and YAGO. Semant. Web **9**(1), 77–129 (2018). https://doi.org/10.3233/SW-170275

10. Hidalgo-Delgado, Y., Xu, B., Mariño-Molerio, A.J., Febles-Rodríguez, J.P., Leiva-Mederos, A.A.: A linked data-based semantic interoperability framework for digital libraries. Revista Cubana de Ciencias Informáticas **13**(1), 14–30 (2019). https://rcci.uci.cu/?journal=rcci&page=article&op=view&path

11. Khan, N.A., Shafi, S., Rizvi, S.Z.: Metadata crosswalks as a way towards interoperability. In: Encyclopedia of Information Science and Technology, 3rd edn., pp. 1834–1842. Data Mining and Databases. IGI Global (2015). https://www.igi-global.com/chapter/metadata-crosswalks-as-a-way-towards-interoperability/112589

12. Martín, A., León, C., López, A.: Enhancing semantic interoperability in digital library by applying intelligent techniques. In: SAI Intelligent Systems Conference, pp. 904–911. IEEE (2015)

13. Mecella, M., Scannapieco, M., Virgillito, A., Baldoni, R., Catarci, T., Batini, C.: Managing data quality in cooperative information systems. In: Meersman, R., Tari, Z. (eds.) OTM 2002. LNCS, vol. 2519, pp. 486–502. Springer, Heidelberg (2002). https://doi.org/10.1007/3-540-36124-3_28

14. Radulovic, F., Mihindukulasooriya, N., García-Castro, R., Gómez-Pérez, A.: A comprehensive quality model for linked data. Semant. Web **9**(1), 3–24 (2018). https://doi.org/10.3233/SW-170267. https://content.iospress.com/articles/semantic-web/sw267

15. Shreeves, S.L., Knutson, E.M., Stvilia, B., Palmer, C.L., Twidale, M.B., Cole, T.W.: Is quality metadata shareable metadata? The implications of local metadata practices for federated collections. In: Proceedings of the Twelfth National Conference of the Association of College and Research Libraries. Association of College and Research Libraries (2005). https://www.ideals.illinois.edu/handle/2142/145. Accepted 2006-10-19T21:25:14Z

16. Singh, T., Sharma, A.: Research work and changing dimensions of digital library. In: Emerging Trends and Technologies in Libraries and Information Services, pp. 39–42. IEEE (2015)

17. Tallerås, K.: Quality of linked bibliographic data: the models, vocabularies, and links of data sets published by four national libraries. J. Libr. Metadata **17**(2), 126–155 (2017). https://doi.org/10.1080/19386389.2017.1355166

18. Villazón-Terrazas, B., Vilches-Blázquez, L.M., Corcho, O., Gómez-Pérez, A.: Methodological guidelines for publishing government linked data. In: Wood, D. (ed.) Linking Government Data, pp. 27–49. Springer, New York (2011). https://doi.org/10.1007/978-1-4614-1767-5_2. http://www.w3.org/TR/ld-bp/

19. Wang, R.Y., Strong, D.M.: Beyond accuracy: what data quality means to data consumers. J. Manage. Inf. Syst. **12**(4), 5–33 (1996). https://doi.org/10.1080/07421222.1996.11518099. https://www.tandfonline.com/doi/abs/10.1080/07421222.1996.11518099

20. Zaveri, A., Rula, A., Maurino, A., Pietrobon, R., Lehmann, J., Auer, S.: Quality assessment for linked data: a survey. Semant. Web **7**(1), 63–93 (2016). http://content.iospress.com/articles/semantic-web/sw175

An Enhanced Meta-model to Generate Web Forms for Ontology Population

Petko Rutesic[1(✉)], Mirjana Radonjic-Simic[1(✉)], and Dennis Pfisterer[2] 📖

[1] Baden-Wuerttemberg Cooperative State University, 68163 Mannheim, Germany
{petko.rutesic,mirjana.radonjic-simic}@dhbw-mannheim.de
[2] Institute of Telematics, University of Luebeck, Luebeck, Germany

Abstract. The process of manually inserting data in ontology instances is usually a cumbersome activity. Editing complex domain ontologies using Protégé and similar tools requires expert knowledge. Despite exhaustive research in this area, the existing ontology population tools are still not user-friendly enough to simplify this activity for end-users. To facilitate this process, we propose an approach to design an ontology to serve as a meta-model for the generation of user interface models. The user interface models are used to create web applications with dialog-based HTML forms, which are eventually used to populate instances of OWL ontologies. Our meta-model includes several patterns used to generate programming control structures used to populate ontology instances. On the one hand, the meta-model describes user interfaces, and on the other hand, it describes the structure of the output ontology instance. We also show a prototype of a tool that loads a simple meta-model file and creates a single-page application that populates an ontology instance.

Keywords: OWL · Knowledge acquisition · Modeling web user interfaces · Ontology · Population of ontology instances · Form generation

1 Introduction

Although ontology engineering and the creation of knowledge graphs are long-established research areas, there is still a high complexity of tooling and languages used in these disciplines. There is a considerable gap between complex vocabularies (in particular, OWL ontologies) and the skills of end-users (being no experts in ontology engineering) willing to describe their products and services using those vocabularies.

In this paper, we propose an approach to use an ontology to describe the graphical user interface and the structure of the output ontology instance. This ontology serves as a meta-model to design models of user interfaces. These user interfaces, in turn, support end-users in creating their knowledge graphs using OWL ontologies.

The original version of this chapter was revised: The references [5] and [9] were extended. The correction to this chapter is available at
https://doi.org/10.1007/978-3-030-91305-2_25

B. Villazón-Terrazas et al. (Eds.): KGSWC 2021, CCIS 1459, pp. 109–124, 2021.
https://doi.org/10.1007/978-3-030-91305-2_9

Our approach differentiates two main groups of users: interface designers and end-users. Interface designers use our *Ontology for Ontology-based Ontology Population* (OBOP, http://purl.org/net/obop) ontology with target (domain) ontologies as vocabularies to define ontology instances, which represent models of the interface. These user interface models are used to generate dialog-based web applications with HTML forms. End-users use those generated web applications to create structured data in the form of ontology instances of the domain ontologies.

This paper is structured as follows: Sect. 2 provides an overview of the related work. Section 3 presents a motivational scenario for the use of our meta-model. Next, Sect. 4 introduces our meta-model structure describing the use of our ontology vocabulary to define both the structure of the collected data and the user interface used to collect that data. The implementation of the form generator for a basic model is described in Sect. 5. Section 6 gives an overview of main aspects of the approach, and Sect. 7 closes this paper with a summary and outlook of the future work.

2   Related Work

Since modeling of user interfaces and ontology engineering are well-developed disciplines, we can find approaches that are similar to our work. Frame-based ontologies were suitable for generating user interfaces for data acquisition. Similarly, in the early days of OWL, as in [4, 12], we have approaches to derive user interfaces from ontologies. However, the use of an ontology vocabulary to generate interfaces, that are further used for the data acquisition of knowledge graphs, which are again instances of OWL ontologies, is not much discussed to the best of our knowledge.

Protege-Frames is a tool that provides the generation of forms for the collection of frame-based domain ontologies. Frame-based ontologies are suitable for the object-oriented representation of knowledge and can be constructed using template-based systems. In contrast to frame-based ontologies, OWL ontologies [1] are axiom-based; the structure of the knowledge graphs is very complex and challenging to fit into template-based systems. For instance, in [5], the authors propose data acquisition of ontologies using models. Nevertheless, those models are generated using a meta-model described as an entity-relationship model. In [5], authors furthermore argue that modeling using ontologies, which use the open-world assumption, is not suitable for their use case that obeys the closed world assumption. In our paper, however, we discuss use cases for which ontology modeling is suitable and gives additional value through reasoning over models.

Our work has a resemblance to the work described in [6], where the authors develop a system, which automatically generates forms from ontology-based form specifications. Unlike their work, that uses a user-defined XML file to configure form layouts and provide bindings of form elements to ontology concepts and properties, we propose a solution where the entire application structure is represented in an ontology instance (e.g., RDF file). Their system focuses on data acquisition in the clinical, functional assessment domain, where HTML forms are used to model particular questionnaires with specific question sections and the question order. Our approach, on the other hand, is focused on a more general case of defining web applications that consist of more HTML forms. Moreover, in our approach, values inserted in a field on one form can influence web application execution and generation of new forms and their elements.

Since our models determine the shape of output ontologies, we use principles of good ontology engineering to define our ontology design patterns, similar to the modeling instructions described in [9] and [10].

Interface models can be beneficial in the context of emerging business models such as *Distributed Market Spaces* [14] as the way to describe complex products and services. This complements the approach described in [8] where the system makes use of SPARQL queries to find suitable complex products and services. Moreover, [13] describes the use of models to generate user interfaces. However, in this paper, we highlight the main ontology parts, and we give an implementation of the form generation software as proof of the concept. An essential aspect of our interface and program models is that they are designed to be shared. On the other hand, shared user interface models with particular domain ontologies can be used as patterns to generate new interfaces (web applications) with new arbitrary domain ontologies.

3   Motivational Scenario

In this section, we present a motivational example used in the next sections to explain the modeling process.

Our motivational scenario describes a simple use case in which a restaurant creates a knowledge graph (OWL ontology instance) containing data about their daily menus. To make the data easily accessible and more useful to the customers, the restaurant management wants to provide additional data about dishes using terms from the FOODON ontology [3]. This enables customers to find food with specific ingredients or to avoid other food products, e.g. the food to which they have developed an intolerance. To make our example as simple as possible we present in Fig. 1 a graphical representation of the knowledge graph (ontology instance) that restaurant staff wants to create.

In the graphical representation, instances of concepts (classes) are depicted as nodes of the graph, instances of object properties as links between nodes, and instances of data properties as links to white rectangles containing their values. Other colored rounded rectangles represent concepts of OWL ontologies. We specifically use concepts and properties from the FOODON ontology (cyan color with prefix foodon:) ENVO [2] (cyan color with prefix envo:), and GoodRelations [7] ontology (orange with prefix gr:).

Since restaurant staff does not usually have ontology experts to create OWL ontology instances (as in our example), we propose an approach by which they get a simple user-friendly dialog-based user interface composed of a series of HTML forms. That user interface is used to create ontology instances like the one outlined in Fig. 1. This paper aims at explaining the main parts of our meta-model (OBOP ontology) for the generation of user interfaces through this

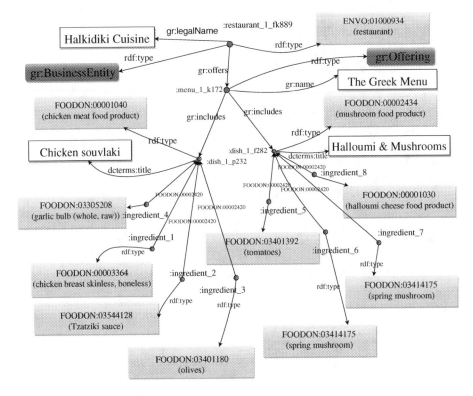

Fig. 1. An example of the output ontology instance

basic example. We do not intend to provide complete ontology describing HTML interfaces but to provide an ontology covering main interface elements and functionalities necessary for simple dialog-based HTML applications.

4   Model Structure

The main purpose of our model is to facilitate the generation of new ontology instances using a user interface such as HTML forms. As mentioned before, the model has two goals: First, to express graphical user interface elements through an ontology instance, and second, to specify the function of the user interface. Therefore, the first part of the model handles the graphical user interface elements and the way how those elements are formatted in HTML. The second part of the model focuses on the logic of interface elements of the corresponding application and the structure of the output ontology instance.

4.1   Graphical User Interface

The part of the meta-model describing HTML elements is explained through main concepts (classes), object properties and data properties. The essential part of the model is the *obop:Block* concept whose instance corresponds to the HTML form element (`<form action=...>`). To model elements that appear visible on an HTML form, we introduce the concept *obop:VisualElement*. For the specific elements, e.g., labels, input fields, buttons, we introduce subclasses of the class obop:VisualElement. One of those subclasses is *obop:Field*, which represents a field on the form in which we can insert data. Thus, an instance of the obop:Field class corresponds to the text input field (`<input type="text">`).

Another important HTML element, used to initiate actions on the form, is the submit button (`<input type= "submit">`). The submit button is modeled using the corresponding concept *obop:Button*. Once that we have elements that build an HTML form, we have to specify their layout and positions. To this end, we define object and data properties that specify to which HTML form an element belongs and its position and properties. The object property *obop:belongsTo* specifies that a obop:VisualElement belongs to a obop:Block. A data property named *obop:hasPositionNumber* specifies the position of an element in the current form. For the sake of brevity, we present here only a simple HTML interface without CSS files or different layouts. Our proposed logic interface ontology contains other basic interface elements necessary to model forms in dialog-based applications. In our code examples, we omit the definition of prefixes for standard ontology vocabularies. When we use column (:) as a prefix, we assume the prefix of the current ontology instance (model of the restaurant application). The prefix *obop:* is used for terms of our OBOP modeling ontology whose main purpose is to explain the logic and control flow of the application execution.

Hence, in the following HTML snippet, we present the first form generated to enter the restaurant name.

```
<form id="block_1" method="post">
 <label>Restaurant name</label><br>
 <input type="text" id="field_1_1" name="field_1_1">
 <input type="submit" value="Save">
</form>
```

A corresponding part of our model which can be used to generate this form is represented by the following triples in RDF Turtle format:

```
:block_1 rdf:type obop:Block .
:restaurant_1 rdf:type gr:BusinessEntity ;
             rdf:type ENVO:01000934;
             obop:modelBelongsTo :block_1 .
:field_1_1 rdf:type obop:Field ;
             obop:containsDatatype gr:legalName ;
             obop:hasLabel "Restaurant name" ;
             obop:hasPositionNumber "1"^^xsd:int ;
             obop:belongsTo :block_1 .
:button_1 rdf:type obop:Button ;
             obop:activatesAction :action_1 ;
             obop:hasLabel "Save" ;
             obop:hasPositionNumber "2"^^xsd:int ;
```

```
            obop:belongsTo  :block_1  .
:action_1  rdf:type  obop:Action .
```

Since our objective is that a Web application generated by the model produces an instance of the domain ontology, we relate our user interface elements to groups of the domain ontology instances that serve as a pattern to create real instances during the use of the application. In our RDF file, an instance (named individual) of the class gr:BusinessEntity having an IRI *:restaurant_1* serves not as a part of the final output instance, but just as a pattern according to which the final output instance will be created. The actual IRI of the individual corresponding to our restaurant, say *:restaurant_1_fk889*, is automatically generated.

Individual *:block_1* is used to specify the form as it can be seen from the value of the id attribute of the HTML form. In the similar way, individual *:field_1_1* is used to model an input text field where the restaurant name should be entered. The object property *obop:containsDatatype* is used to specify that the value entered in the input field field_1_1 is inserted in the output instance as the value of *gr:legalName* data property. Data property *obop:hasPosition* defines the position of the element in our default grid layout. Individual *:button_1* corresponds to the submit button of the form and the object property *obop:action_1* specifies an action that corresponds to the click on the submit button and leads us to a new form. *obop:activatesAction* indicates that the click on the Save button initiates the action :action_1.

Therefore, if the end-user types in the string "Halkidiki Cuisine" in the input field for the name of the restaurant then the result of the application is an ontology instance with the following RDF triples:

```
:restaurant_1_fk889  rdf:type  gr:BusinessEntity  ;
         rdf:type  ENVO:01000934;
         gr:legalName  "Halkidiki  Cuisine"@en  .
```

Here we have an individual :restaurant_1_fk889 that belongs to the concepts gr:BusinessEntity and ENVO:01000934 and has the name "Halkidiki Cuisine".

To explain our model stepwise, we augment it in each step with new constructions, and we use schematic representations of the model instance instead of RDF graphs. Schematic representation of the current model is outlined in Fig. 2.

4.2   Interface Logic

The second part of our model ontology takes care of the interface logic (i.e., the functionality of the application). Essential concepts distinguished in this part of our vocabulary are *obop:Connection, obop:Condition, obop:Loop*, etc.

An instance of the obop:Connection class specifies an object property that will be created during the use of the model (web application execution). Since an object property relates instances of two classes, we have to specify the domain and range of the modeled object property. Accordingly, each obop:Connection

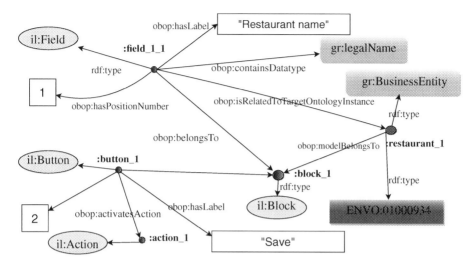

Fig. 2. The model of the first HTML form.

instance can be the domain of two kinds of object properties: *obop:hasSource* property that indicates the "source" of the planned object property (subject of the triple) and the *obop:hasDestination* property that indicates the "destination" of the object property (object of the triple) that obop:Connection models.

During the usage of the model, an instance of class obop:Connection induces the generation of a new instance of the object property that it models. Additionally, instances of classes specified as the subject or object of data property will be created in case they do not exist in the current output ontology instance.

In Fig. 3 we provide a graphical representation of the connection that models adding an instance of the *gr:Offering* class to the restaurant ontology. Nodes representing individuals that belong to the domain ontologies have a blue color, while nodes comprising the model are colored in grey. In the part of the model that belongs to the domain ontology, our instance :restaurant_1 is related to a new instance of the class gr:Offering from the GoodRelations ontology.

The gr:Offering instance named :menu_1 in the diagram indicates that a new gr:Offering instance will be generated by the application. The actual name of the output instance is not :menu_1, but it is named using a particular naming convention (:menu_1_k172 in Fig. 1). It can be noted that new instances are created only for those parts of the model that do not already exist. Since an instance corresponding to the model instance :restaurant_1 would exist at the time when this part of the model is considered, it implies that only instances corresponding to the remaining part of the model would be generated, i.e., those that correspond to the gr:Offering and gr:offers.

Object properties *obop:hasSource* and *obop:hasDestination* specify the subject and predicate of the gr:offers property instantiated when the model is used in an application. Even though there is gr:offers connection in the model, it is

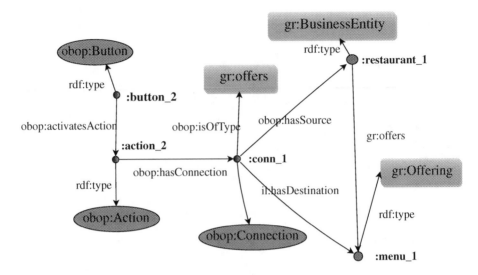

Fig. 3. Diagrammatic represetation of the relation between obop:Action and obop:Connection instances.

necessary to specify again the type of newly created object property. For this reason, we define *obop:isOfType* object property that stipulates that object property of type gr:offer should be generated between instances generated according to :restaurant_1 and :menu_1. This is necessary because a model can have more different object properties between the same instances.

In Fig. 3 we illustrate the button :button_2 and the action :action_2 to model the fact that clicking on the submit button on the corresponding form initiates the creation of a new connection (making a new object property) during the application execution. This action initiates the generation of a new form and switching the control flow of the application to that form. This is due to the fact that a new block is related to the newly generated instances (:menu_1). In our example, the obop:Action instance has only one obop:Connection. However, a model can establish more connections at the same time. This is particularly useful for an example scenario in which a new form with many fields is opened. This situation requires that an entire subgraph be created using an obop:Action with many obop:Connection instances.

The other option to insert a subgraph as a part of an ontology is a concept named *obop:Subgraph*. Using this element, the designer can prepare a chunk of an ontology (implant) that can include instances of concepts from different vocabularies. That chunk is inserted in the output ontology when a specific action (obop:Action) is executed.

In order to preserve information on the part of model used to generate some part of the output ontology instance, we propose one mechanism with a stamp attached to some nodes of the output ontology. These stamps are attached using an object property called *obop:generatedAccordingToModel*. Stamps are used in the process of modification of the output ontology. The system can search in the database of models for the part of the model that has been used to generate particular output ontology instance.

4.3   Modeling of the Control Flow Instructions

In this section, we look at the structures that determine the shape of the resulting ontology instance. These structures resemble to the standard control flow structures in programming languages.

Following the structure of the ontology instance in Fig. 1, the next step is to define a form to collect information on a specific food on the created menu. In Fig. 4 we can take a look at the form for inserting the name of the dish and food type.

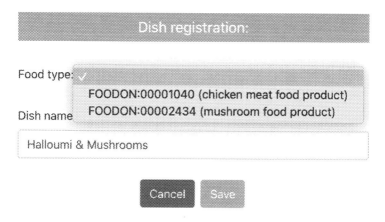

Fig. 4. Part of the application to insert a new dish name and food type.

Depending on the chosen option in the drop-down list, the end user decides on the type of food the restaurant offers, i.e., the class from FOODON ontology to which the instance belongs and type of dish as specified in Fig. 1. In order to implement this in the model, we need to specify selecting one among more options as described in the next section.

Branching Instructions. An important element of our interface ontology is the branching instruction. We introduce a class *obop:Branching* whose instances are used to make decisions as to which part of the model to assign to the existing ontology instance. To this aim, each branching has an *obop:Condition* instance with a condition test that is represented by the value of the class name. The satisfied condition causes a specific path to be followed during the application execution. Each branch can contain connections to specify how a new part of the ontology instance will be related to the existing part.

Figure 5 describes two different possibilities presented to the user inserting a new dish in the existing menu. An important task for the application designer is to chose a subset of possible ontology classes that would be available to the end user to select. Here we chose to present just two possibilities, namely, FOODON:00002434 (mushroom food product) and FOODON:00001040 (chicken meat food product).

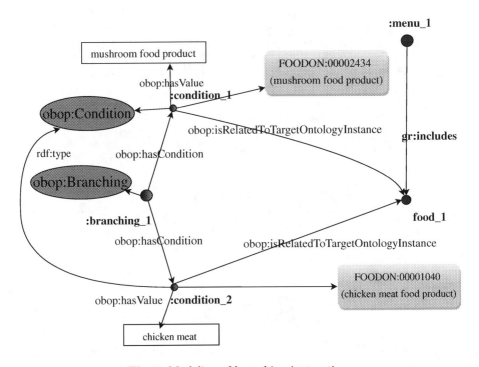

Fig. 5. Modeling of branching instruction.

Depending on the option chosen by the user in the dropdown list it is decided what type of food to enter in the menu. For example, the FOODON ontology offers many possibilities for the food products and it is often reasonable to enable end users to chose additional concepts (e.g., only those subsumed by specific concepts) from the original ontology. However, in Fig. 5 we present only two options to make it readable. Each condition instance has a data property *obop:hasValue* indicating the branch to be followed in the case that the corresponding field is selected in the HTML form.

Figure 6 illustrates the remaining part of the model, related to the branching instruction *:branching_1*. In the model, we have that *:dropdown_1*, an instance of the *obop:Dropdown* concept, describes an HTML drop down list that takes options belonging to the conditions defined for the :branching_1 and it initiates creating an instance of food corresponding to the selected option. The

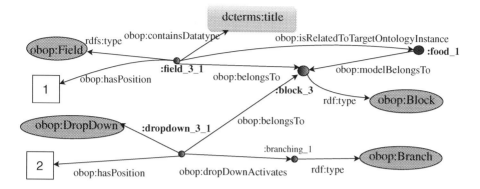

Fig. 6. The value of the drop down field intiates the brunching.

drop-down list has values corresponding to the values described in the conditions of :branching_1 in Fig. 5. Hence, if one of the values in the drop-down element has been chosen, say "mushroom food product", then in output ontology instance the :menu_1_k172 gets a new dish of the type FOODON:00002434 named :dish_1_p232 (Fig. 1).

Iterations. To specify actions that can be executed many times the model uses instances of the *obop:Loop* concept. The number of iterations can be determined by the value that the end-user enters in a field on the form or it can be specified in the model by the designer. In Fig. 7, we model a loop that facilitates entering food ingredients to the current dish. Here we model the case, where the end-user has an input field (*:field_4_1*) to specify the number of ingredients. For example, if the dish has four ingredients, then the user is obliged to select four times new ingredient (specific class from the FOODON ontology) .

As outlined in Fig. 7, the instance *:loop_1* has an instance of the class *obop:LoopCondition* called *:loop_cond_1*. In fact, :loop_cond_1 specifies the number of iteration within the loop. Each iteration adds a new ingredient instance modeled by *:ingredient_1*. In order to chose a proper class from the FOODON ontology, the end-user is presented with the list of options like drop down list and each iteration initiates a new branching represented with the :branching_2 to decide on the class to which the ingredient belongs. In the diagram we omitted drop down element for the sake of clarity. The previously created instance corresponding to :dish_1 is related to ingredients by the FOODON:00002420 (has ingredient) object property. Additionally, there is an input field in the application to enter an additional title for the ingredient and it is inserted as dcterms:title data property of the ingredient instance.

In the case when each iteration has to create more instances, object properties and data properties, it is used an instance of the *obop:Subgraph* class to model the entire part of the target ontology to be inserted (e.g., instance :subgraph_1 in Fig. 7). This subgraph has to be modeled by the designer, and for each

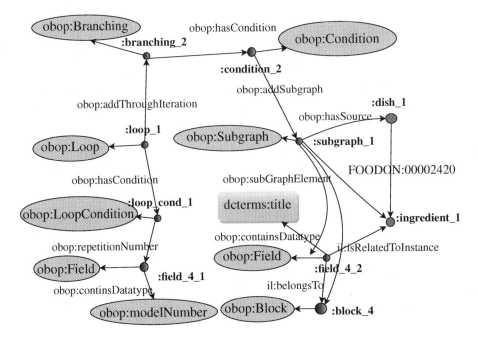

Fig. 7. Entering a specific number of ingredients using iterations.

iteration of the loop, it adds a new group of instances generated by the model. In order to distinguish subgraph from the other part of the model we introduce the *obop:subGraphElement* object property related to all instances of classes included in the subgraph. Additionally, all object properties between subgraph instances and data properties related to those instances in the model are assumed to be the inclusive part of the subgraph. A subgraph can contain parts of target domain ontologies as well as parts of the OBOP ontology (obop:Block and obop:Field). Property *obop:hasSource* indicates that the corresponding instance is outside of the scope of subgraph and will be already generated when the execution of the application comes at this point. All other instances in the subgraph of the model are cloned in each iteration.

4.4 Axiomatization

Diagrams in previous sections do not represent an ontology fully but depict its main parts. To further describe the OBOP ontology, we introduce in this section a part of axiomatization for the case of iterations. The purpose of axioms is to ensure that model instances are properly formed and can be used by a tool (form generator) to generate functional HTML applications. In Fig. 8, we use description logics to describe axioms and we omit prefixes in front of class and property names.

$$Loop \sqsubseteq (= 1 \; addThroughIteration.SubGraph) \tag{1}$$

$$Loop \sqsubseteq (= 1 \; hasLoopCondition.LoopCondition) \tag{2}$$

$$\exists hasLoopCondition.LoopCondition \sqsubseteq Loop \tag{3}$$

$$\exists addThroughIteration.SubGraph \sqsubseteq Loop \tag{4}$$

$$Loop \sqsubseteq \forall addThroughIteration.SubGraph \tag{5}$$

$$Loop \sqsubseteq \forall hasLoopCondition.LoopCondition \tag{6}$$

$$DisjointClasses(Loop, LoopCondition, SubGraph) \tag{7}$$

Fig. 8. Axiomatization for iterations

Axioms (1)–(4) capture domains and ranges of data properties in our ontology. In particular, axioms (1) and (2) express that a loop can have exactly one Subgraph instance and exactly one LoopCondition instance. Axiom (3) specifies that if there exist two individuals x and y such that (x hasLoopCondition y) and x is an instance of the class Loop then y must be a LoopCondition. Finally, axiom (7) asserts that any two different classes among Loop, LoopCondition, and Subgraph are pairwise disjoint. This ensures, for example, that an instance of the Loop cannot be also an instance of the LoopCondition.

5   Implementation

In order to test our approach we implement a prototype of form generator that takes an ontology instance as input, generates HTML application and can export the output ontology instance. The output ontology instance contains data acquired during the operation of the web application. The source code of the form generator and OBOP[1] ontology can be found on Github[2].

Fig. 9. A form generated to insert restaurant name.

---

[1] www.purl.org/net/obop.

[2] https://github.com/ontosoft/logic-interface.git.

Since our approach has to simplify the process of ontology population to end users, generated web applications should work on the client side. To this end, we use JavaScript with the JavaScript framework React for the implementation. Handling the contents produced by React components and reconciliation process proved to be useful to implement our approach by minimizing the changes to the Document Object Model (DOM). Our application uses reconciliation as a part of React lifecycle to update only those components that are changed and to go from one form to another with changing only that part of the application. To manipulate RDF graphs on the client side we use a Javascript RDF library rdflib.js [11].

To start the application, the end-user loads an input file containing the model (e.g. restaurant-example.owl). The system creates internal representation of the application functionality and generates the starting form, as shown in Fig. 9. During the application runtime, the system constantly maintains the current form. The system has first to internally load a description of the next form that has to be generated and presented to the end-user. If an action on the form is executed (e.g. click on the submit button), this action initiates the corresponding activity that, for example, stores entered data and opens the next form.

6 Discussion

One of the features of our interface models is that they additionally constraint the structure of the ontology instances that can be created as a result. At the theoretical level, this can lead us to the question of how axioms of our interface patterns fit to the axioms of the target domain ontologies.

As can be seen in our motivational example in Sect. 3 our output ontology instance has dominantly the tree structure. So far, we provided one model that is handling the process of creating a new instance of the ontology. However, enabling users to make changes to the existing ontology is a more complicated task. In our case, we can make use of the same model to make a particular modification. For instance, deleting part of the ontology instance can prune the entire subtree. It is not surprising that deleting the part of the ontology instance with a non-tree structure can be more involved because the system should make sure which parts of the knowledge graph can be deleted.

Modification can be done at three different levels. At the first level, end-users modify the existing output ontology instance using the model. At the second level modifications can occur to the model itself. An ontology designer, for example, wants to change the structure of interface patterns. At the third level, modifications can occur at the meta-model level if the OBOP ontology (patterns) has to be changed. For the last two types of modification, we propose that the output ontology instance keeps track of the version of the model used for the ontology instance creation. For this we can use constructions similar to the TimeInstant concept used with the AgentRole ontology design pattern [10].

It can happen that end-users who use a particular model want to add additional elements to their ontology instance that designers did not include in the model. If these changes are provided, then it opens new issues related to the scaling of models.

7   Conclusion and Future Work

The main contribution of our approach for modeling of Web applications is the use of OWL ontologies as models. In contrast to other authors, we use ontology instances to model both our graphical user interface and the output domain ontology instances. To this aim, we proposed a new modeling ontology called OBOP used as a meta-model to define our models.

An important advantage of using OWL ontology models could be OWL reasoning over those models of user interfaces and domain ontologies. The reasoner would possibly detect that a given model could produce inconsistent output ontologies. Another advantage is the reuse of the existing models and their sharing and querying using SPARQL. Additionally, applying machine learning algorithms over existing models would facilitate the automatic or semi-automatic generation of new interfaces for a particular problem. The topic for our future work is how to create a tool for semi-automatic and automatic generation of interface models using the OBOP ontology and domain ontologies.

Furthermore, we plan to investigate the relation of our modeling ontology control structures and design patterns[3]. In addition, we plan to develop a graphical tool to generate interface models according to our modeling ontology, which would facilitate designers to create models of both user interfaces and ontologies. This tool could enable designers to combine our control structures with the existing design patterns.

References

1. Owl 2 web ntology Language: Structural Specification and Functional-Style Syntax, 2nd edn. (2012). http://www.w3.org/TR/owl2-syntax/
2. Buttigieg, P.L., Pafilis, E., Lewis, S.E., Schildhauer, M.P., Walls, R.L., Mungall, C.J.: The environment ontology in 2016: bridging domains with increased scope, semantic density, and interoperation. J. Biomed. Seman. **7**(1), 1–12 (2016)
3. Dooley, D.M., et al.: Foodon: a harmonized food ontology to increase global food traceability, quality control and data integration. NPI Sci. Food **2**(1), 1–10 (2018)
4. Furtado, E., et al..: An ontology-based method for universal design of user interfaces, September 2001
5. Girardi, D., Arthofer, K., Giretzlehner, M.: An ontology-based data acquisition infrastructure - using ontologies to create domain-independent software systems. In: Filipe, J., Dietz, J.L.G. (eds.) Proceedings of the International Conference on Knowledge Engineering and Ontology Development, pp. 155–160. SciTePress, Barcelona (2012)
6. Gonçalves, R., Tu, S., Nyulas, C., Tierney, M., Musen, M.: An ontology-driven tool for structured data acquisition using web forms. J. Biomed. Seman. **8**, (2017). https://doi.org/10.1186/s13326-017-0133-1

---

[3] http://ontologydesignpatterns.org.

7. Hepp, M.: GoodRelations: an ontology for describing products and services offers on the web. In: Gangemi, A., Euzenat, J. (eds.) EKAW 2008. LNCS (LNAI), vol. 5268, pp. 329–346. Springer, Heidelberg (2008). https://doi.org/10.1007/978-3-540-87696-0_29

8. Hitz, M., Kessel, T., Pfisterer, D.: Towards sharable application ontologies for the automatic generation of UIS for dialog based linked data applications. In: Proceedings of the 5th International Conference on Model-Driven Engineering and Software Development February 2017, pp. 65–77, February 2017. https://doi.org/10.5220/0006137600650077

9. Hitzler, P., Krisnadhi, A.: A tutorial on modular ontology modeling with ontology design patterns: the cooking recipes ontology (2018). http://arxiv.org/abs/1808.08433

10. Krisnadhi, A., Hitzler, P.: Modeling with ontology design patterns: chess games as a worked example. In: Ontology Engineering with Ontology Design Patterns, pp. 3–21. IOS Press, Amsterdam (2016)

11. Linked Data API for JavaScript: reactlib.js. https://github.com/linkeddata/rdflib.js.git

12. Liu, B., Chen, H., He, W.: Deriving user interface from ontologies: a model-based approach. In: 17th IEEE International Conference on Tools with Artificial Intelligence (ICTAI 2005), vol. 2005, December 2005. https://doi.org/10.1109/ICTAI.2005.55

13. Radonjic-Simic, M., Pfisterer, D., Rutesic, P.: Arising internet of everything: business modeling and architecture for smart cities in recent developments in engineering research, vol. 8 Chapter 7 (2020)

14. Hitz, M., Radonjic-Simic, M., Reichwald, J., Pfisterer, D.: Generic UIs for requesting complex products within distributed market spaces in the internet of everything. In: Buccafurri, F., Holzinger, A., Kieseberg, P., Tjoa, A.M., Weippl, E. (eds.) CD-ARES 2016. LNCS, vol. 9817, pp. 29–44. Springer, Cham (2016). https://doi.org/10.1007/978-3-319-45507-5_3

An Ontology-Based Source Selection for Federated Query Processing: a Case Study

Yoan A. López[1]([⊠]) [ID], Hector Gonzalez[1] [ID], Yusniel Hidalgo-Delgado[1] [ID], and Erik Mannens[2] [ID]

[1] Departamento de Informática, Universidad de las Ciencias Informáticas, Havana, Cuba
{yalopez,hglez,yhdelgado}@uci.cu
[2] Ghent University - iMinds, Sint-Pietersnieuwstraat, Gent 9000, Belgium
erik.mannens@ugent.be

Abstract. An important step in federated query execution frameworks is source selection, determining which endpoints are relevant to evaluate a given query. Source selection process happens as a separate step before the federated query by executing SPARQL ASK queries, updating catalog/index, or collecting heuristic information as a pre-processing stage, however, in domains as the Linked Open University context, these strategies involve some issues. On the other side, the DCAT metadata vocabulary enables a publisher to describe datasets and data services in a catalog using a standard model and vocabulary that facilitates their consumption. In addition, data summarizations are a lightweight form of representing crucial dataset information. Moreover, the Hydra hypermedia vocabulary along with its Hydra API Documentation allow describing RDF Web APIs facilitating the automation of the client-server communication. This work focuses on using the former semantic vocabularies, along with a context-based unified well-accepted vocabulary, in favor of facilitating the source selection process. In order to explain our proposal, a case study in the Linked Open University context was presented. The case study showed that our proposal allows to select the right sources per triple pattern without further processing complexity as the usage of SPARQL ASK queries and, in turn, it is tailored not only to established query interfaces as SPARQL endpoints, but also to new query interfaces.

Keywords: DCAT · Federated queries · Hydra · Linked open university · Source selection

1 Introduction

Besides large and general-purpose open knowledge graphs, such as Dbpedia, Freebase, Wikidata, and Yago, on the Web there exist specific domain knowledge graphs included those whose underlying data source is an RDF dataset

© Springer Nature Switzerland AG 2021
B. Villazón-Terrazas et al. (Eds.): KGSWC 2021, CCIS 1459, pp. 125–137, 2021.
https://doi.org/10.1007/978-3-030-91305-2_10

[8]. Schmachtenberg et al. [19] classifies these linked open datasets into different topical categories and such a classification is very significant because each context entails widely used ontologies/vocabularies. The creation of university-linked data platforms has been a trend in recent years [15]. In the Linked Open University context (LOU context), each university publishes several datasets such as courses, scientific publications, and staff profiles following the linked data principles [2]. Besides, such a university also publishes those datasets integrated under a SPARQL endpoint [5,11,21].

SPARQL endpoints have been presented as the main option for live query execution for Web applications [23,25]. However, their shortcomings have caused a search for other query interfaces. The low-cost interface to triples called Triple Pattern Fragment (TPFs) aimed to lower the cost for knowledge publishers to offer live queryable data on the open Web [25]. The idea of TPFs has been strongly accepted by the Semantic Web Community and other interfaces have been developed. Indeed, some of them have come to cope with its limitations [23,24].

Like in federated databases, it is not trivial to implement answering complex queries across different RDF data sources [7]. An important step in federated query execution frameworks is source selection, determining which interfaces are relevant to evaluate a given query. Existing source selection strategies are based on SPARQL ASK queries, catalog/index, and heuristic information [7,16,20]. These strategies present shortcomings, e.g., SPARQL ASK queries only take place over SPARQL endpoints [17]. However, in domains as the LOU context, besides one integrated dataset under a SPARQL endpoint, it is also desirable to have other access methods for each dataset separately. Regarding catalogs/index-assisted solutions, they need to be constantly updated to ensure complete results retrieval.

As such, we explore other ways to support the source selection process in the LOU context, regardless of the kind of query interface that is used. The DCAT metadata vocabulary enables a publisher to describe datasets and data services in a catalog using a standard model and vocabulary that facilitates their consumption. The Hydra hypermedia vocabulary [10] along with its Hydra API Documentation [9] allow describing RDF Web APIs facilitating the automation of the client-server communication. Hypermedia controls provide the user with a guidance on what type of content they can retrieve, or what actions they can perform upon it. In addition, data summarizations are a lightweight form of representing crucial dataset information [18], which in turn, benefit from a context-based unified, well-accepted vocabulary in controlled contexts.

This work aims to show the benefits of the DCAT and other semantic vocabularies to facilitate the source selection process as part of the federated query processing in controlled domains. The contributions of our proposal are the following: i) instead of using SPARQL ASK queries, catalog/index, heuristic information, we propose using some semantic vocabularies to describe datasets and dataset access methods to carry out the source selection process without demanding further processing complexity, ii) our proposal strengthens the route of using established semantic vocabularies as DCAT, Hydra, Hydra API Documentation, and Capacity Summaries, in favor of the source selection process as a step of the federated SPARQL queries. Moreover, iii) we highlight the LOU context as an important scenario of Linked Data.

The remaining of this paper is organized as follows: First, in Sect. 2, related work is described. Then, we present the problem statement in Sect. 3. After that, we introduce our source selection proposal in the LOU context in Sect. 4 and, in Sect. 5, a case study of source selection in the LOU context is shown. Next, we discuss about the case study in Sect. 6 and finally, the Conclusions and future work are presented in Sect. 7.

2   Related Work

The SPARQL query language[1] is the W3C standard to express declarative queries over collections of RDF triples. There are three common interface types to RDF triples: data dumps, SPARQL endpoints, and Linked Data documents. Specifically, about live query execution from Web applications, SPARQL endpoints have been presented as the main option [24,25].

2.1   SPARQL Endpoints

From the point of view of the client, the easiest way to execute a SPARQL query is to dispatch queries to the SPARQL endpoint [25]. Whereas enabling clients to send arbitrary SPARQL queries leads to low bandwidth consumption and low client cost, the processing of individual requests is potentially very expensive in terms of server CPU time and memory consumption. This likely contributes to the low availability of public SPARQL endpoints [3]. As such, SPARQL endpoints shortcomings have caused the search for other interfaces.

2.2   Triple Pattern Fragments

The low-cost interface to triples called Triple Pattern Fragment (TPFs) [25] was developed to overcome the SPARQL endpoint limitations. TPFs divides the query processing between clients and servers and allows to restrict the kinds of queries the client can send to the server. TPF is a hypermedia-driven REST API that represents the hypermedia controls through the Hydra Core Vocabulary [10]. TPF clients can directly reach and retrieve all fragments of the collection. TPFs have been strongly accepted by the Semantic Web Community and other interfaces have been developed based on it. Some of them have come to solve its limitations. As such, Van Herwegen et al. [23] proposed Substring matching from TPFs, which allows the user to request all literal objects that contain a given string pattern. In the case study presented later on, an implementation with filters can be seen in order to meet the client requirements. Van Herwegen [24] proposed a new query execution algorithm that reaches solutions with fewer HTTP requests than basic TPFs based on a combination of metadata and intermediate results.

---

[1] http://www.w3.org/tr/sparql11-query/.

2.3   Source Selection in Federated Queries

Like in federated databases, it is not trivial to implement answering complex queries across different RDF data sources, and more with the increasing heterogeneity of query interfaces [7]. To cope with the challenge of localizing the desired RDF graphs, centralized architectures have been created. Inside this kind of architecture, we have repositories like Laundromat [1] and CKAN[2], which centralize SPARQL endpoints to facilitate data search and discoverability. On the other side, decentralized architectures like Solid [12], and KBox [13] have been also created. This kind of architecture is often used in highly reliable, scalable and available systems. Once, they have been identified the candidate interfaces, Comunica [22] was presented as a highly modular meta engine for federated SPARQL query evaluation over heterogeneous interfaces, with appreciable results. Yet, an important step in federated query execution frameworks which continues attracting a significant amount of research is triple pattern-wise source selection or source selection for short, determining which endpoints are relevant to evaluate a given query.

It has been proved that source selection runtime greatly affects the overall query execution time [17]. This process happens as a separate step before the actual execution. While this step is intended to reduce the number of requests to servers, and hence the overall query evaluation time, source selection itself also takes time [25]. There are several source selection approaches, e.g., DARQ [16] makes use of an index known as service description to perform source selection. Each service description provides a declarative description of the data available in a data source, including the corresponding SPARQL endpoint along with statistical information. The source selection algorithm used in DARQ for a query simply matches all triple patterns against the capabilities of the data sources. SPLENDID [7] makes use of VoID descriptions as index along with SPARQL ASK queries to perform the source selection step. FedX [20] relies completely on SPARQL ASK queries and a cache. The cache is used to store recent SPARQL ASK operations for relevant data source selection. Besides, LHD [26] only makes use of the VoID descriptions to perform source selection.

3   Problem Statement

Previous source selection strategies, which are based on SPARQL ASK queries, catalog/index, and heuristic information present shortcomings, such as [17] i) SPARQL ASK queries are only intended for SPARQL endpoint interfaces. However, many sources are published under other types of interfaces, for instance, in the LOU context, besides one integrated dataset under a SPARQL endpoint, it is also desirable to have other access methods for each dataset separately, ii) trying to lower the overestimation of source selection, sometimes a high number of SPARQL ASK queries are dispatched to servers, which provokes delay

---

[2] http://ckan.org/.

to the process, iii) regarding catalogs/index-assisted solutions, they need to be constantly updated to ensure complete results retrieval.

Focused on the relevance of the source selection process as part of the federated queries in scenarios as the LOU context, we define our research question as follows: How to improve the source selection process as part of the federated query processing in the LOU context?

Vander Sande presented a novel hypermedia-based discovery method for source selection using Low-Cost Linked Data Interfaces [25]. This method relies on data summaries to announce the data contained in the source. It reuses summaries based on grouping authorities of subjects and objects per distinct predicate. To describe the data contained in the datasets, our proposal, also reuses this kind of data summary. Nevertheless, instead of discovering relevant sources in the whole Web of Data from seed TPFs interfaces, we concentrate on offering a source selection way in controlled domains as the LOU context, where counting on a shared vocabulary/ontology and a group of candidate sources beforehand is possible.

The DCAT metadata vocabulary enables a publisher to describe datasets and data services in a catalog using a standard model and vocabulary that facilitates their consumption. In controlled domains, the use of a unified, well-accepted vocabulary enables the announcement of data summaries unambiguously through hypermedia controls. A hypermedia control is a declarative construct that informs client applications of a hypermedia interface of possible application and/or session state changes in their interaction with a server and explains how to effectuate such changes [25]. The Hydra Core Vocabulary [10] allows Web APIs to describe the equivalence of links and forms in RDF. Web APIs have been designed for an automated, machine-based consumption of Web content. Hydra supports such process automation via its Hydra API Documentation[3] which describes the structure and capabilities of a Hydra Web API. A Hydra API Documentation enables clients to interact with the API and make those interactions more efficient.

By placing the above semantic vocabularies in favor of the dataset descriptions and the client-server communication to facilitate the source selection, we define the hypothesis of this work as follows: Using the DCAT vocabulary, and the Hydra hypermedia vocabulary, and a context-based, unified, well-accepted vocabulary to describe dataset and dataset access methods along with a data summary vocabulary to describe dataset capacities, it will improve the source selection process as part of the federated query processing in the LOU context.

4   Source Selection in the LOU Context

Implementing LOD can be summarized as using the web both as a channel to access data (through URIs supporting the delivery of structured information) and as a platform for the representation and integration of data (through creating

---

[3] http://www.hydra-cg.com/drafts/use-cases/2.api-documentation.md.

a graph of links between these data URIs) [6]. Having educational linked datasets facilitates the effective reuse of data and increases the opportunities to build more effective, integrated, and innovative applications based on these datasets [4]. It is also a trend revealing the contributions and achievements of the universities and makes them visible on the Web as LOD as it is a means to measure the university's reputation and standing among other international universities and institutions [14,15].

In 2010, the Open University in the UK was launched as the first initiative to expose public information from the university in an accessible, open, integrated, and Web-based format [5]. Since then, universities around the world have been joining that initiative by deploying their own LOD platforms [11,21]. The process of generating linked datasets in universities consists of the following stages [15]: i) raw data collection, ii) defining the vocabulary model based on reusing existing ontologies and extend them when it is needed, iii) extracting and generating RDF datasets according to the defined vocabulary, iv) achieving interlinking among datasets internally and externally, v) storing the outcome datasets and exposing them via SPARQL endpoints, vi) exploiting datasets by developing applications and services on top, and, vii) providing optimization and quality to improve data querying and retrieving.

Traditionally, the consumption of triples in the LOU context is resolved via a SPARQL endpoint. Each university stores its triples on a server and offers the query service to clients. However, this situation does not benefit universities with medium or small platforms that just have a few linked datasets because they are required to set up a SPARQL endpoint with all the costs that it entails. Recently, novel solutions have been developed to offer more affordable options. One example is the low-cost query interface TPFs [25] which has been used to publish and consume RDF dataset like the DBpedia knowledge graph [4]. Linked Connections[5] is another example, which offers a lightweight data interface for the consumption of open data in the Transportation area. Linked Connections aims to publish RDF triples in an optimized way gaining in data reuse and getting the service close to the client requirements. Both, Linked Connections and TPFs benefit from the usage of semantic vocabularies such as DCAT and Hydra.

Similar to other domains, in the LOU context, there exist client applications demanding the optimization of the services. University course data are a special segment of open data at the university given the public nature of the data. With the increase of distance learning, there are a lot of course recommender applications that assist clients to find suitable courses. Publishing course data in a standardized way allows such applications to reach a broader course dataset range through federated queries. Next, we formalize our source selection proposal for federated SPARQL queries in the LOU context.

Given a set of LOU platforms denoted by the set $\{x_1, \ldots, x_n\}$ of DCAT files, where each platform has one DCAT file. In turn, each DCAT file x_k includes a set of datasets denoted by $\{d_1, \ldots, d_{mk}\}$. Each dataset d_{zk} is associated with

---

[4] http://fragments.dbpedia.org.

[5] https://github.com/linkedconnections/linked-connections-server.

the properties: *dcterm:subject* and *dcterm:conformsTo* whose values are denoted by s_{zk} and c_{zk} respectively. s_{zk} represents the type of data of d_{zk} while c_{zk} represents the Hydra API Documentation associated with d_{zk}. In addition, c_{zk} has a set of $ds : predicate$ denoted by $\{p_1, \ldots, p_{zk}\}$ to describe the d_{zk} capacities and a set of *hydra:IriTemplate* denoted by $\{h_1, \ldots, h_{zk}\}$ to describe the d_{zk} query interfaces respectively. So, the source selection procedure upon a triple pattern *tp* is defined as follows:

Given a *tp* denoted by *<subject, predicate, object>* of a SPARQL query $q \in \mathcal{Q}$. In turn, given *predicate* can be either a variable or a URI:

- if *predicate* is a variable, all x_i are selected,
- if *predicate* is equal to *rdf:type*, x_i that contains a d_{zk} whose s_{zk} is equal to *object* will be selected,
- if *predicate* es different to *rdf:type*, the domain of *predicate* should be found in the shared LOU ontology, and x_i that contains one d_{zk} whose s_{zk} is equal to the domain of *predicate* and one p_{zk} equal to *predicate* will be selected.

Our source selection proposal has been conceived to both: i) carry out the source selection as a previous step of the federated queries to get a list of sources to query and, ii) include source selection within federated queries as a single algorithm. The former is exactly what we formalized before whereas, the second one, entails in addition, client apps to be aware of choosing the suitable h_i due to each dataset may have several query interfaces. In order to demonstrate our source selection proposal, a case study in the LOU context is presented in the next section.

5   Case Study

To show our proposal of source selection based on semantic vocabularies in the LOU context, we rely on the University of Informatics Sciences LOU platform to explain the creation of datasets from the beginning. This platform includes six important linked datasets: university staff, academic courses, internal places, scientific production, productive and research projects, and real-time streaming data (daily water and energy consumption). Hereafter, the case study that is presented focuses on the academic courses dataset which is a very common dataset for any LOU platform.

5.1   Semantic Modeling Process

A standard set of vocabularies provides unified access to data consumers [11]. The semantic modeling process in the LOU context aims at getting a unified schema where different universities can exchange data in a standard way [11,15]. Vocabularies (or ontologies, more strictly), define the concepts and relations used to describe and represent an area of concern. Intending to find out the most popular vocabularies/ontologies for describing university courses, we carried out a state-of-the-art study over existing LOU platforms [5,11,21]. As outputs of the review: i) AIISO ontology is applied in most works while other vocabularies such as Teach and Courseware include crucial terms about university courses [5,11]; ii) most works followed the principle of reusing existing ontologies as much as possible, however, all of them had to extend these vocabularies to fulfill their requirements; iii) general ontologies such as Dublin Core Metadata Element Set, FOAF, W3C Basic Geo Vocabulary, and W3C Ontology for Media Resources had a common usage along with the above vocabularies.

For covering the missing terms and relations, similar to the state-of-the-art works, we decided to implement a new ontology reusing and extending some above ontologies (considered as a core schema). A university course is associated with teachers, subjects, students, materials, and institutions. In turn, it is described by properties such as *name, language, location, teaching method, assessment method*, etc. The Protege tool was used to implement the ontology *CourseOntology*[6] while Turtle was the serialization format to its publication because of its dual human machine-readable capacity.

5.2 DCAT Metadata Vocabulary

The DCAT metadata vocabulary is used to describe datasets. The DCAT-catalog file is located on the homepage of the platform accessible by client applications. In the catalog file are defined: catalog metadata (*URI, title, description, license, publisher, accessRights, datasets*); dataset metadata (*URI, subject, description, title, keyword, conformsTo, accessRights, license, temporal Range*); and distribution metadata (*URI, accessURL, mediaType, issued*). By accessing the dataset through the *subject* property, clients can distinguish one dataset from many other ones.

5.3 Hydra Web API and Hydra API Documentation

Additionally, by getting to the dataset distribution, clients find out where to retrieve the dataset (URL via the distribution *accessURL* property) and how to retrieve it (serialization format via the distribution *mediaType* property). DCAT distributions are usually related to data services (Web APIs) that resolve the service indicated at the distribution. Clients normally have two purposes when they access a dataset: i) to download it as a dump, ii) to perform a live query over it. Whether the client needs a dump, by getting to the dataset distribution *accessURL* property, the client can obtain the dump in one of the serialization formats offered in the distribution *mediaType* property.

On the other hand, if the client aims to perform a live query, a description of the service can be obtained from the Hydra API Documentation which is connected to the dataset *conformsTo* property. At the Hydra API Documentation, the API services are described through the *hydra : IriTemplate* class. Moreover, a summary of the triples contained in the dataset is also included in the API Documentation via *ds : capability*.

---

[6] https://github.com/yalopez84/coursesld_server/blob/master/files/ld/ontologies/courseontology.ttl.

5.4   Source Selection Scenario

To demonstrate our proposal, besides the University of Informatics Sciences' LOU platform denoted by PL_1, we create a scenario where two more LOU platforms take place: Central University Marta Abreu de las Villas' LOU platform denoted by PL_2 and West University's LOU platform denoted by PL_3. Thus, we count on a scenario of three LOU platform DCAT-catalogs as depicted in Fig. 1, which can be queried by client applications to find courses via federated queries. PL_1 presents a DCAT catalog with one dataset of courses, and such a dataset is associated with a Hydra API Documentation with a set of three predicates as capacities and three dataset access methods: a customized query interface discussed later on called *coursesld_server*, a Triple Pattern Fragment interface, and a SPARQL endpoint interface.

In addition, PL_2 presents a catalog with two datasets, one for courses and the other for journal articles. In turn, each dataset is associated with a Hydra API Documentation. The course dataset Hydra API Documentation includes a set of three predicates as capacities and one dataset access method: a SPARQL endpoint interface while the journal article dataset Hydra API Documentation includes a set of two predicates as capacities and one dataset access method: a SPARQL endpoint interface as well. On the other hand, PL_3 presents a catalog with two datasets, one for projects and the other for journal articles. In turn, each dataset is associated with a Hydra API Documentation. Each Hydra API Documentation includes a set of two predicates as capacities and one dataset access method: a SPARQL endpoint interface.

Normally, course recommender apps ask for courses about one specific subject that start on a certain date. Hence, a possible set of triple patter is *<course, rdf:type, teach:Course>* denoted by tp_1, *<course, dbpedia: startDate, 2021-04-04T00:00:00>* denoted by tp_2, and *<course, dcterm:subject, Semantic Web>* denoted by tp_3. Following the earlier on formalization, given tp_1 has *rdf:type* as the predicate therefore, $PL_1 - coursedataset$ and $PL_2 - coursedataset$ are selected. In turn, given tp_2 has *dbpedia:startDate* as the predicate, by looking for the domain of such a predicate in the *CourseOntology* and according to the formalization, $PL_1-coursedataset$, $PL_2-coursedataset$, and $PL_3-projectdataset$ are selected. Finally, tp_3 has *dcterm:subject* as the predicate, and looking for the domain of such a predicate in the *CourseOntology* and according to the formalization, $PL_1-coursedataset$, $PL_2-coursedataset$, $PL_2-journalarticledataset$, and $PL_3 - journalarticledataset$ are selected. So, if those three triple patterns belong to the same SPARQL query, a logic source intersection would take place and only $PL_1 - coursedataset$ and $PL_2 - coursedataset$ would be successfully selected.

5.5   A Customized Query Interface *coursesld_server*

Regarding dataset access methods, since most developers are familiar with APIs with descriptions more than SPARQL endpoints over the RDF format, customized interfaces can serve to pave that issue. Therefore, besides established

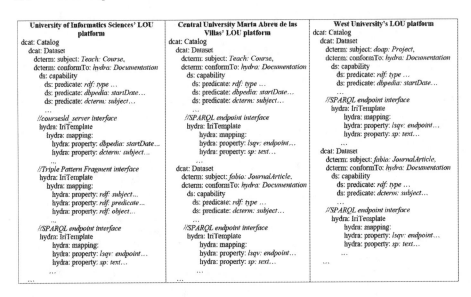

Fig. 1. A scenario of three LOU platform DCAT-catalogs

query interfaces as SPARQL endpoints and Triple Pattern Fragments, we also developed a customized query interface called *coursesld_server* in the PL_1. It was developed specifically to query the course dataset and, in turn, it demonstrates that our source selection proposal is worth it regardless of the kind of query interface. Next, a brief description of *coursesld_server*.

The customized query interface *coursesld_server*[7] was implemented in Node.js and transforms raw data on JSON files to courses files on the RDF serializations: JSON LD, TTL, N3, and CSV. It is a Hydra REST API that offers clients the possibility of obtaining courses filtered by two fields: subject and start date. It also delivers courses ordered by the start date. To deal with the client memory requirements and contribute to data reuse, this interface splits the answer into fragments with no more than 100 courses per fragment.

By using *coursesld_server*, client applications can request the server each fragment through Hydra Hypermedia controls without any human intervention. It allows clients to reuse previous fragmentations. The fragmentation lifetime depends on the server cache. On every fragmentation page, the description can be found of how to get to a page describing another course fragment. Since the same page describes how to get to the next or previous page, the client can be certain about which page to ask next. Besides delivering the course fragment with its URI, the response contains Hydra Hypermedia controls to guide the client-server communication, such as *hydra : next* and *hydra : previous* properties.

---

[7] https://github.com/yalopez84/coursesld_server.

6 Results and Discussion

The case study starts with showing a search for a context-based unified well-accepted vocabulary for the semantic modeling process in the LOU context. Thus, CourseOntology extends and reuses existing ontologies, and in turn, covers the missing terms and relations according to some Cuban universities. The DCAT metadata vocabulary with its centralized catalog conception was used to describe datasets, while Hydra, Hydra API Documentation, and Capacity Summaries complement DCAT to describe dataset and dataset access methods. As main findings of the case study, we can mention the following:

- By using DCAT, Hydra, Hydra API Documentation and, Capacity Summaries, it is possible to describe sources at the dataset level, still keeping the catalog conception, in order to facilitate the source selection process as a step of the federated queries. Of course, several datasets integrated under the same SPARQL endpoint is very common, but we defend the idea of describing them at the dataset level,
- The source selection formalization presented earlier on allows selecting the right sources per triple pattern without further processing complexity.
- Our proposal is tailored not only to established query interfaces as SPARQL endpoints, but also, to new query interfaces.

7 Conclusions and Future Work

An important step in federated query execution frameworks is source selection determining which endpoints are relevant to evaluate a given query. However, existing source selection strategies involve some issues in domains as the LOU context. The proposal presented in this work is consistent with the idea that using DCAT, Hydra, Hydra API Documentation along with a context-based unified well-accepted vocabulary and data summaries, it is possible to improve the source selection as a step of the federated query execution. In this sense, a case study in the LOU context was presented.

As a result, we showed that the usage of former semantic vocabularies along with a context-based unified well-accepted vocabulary does allow the selection of the relevant sources in a federated query environment regardless of the kind of query interface that is used, without ambiguity and further processing complexity.

As ongoing work, we plan to continue with the evaluation of our proposal and explore the usage of the Tree vocabulary[8] in our solution. Such a vocabulary is based on the Hydra vocabulary and allows to further describe the relations between fragments via math operators. On the other hand, an interesting opportunity to research may be the definition of a DCAT profile in the LOU context. A DCAT profile adds additional constraints to DCAT such as controlled vocabularies. Several DCAT profiles for specific countries and domains have already been defined and we consider the LOU context deserves special attention.

---

[8] https://treecg.github.io/specification.

Acknowledgment. This research has been partially sponsored by VLIR-UOS Network University Cooperation Programme-Cuba.

References

1. Beek, W., Rietveld, L., Bazoobandi, H.R., Wielemaker, J., Schlobach, S.: LOD laundromat: a uniform way of publishing other people's dirty data. In: Mika, P., et al. (eds.) The Semantic Web - ISWC 2014. pp. 213–228. Lecture Notes in Computer Science, Springer International Publishing, Cham (2014). https://doi.org/10.1007/978-3-319-11964-9

2. Berners-Lee, T.: Linked data-design issues (2006). https://www.w3.org/DesignIssues/LinkedData.html

3. Buil-Aranda, C., Hogan, A., Umbrich, J., Vandenbussche, P.Y.: SPARQL web-querying infrastructure: ready for action? In: Alani, H., et al. (eds.) The Semantic Web - ISWC 2013. pp. 277–293. Lecture Notes in Computer Science, Springer, Berlin, Heidelberg (2013). https://doi.org/10.1007/978-3-642-41338-4

4. Cifuentes-Silva, F., Labra Gayo, J.E.: Legislative document content extraction based on semantic web technologies. In: Hitzler, P., et al. (eds.) The Semantic Web. pp. 558–573. Lecture Notes in Computer Science, Springer International Publishing, Cham (2019). https://doi.org/10.1007/978-3-030-21348-0

5. Daga, E., d'Aquin, M., Adamou, A., Brown, S.: The open university linked data - data.open.ac.uk. Semantic Web **7**(2), 183–191 (2016). https://doi.org/10.3233/SW-150182, https://content.iospress.com/articles/semantic-web/sw182

6. dAquin, M., Dietze, S.: Open education: a growing, high impact area for linked open data. ERCIM News (96) (2014)

7. Görlitz, O., Staab, S.: SPLENDID: SPARQL endpoint federation exploiting VOID descriptions. In: Proceedings of the Second International Conference on Consuming Linked Data, Vol. 782. pp. 13–24. COLD 2011, CEUR-WS.org, Aachen, DEU (2011)

8. Hogan, A., et al.: Knowledge graphs. ACM Comput. Surv. (CSUR) **54**(4), 1–37 (2021)

9. Lanthaler, M.: Hydra core vocabulary (2021). https://www.hydra-cg.com/spec/latest/core

10. Lanthaler, M., Gütl, C.: Hydra: a vocabulary for hypermedia-driven web APIS. In: LDOW (2013)

11. Ma, Y., Xu, B., Bai, Y., Li, Z.: Building Linked Open University Data: Tsinghua University Open Data as a Showcase. In: Pan, J.Z., et al. (eds.) The Semantic Web. pp. 385–393. Lecture Notes in Computer Science, Springer, Berlin, Heidelberg (2012). https://doi.org/10.1007/978-3-642-29923-0

12. Mansour, E., et al.: A demonstration of the solid platform for social web applications. In: Proceedings of the 25th International Conference Companion on World Wide Web, WWW 2016 Companion, pp. 223–226. International World Wide Web Conferences Steering Committee, Republic and Canton of Geneva, CHE (2016). https://doi.org/10.1145/2872518.2890529

13. Marx, E., Baron, C., Soru, T., Auer, S.: KBox - transparently shifting query execution on knowledge graphs to the edge. In: 2017 IEEE 11th International Conference on Semantic Computing (ICSC), pp. 125–132. IEEE, USA (2017). https://doi.org/10.1109/ICSC.2017.77, https://ieeexplore.ieee.org/abstract/document/7889519

14. Meymandpour, R., Davis, J.G.: Ranking universities using linked open data. In: LDOW (2013)

15. Nahhas, S., Bamasag, O., Khemakhem, M., Bajnaid, N.: Added values of linked data in education: a survey and roadmap. Computers **7**(3), 45 (2018)
16. Quilitz, B., Leser, U.: Querying Distributed RDF Data Sources with SPARQL. In: Bechhofer, S., Hauswirth, M., Hoffmann, J., Koubarakis, M. (eds.) The Semantic Web: Research and Applications. pp. 524–538. Lecture Notes in Computer Science, Springer, Berlin, Heidelberg (2008). https://doi.org/10.1007/978-3-540-68234-9
17. Saleem, M., Khan, Y., Hasnain, A., Ermilov, I., Ngonga Ngomo, A.C.: A fine-grained evaluation of SPARQL endpoint federation systems. Seman. Web **7**(5), 493–518 (2016). https://doi.org/10.3233/SW-150186
18. Sande, M.V., Verborgh, R., Dimou, A., Colpaert, P., Mannens, E.: Hypermedia-based discovery for source selection using low-cost linked data interfaces. In: Information Retrieval and Management: Concepts, Methodologies, Tools, and Applications, vol. 1, pp. 502–537. IGI Global, USA (2018). https://doi.org/10.4018/978-1-5225-5191-1.ch023
19. Schmachtenberg, M., Bizer, C., Paulheim, H.: Adoption of the Linked Data Best Practices in Different Topical Domains. In: Mika, P., et al. (eds.) The Semantic Web - ISWC 2014. pp. 245–260. Lecture Notes in Computer Science, Springer International Publishing, Cham (2014). https://doi.org/10.1007/978-3-319-11964-9
20. Schwarte, A., Haase, P., Hose, K., Schenkel, R., Schmidt, M.: FedX: Optimization Techniques for Federated Query Processing on Linked Data. In: Aroyo, L., et al. (eds.) The Semantic Web - ISWC 2011. pp. 601–616. Lecture Notes in Computer Science, Springer, Berlin, Heidelberg (2011). https://doi.org/10.1007/978-3-642-25073-6
21. Szász, B., Fleiner, R., Micsik, A.: A Case Study on Linked Data for University Courses. In: Ciuciu, I., et al. (eds.) On the Move to Meaningful Internet Systems: OTM 2016 Workshops. pp. 265–276. Lecture Notes in Computer Science, Springer International Publishing, Cham (2017). https://doi.org/10.1007/978-3-319-55961-2
22. Taelman, R., Van Herwegen, J., Vander Sande, M., Verborgh, R.: Comunica: A Modular SPARQL Query Engine for the Web. In: Vrandečić, D., et al. (eds.) The Semantic Web - ISWC 2018. pp. 239–255. Lecture Notes in Computer Science, Springer International Publishing, Cham (2018). https://doi.org/10.1007/978-3-030-00668-6
23. Van Herwegen, J., De Vocht, L., Verborgh, R., Mannens, E., Van de Walle, R.: Substring Filtering for Low-Cost Linked Data Interfaces. In: Arenas, M., et al. (eds.) The Semantic Web - ISWC 2015. pp. 128–143. Lecture Notes in Computer Science, Springer International Publishing, Cham (2015). https://doi.org/10.1007/978-3-319-25007-6
24. Van Herwegen, J., Verborgh, R., Mannens, E., Van de Walle, R.: Query Execution Optimization for Clients of Triple Pattern Fragments. In: Gandon, F., et al. (eds.) The Semantic Web. Latest Advances and New Domains. pp. 302–318. Lecture Notes in Computer Science, Springer International Publishing, Cham (2015). https://doi.org/10.1007/978-3-319-18818-8
25. Verborgh, R., et al.:Triple pattern fragments: a low-cost knowledge graph interface for the Web. J. Web Seman. **37–38**, 184–206 (2016)
26. Wang, X., Tiropanis, T., Davis, H.C.: Lhd: Optimising linked data query processing using parallelisation. In: Proceedings of the WWW2013 Workshop on Linked Data on the Web (2013). http://ceur-ws.org/Vol-996/papers/ldow2013-paper-06.pdf

OntoKnowNHS: Ontology Driven Knowledge Centric Novel Hybridised Semantic Scheme for Image Recommendation Using Knowledge Graph

N. Roopak[1(✉)] and Gerard Deepak[2]

[1] SRM Institute of Science and Technology, Ramapuram, Chennai, India
[2] National Institute of Technology, Tiruchirappalli, Tiruchirappalli, India

Abstract. Multimedia content is increasing immensely as there are various websites available to upload images. Image retrieval is a method of searching for, viewing, and retrieving images from a database. Close text choices are often accepted by image search engines. It is difficult for search engines to comprehend users' search intent merely through terms, resulting in unclear and quavering search results that are far from satisfying. To solve the dilemma in text-based picture retrieval, it is important to employ content-first search. The proposed OntoKnowNHS model is composed of Domain Ontology based query term enrichment and Knowledge enrichment of the images with the help of Google's Knowledge Base API and Wikidata, incorporated with the Knowledge Graph of images which is compared using Convolutional Neural Networks and, the semantic similarity is computed using Kullback Leibler Divergence, Concept Similarity, and Normalised Compression Distance which recommends images from both Knowledge Graphs and Redefined Image Tag set. All of these factors work together to improve accuracy. The Flickr30k dataset is used to integrate user preferences for picture suggestions, which are then categorized using Convolutional Neural Networks with the aid of extracted query terms from the user information using domain ontology. The developed approach has an accuracy of 96.41% and outperforms the alternative reference models by weakening the robustness of conventional image Recommender Systems.

Keywords: Concept similarity · Convolutional neural networks · Domain ontology · Normalised compression distance

1 Introduction

The multimedia content of web pages is exponentially increasing day by day. There are so many popular websites like Instagram, Flickr, Picasa, Pinterest, etc. where multimedia contents like images are uploaded in humongous amounts. The

B. Villazón-Terrazas et al. (Eds.): KGSWC 2021, CCIS 1459, pp. 138–152, 2021.
https://doi.org/10.1007/978-3-030-91305-2_11

retrieval of multimedia information from web pages is quite tedious. Analyzing the context of the image is an intricate process, that is to identify individual objects and describe the subject of the image. There are various types of web image search techniques namely content-based and annotation-based. The paradigm of content-based image retrieval is based on a visual examination of the contents of the query picture. The method of content-based picture retrieval focuses on debased visual attributes such as colour, shape, or texture. Annotation-based image retrieval is a new type of retrieval mechanism based on text or user queries. The major step of annotation-based image retrieval is split into two categories namely automated image annotation and query processing. Picture segmentation and labelling methods can be used to do automatic image annotation. Web Image Retrieval employs web information to retrieve images such as image URL, image title, ALTtag, hyperlinks, and so on. Visual information is presented as stand-alone items as well as incorporated in web pages. It is represented through pictures, graphics, bitmaps, animations, and videos. As a result, web image search engines are in high demand. Law enforcement, picture copyright protection, filtering of unsuitable adult content, crime monitoring, etc. are all applications for such engines. Semantic technologies, which attempt to connect low-level picture characteristics to high-level ontology ideas, provide a promising approach to image retrieval. One of the concepts that has come to public attention as a result of this development is the Knowledge Graph (KG). Furthermore, with that booming development, particularly in the previous two decades, there is a greater requirement to analyse and extract important information in a more effective manner [1,2].

Web-users require automatic picture retrieval tools; yet, while creating and implementing such tools, individuals encounter a variety of issues linked to two elements. The primary concern of elements of image retrieval is the volume of information included in an image and its details. The second is associated with the characteristics of the Web, specifically its massive size, lack of organization, and bewildering scale, which limits the retrieval and indexing techniques that could be deployed. The context of the image cannot be predicted always and annotation of images is necessary for proper retrieval. In this proposed Onto-Know model analyzing both context and the background context along with other annotations using ontology and folksonomy for the web image search is incorporated. The Semantic Web is a concept of a widening of the preexisting World Wide Web that gives machine-interpretable metadata of published information and data to software programs. The proposed OntoKnowNHS model is composed of Domain Ontology-based query term enrichment and Knowledge enrichment of the images with the help of Google Knowledge Graph API and Wikidata, incorporated with the Knowledge Graph of images which are compared using Convolutional Neural Networks (CNN) and, the semantic similarity is computed using Kullback Leibler (KL) Divergence, Concept Similarity, and Normalised Compression Distance (NCD) which recommends images from both Knowledge Graphs and Redefined Image Tag set.

Motivation: There is a need for better techniques for the mining of pictures from the world wide web. Images and multimedia content on the world wide web is increasing, so it is difficult to mine pics from the semantic web. Most of the web image retrieval techniques are gleaned from the traditional world wide web, not the semantic web. An approach for considering the background textual information, and for determining the context, and to consider the image contents, as well as the annotations of the images. A machine learning infused semantic approach has been incorporated for web image retrieval.

Organization: The remainder of the paper is organized as follows. Section 2 is devoted to Related Work. The Proposed System Architecture is profiled in Sect. 3. Implementation and the algorithm of the proposed model are presented in Sect. 4. The Performance Analysis is exhibited in Sect. 5. Eventually, Sect. 6 brings the paper to a conclusion.

2   Related Works

Maha Saddal et al. [3] recommended browsing and exploring recommendations of images while reducing the related reachability issues. The multimedia graph is being used as a method for non-linear web image exploration outcomes. A search engine is also being developed to give a synergistic search user interface for exploring image results in a useful manner. Divakar Yadav et al. [4] have proposed a search engine paradigm in which an image may be uploaded from the user's local database to get information about it from the web by using the content retrieval method to recommend images. A.F. Adrakatti et al. [5] have proposed a study to describe the concept and operation of the most popular nonprofit Reverse Image Search Engines by picking S.R. Ranganathan's picture to assess the performances of the image retrieval systems. Bernard J. Jansen [6] has focused on online users' information demands as reflected by image searches. They made recommendations for enhancing picture indexing and retrieval systems in order to fulfill the information demands of real-world consumers. Umesh K.K. et al. [7] presented a semantic-based image mining system to obtain a group of pertinent pictures from the Web for a specified query image by using a global color space model and Dense SIFT feature extraction technique. Furuta et al. [8] has proposed a system that considers both spatial and semantic information since it uses FCN and product quantization techniques. Ritika Hirwane [9] presented many Semantic Image Retrieval methods for retrieving images related to the user query. R. Gupta et al. [10] presented a framework in which debased characteristics of the image are extracted. This study provides an in-depth examination of patch recognition, which is a key component of content-based image retrieval. Khodaskar A. et al. [11] this study provides a strategy for optimal CBIR with good performance semantic characteristics using object ontology. Sejal et al. [12] proposed a model which recommends an image based on user queries using Markov chain technique and image visual features. Umar Manzoor et al. [13] present an image recommendation system that uses domain-specific ontology by considering shape, colour and texture-based for classification. Ronak Panchal et al. [13] developed an ontology-based case study for public higher education, and SPARQL queries are utilised for reasoning.

3   Proposed System Architecture

The presented system architecture includes knowledge production and semantic awareness, which are calculated by combining semantic similarity models with CNN. Figure 1 depicts a knowledge-centric image recommendation system based on both image features and image labels or annotations. According to the criteria of this suggested model, the query is pre-processed using different approaches such as tokenization, lemmatization, and stop word removal. Tokenization is the

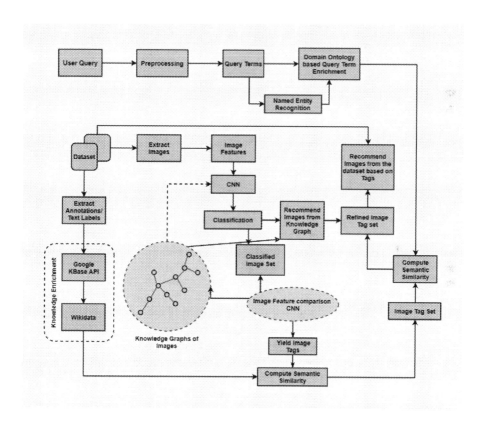

Fig. 1. The proposed system architecture of OntoKnowNHS.

process of dividing a set of words into smaller parts known as tokens. Tokens can be words, letters, or subwords in this context. Lemmatization enables users to query any form of a base term and receive relevant results where users can query any adverbial form of a word and receive appropriate results. Stop word removal is also done in order to get the results more appropriate to the user's needs. Following data pre-processing, individual query terms are obtained. These query terms are subjected to Named Entity Recognition (NER), identifying the key elements. Then the Domain ontology-based query term enrichment takes place where domain ontologies that are relevant to the queried domain are included. The Ontologies are formulated based on the domains to which the query terms belong. The query terms are chosen from the categories of the domain which belong to the dataset. The categories, annotations as well as labels from the dataset are extracted and domain ontology is generated by using OntoCollab. Since the domain ontologies are based on distinctive domains and generated mainly using OntoCollab, the scale of the ontologies is definitely unknown as it is intrinsic. However, the ontology which is generated for all the domains of the dataset is comprised of concepts that were 14,872 in number and individuals which were 21,627 in number. The ontology is automatically generated using OntoCollab and it is difficult to describe the highly linked data but it is relevant to the domain and is generated from the World Wide Web content. This is the overall number of concepts used in this model. The dataset comprises both image annotations and images. Image features are automatically extracted by using CNN and it is subjected to classification.

To classify the images, highly relevant simple images which are present in the dataset based on the images with quite an amount of simplicity and with individual or pair of objects, are taken and the knowledge graph of the image which is relevant to the problem domain is extracted from the dataset and the annotations are modeled. Knowledge Graph of images refers to images that are highly relevant which have some amount of correlation with each other. A knowledge graph is a knowledge base that integrates data using a graph-structured object model or architecture. Knowledge graphs are frequently used to hold interconnected models of entities with free-form semantics, such as objects, events, etc. It contextualizes data by connecting and semantic metadata, providing a framework for data integration and analytics. The Knowledge graph of images and Knowledge graphs of annotations are highly synonymous.

From the dataset, the annotations or the text labels are obtained and are subjected to Google Knowledge Graph API, where highly relevant words to the annotations in the form of a knowledge graph are obtained. Further, the knowledge enrichment takes place with the help of both Google Knowledge Graph API and Wikidata. In Wikidata, an agent is modeled in order to extract highly relevant terms and annotations. These knowledge enriched annotation or text labels with the help of Google Knowledge Graph API and Wikidata is further used for semantic similarity between text labels. Google Knowledge Graph API and Wikidata are used for knowledge enrichment. They are knowledge stores and not the ontology which is used in this proposed model. There is a clear-cut demarcation between domain ontologies as well as the knowledge stores.

Google Knowledge Graph API and Wikidata is used for knowledge enrichment by corporating the hierarchically related entities from the Wikidata as well as the open linked data in the form of a subgraph from the Google Knowledge Graph API. However, they are not the ontologies used, the ontologies formulated are the domain ontology that belongs to the query term domain that is extracted from the annotations in the dataset. In total there are 14,618 concepts and individuals were around 17,877.

On the other hand, the images are extracted from the dataset, image features are taken which are then loaded into CNN along with the images that are yielded from the knowledge graph. Then the classification of the extracted images along with the knowledge graph of images is done. As a result, a classified image set is yielded. Now, this model compares the features of the images that are obtained from the dataset and from the knowledge enriched images with the help of CNN, which yields image tags. The Semantic similarity is calculated between the yielded image tags and with the images obtained with enriched knowledge. Again, the semantic similarity is reckoned between knowledge graphs of annotations and the tag set, i.e. the initial tag set.

From the images that are obtained from the classification using CNN, where the extracted images from the dataset and the Knowledge Graph of images are compared, recommendation of images from the Knowledge Graph is done. These recommended images are then labeled as Refined Image Tagset, which is a cluster of recommended images from the Knowledge Graphs and the secondary image tag set, and the domain ontology-based query term enrichment. The secondary image tag set is obtained as a result of semantic computation between the knowledge enriched images from the data set and the yielded images tags obtained after the image feature comparison using CNN. So from the Refined image tag set, recommendation of images is done based on the dataset and the tag set.

The recommendation of images from the dataset and the tag set is recommended first and then the recommendation of images from the Knowledge Graphs happens. All of these recommended images will be arranged based on the semantic similarity of the tags. The semantic similarity is computed using three different algorithms namely KL Divergence which measures the difference between two probability distributions over the same variable x, Concept similarity which is computed based on distance, content, and property. The final method involved in computing semantic similarity is the NCD which determines the similarity of two items, such as two images, documents, etc. It is not application-specific or arbitrary. So finally, the images are recommended to the users.

4   Implementation

The suggested OntoKnowNHS method is implemented in the Windows 10 Operating System using Python 3.9.0. The appropriate IDE is Google Colaboratory, and the backend is MySQL lite. The procedure is carried out on an i9 Intel Core

CPU with 16 GB of Random Access Memory and a 16 GB Nvidia graphics card. Flickr30k Dataset is used for web image recommendation research, which adds 244k coreference chains to the 158k captions from Flickr30k, connecting mentions of the same entities across various descriptions for the same image, and associates them with 276k carefully annotated input images. Google's Knowledge Graph API and the Wikidata were accessed via already available API libraries and the auxiliary knowledge is included in the framework. The Knowledge Graph of images was modeled using OntoCollab, which is a platform constructed for knowledge bases using ontology modeling [11]. OntoCollab models ontologies manually for images and generating ontologies for large amounts of images. So images with labels were taken into consideration and label-label associations were computed in order to associate the images. For CNN, Google Colaboratory is used thereby domain ontology was also dynamically generated using OntoCollab. A lot of domain-related terms were crawled using Beautiful Soup and enriched. An agent was modeled, which included agent speak and further adhered to the framework. The proposed OntoKnowNHS model was tested for 4782 queries out of which 672 queries were single word and the rest were multi-word queries. The ground truth was collected from 1418 participants who were given 10 to 18 queries each and were asked to give their top 10 images extracted from their favorite image search engines. Also, they were asked to give as many text markers and annotations as possible for each query. The algorithm of the presented system is illustrated in Algorithm 1.

The user's queries are gathered and those queries are subjected to preprocessing with various techniques like tokenization, lemmatization, stop word removal, and also subjected to NER by identifying the key elements. Then the Domain ontology-based query term enrichment takes place where domain ontologies that are relevant to the queried domain are included. Image features are automatically extracted from the dataset by using the CNN and it is subjected to classification. The annotations or the text labels are obtained from the and are subjected to Google's Knowledge Graph API, Wikidata for knowledge enrichment. Image features are taken from the dataset which is then loaded into CNN along with the images that are yielded from the Knowledge Graph. As a result, a classified image set is yielded. The semantic similarity is computed between the knowledge enriched annotation extracted from the dataset and the image tags using 3 schemes namely KL Divergence, Concept Similarity, and NCD, which yields an image tag set. Again the semantic similarity is calculated between the image tag set and the domain ontology-based enriched query term, which yields a refined image tag set which is then used in recommending the images to the users. The recommendation is done twice, one from the Knowledge graph of images and the other one from the dataset based on tags.

Algorithm 1. Proposed algorithm for OntoKnowNHS model.

Input : Queries collected from the user and the Flickr30k dataset are used.
Output : Image recommendations from web pages depending on user inputs.

Begin,

Step 1: Query q obtained from the user is preprocessed by tokenization, lemmatization, stop word removal.

Step 2: Extracting the query words q1 and creating a Domain Ontology for Query term enrichment q3 using Named Entity Recognition.

Step 3: From the dataset, the image features Img are extracted. And at the same time, Text labels or annotations are extracted from the dataset, and knowledge enrichment is done with the help of Google's knowledge base API and Wikidata.

Step 4: A knowledge graph of images is created which is then compared with the extracted image features Img from the dataset using Convolutional Neural Networks. Classification of images is done as a result.

Step 5: A classified image set A is created as the result of CNN1 and image feature comparison is done with the knowledge graphs of images using another CNN2 model.

Step 6: As a result of image feature comparison using CNN, image tags B is yielded. Then the semantic similarity is computed between the knowledge enriched annotation extracted from the dataset and the image tags B using 3 schemes:

    Step 6.1: Set X = when Normalised compression Distance and the Concept similarity between Image tag B and the enriched annotation of dataset > 0.75.

    Step 6.2: Set Y = When the NCD is low.

    Step 6.3: Set Z = when KL divergence < 0.25.

    Step 6.4: Set P = (Set X Set Y Set Z)

Step 7: Result of Step 6 yields Image tag set C.

Step 8: Again the semantic similarity is calculated between the image tag set C and the domain ontology-based enriched query term.

    Step 8.1: Set X = when Normalised compression Distance and the Concept similarity between Image tag C and the enriched query term q3s> 0.75.

    Step 8.1: Set Y = When the NCD is low between Set C and q3.

    Step 8.2: Set Z = when KL divergence < 0.25.

    Step 8.3: Set P = (Set Y Set Z Set P).

Step 9: Result of Step 8 yields Refined image tag set D.

Step 10: Images are Recommended from both, the dataset based on Image tag set D and from the Knowledge Graph.

End

---

5   Results and Performance Evaluation

The proposed OntoKnowNHS approach has been baselined with four distinct models namely BAEWIS [1] KRMAIF [10], OBA [14], and Neural Net Descriptors [15]. Performance metrics include Average Precision, Average Recall, Accuracy, F-Measure, False Discovery Rate (FDR), and Discounted Cumulative Gain (nDCG). Equation (1) is used to compute the model's accuracy percentage.

Equation (2) computes the OntoJudy model's recall percentage. The percentage of accuracy is calculated using Eq. (3). Equations (4) and (5) calculate the suggested approach's F-Measure and FDR. Accuracy is accustomed to determine the model's anticipated accuracy. The proposed model's nDCG is computed using Eq. (6). The F-Measure is an approach of combining the model's accuracy and recall, and it is characterized as the harmonic mean of the precision and recall of the model. Precision, Recall, Accuracy, F-Measure computes the relevance of the results yielded. Whereas, FDR quantifies the number of false positives yielded by the proposed system. While nDCG measures the diversity in the results which is furnished by the proposed OntoKnowNHS model. To compare the performances of the proposed OntoKnowNHS, the baseline approaches are also evaluated in the same environment as done in the proposed approach, with the same dataset for 8816 queries whose ground truth has been collected. The Knowledge Base is large, and it is mostly employed in this case for entity population and boosting the density of incoming auxiliary knowledge into the framework. The Recall computation is carried out with respect to the dataset and not with respect to the Knowledge Base. The number of relevant images in the dataset is already known for each query that has been tested, as the ground truth collection was carried out by a simple voting mechanism by 1418 candidates and the top 10–18 relevant images for each query were taken. However, 10 coherent images, based on the maximum voting, were shortlisted and considered relevant for each subsequent query. The queries were distributed such that each candidate had to answer 20 queries and the top 20 relevant documents from the dataset had to be recommended by them. Instead of using a query tool, a human-in-the-middle approach was followed for the collection of ground truth based on the documents in the dataset. For the query expansion, the keywords in the documents based on the frequency of occurrences and the uniqueness of terms were considered to be relevant.

$$Precision\% = \frac{Retrieved \cap Relevant}{Retrieved} \tag{1}$$

$$Recall\% = \frac{Retrieved \cap Relevant}{Relevant} \tag{2}$$

$$Accuracy\% = \frac{Precision + Recall}{2} \tag{3}$$

$$F-Measure\% = \frac{2(Precision + Recall)}{Precision + Recall} \tag{4}$$

$$False Discovery Rate = 1 - Precision \tag{5}$$

$$nDCG = \frac{DCG\alpha}{IDCG\alpha} \tag{6}$$

$$DCG = \sum_{i=1}^{\alpha} \frac{Rel_i}{log(i+1)} \tag{7}$$

Figure 2 depicts the performance metrics of OntoKnowNHS which is compared with other approaches in terms of Avg Precision %, Avg Recall %,

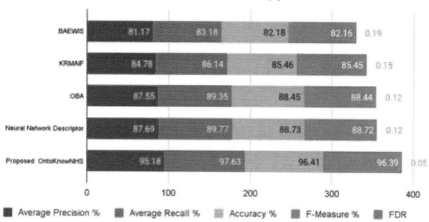

Fig. 2. Comparison of performance of OntoKnowNHS model with other approaches.

Accuracy %, F-Measure %, and FDR. From Fig. 2, it is expressive that the propounded OntoKnowNHS model is extra coherent in contrast with the baseline approaches. The propounded OntoKnowNHS model is composed of Domain Ontology-based query term enrichment and Knowledge enrichment of the images with the help of Google's Knowledge Graph API and Wikidata, incorporated with the Knowledge Graph of images which are compared using CNN and, the semantic similarity is computed using KL Divergence, Concept Similarity, and NCD which recommends images from both Knowledge Graphs and Redefined Image Tag set. The image recommendation using BAEWIS, which is a browsing aware system where a dynamically modeled graph or a multi-modeled graph is generated between the text and the images. The concept of multi-modeled graphs is absolutely novel because clustering is used for a noncategorical dataset which results in minimization of the number of entities in the graph that caves a precision of 88.17% and a recall of 83.18% and an accuracy percentage of 82.18 with an F-Measure of 82.16% and FDR of 0.19. The web image recommendation by KRMAIF is done by incorporating the Markovian Semantic Index along with image features which are mainly targeted rather than the textual features. It ensures that the indexes are generated, while it is not much effective for this dataset as it fails to address the textual features which in result furnishes an 84.78% precision value, a recall value of 86.14%, an accuracy percentage of 85.46, and an F-Measure of 85.45% including FDR of 0.15.

Web image retrieval by OBA provides auxiliary knowledge which makes sure it furnishes a precision of 87.55%, a recall of 89.35%, an accuracy of 88.45%, and an F-Measure of 88.44% with an FDR of 0.12 which is higher than the above-mentioned models, but static ontology alone cannot make the system very effective as the relevance computation is quite low. The large-scale image recommendation by Neural Network Descriptor embeds both Neural Networks and the descriptors which produce a precision of 87.69%, a recall of 89.77%, an accuracy of 88.73%, and F-Measure of 88.72% with an FDR of 0.12. But the mechanism of the Neural Network Descriptor is computationally complex; above all, it also results in the over-fitting problem. The proposed OntoKnowNHS model uses text-based annotations as well as image-based features with knowledge expansion by means of annotations derived from the dataset. Google's Knowledge Graph API increases the size of the entities of the graph and the Wikidata increases the knowledge density which altogether is used to build the Knowledge Graph of images. Three distinct semantic similarities are used and image classification is done with the help of CNN along with the domain ontology for initial query extraction. So all of these increase the performance metrics of the model. OntoKnowNHS yields a higher precision of 95.18%, a higher recall of 97.63%, with higher accuracy of 96.41%, and a higher F-Measure of 96.39% with a lower FDR of 0.05.

Figure 3 illustrates Precision vs. No. of recommendations in increments of 10 up to 50. OntoKnowNHS has a greater Precision distribution than other baseline models as seen in Fig. 3. The suggested OntoKnowNHS model has a precision of 97.84% for ten suggestions, whereas the other baseline models have a lower precision for ten recommendations. According to Fig. 2, the FDR for the suggested OntoKnowNHS model is the lowest, indicating that baseline models are inefficient when evaluated to this proposed model. According to Fig. 3, the proposed method has proven to be beneficial concerning precision for recommendations. The OntoKnowNHS is coherent in contrast with the baseline approaches for image recommendations as it uses Domain Ontology-based query term enrichment and Knowledge enrichment of the images with the help of Google's Knowledge Graph API and Wikidata, incorporated with the Knowledge Graph of images which are compared using CNN, and the semantic similarity is calculated with KL Divergence, Concept similarity and NCD which recommends images from both Knowledge Graphs and Redefined Image Tag set (Fig. 4).

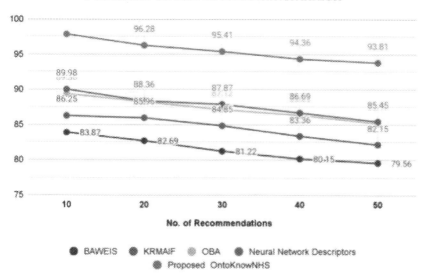

Fig. 3. Precision vs No. of recommendations

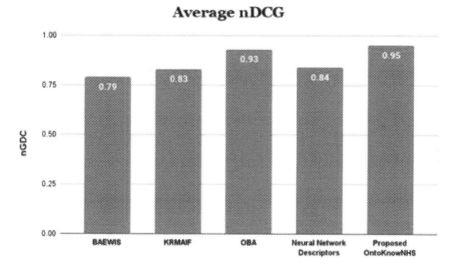

Fig. 4. Average nDCG for the proposed OntoKnowNHS and the baseline models.

Figure 5 clearly shows that the proposed OntoKnowNHS model has a greater Normalized Discounted Cumulative Gain (nDCG) than the other baseline methods that employ Domain Ontology-based query term enrichment and Knowledge enrichment of the images with the help of Google's Knowledge Graph API and Wikidata, incorporated with the Knowledge Graph of images which is then compared using CNN, and the semantic similarity is computed using KL Divergence, Concept Similarity, and NCD which recommends images from both Knowledge Graphs and Redefined Image Tag set. Because of the combination of several ideas for image recommendation, the suggested model has a larger nDCG. Since incorporating several principles inside the model, nDCG in Eq. (7) produces greater results than previous baseline models. nDCG value is comparatively low for the BAEWIS model because of the absence of a high density of knowledge. Since the knowledge density is higher in the OBA model, it yields higher nDCG than BAEWIS, KRMAIF. The RS is evaluated using nDCG. DCG is determined as shown in Eq. (6) where it represents response possibilities for ground-truth significance which is more than 0. The nDCG assesses the grade standard of Recommender System using DCG by highlighting the variety of outcomes and provides a high level of variety. As a result, nDCG is proportional to the variety of the recommendation.

Fig. 5. Output for the query "Taj"

Figure 5 shows the top 5% of the images recommended by the proposed model. The query word used for image retrieval is "Taj" and the images are recommended not only from the Flickr30k dataset but also from the Knowledge Graph of images created using Google's Knowledge Graph API and Wikidata. The major benefit of this hybridization is improved accuracy and precision in image recommendations from the web [16]. Since the approach is knowledge-centric, it is a mandate that knowledge bases like Google Knowledge Graph API and Wikidata as well as the knowledge graph of images have to be incorporated.

Without the categorical knowledge in the form of texts or images, the system would not function as there is a sparsity of knowledge. So, the more the aggregation of knowledge the better the results. This is a knowledge accelerated system, and there is a need for knowledge enrichment by Google Knowledge Graph API and Wikidata, which acts as a shortcoming for this proposed model.

6   Conclusions

An effective technique for browsing photos yields multimodal information retrieval systems, which has to be researched further. This article described a technique for viewing picture results that make use of language and visual information, as well as image characteristics. The suggestions are established on the input queries provided by the user and the dataset, which are carefully satisfied to flex aloft accuracy and F-Measure than other baseline approaches. OntoKnowNHS is composed of Domain Ontology-based query term enrichment and Knowledge enrichment of the images with the help of Wikidata and Google's Knowledge Graph API. The semantic similarity is quantified using KL Divergence, Concept similarity, and NCD which recommends images from both Knowledge Graphs and Redefined Image Tag set. The model is also incorporated with the Knowledge Graph of images which are compared using CNN to yield image tag sets. When all of these approaches are used together, the precision, recall, accuracy, and F-Measure percentages with a low FDR improve. The suggested model obtained 96.41% accuracy with a low FDR of 0.05 and a higher nDCG of 0.95.

References

1. Tiwari, S., Al-Aswadi, F.N., Gaurav, D.: Recent trends in knowledge graphs: theory and practice. Soft. Comput. **25**(13), 8337–8355 (2021). https://doi.org/10.1007/s00500-021-05756-8
2. Villazón-Terrazas, B., Ortiz-Rodríguez, F., Tiwari, S.M., Shandilya, S.K.: Knowledge Graphs and Semantic Web. Communications in Computer and Information Science, vol. 1232, pp. 1–225. Springer, Cham (2020). https://doi.org/10.1007/978-3-030-65384-2
3. Saddal, M., Rashid, U., Khattak, A.S.: A browsing approach to explore web image search results. In: 2019 22nd International Multitopic Conference (INMIC), pp. 1–6 (2019). https://doi.org/10.1109/INMIC48123.2019.9022781
4. Ragatha, D.V., Yadav, D.: Image query based search engine using image content retrieval. In: International Conference on Modeling and Simulation (2012). https://doi.org/10.1109/UKSim.2012.48
5. Adrakatti, A.F., Wodeyar, R.S., Mulla, K.R.: Search by image: a novel approach to content based image retrieval system. Int. J. Libr. Sci. **14**, 41–47 (2016)
6. Jansen, J.: Searching for digital images on the web. J. Doc. **64** (2008). https://doi.org/10.1108/00220410810844169

7. Umesh, K.K., Suresha: Semantic based image retrieval system for web images. In: Meghanathan, N., Nagamalai, D., Chaki, N. (eds.) Advances in Computing and Information Technology. Advances in Intelligent Systems and Computing, vol. 178, pp. 491–499. Springer, Heidelberg (2013). https://doi.org/10.1007/978-3-642-31600-5_48

8. Furuta, R., Inoue, N., Yamasaki, T.: Efficient and interactive spatial-semantic image retrieval. Multimed. Tools Appl. **78**(13), 18713–18733 (2019). https://doi.org/10.1007/s11042-018-7148-1

9. Hirwane, R.: Semantic based image retrieval. Int. J. Adv. Res. Comput. Commun. Eng. 6(4) (2017). ISO 3297:2007 Certified. https://doi.org/10.17148/IJARCCE.2017.6423

10. Gupta, R., Singh, V.: A framework for semantic based image retrieval from cyberspace by mapping low level features with high level semantics. In: 2018 3rd International Conference on Internet of Things: Smart Innovation and Usages (IoT-SIU), pp. 1–6 (2018). https://doi.org/10.1109/IoT-SIU.2018.8519882

11. Khodaskar, A., Ladke, S.A.: Content based image retrieval with semantic features using object ontology. Int. J. Eng. Res. Technol. **1**, 1–6 (2012)

12. Sejal, D., Rashmi, V., Venugopal, K.R., Iyengar, S.S., Patnaik, L.M.: Image recommendation based on keyword relevance using absorbing Markov chain and image features. Int. J. Multimed. Inf. Retr. **5**(3), 185–199 (2016). https://doi.org/10.1007/s13735-016-0104-9

13. Panchal, R., Swaminarayan, P., Tiwari, S., Ortiz-Rodríguez, F.: AISHE-Onto: a semantic model for public higher education universities, pp. 545–547 (2021). https://doi.org/10.1145/3463677.3463750

14. Manzoor, U., Balubaid, M., Zafar, B., Umar, H., Khan, M.S.: Semantic image retrieval: an ontology based approach. Int. J. Adv. Res. Artif. Intell. **4** (2015). https://doi.org/10.14569/IJARAI.2015.040401

15. Novak, D., Batko, M., Zezual, P.: Large-scale image retrieval using neural net descriptors. In: SIGIR 2015: Proceedings of the 38th International ACM SIGIR Conference on Research and Development in Information Retrieval, pp. 1039–1040, August 2015. https://doi.org/10.1145/2766462.2767868

16. Gupta, S., Tiwari, S., Ortiz-Rodriguez, F., Panchal, R.: KG4ASTRA: question answering over Indian missiles knowledge graph. Soft. Comput. **25**, 13841–13855 (2021). https://doi.org/10.1007/s00500-021-06233-y

The Covid-19 CODO Development Process: an Agile Approach to Knowledge Graph Development

Michael DeBellis[1]([✉]) [ID] and Biswanath Dutta[2] [ID]

[1] San Francisco, CA, USA
mdebellissf@gmail.com
http://michaeldebellis.com/
[2] Indian Statistical Institute, Bangalore, India
bisu@isibang.ac.in

Abstract. The CODO ontology was designed to capture data about the Covid-19 pandemic. The goal of the ontology was to collect epidemiological data about the pandemic so that medical professionals could perform contact tracing and answer questions about infection paths based on information about relations between patients, geography, time, etc. We took information from various spreadsheets and integrated it into one consistent knowledge graph that could be queried with SPARQL and visualized with the Gruff tool in AllegroGraph. The ontology is published on Bioportal and has been used by two projects to date. This paper describes the process used to design the initial ontology and to develop transformations to incorporate data from the Indian government about the pandemic. We went from an ontology to a large knowledge graph with approximately 5M triples in a few months. Our experience demonstrates some common principles that apply to the process of scaling up from an ontology model to a knowledge graph with real-world data.

Keywords: Ontology · Knowledge graph · Healthcare · Covid-19 · Agile methods · Software Development Life-Cycle (SDLC) · OWL · SPARQL · Transformations

1 Introduction

At the beginning of the Covid-19 pandemic (March 2020) we began to develop an ontology called CODO, an Ontology for collection and analysis of COVID-19 data. The ontology followed the FAIR model for representing data and incorporated classes and properties from standard vocabularies such as FOAF, Dublin Core, Schema.org, and SNOMED CT. While other Covid ontologies, such as CIDO, VIDO, CoVoc, etc. (more detail provided in Sect. 1.1) focus on analyzing the virus, CODO focuses on epidemiological issues, such as tracking how the virus was spread based on data about relationships, geography, temporal relations, etc. For more details on the FAIR principles and the general structure of the CODO ontology see [1]. We evolved what started as a small ontology

© Springer Nature Switzerland AG 2021
B. Villazón-Terrazas et al. (Eds.): KGSWC 2021, CCIS 1459, pp. 153–168, 2021.
https://doi.org/10.1007/978-3-030-91305-2_12

in Protégé to a large knowledge graph (KG) in the AllegroGraph triplestore product from Franz Inc[1]. We use the term *ontology* to refer to the CODO Web Ontology Language (OWL) model with only basic example test data. We use the term *knowledge graph* to refer to the ontology populated with large amounts of real-world data.

1.1   Relation to Other Work

There has been extensive work in the Semantic Web community to add value to the vast amount of data produced by the pandemic. The existing Covid-19 ontologies can broadly be classified into three categories:

1. High level statistics that illustrate the number of patients infected and the number of deaths per region for various time intervals.
2. Modeling of concepts required to analyze the virus in order to develop treatments and vaccines. This includes modeling the Covid-19 virus and how it is similar and different from related viruses such as SARS and modeling drugs used to treat and develop vaccines for viruses and other illnesses similar to Covid-19.
3. Modeling the space of scientific articles on topics related to Covid-19 in order to provide semantic search capabilities for researchers developing treatments and vaccines.

Examples of the first category include the Johns Hopkins [2] and NYTimes [3] knowledge graphs. Examples of the second category include CIDO [4], IDO-COVID-19[2], COVID-19 Surveillance Ontology[3], and CoVoc[4]. These ontologies all extend the Infectious Disease Ontology (IDO) [5]. Examples of the third category include the Covid-19 Knowledge Graph [6].

   CODO fills a specific niche that is different from these categories. It focuses on modeling epidemiology and the various ways that the virus has spread throughout the population, with a case study of India. For example, the demographics of the patients who were infected by the virus (age, sex, family and social relations, geographic home, travel history) and contact tracing from one patient to another. The graphical features of the AllegroGraph Gruff tool are especially useful for this type of analysis. Information such as the graph of which patient infected which other patients can be generated automatically with Gruff (see Figs. 6 and 7 below). Information that is implicit in the data but difficult to understand without a knowledge graph model can be made explicit and obvious with a knowledge graph and visualization tools. This allows medical professionals to conduct contact tracing and perform epidemiological research. Although, the focus of the current work has been on the pandemic in India, CODO can be applied to any location and indeed to the spread of any infectious disease.

---

[1] http://www.allegrograph.com.
[2] https://bioportal.bioontology.org/ontologies/IDO-COVID-19.
[3] https://bioportal.bioontology.org/ontologies/COVID19.
[4] https://www.ebi.ac.uk/ols/ontologies/covoc.

In addition, the CODO team has been taking part in a harmonization process with many of the designers of the ontologies described above [7]. As part of the harmonization process, we have altered the design of the ontology to be more consistent with and more easily integrate with other ontologies that deal with different aspects of the Covid-19 pandemic such as the CIDO ontology.

The main contributions of this paper are:

1. Details the CODO Agile knowledge graph development processes.
2. Describes the issues related to the real world COVID-19 data we incorporated and its transformation to a knowledge graph.
3. Demonstrates some of the visualization capabilities provided by the CODO knowledge graph.

The rest of the paper is organized as follows: Sect. 2 discusses the CODO ontology design process and its lifecycle. Section 3 discusses the five phases of CODO KG development activity. The issues related to the pandemic data and their transformations to the graph are discussed in Sect. 4. Section 5 provides example results. Finally, Sect. 6 concludes with the future plans to enhance CODO and to harmonize it with other ontologies designed for the pandemic, especially those in the OBO foundry.

2   CODO Processing Lifecycle

Our development process was a hybrid of two different methods. We utilized the YAMO process for ontology development [8] and Agile Methods [9] to drive our iterations and overall approach to analysis, design, implementation, and testing. These two are complimentary, they address different aspects of the development process. YAMO addresses the specific details of how to design an ontology rather than say an Object Oriented Programming (OOP) or transactional database system. Agile Methods defines the approach to development issues that apply to all software development processes such as length of iterations and interaction between analysis, design, testing, and implementation. It is possible to practice the YAMO methodology in a Waterfall or Agile process. This is similar to the Rational Unified Process (RUP) which defines the design artifacts and processes to develop an OOP system. Although RUP is typically done in an iterative manner it can be used in a Waterfall manner as well [10].

We have created a hybrid approach that is well suited to knowledge graph development in general. The specific Agile methods that we applied were:

– Test Driven Development. We had test data from the very first ontology as well as various competency questions (stories in Agile terminology) that we used to practice test-driven development of the ontology. As we began to acquire more data it was clear that simply visually inspecting the ontology to validate it was inadequate. Hence, we developed SPARQL queries and Lisp functions[5] to facilitate the testing process.

- Rapid Iterations. Our iterations were approximately on a weekly basis. To present the path of our development we have abstracted these iterations into monthly phases where we describe the major development done in each phase.
- Refactoring. Our goal was to deliver technology that could be usable from the very beginning. However, as we scaled up the ontology to support larger data, we needed to refactor the model and the transformations we used to transform tabular data into a knowledge graph. As an example of how we used refactoring of the model (as opposed to refactoring the transformations described below), in our initial model the diagnosis date and the date that the patient was released from the hospital were simply stored on the Patient class. When we decided to take advantage of the temporal reasoning in AllegroGraph we refactored these properties onto the Disease class and made Disease a subclass of the Event class which had the appropriate properties for temporal reasoning such as the start and end time of an Event. We used this information to generate visualizations and summary data such as the average length of hospitalization and temporal relations among patients graphed on a timeline.
- Bottom Up and Top-Down Design. A key concept of Agile is that design emerges over time rather than being set in stone at the end of an Analysis and Design phase as in the Waterfall model. We designed an initial ontology based on our best understanding of the problem and the existing data but refactored that design as we acquired more data and added new ways to utilize the data.
- Story driven development. The YAMO methodology is designed around competency questions that the model is meant to answer. These competency questions are essentially the same as stories in Agile development.

Figure 1 illustrates the complete life cycle as data goes from heterogeneous input formats to a knowledge graph. These processes consist of:

1. The Upload process
2. Data Transformation
3. Reasoning
4. Publication

The Upload process imports data into the initial version of the triplestore. The inputs to this process are various documents and the CODO ontology. The output of this process is an initial triplestore knowledge graph. An additional output of this process are suggested standards fed back to the user communities that recommend canonical formats to standardize future input data in order to make it more amenable to conversion into a knowledge graph. The Data Transformation process transforms text strings from the Upload process into objects and

---

[5] We utilized Lisp because our team was very small (2 people), and the lead developer had the most experience in Lisp and we wanted to work as rapidly as possible to meet the needs of the pandemic. In future versions we will re-implement the functions in Python.

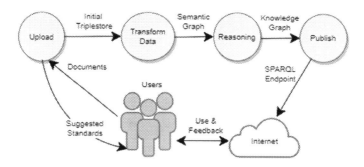

Fig. 1. CODO data processing life-cycle

property values. The boundary between the Upload and Transformation process is not rigid. It is possible to do a significant amount of conversion into objects and properties via the initial Upload process using tools such as Cellfie [11]. However, due to the varied nature of our input data we often required the power of a programming language and SPARQL to transform data over those available in tools designed for initial uploading. Thus, we would often simply transfer strings from columns directly to data properties (which we call *utility properties*) in the initial knowledge graph and then apply more sophisticated transformations to the graph that converted these data properties into objects and object properties. We deleted each utility property string after it had been transformed. The output of the transformation process is the initial semantic knowledge graph model.

The Reasoning process utilizes OWL and rule-based reasoners. This is required for reasoning about social and family relations as well as other kinds of relations. For example:

- Reasoning about inverse values. E.g., if a patient X is the father of patient Y then patient Y is the child of patient X.
- Reasoning about property hierarchies. E.g., if patient X is the father of patient Y then patient X is also the parent of patient Y.
- Reasoning about transitive place relations. E.g., if city X is contained in state Y and state Y is contained in nation Z then city X is contained in nation Z.
- SWRL (and later SPARQL) rules to cover reasoning that can't be done with OWL. E.g., if patient X is the brother of patient Y and patient Z is the daughter of patient Y then patient X is the uncle of patient Z.

For the early iterations of CODO this process consisted of running the Pellet reasoner which included execution of SWRL rules. For later iterations of CODO where Protégé could not support the large number of objects in the knowledge graph we utilized the AllegroGraph triplestore. In these later iterations we utilized the Materializer reasoner in AllegroGraph. In addition, since SWRL is currently not supported in AllegroGraph we replaced SWRL rules with equivalent SPARQL rules.

Finally, the publication process consists of making the knowledge graph available as a SPARQL endpoint. In addition, we publish and update the CODO ontology on Bioportal and the transformation rules and Lisp code on Github.

3   The CODO KG Development Phases

The CODO[6] project was divided into 5 phases, beginning with a basic ontology in Protégé with only a handful of test data to an AllegroGraph knowledge graph with over 3M triples.

3.1   Phase 1: Protégé Ontology

The initial phase consisted of defining the basic competency questions that we wanted the ontology to answer and building the initial ontology in the desktop version of the Protégé ontology editing tool [12]. Competency questions are a concept from YAMO [8]. Example competency questions are:

- What is the travel history of patient p (see Fig. 6)?
- What is the transitive closure for any patient p of all patients who infected and were infected by patient p (see Fig. 7)?
- Who are the people with any known relationship (family, co-workers, etc.) to patient p?
- What was the average length of time from infection to recovery for all patients or for patients in a given geographic area or time span?
- What are summary statistics for the incidents of infection, both globally and in different geographic areas and time periods?

This version of the ontology had no real data. However, as part of our test-driven approach we created representative individuals as example test data. Primarily patients but also test results, cities, etc. These individuals were used to validate the ontology. This version included rules in the Semantic Web Rule Language (SWRL) [13] to define concepts beyond basic OWL Description Logic such as Aunts and Uncles.

3.2   Phase 2: Cellfie and AllegroGraph

In phase 2 we began to use the Cellfie plugin for Protégé to load data from the Indian government about the pandemic. As we loaded our initial data it soon became clear that we required a true database to get acceptable performance. Protégé is a modeling tool and is not designed to accommodate large data sets. We chose the free version of the AllegroGraph triplestore from Franz Inc. As a result, we refactored our SWRL rules into SPARQL as SWRL is not currently supported by AllegroGraph.

---

[6] The details of the CODO project can be found at: https://github.com/biswanathdutta/CODO. The CODO ontology can be found at: https://bioportal.bioontology.org/ontologies/CODO.

We also began to use Web Protégé to store the CODO ontology. This made collaboration much easier. Prior to using Web Protégé we had issues with consistency between the various changes we each made to the ontology. Web Protégé eliminated these issues and also allowed further collaboration capabilities such as having threaded discussions about various entities stored with the ontology. However, there are also capabilities that are currently only supported in the desktop version of Protégé, most significantly the ability to run a reasoner to validate the model. Thus, at regular intervals we would download the ontology into the desktop version of Protégé to run the Pellet reasoner and make other changes not currently supported in Web Protégé.

3.3   Phase 3: SPARQL Transformations

In phase 3 we began to use SPARQL to transform the strings that were too complex for Cellfie to process. This is discussed in more detail in the next section.

3.4   Phase 4: Pattern Matching and LISP

Although we performed pattern matching in phase 3, the majority of our early SPARQL transformations were specific (ad hoc, discussed below). In phase 4 we eliminated most of these transformations with fewer pattern matching transformations in SPARQL and Lisp. In this phase we also wrapped all of our SPARQL transformations in Lisp code. This eliminated the tedious and potentially error filled task of manually running each SPARQL transformation in AllegroGraph's Gruff editor [14]. Instead, we could run Lisp functions which executed several SPARQL transformations automatically.

We also began to use Lisp to do more complex transformations that were too difficult to do in SPARQL such as iterating through a sequence of patient IDs. We created Lisp functions that utilized the regex extensions in Franz's version of Common Lisp and directly manipulated the knowledge graph.

3.5   Phase 5: Test Harness and Additional Refactoring of Transformations

One issue we identified when testing the transformations developed in the previous phase was that in some cases a general pattern matching transformation might make an inappropriate transformation to a string it wasn't designed to match. In order to facilitate testing we developed a test harness in Lisp. In testing mode when we deleted a utility property, we would copy it to another test utility property. Thus, we could still take advantage of our strategy of working from specific to more general transformations (see Fig. 4) which required deleting utility property values once they were processed but we could retain an audit trail so that we could inspect objects to ensure that the processed strings were appropriately transformed.

In addition, we further refactored our SPARQL and Lisp transformations to eliminate multiple specific transforms with individual pattern matching transforms. We also imported data on longitude and latitude for the various places (cities, states, nations, etc.) in the CODO ontology. A significant part of our data involves geographic information such as where patients were infected, where they live, travel, etc. We added various SPARQL queries that could provide statistical information and connectivity among patients which could be visualized via the Gruff graph layout tool. Finally, we took advantage of the temporal reasoning capabilities in AllegroGraph. Allegro has a temporal reasoning model based on the well-known Allen model for reasoning about time [15]. We added the required properties from the Allegro model to the CODO ontology so that we could take advantage of the capabilities in Gruff for displaying graphs along a timeline and could also use SPARQL queries to create additional summary data and visualizations about the spread of the pandemic over time.

4   Transforming Strings to Objects

The most difficult part of transforming data from documents, spreadsheets, and relational databases into a knowledge graph is transforming data represented by strings and tables into objects and property values [16]. This is because much of the information required for a useful knowledge graph is implicit in the context of a document. One of the main benefits added by a knowledge graph is to take this implicit context information that users apply when reading the document and make it explicit in the knowledge graph.

For example, one of the columns in the spreadsheets that we used as a data source had the heading *Reason*. This was meant to be the reason that the patient in that row contracted the virus. Examples of values were:

1. "Travel to Bangalore"
2. "Contact with P134-P135-P136-P137 and P138"
3. "Father"
4. "Policeman on duty"

The meaning for these strings is implicit but easy for humans to understand. Example 1 means that the patient travelled to Bangalore and caught the virus as a result of this trip (information about travel companions was captured in another column). Example 2 means that the patient had contact with a certain group of other patients and caught the virus from one of them. Example 3 means the patient caught the virus from their father (family relations were captured in another column). Example 4 means that the patient was a policeman on duty and caught the virus in the course of their duties. In the CODO ontology this kind of information results in creation of several different objects and property values. In addition to transforming strings in each column our transformations needed to integrate relevant information from other columns.

As an example of the kinds of transformations we developed, ExposureToCOVID-19 is a class with several sub-classes for the different kinds of potential exposures to the virus. Figure 2 shows a partially expanded view of the subclasses of this class in Protégé. For each string in the *Reason* column, we need to create an instance of the appropriate subclass of ExposureToCOVID-19 and then make that new individual the value of the suspectedReasonOfCatchingCovid-19 property for the patient. We also need to integrate information such as family relations and travel companions from other columns.

Relating back to the examples above, Example 1 should result in an instance of InfectedCo-Passenger. Example 2 should result in an instance of CloseContact. Example 3 should result in an instance of InfectedFather (a subclass of InfectedFamilyMember). Example 4 should result in an instance of InfectedViaPoliceWork.

In addition, depending on the specific instance, other objects or property values may need to get instantiated. For example, for the InfectedCo-Passenger class there is a property to define the place that was the travel destination, in this case the city Bangalore India. For strings such as Example 2 the contractedVirusFrom property on the Patient needs to have values for each Patient referenced in the string as a value. The difficulty with processing these types

Fig. 2. Exposure to Covid class hierarchy

of strings is that the input data does not adhere to standardized patterns. In some cases, someone may simply enter "Bangalore" in other cases "Travel to

Bangalore". Similarly, when the reason is contact with other patients there are many different patterns used to enter the data. Example 2 can also be entered as: "Contact with P134-P138", "Contact with P134, 135, 136, 137, and 138", "Contact with P134-138", and other formats.

While upload tools such as Cellfie can do simple pattern matching these more complex examples are difficult to process with upload tools. As a result, we utilized a two-step process for uploading and transforming data as illustrated in Fig. 1. During the Upload process we would where possible directly transform strings to data types or objects. However, where there were many patterns to the data, we would simply upload those strings into data properties we defined as *utility properties*. Then in the Transformation process we would use tools such as SPARQL and Lisp to perform more complex pattern matching on the strings uploaded into the utility data properties. The Lisp and SPARQL files can be found at [17].

Our process for transforming these types of strings illustrates our Agile development approach. To begin with when we had a small amount of sample data, we wrote specific SPARQL queries. We call these queries transformations because they don't just query the data but change it via INSERT and DELETE statements. To begin we had many SPARQL transformations in a text file which we would execute by hand via AllegroGraph's Gruff tool. These included transformations (which we call *ad hoc transformations*) that directly match for specific strings via WHERE clauses in SPARQL and then perform the appropriate creation of objects and property values via INSERT clauses.

Figure 3 shows an example of an ad hoc transformation. The FILTER statement exactly matches a specific string, and the INSERT statement adds the appropriate new triples. E.g., it creates a new instance of the CloseContact class shown in Fig. 2 and adds that to the suspectedReasonOfCatchingCovid-19 property for the patient. The DELETE statement removes the utility string value.

```
DELETE {?p codo:reasonString ?rs.}
INSERT {?nexp a codo:CloseContact.
        ?p codo:suspectedReasonOfCatchingCovid-19 ?nexp;
        codo:contractedVirusFrom ?pc1; codo:hasRelationship ?pc1;
        codo:contractedVirusFrom ?pc2; codo:hasRelationship ?pc2.}
WHERE {?p codo:reasonString ?rs; codo:statePatientID ?pid.
        ?pc1 codo:statePatientID "485". ?pc2 codo:statePatientID "483".
        BIND (IRI((CONCAT("http://www.isibang.ac.in/ns/codo#CloseContact-",
        ?pid))) AS ?nexp).
FILTER(?rs = "Contact of P485 and P483")}
```

Fig. 3. An Ad hoc SPARQL transformation

Of course this approach was not scalable. As a result, we defined a more scalable approach to transforming our data. That process was as follows:

1. Delete each utility data property value after it has been transformed (in Fig. 3 the reasonString property is a utility property).
2. Apply transformations in an order from the most specific transformations to more general transformations. See Fig. 4.

This process illustrated in Fig. 4 allowed us to write pattern matching transformations that were very general and would not correctly process certain unusual strings. These more specific strings were processed first by less general pattern matching transformations. After processing, the value for the processed utility property was deleted so that the more general pattern matching transformations could be applied without risk of error on the more unusual strings.

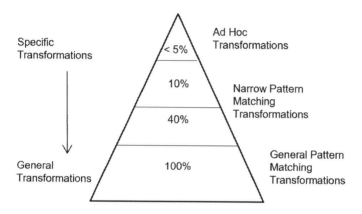

Specific Transformations

General Transformations

Ad Hoc Transformations

< 5%

10%

40%

100%

Narrow Pattern Matching Transformations

General Pattern Matching Transformations

Fig. 4. Specific to general transformation

Figure 5 shows a pseudo code fragment[7] from a Lisp function that does general pattern matching. This function matches strings such as: "Contact of P6135-6139". The function first executes a SPARQL query to find all the patients with a reasonString that matches the pattern. It then uses the Allegro CL function *match-re* to extract the sub-string required for the transformation (e.g., "6135-6139"). It then uses the function *split-re* to extract the two patient ID strings, in this case "6135" and "6139". It then converts these strings to integers and loops from the first to last integer. Within the loop it performs the appropriate manipulation of the knowledge graph. This requires converting each integer back into a string and performing a lookup of the Patient object that matches the ID. Finally, it calls the function make-close-contact-object which does the equivalent of the part of the SPARQL transformation in Fig. 3 to create an instance of the CloseContact class and fill in appropriate property values. The make-close-contact-object function also deletes the utility property value. If the system is running in test mode it saves a copy of the value on a testing utility property.

---

[7] See [17] for the actual Lisp and SPARQL code for this and all transformations.

```
results = run-sparql("SELECT ?p ?rs WHERE {?p codo:reasonString ?rs.
FILTER(REGEX(?rs, 'Contact of P\\\d+-\\\d+'))}")
    for result in results do
        patient = first(result)
        rs = second(result)
        patient-ids = match-re("\\d+-\\d+", rs)
    first-and-last-list = split-re("-", patient-ids)
    first-id-num = integer(first(first-and-last-list))
    last-id-num = integer(second(first-and-last-list))
    for id-index from first-id-num to last-id-num do
        contact-patient = freetext-get-unique-subject(string(id-index))
        add-triple(patient, codo:contractedVirusFrom, contact-patient)
        make-close-contact-object(patient, contact-patient)
```

Fig. 5. Pseudo code fragment for a general pattern matching lisp function

The most general pattern matching function for these types of contact strings (a transformation at the bottom of Fig. 4) simply uses the Allegro CL function: *(split-re "\\D+" rs)* where *rs* is bound to the reasonString to extract all the numeric substrings in the string. This function needs to be run after other functions that match patterns for locations, relatives, etc. since those strings may have numbers in them that are not related to patient ID's. It also needs to run after transformations that have patterns such as "P6135-6139" since it only finds each individual numeric string and would not correctly process the iteration implied in those types of strings. When run at the appropriate time, after the more specific strings have been removed this general pattern matching function processes a great deal of the strings that were previously handled by several more specific transformations. This is an example of how refactoring can help us build a knowledge graph capable of handling increasing amounts of data.

5   Results

The CODO knowledge graph has over 71 thousand patients and approximately 5M triples after running the Materializer reasoner. We implemented 100% of the initial competency questions defined in the original phase of the project via SPARQL queries. These queries can be found at [17]. In addition, we found countless opportunities for providing new ways to visualize the data once it is in one integrated graph format. Just three of these are shown in Figs. 6 and 7 below. These visualizations come from simple SPARQL queries. Typically, (as in these figures) we use Gruff to automatically transform the results of the SPARQL query into a visualization. We have also imported the output of SPARQL queries into Excel to create pie and other charts.

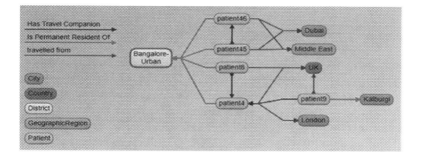

Fig. 6. Visualization of geographic and travel data

5.1   Evaluation of CODO

The most significant failure of the team to follow an Agile process is that as much as we tried, it was very difficult to find medical professionals to define requirements and to utilize the ontology and give us feedback. The reason is analogous to the classic Knowledge Acquisition Bottleneck problem. Healthcare professionals in India were so overwhelmed with simply dealing with the pandemic that they were unable to participate in research. As part of the Covid harmonization process [7], Dr. Sivaram Arabandi MD reviewed the ontology. CODO was also used as a test ontology for the OOPS! Ontology evaluation tool [18]. Design changes were made as a result of both these reviews. We hope that future versions of CODO will be utilized and evaluated by more healthcare professionals as their time is freed from the crisis of the pandemic.

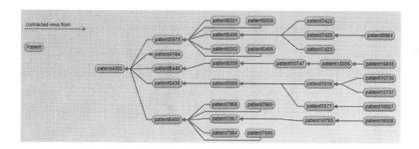

Fig. 7. Visualization of infection paths among patients in the CODO knowledge graph

5.2   Privacy Issues

Although the data in CODO was anonymous, legislation such as the US Health Insurance and Portability Act (HIPAA) and the European Union's Regulation 2016/679 may make utilization of CODO for functions such as contact tracing problematic. However, as [19] points out, Google and Apple have released voluntary contact tracing apps and nations such as Singapore and Ireland have had success in the voluntary usage of these apps by patients and consumers.

6 Conclusions

Most current ontology design methods (e.g., [20,21], the models surveyed in [22]) emphasize an approach that is essentially a Waterfall model where all the emphasis is on designing the model (essentially the T-Box). For example, in the evaluation of the productivity of upper models in [23] the evaluation criteria were focused only on the model with no consideration of the model's ability to incorporate and provide value to actual data. These approaches have the same problems for designing ontologies as the waterfall model in general has shown for most software development projects [9]. The emphasis on getting a "perfect" design the first time is doomed to failure. This insight goes back to Boehm's spiral model [24]. What might be a correct ontology in terms of the actual domain may turn out to be difficult to use because of issues with existing data or other non-functional requirements. In the real-world good software design comes both from the bottom up (from constraints imposed by legacy data, business processes, etc.) as from the top down (by analysis of the problem domain). Our experience with CODO, where only two developers developed a large knowledge graph in a few months, is evidence that the Agile approach provides the same benefits for the design of knowledge graphs as it has demonstrated for many other types of software systems [25]. In addition, our experience demonstrates principles that apply to real-world knowledge graph development in general:

- Use of pattern matching transformations. In transforming from "strings to things" [16] the basic capabilities of upload tools may not be sufficient and may require transformations that utilize features such as iteration in programming languages.
- Transforming from specific to general. In developing transformations, the most productive strategy is to begin with the most specific types of patterns and then use more general transformations after ensuring that outliers that would be incorrectly processed by the general transformations have been processed and removed.

In the future we plan to investigate the use of ML and NLP for these transformations.

Acknowledgement. This work has been supported by Indian Statistical Institute, Kolkata. This work was conducted using the Protégé resource, which is supported by grant GM10331601 from the National Institute of General Medical Sciences of the United States National Institutes of Health. Thanks to Franz Inc. (http://www.allegrograph.com) for their help with AllegroGraph and Gruff. Thanks to Dr. Sivaram Arabandi, MD for his feedback on the CODO ontology.

References

1. Dutta, B., DeBellis, M.: CODO: an ontology for collection and analysis of COVID-19 data. In: Proceedings of the 12th International Joint Conference on Knowledge Discovery, Knowledge Engineering and Knowledge Management (2020)

2. Gardner, L.: Modeling the spreading risk of 2019-nCov (2020). https://systems. jhu.edu/research/public-health/ncov-model-2/

3. Sirin, E.: Analyzing COVID-19 data with SPARQL (2020). https://www.stardog. com/labs/blog/analyzing-covid-19-data-with-sparql/

4. He, Y., et al.: CIDO, a community-based ontology for coronavirus disease knowledge and data integration, sharing, and analysis. Sci. Data **7**(1), 1–5 (2020)

5. Cowell, L.G., Smith, B.: Infectious disease ontology. In: Sintchenko, V. (ed.) Infectious Disease Informatics, pp. 373–395. Springer, New York (2010). https://doi. org/10.1007/978-1-4419-1327-2_19

6. Domingo-Fernández, D., et al.: COVID-19 knowledge graph: a computable, multimodal, cause-and-effect knowledge model of COVID-19 pathophysiology. Bioinformatics **37**(9), 1332–1334 (2021)

7. Lin, A., et al.: A community effort for COVID-19 ontology harmonization. In: The 12th International Conference on Biomedical Ontologies (2021)

8. Dutta, B., Chatterjee, U., Madalli, D.P.: YAMO: yet another methodology for large-scale faceted ontology construction. J. Knowl. Manag. **19**(1), 6–24 (2015)

9. Beck, K.: Extreme Programming Explained: Embrace Change. Addison-Wesley Professional, Boston (2000)

10. Kroll, P., Kruchten, P.: The Rational Unified Process Made Easy: A Practitioner's Guide to the RUP: A Practitioner's Guide to the RUP. Addison-Wesley Professional, Boston (2003)

11. O'Connor, M.J., Halaschek-Wiener, C., Musen, M.A., et al.: Mapping master: a flexible approach for mapping spreadsheets to OWL. In: Patel-Schneider, F. (ed.) ISWC 2010. LNCS, vol. 6497, pp. 194–208. Springer, Heidelberg (2010). https:// doi.org/10.1007/978-3-642-17749-1_13

12. Musen, M.A.: The protégé project: a look back and a look forward. AI Matters **1**(4), 4–12 (2015)

13. SWRL: A semantic web rule language combining OWL and ruleML. W3C Member Submission 21 May 2004 (2016). Accessed Feb 2016

14. Aasman, J., Cheetham, K.: RDF browser for data discovery and visual query building. In: Proceedings of the Workshop on Visual Interfaces to the Social and Semantic Web (VISSW 2011), Co-located with ACM IUI, p. 53 (2011)

15. Aasman, J.: Unification of geospatial reasoning, temporal logic, & social network analysis in event-based systems. In: Proceedings of the Second International Conference on Distributed Event-Based Systems, pp. 139–145 (2008)

16. Singhal, A.: Introducing the knowledge graph: things, not strings. Official Google Blog **5**, 16 (2012)

17. Debellis, M.: Lisp and SPARQL files for CODO ontology (2020). https://github. com/mdebellis/CODO-Lisp

18. Chansanam, W., Suttipapa, K., Ahmad, A.R.: COVID-19 ontology evaluation. Int. J. Manag. (IJM) **11**(8), 47–57 (2020)

19. Kejriwal, M.: Knowledge graphs and COVID-19: opportunities, challenges, and implementation. Harv. Data Sci. Rev. (2020)

20. Arp, R., Smith, B., Spear, A.D.: Building Ontologies with Basic Formal Ontology. MIT Press, Cambridge (2015)

21. de Almeida Falbo, R.: SABiO: systematic approach for building ontologies. In: CEUR Workshop Proceedings, vol. 1301 (2014)

22. Garcia, A., et al.: Developing ontologies within decentralised settings. In: Chen, H., Wang, Y., Cheung, K.H. (eds.) Semantic e-Science. AOIS, vol. 11, pp. 99–139. Springer, Boston (2010). https://doi.org/10.1007/978-1-4419-5908-9_4

23. Keet, C.M., et al.: The use of foundational ontologies in ontology development: an empirical assessment. In: Antoniou, G. (ed.) ESWC 2011. LNCS, vol. 6643, pp. 321–335. Springer, Heidelberg (2011). https://doi.org/10.1007/978-3-642-21034-1_22
24. Boehm, B.W.: A spiral model of software development and enhancement. Computer **21**(5), 61–72 (1988)
25. Pallozzi, D.: The word that took the tech world by storm: returning to the roots of agile (2018). https://www.thoughtworks.com/en-in/perspectives/edition1-agile/article

Selecting Ontologies for Reuse: Case of Constructing Hotel Room Ontology

Ronald Ojino[1(✉)] , Luisa Mich[2] , and Nerey Mvungi[1]

[1] University of Dar es Salaam, Dar es Salaam, Tanzania
rojino@cuk.ac.ke
[2] University of Trento, Trento, Italy

Abstract. In line with the goal of promoting interoperability among applications, ontology reuse is an encouraged practice. Selecting appropriate ontologies for reuse when constructing a domain ontology is a critical activity. It calls for the use of formal methodologies and quality metrics in order to provide a comprehensive rationale for the selection process. This research employs NeOn methodological guidelines and CLeAR in selecting and assessing ontologies for reuse while building a domain-specific ontology, the Hotel Room Ontology. Results of the ontology selection and assessment exercise led to the selection of Hontology, DogOnt and SOSA/SSN. The integrated approach to ontology selection gives a justifiable basis for decisions made in identifying ontologies for reuse.

Keywords: Ontology selection · Ontology assessment · Ontology reuse

1 Introduction

Ontologies represent knowledge in a machine-interpretable way, and as such are an invaluable component of many knowledge-based applications [1]. They are currently adopted in a range of fields such as tourism, education, biomedicine and other domains for unification, enhancing experiences and easing data retrieval among other functions. In line with the goal of promoting interoperability among applications, ontology reuse is an encouraged practice, in particular to optimise the implementation of domain-specific ontologies. Ontology reuse is the task of taking some existing ontologies and manipulating them in some way in order to integrate different knowledge sources. Such integration has to be planned taking into account design requirements related to specific use cases [2]. It promotes data interoperability among multiple applications by providing a common semantic background for data interpretation. For instance when new datasets are linked to existing vocabularies e.g. Schema.org, the datasets become intelligible to online applications thereby promoting interoperability. Ontology reuse is therefore a recommended practice in a number of ontology development methodologies due to the significant gains it offers including reduction of costs, increasing interoperability of applications, speeding up development time, and elimination of redundancy.

© Springer Nature Switzerland AG 2021
B. Villazón-Terrazas et al. (Eds.): KGSWC 2021, CCIS 1459, pp. 169–181, 2021.
https://doi.org/10.1007/978-3-030-91305-2_13

There is a proliferation of ontologies online that knowledge engineers have to sift through when selecting appropriate ones to use. However, some of the existing ontologies are not of adequate quality due to a range of flaws [3]. Most developers use their intuition and experience when looking for ontologies to incorporate in their systems [4] while others disregard previous knowledge sources [5], thereby hampering interoperability efforts. This situation is exacerbated by the lack of consensus within the community on evaluation criteria for ontologies [6]. The result therefore is that ontology reuse across a range of projects is not a consolidated practice [7], leading to ambiguities and inconsistencies across various domains.

It is noteworthy that, ontology reuse is a non-trivial process that re-quires knowledge about available tools and methods supporting the process [8]. Moreover, comprehensive and high-quality ontologies are required to solve the problems involving semantic issues [9]. NeOn, a scenario-based methodology that addresses the definition and formalization of ontology [10] is one of the few ontology methodologies that supports ontology reuse. However, Campos et al.,[5] contend that it provides only generic guidelines for the search and selection of reusable knowledge resources. To fill this gap there is need to integrate NeOn methodology with other structured methods.

In our study we enriched the NeOn methodology with modified CLeAR (Conducting Literature Search for Artifact Reuse) by Campos et al., [5], in order to provide a comprehensive rationale for finding the most-fit-for use ontologies in constructing a domain-specific ontology. To illustrate the application of a structured method based on NeOn and CLeAR in assessing the suitability of ontologies for reuse, we describe the development of HoROnt, a Hotel Room Ontology.

The case study has shown that the application of the two methods can be used as a basis to support decisions made in selecting, comparing and assessing candidate ontologies for reuse; a key aspect lacking in many ontology development papers.

This paper is organized as follows: Sect. 2 provides an overview of previous works done in ontology assessment for reuse. Section 3 presents the methodology used to evaluate candidate ontologies. Section 4 reports on the results obtained during the ontology selection and evaluation exercise. Section 5 summarizes and concludes the paper.

2   Related Work

Reusing knowledge resources for constructing ontologies plays a key role in facilitating inclusion, expansion and eventual standardization in many software systems and web applications, and more recently in the web of things. Cota [11] states that the motivation to select any ontology for reuse is guided by standardization, popularity or cognitive analysis.

Some ontologies have been reused in a number of projects and tend to be quite popular; while there are others, which are reused without following any formal guidelines and therefore they end up striking blows to efforts being made towards promoting data and semantic interoperability. The current situation paints a grim picture where most ontologies created are rarely aligned or inspired by upper-level ontologies [6]. The cognitive analysis motivation for ontology reuse is intuitive and catches the concepts of a domain [11]; it thus results in cognitively relevant, linguistically relevant, small and hierarchical ontologies that follow best practices. We use the cognitive analysis approach in selecting ontologies for reuse due to the nature of our project.

Katsumi and Gruninger [2] state that reuse of ontology can be carried out as follows: (a) As-is i.e. without modifying it. (b) Through extraction which entails removing some original axioms (c) Via extension, i.e., adding new axioms to the ontology (d) Through combination, which is reuse by merging several ontologies.

Ultimately the choice of how to implement reuse of ontologies lies with the knowledge engineer who makes an informed decision based on his goals and options available.

Although most methodologies propose reusing existent ontologies, they do not quantify the suitability of these ontologies for a given system [4]. Ontology development methodologies such as NeOn and the System Approach for Building Ontologies (SABiO) support reuse of knowledge resources to speed up the ontology development process. These methodologies propose activities for the identification and integration of knowledge resources but do not show how to perform the search and record the search results [5]. This therefore calls for complementing of such methodologies with other guidelines that would make the processes more comprehensive.

Ontology development guidelines such as the ones by Chaves and Trojahn [12], and Noy and McGuinness [13] mention ontology reuse as one of the steps in ontology construction but do not stipulate how the process is to be achieved. They therefore leave it upon the knowledge engineer to decide on how to approach the reuse step.

Ontology Design Patterns (ODPs) capture common modeling problems, help facilitate ontology development and avoid common mistakes [14] by providing successful reusable solutions to recurrent modeling problems. They ensure that modules tackling specific requirements are clearly and formally defined in a dedicated ontology, and have been explicitly designed for reuse [11]. We can explore the use of ODPs in candidate ontologies programmatically and then base the selection either on entire ontologies or particular modules. In spite of the availability of ODPs, representation incompatibilities between ontologies [15], lack of relevant patterns, unavailability of a pattern discovery service, and hidden patterns in upper level ontologies [16] hamper reuse.

There exist methods that complement ontology development methodology processes such as selection, assessment and comparison. For instance, CLeAR, is a systematic approach to find and select reusable knowledge resources for building ontologies with the purpose of scientific research data integration [5]. CLeAR proposes the evaluation of reusable knowledge resources based on objective quality attributes, which can lead to justification of choices made during ontology reuse.

The FAIR principles by Wilkinson et al., [17] defined as a guide for enhancing scientific data management and stewardship; can be applied to ontologies to make them: (a) Findable (b) Accessible (c) Interoperable (d) Reusable. However Poveda-Villalón et al., [18] suggest that for FAIR principles to be adopted by the Ontology Engineering community, some considerations must be made including: (a) Whether mechanisms and authorities should be established to coin persistent identifiers (PIDs) for ontologies to make them findable. (b) If PIDs should refer to ontologies as a whole or also to each of their components. (c) The minimum set of metadata that semantic artefacts should have etc.

Focusing on the hotel domain, there exist few hotel ontologies and all the ones we studied reused knowledge resources. For instance, RoomFort ontology was constructed using the NeOn methodology, and it reused Acco, DogOnt, SAREF and IFC ontologies [19]. Hontology[1] was developed using the seven phases of ontology development described by Chaves and Trojahn [12] and it reused the QALL-ME ontology, DBPedia.org and Schema.org vocabularies [20]. All the studied hotel domain ontologies did not follow comprehensive methods and metrics in selecting knowledge resources for reuse. The availability of a few ontologies in the hotel domain creates a window of opportunity for creating domain ontology such as HoROnt, which uses formal methodologies and guidelines in selecting ontologies for reuse.

3   Methods

The development of a domain-specific ontology as HoROnt requires that it is grounded in authoritative ontologies which would increase its acceptance and use in the ontology community.

We selected NeOn methodology of ontology development for the achievement of the goals of our project, as it is one of the few rigorous methodologies that offers guidelines for the search and selection of reusable knowledge resources. It was combined with CLeAR to provide a systematic way of carrying out the search activities outlined in NeOn. This is because finding an appropriate ontology is one of the challenges that lead to low reuse of knowledge resources [21]. While developing HoROnt, we combined two scenarios of the NeOn methodology, namely, Scenario 1 (from specification to implementation) and Scenario 3 (reuse of ontological resources). NeOn methodology divides the ontology reuse phase into steps, which have been modified to include some guidelines from CLeAR as follows:

1. Ontology search: It involves identifying a set of ontologies that best match the requirements specification from a collection of ontologies. Incorporating CLeAR guidelines, the step is further subdivided into:
   - Selection of keywords to compose the search string.
   - Selection of search engines and online repositories.

---

[1] https://portulanclarin.net/repository/browse/hontology/a83c9d04cb7a11e1a404080 027e73ea2359e10ea62b940109aabe03684aa5ea4.

- Definition of inclusion and exclusion criteria.
- Definition of structured resources identification procedure.
2. Ontology assessment: We inspected the content and granularity of the ontological resources sought in order to check if they satisfy the needs of the proposed ontology.
3. Ontology comparison: We measure the differences and similarities against identified set of criteria in the specification requirements. Ontology comparison in terms of *reuse cost, understandability effort, integration effort* and *reliability* is carried out on candidate ontologies.
4. Ontology selection: Based on the assessment and comparison done, ontologies are selected for re-use in our project.

4 Results and Discussion

4.1 Ontology Search

In order to achieve better selection results, we pre-processed the do-main name 'hotel room' and expanded it into a set of terms that best represent the domain. Other terms were also gotten from the hotel room ontology competency questions (CQs) presented in Ojino [22]. The terms yielded from the process included: "guest", "hotel", "hotel room", "sleeping", "bedroom", "context", "sleeping room" etc.

We selected Google Scholar as the search engine of choice to find reference papers as it hosts a large variety of scientific papers. Popular ontology search engines and libraries selected for the retrieval of ontologies included: *OntoHub, Schema.org, DBpedia.org, Swoggle, FalconS* and*Linked Open Vocabularies*. As a strategy, we begun by retrieving publications from online repositories using keywords such as *"hotel room ontology, "hotel reference model"*etc. Such a strategy reduces bias and increases the scope of the search [5]. To enhance the quality of the search, we also checked knowledge imported by the retrieved ontologies including cited ontologies.

The inclusion criteria for the candidate ontologies and publications were defined as follows: (a) The ontology and publications should address the hotel room domain or its aspects. (b) The publications must be available in English.

The exclusion criterion was that candidate ontologies and publications whose content is not fully available online must be excluded.

As part of defining the structured resource identification procedure, we began by searching for publications in Google Scholar in October 2020 and the process yielded 87 publications. After applying the exclusion and inclusion criteria, 27 publications were selected. It is important to note that on reading the papers, some of the relevant referenced articles were also sought and included in the results.

Ontologies were directly obtained from the ontology libraries and search engines. We realized that a range of issues existed in some of the ontology libraries and search engines including: (a) Popular ontology search engines in literature e.g., FalconS[2] and Swoogle[3] are unavailable online. (b) OntoHub listed a range of ontologies some of which lacked unique names while a number of ontologies are not categorized. The repository could be improved if the issues noted are addressed. (c) Schema.org gives a listing of different resources in a hierarchy and as properties. The representation of the results would have been better if categorized as classes, object properties etc. for ease of use.

The ontologies mentioned in the publications were identified and recorded. We then checked the abstract section of the publications in order to get more information about the ontologies. The ontologies were then analyzed by applying the inclusion and exclusion criteria. Of the 11 ontologies retrieved after applying the inclusion and exclusion criteria, 9 were selected. *RoomFort* and *SmartEnv* ontologies were excluded from the study, as they were unavailable online. The ontologies selected for the study include: *Acco*[4], *BOT (Building Topology Ontology)*[5], CODAMOS (Context-Driven Adaptation of Mobile Services)[6] , DogOnt[7], Hontology, SAREF (Smart Appliances REFerence)[8], SAREF4BLDG[9], SOSA/SSN[10] and *SSNx*[11] (see Table 1).

4.2   Ontology Assessment

At this phase of the NeOn methodology, we inspected the content and granularity of the selected ontological resources in order to check if they satisfy both functional and non-functional needs of HoROnt. As input, we used the 9 ontologies obtained during the ontology search and checked whether a set of criteria are met.

From the ontology assessment exercise done, 7 ontologies *(ACCO, BOT, CODAMOS, DogOnt, Hontology, SAREF4BLDG, and SOSA/SSN)* were found to be suitable as they partially or totally satisfied the ontology requirements specification. The scope of SAREF was found to be broad and thus its extension SAREF4BLDG would be better placed for reuse as it models the building device concepts in a better way. SSNx ontology was dropped due to its complexity and vocabulary inconsistencies [23] that have been fixed in SOSA/SSN.

---

[2] http://ws.nju.edu.cn/falcons
[3] http://swoogle.umbc.edu
[4] http://ontologies.sti-innsbruck.at/acco/ns.html
[5] https://w3c-lbd-cg.github.io/bot
[6] https://distrinet.cs.kuleuven.be/projects/CoDAMoS
[7] http://iot-ontologies.github.io/dogont
[8] https://saref.etsi.org/
[9] https://saref.etsi.org/saref4bldg/v1.1.2
[10] http://www.w3.org/ns/sosa
[11] http://www.w3.org/ns/ssn

Table 1. Candidate ontologies

Name	Description	Key concepts	Ontologies reused
ACCO	An extension of GoodRelations providing additional vocabulary for describing hotel and other accommodation rooms.	Accommodation Feature, Bed details, Brand, Delivery method, Price specification, Warranty scope, Offering	GoodRelations
BOT	Defines reoccurring design patterns in domain ontologies for Architecture, Engineering, Construction and Facility Management.	Building, Storey, Space Zone, Element, Interface, Site	DogOnt, BRICK, DEDIROOMS, DUL, ThinkHome, IFCOwl, SAREF4Bldg
CODAMOS	An adaptable and extensible context ontology for creating context-aware computing infrastructures.	User, Platform, Service, Environment	-
DOGONT	Designed to tackle interoperability issues in home automation networks. DogOnt empowers projects needing semantic access to environment sensors and actuators.	Building Environment, Building Thing, Domotic Network component, Functionality, State	DomoML
HONTOLOGY	A multi-lingual ontology for the hotel domain. Helps travellers to find accommodation.	Accommodation, Facility, Room, Service/ Staff and Guest type	QALL-Me, DBpedia.org, Schema.org
SAREF	It is a reference ontology representing smart appliances focusing on smart home. It mainly focuses on the concept of a device.	Command, Commodity, Device, Feature of Interest, Function, Measurement, Profile, Property, Service, State, Task, Unit of Measurement	SSN, OMA Lightweight M2M, PowerOnt, UPnP, Z-Wave, ECHONET, FAN
SAREF4BLDG	A SAREF extension based on the Industry Foundation Classes standard. It is limited to devices and appliances within the building domain.	Spatial Thing, Building, Measurement, Building Device, Distribution Device, Distribution, Control Device, Distribution Flow Device	SAREF
SOSA/SSN	It extends SSNx and supports household infrastructures and allow humans and animals to act as agents.	Sensor, Observation, Sample, Actuator, Sampling and Actuations	SSNx
SSN	Initial Semantic Sensor Network ontology; proposes a schema for describing sensors, observations and methods of observation.	Sensors, Sensing, Sensor measurement capabilities, Observations and Deployments	Dolce Ultralite ontology (DUL)

4.3   Ontology Comparison

Ontology comparison is an important step as it will determine the quality of the proposed ontology. Using NeOn, the ontology developer measures the differences and similarities against the identified set of criteria in the specification requirements. Ontology comparison in terms of *reuse cost, understandability effort, integration effort* and *reliability* is carried out on ACCO, BOT, CODAMOS, DogOnt and SAREF4BLDG ontologies. According to the results of the comparison, we chose the ontologies satisfying more requirements as this would help in develop HoROnt with minimal cost and effort.

We adopt the following quality attributes that can be objectively evaluated:

1. **Reuse Economic Cost:** This is the estimate of the cost needed for accessing and using the candidate ontologies. We determine the reuse economic cost based on the type of license utilized. Ontology licenses determine the permissions that surround an ontology. ACCO, Hontology and SAREF4BLDG use creative commons licenses, DogOnt uses Apache 2.0 license, BOT uses W3C community contributor license and SOSA/SSN uses W3 software license. CODAMoS is the only ontology that lacks a license; a factor that may hamper its reuse. The rest of the ontologies have open licenses that encourage reuse making it possible to utilize the ontologies without having to submit payments or following up other legal requirements.

2. **Understandability Effort:** We compared the candidate ontologies understandability effort in terms of quality of the documentation, whether the candidate ontology has references to external knowledge sources and if experts are easily available. The results in Table 2 shows that DogOnt requires the least effort to understand as it has all resources available online for anyone who intends to reuse it. CODAMOS and Hontology lack user guides and glossaries making them require more effort to understand. Lack of documentation makes it difficult to locate and understand an ontology [11]. All resources that make it easy to understand an ontology must be availed to increase reuse.

Table 2. Understandability effort required to reuse candidate ontologies

Understandability effort						
Candidate Ontology	Overview	User guide	Glossary	Documentation on ontology metadata	Reference to external knowledge source	Expert availability
ACCO	X	-	X	X	X	X
BOT	X	-	X	X	X	X
CODAMOS	X	-	-	X	X	
DOGONT	X	X	X	X	X	X
HONTOLOGY	X	-	-	X	X	X
SAREF4BLDG	X	-	X	X	X	X
SOSA/SSN	X	-	X	X	X	X

3. **Integration Effort:** For the integration effort required in reusing the candidate ontologies, we checked the adequacy of the naming convention and implementation language. The axiomization of ontology in a standard language such as OWL with open implementations of translators between these languages has gone a long way to making ontologies interoperable [6]. The results in Table 3 show that all the candidate ontologies are available in OWL, a broadly applicable language for knowledge representation, which enhances their semantic interoperability and reuse. However reusing DogOnt may require more integration effort as it does not use a standard modelling

notation. Furthermore the CamelCase notation utilized across 6 of the ontologies can easily unify reused ontology resources [24] thereby reducing the effort required in developing HoROnt.

Table 3. Integration effort required to reuse the candidate ontologies

Integration effort		
Candidate ontology	Implementation language	Notation
ACCO	OWL, RDF	Camelcase
BOT	OWL-DL, Turtle and RDF	Camelcase
CODAMOS	OWL	Camelcase
DOGONT	OWL2, RDF	Not defined
HONTOLOGY	OWL, RDF	Camelcase
SAREF4BLDG	OWL DL, RDF	Camelcase
SOSA/SSN	OWL, RDF	Camelcase

4. **Ontology Reliability:** We checked the candidate ontologies' reliability based on development team reputation, purpose reliability and practical support. Table 4 shows that all the 6 ontologies have been used in real world projects and were not just built as academic examples. SOSA/SSN and DogOnt have been reused in many ontologies and projects, demonstrating the high quality of knowledge they possess [25] in comparison to the rest. Reliable ontologies are well established; meaning their terms and content have been reused in projects without failure in turn promoting their common usage by the ontology community.

5. **Domain Aspect Coverage:** We also grouped some the key terms in the glossary derived from the CQs using a bottom-up approach to determine the key domain aspects coverage in the hotel room domain (see Table 5) by the candidate ontologies. We performed domain analysis using a matrix such as the one presented in CLeAR as it is quite comprehensive. Based on the results in Table 5, Hontology covers most of the aspects in the hotel room domain followed by SOSA/SSN and DogOnt and so demonstrate their appropriateness for reuse in building HoROnt. ACCO and BOT cover the least domain aspects.

4.4   Ontology Selection

Ontology selection is done based on a comprehensive evaluation process discussed in ontology assessment and comparison.

From the ontology assessment and comparison activities, we selected DogOnt, Hontology, and SOSA/SSN. Hontology was selected because of its ability to represent hotel room concepts with a high level of detail, effectively showing its

Table 4. Reliability of the candidate ontologies

Ontology reliability

Candidate ontology	Development team	Some ontologies utilizing candidate ontology	Sample projects where the candidate ontology has been reused
ACCO	STI Innsbruck (Fensel, Martin)	RoomFort	Tourpedia[a]
BOT	Linked Building Data Community Group	Building Automation and Control System Ontology (BACS)	AECOO[b] (Architecture, Engineering, Construction, Owner, Operator) application plugins
CODAMOS	IMEC-Distrinet Research Group, KU Leuven (Preuveneers, Van den Bergh, Wagelaar, Georges, and De Bosschere)	A context ontology for mobile environments, and mIO ontology network	Digital Environment Home Energy Management System (DEHEMS[c])
DOGONT	Politecnico di Torino (Bonino and Corno)	RoomFort, BOT, SmartHome, Energy Efficiency Ontology, PowerOnt, Thinkhome, SAREF	DEHEMS, EGNIAS and VICINITY[d]
HONTOLOGY	Universidade Atlântica - Fábrica da Pólvora de Barcarena (Chaves, de Freitas, and Vieira)	Touringology	Tourpedia
SAREF4BLDG	European Telecommunications Standards Institute	SAREF4INMA	VICINITY
SOSA/SSN	World Wide Web Consortium and Open Geospatial Consortium	Semantic SSN (S3N), SmartEnv, SEAS, The Vehicle Signal and Attribute (VSSo), BACS, BCI Ontology (BCI-O), LHR	VICINITY, EUREKA ITEA 12004 SEAS project[e], Weather Data publication in LOD[f]

[a] http://tour-pedia.org
[b] https://orbit.dtu.dk/en/publications/bot-the-building-topology-ontology-of-the-w3c-linked-building-dat
[c] http://www.dehems.org
[d] http://vicinity.iot.linkeddata.es
[e] https://itea4.org/project/seas.html
[f] https://www.davisinstruments.com/solution/vantage-pro2

maturity and closest fit to what is needed in the hotel room domain. Furthermore, it has practical support, is easy to integrate and has no cost implications.

SOSA/SSN was selected due to its suitability to model activities, environmental conditions and observations especially in the IoT environment; a key infrastructure for smart hotels. SOSA/SSN is highly reliable, having been used in a range of projects and ontologies.

Table 5. Domain coverage by candidate ontologies

Domain aspects coverage										
Candidate ontology	Activity	Environmental characteristics	Guest	Guest type	Observation	Room	Room spaces	Room type	Sensor	Service	View
ACCO		-	X	X	-	X	-	-	-	-	-
BOT	-	-	-	-	-	X	X	-	X	-	-
CODAMOS	X	X	X	-	-	-	-	-	-	X	-
DOGONT	-	X	-	-	X	X	X	-	X	-	-
HONTOLOGY	-	-	X	X	-	X	X	X	-	X	X
SAREF4BLDG					X	X	X		X		
SOSA/SSN	X	X	X		X	X			X		

DogOnt was used to complement Hontology by modelling other room elements not defined therein and due to its widespread re-use across many ontologies.

5   Conclusion

Ontology reuse though encouraged during development of knowledge resources is not often practiced due to the lack of proper methodology and tools. Reusing ontologies has benefits such as reduction of costs, increasing interoperability of applications, speeding up development time/effort, and elimination of redundancy. Our work has demonstrated how the potential of existing ontologies can be tapped by applying NeOn methodology, and CLeAR guidelines.

The case study has shown that the application of various methods can be used as a basis of justifying decisions made in selecting, comparing and assessing candidate ontologies for reuse; a key aspect lacking in many ontology development papers. Based on the study, we have selected reliable ontologies like DogOnt, Hontology, and SOSA/SSN for reuse in building HoROnt as they would increase its chances of being utilized in other projects.

The reuse of ontologies in the development of HoROnt will facilitate standardization of terminology used by various hotel information systems and the exploitation of resources for knowledge discovery and recommendations.

Our study provides a practical resource that can be utilized in promoting the reuse of knowledge resources in building ontologies.

In the next steps, we shall consider introducing changes to the selected ontologies due to their incompleteness or heterogeneity. This is due to the fact that existing ambiguities, heterogeneities and inconsistencies in the selected ontologies may affect HoROnt at different dimensions during the integration process. Furthermore, we shall also decide on the ODPs and concepts to reuse from the selected ontologies or whether we shall reuse the ontologies as-is.

References

1. Schindler, S., Keil, J.M.: Building ontologies for reuse. In: 2nd International Workshop on Bad Or Good Ontology (2019)

2. Katsumi, M., Grüninger, M.: What is ontology reuse? In: FOIS, pp. 9–22 (2016). https://doi.org/10.3233/978-1-6149-660-6-9
3. Guarino, N., Welty, C.A.: An overview of ontoclean. In: Staab, S., Studer, R. (eds) Handbook on Ontologies. International Handbooks on Information Systems. Springer, Berlin (2004)
4. Lozano-Tello, A., Gómez-Pérez, A., Sosa, E.: Selection of ontologies for the semantic web. In: Lovelle, J.M.C., Rodríguez, B.M.G., Gayo, J.E.L., del Puerto Paule Ruiz, M., Aguilar, L.J. (eds.) ICWE 2003. LNCS, vol. 2722, pp. 413–416. Springer, Heidelberg (2003). https://doi.org/10.1007/3-540-45068-8_77
5. Campos, P.M.: Finding reusable structured resources for the integration of environmental research data. Environmental Modelling Software **133**, 104813 (2020). https://doi.org/10.1016/j.envsoft.2020.104813
6. Ferrario, R., Grüninger, M.: Proposed guidelines for publishing ontology papers. Appl. Ontology **15**(1), 1–5 (2020). https://doi.org/10.3233/AO-200227
7. Fernández-López, M., Poveda-Villalón, M., Suárez-Figueroa, M.C., Gómez-Pérez, A.: Why are ontologies not reused across the same domain? J. Web Seman. **57**, 100492, (2019). https://doi.org/10.1016/j.websem.2018.12.010
8. Jarosław, W.: An attempt to knowledge conceptualization of methods and tools supporting ontology evaluation process. Proc. Comput. Sci. **126**, 2238–2247 (2018). https://doi.org/10.1016/j.procs.2018.07.225
9. Reginato, C., Salamon, J., Nogueira, G., Barcellos, M., Souza, V., Monteiro, M.: Go-for: a goal-oriented framework for ontology reuse. In: 2019 IEEE 20th International Conference on Information Reuse and Integration for Data Science (IRI), pp. 99–106. IEEE (2019). https://doi.org/10.1109/IRI.2019.00028
10. Suárez-Figueroa, M.C., Gómez-Pérez, A., Fernández-López, M.: The neon methodology for ontology engineering. In: Suárez-Figueroa, M.C., Gómez-Pérez, A., Motta, E., Gangemi, A. (eds.) Ontology Engineering in a Networked World, pp. 9–34. Springer, Heidelberg (2012). https://doi.org/10.1007/978-3-642-24794-1_2
11. Cota, G., et al.: The landscape of ontology reuse approaches. Appl. Practices Ontol. Des., Extraction, Reason. **49**, 21 (2020). https://doi.org/10.3332/SSW200033
12. Chaves, M., Trojahn, C.: Towards a multilingual ontology for ontology-driven content mining in social web sites. In: Proceedings of the ISWC 2010 Workshops, vol. I, 1st International Workshop (2010)
13. Noy, N.F., et al.: Ontology development 101: a guide to creating your first ontology (2001)
14. Mortensen, J.M., Horridge, M., Musen, M.A., Noy, N.F.: Applications of ontology design patterns in biomedical ontologies. In: AMIA Annual Symposium Proceedings, vol. 2012, p. 643. American Medical Informatics Association (2012)
15. Fillottrani, P.R., Keet, C.M.: Dimensions affecting representation styles in ontologies. In: Iberoamerican Knowledge Graphs and Semantic Web Conference, pp. 186–200. Springer, Cham (2019). https://doi.org/10.1007/978-3-030-21395-4_14
16. Blomqvist, E., Hitzler, P., Janowicz, K., Krisnadhi, A., Narock, T., Solanki, M.: Considerations regarding ontology design patterns. Seman. Web **7**(1), 1–7 (2016)
17. Wilkinson, M.D., et al.: The fair guiding principles for scientific data management and stewardship. Scientific data **3**(1), 1–9 (2016). https://doi.org/10.1038/sdata.2016.18
18. Poveda-Villalón, M., Espinoza-Arias, P., Garijo, D., Corcho, O.: Coming to terms with FAIR ontologies. In: Keet, C.M., Dumontier, M. (eds.) EKAW 2020. LNCS (LNAI), vol. 12387, pp. 255–270. Springer, Cham (2020). https://doi.org/10.1007/978-3-030-61244-3_18

19. Spoladore, D., Arlati, S., Carciotti, S., Nolich, M., Sacco, M.: Roomfort: an ontology-based comfort management application for hotels. Electronics **7**(12), 345 (2018). https://doi.org/10.3390/electronics7120345
20. Chaves, M., Freitas, L. Vieira, R.: Hontology: a multilingual ontology for the accommodation sector in the tourism industry (2012)
21. Tudorache, T.: Ontology engineering: current state, challenges, and future directions. Seman. Web **11**(1), 125–138 (2020). https://doi.org/10.3233/SW-190382
22. Ojino, R.O.: Towards an ontology for personalized hotel room recommendation: student research abstract. In: Proceedings of the 35th Annual ACM Symposium on Applied Computing, pp. 2060–2063. (2020). https://doi.org/10.1145/3341105.3374230
23. Haller, A. et al.: The modular SSN ontology: A joint w3c and OGC standard specifying the semantics of sensors, observations, sampling, and actuation. Seman. Web **10**(1), 9–32 (2019). https://doi.org/10.3233/SW-180320
24. Cuenca, J., Larrinaga, F., Curry, E.: A unified semantic ontology for energy management applications. In: WSP/WOMoCoE@ ISWC, pp. 86–97 (2017)
25. Missikoff, Michele, Navigli, Roberto, Velardi, Paola: The usable ontology: an environment for building and assessing a domain ontology. In: Horrocks, Ian, Hendler, James (eds.) ISWC 2002. LNCS, vol. 2342, pp. 39–53. Springer, Heidelberg (2002). https://doi.org/10.1007/3-540-48005-6_6

Fabula: Hybridized Weightage Based Book Recommendation System

Debajyoty Banik(✉), Utkarsh Dixit, Rudra Narayan Mishra,
Manoranjan Maharana, Ritesh Mishra, and Suresh Chandra Satapathy

KIIT University, Bhubaneswar, Odisha, India

Abstract. This paper is about an all in one approach for an industrial level implementation of a recommendation system by applying different recommendation approaches, studying and making a comparison with the state of the art and proper implementation which can be a prototype on an industrial level. In this paper we describe the usage of a hybrid weightage based recommender system focused on books and putting a model into the most used platform application. To make it available for the book readers by making an all in one approach to improvise the state of the art and resolve the cold start problem, making the user experience a major standard for the recommendations. The paper deals with the phases of Software Engineering from the analysis of the requirements, the actual making of the recommender model to deployment and testing of the Application at the user end.

1 Introduction

In recent times the recommendation has become a major point of interest for all social businesses like entertainment, movies, music, books, shopping etc. Not even that but the social feeds of a user on the social networking platforms like Facebook, Twitter, Linked In, Instagram and many others. In the industry, recommender systems are critical tools to enhance user experience and promote sales/services [4–6,8,11]. But the recommendations need a diverse outlook which has to be taken into consideration for a satisfactory experience of a user or to showcase all the available products related to a particular item in the market. Thus, being fruitful in promoting its value and becoming an easy and attractive place for a user to spend their time. As the new users are getting introduced in huge numbers to the social platforms thus increasing the variety of prospects and intentions among the user. But not all recommendation systems are implementable [15]. With our survey, we came to some basic conclusions for building a reliable recommender system. For our model, we decided to have an interactive application for users to receive more data regarding the users and putting our model on self-trained mode for reducing the error and familiarizing with the behaviour of a particular user. To implement, we went for the Collaborative and Content-Based filtering model as a basic backbone for user-user, user-item and item-item recommendations [7,18]. The available methods can be categorized as

B. Villazón-Terrazas et al. (Eds.): KGSWC 2021, CCIS 1459, pp. 182–196, 2021.
https://doi.org/10.1007/978-3-030-91305-2_14

Hypothetical (Proposed Discussed but theoretical with no practical Implementation) which are not generalized over a mass and the Industrially implemented which are not very accurate as most of them suffer from the cold start problem, few drawbacks; one of them being, it is based only on the explicit feedback given by the user in the form of a rating. The real needs of a user are also demonstrated by various implicit indicators such as views, read later lists, etc. [12] and models reached are very heavy in their attributes to be deployed as an actual application among general people. The majority of research in recommender systems is focused on improving recommendation algorithms, without a specific focus on user experience. In this paper we describe an effort to achieve its motive by putting a recommender system model into the actual application and to make it available for the book readers by making an all in one approach to improvise the state of the art and resolve the cold start problem, making the user experience a major standard for the recommendations.

1.1 Dataset

This dataset contains six million ratings for ten thousand, most popular (with most ratings) books. There are books marked to read by the user's book metadata (author, year, etc.) tags/shelves/genres. The datasets were collected in late 2017 from goodreads.com, where only users' public shelves were scraped, i.e. everyone can see it on the web without login. User IDs and review IDs were anonymous. These datasets are for academic use only [16,17]. booktags.csv contains tags/shelves/genres assigned by users to books. Tags in this file are represented by their IDs. They are sorted by goodreads_book_id ascending and count descending. books.csv has metadata for each book (good reads IDs, authors, title, average rating, etc.). The metadata has been extracted from good reads XML files, available in books_xml, as shown in Table 1. best_book_id is the most popular edition for a given work. Generally, it's the same as goodreads_book_id and differs occasionally.books_count is the number of editions for a given work. Each book may have many editions.Goodreads_book_id and best_book_id generally point to the most popular edition of a given book, while good reads work_id refers to the book in the abstract sense.Note that book_id in ratings.csv and to_read.csv maps to work_id, not to goodreads_book_id, meaning that ratings for different editions are aggregated.

Table 1. The books dataset containing all the details of the books.

id	Book_id	Best_book_id	Work_id	Books_count	Isbn	Isbn13	Authors	Original_publication_year
1	2767052	2767052	2792775	272	4.39E+08	9.78E+12	Suzanne Collins	2008
2	3	3	4640799	491	4.4E+08	9.78E+12	J.K. Rowling, Mary GrandPr	1997
4	2657	2657	3275794	487	61120081	9.78E+12	Harper Lee	1960
5	4671	4671	245494	1356	7.43E+08	9.78E+12	F. Scott Fitzgerald	1925

Original_title	Title	Language_code	Average_rating	Ratings_count
The Hunger Games	The Hunger Games	eng	4.34	4780653
Harry Potter and the Philosopher's Stone	Harry Potter and the Sorcerer's Stone	eng	4.44	4602479
To Kill a Mockingbird	To Kill a Mockingbird	eng	4.25	3198671
The Great Gatsby	The Great Gatsby	eng	3.89	2683664

Work_ratings_count	Work_text_reviews_count	Ratings_1	Ratings_2	Ratings_3	Ratings_4	Ratings_5
4942365	155254	66715	127936	560092	1481305	2706317
4800065	75867	75504	101676	455024	1156318	3011543
3340896	72586	60427	117415	446835	1001952	1714267
2773745	51992	86236	197621	606158	936012	947718
2478609	140739	47994	92723	327550	698471	1311871

2   Modern Recommendation

In recent years, many researchers have hypothesized, proposed and intended to implement some of their architectures. Over this period, some of these architectures have shown better results but it is not always better in every situation. As many are just ideas that were never implemented as a product. Thus we have compiled some state-of-the-art architectures and come up with our model which could be used in real-life scenarios being generalized to the major population and their perspectives.

2.1   Hypothetical Model

These are the models which are proposed as a concept but with no actual implementation at the users' end or the model not put to actual application. James Schaffer et al. (2016) proposed a model to evaluate the impact of different types of low-cost, exploratory manipulations on a preference profile for Collaborative Filtering (CF) recommender systems. The experiment tested one condition in which dynamic feedback on profile manipulations was provided, and one with no feedback [7]. Their data supported the following claims: (i) The presence of dynamic feedback elicits marginally more profile additions. (ii) The addition of new items to a profile reduces recommendation error, and when dynamic feedback is present, deletes become significantly more effective. (iii) Profile update tasks improve perceived accuracy and trust, regardless of any change in actual recommendation error. In this study, the interactive recommender system was presented to participants, and they were asked to add, delete or re-rate items in their profile. This step was done to gather various data regarding the behaviour of the users based on the interactive system. After gathering the data, a simple Collaborative Filtering (CF) model based on the K-nearest neighbours' algorithm was designed and trained to get top recommendations for those users. A simple recommendation algorithm was used, so the results were not so great but this proved all their claims regarding an interactive system for recommendations.

Table 2. This particular is a major dataset used for training.

0	Book_id	User_id	Rating
370571	3711	7	5
153478	1536	7	4
379138	3797	7	2
666661	6701	7	3
324203	3246	7	4

Table 3. This is a to-read dataset.

User_id	Book_id
1	112
1	235
1	533
1	1198
1	1874

2.2 Previously Implemented Models

A Hybrid Book Recommender System Based on Table of Contents (ToC) and association Rule Mining, proposes a concept of a hybrid book recommender system that recommends books by using a book table of contents (TOC) along with association rule mining and opinions of similar users [1]. They implemented this hybrid model by using CB and CF approaches. Their proposed system went through different phases namely: CF recommendation; CB recommendation that uses term frequency-inverse document frequency (TF-IDF) in dealing with book content; and association rule-mining that is combined with the scores obtained from CB and CF filtering. In the CB phase, To minimize problems related to CB filtering their system considered ratings provided by users' friends in the recommendation process. After identifying user preferences, the system then applies an adjusted cosine similarity [5] approach for finding other books in which a particular user might be interested.

The formula for adjusted cosine similarity is given in Eq. 1.

$$sin(x,y) = \frac{\sum s\epsilon S_{xy}(R_{xs} - R_x)(R_{ys} - R_y)}{\sqrt{\sum s\epsilon S_{xy}(R_{xs} - R_x)}\sqrt{\sum s\epsilon S_{xy}(R_{ys} - R_y)}}$$

In the CF phase, The features are represented either by using Boolean values representing the presence or absence of terms in the descriptions or by using an integer value such as term frequencies (TF) [3,19]. To find term weights and their relevance to document/documents, term frequency-inverse document frequency (TF-IDF) [7] is used that measures the importance of a term in a document concerning document collection or corpus. After finding the TF-IDF vectors, cosine similarity [7] is used to find similarity between books, which can be calculated using Eq. 2 that finds the cosine similarity between two books as given below:

$$Similarity(Book_a, Book_b) = \frac{DotProduct(Book_a, Book_b)}{||Book_a|| * ||Book_b||}$$

In the association rule mining phase, the aim is to discover such rules that satisfy user-specified minimum support and confidence score. Confidence indicates the number of times the if/then statements are true. While confidence of the association rule can be calculated by applying the formula as

$$Confidence(X \Rightarrow Y) = \frac{Support\ of(X \bigcup Y)}{Support(X)} * 100\%$$

When the rule fulfils the required criteria of minimum support and confidence value, it is considered useful for recommendation purpose [9]. In 2018, "Recommendation system for Netflix", the researchers proposed another state-of-art architecture that also revolved around hybridized approach of recommendation but the methods of implementations were different. According to the paper, the main types of recommenders. Algorithms are Popularity, Collaborative Filtering (CF), Content-based Filtering and Hybrid Approaches. For Model-based techniques, the SVD approach was executed. The user-item matrix defined here as X (before we named it V) can be expressed as a composition of U, S and V. Where U is representing the feature vectors corresponding to the users in the hidden feature space and V is representing the feature vectors corresponding to the items in the hidden feature space.

$$X_{n \times m} = U_{n \times r} \times S_{r \times r} \times V^{t}_{r \times m}$$

Before applying the content-based recommendations, they implemented a TF-IDF approach to the dataset. Consequently, for Memory-based, just Item-based CF will be implemented using similarity measures the cosine and Pearson correlation [1, 14, 19]. The Cosine Similarity (Eq. 2.1) computes the cosine of the angle between these two users' vectors.

$$cos(u_i, u_k) = \frac{\sum_{j=1}^{m} v_{ij} v_{kj}}{\sqrt{\sum_{j=1}^{m} v_{ij}^2 \sum_{j=1}^{m} v_{kj}^2}}$$

Pearson correlation (Eq. 2.2), which measures the strength of a linear association between two vectors.

$$S(i, k) = \frac{\sum_{j}(v_{ij} - \overline{v_i})(v_{kj} - \overline{v_k})}{\sqrt{\sum_{j}(v_{ij} - \overline{v_i})^2 \sum_{j}(v_{kj} - \overline{v_k})^2}}$$

From the above equation, S (i, k) calculates the similarity between two users ui and uk, where vij is the rating that the user ui gave to the movie pj, vi is the mean rating given by the user ui. With this similarity score, we can compare each user among the rest of n X 1 users. The higher the similarity between vectors, the higher the similarity between users. As a result, we obtain a symmetric matrix n x n with the similarity score of all the users, defined as similarity matrix S.

The higher the similarity between vectors, the higher the similarity between users. As a result, we obtain a symmetric matrix n x n with the similarity score of all the users, defined as similarity matrix S.

$$u_1 \quad u_2 \qquad u_i \qquad u_n$$

$$\begin{bmatrix} 1 & S(1,2) & \dots & S(1,i) & \dots & S(1,n) \\ & & & & & S(2,n) \\ & & \ddots & & & \\ & & & 1 & & \\ & & & & \ddots & \\ & \dots & & & \dots & 1 \end{bmatrix} \begin{matrix} u_1 \\ u_2 \\ \\ u_i \\ u_n \end{matrix}$$

Use of K-nearest neighbor concept of Item-based Collaborative Filtering (CF) here, the content-based approaches are built on neighbors of a target item. Exemplify finding neighbors of a target item. Here, D_ is set/group of all items in training set and D_ is set of items rated by active user. In order to predict rating of a target item for active user, proposed algorithm first searches the K-nearest movies of a target item in the domain of D_ set. Adjusted cosine similarity between target item and all items in D_ set is computed using equation given below:

$$sin(u_a, u_b) = \frac{\sum_{i \epsilon I_{u_a,u_b}} \mu_{i,u_a} \mu_{i,u_b}}{\sqrt{\sum_{i \epsilon I_{u_a,u_b}} \mu_{i,u_a}^2 \sum_{i \epsilon I_{u_a,u_b}} \mu_{i,u_b}^2}}$$

where i is test item, j is one of the item from D_ set, U are the users in training set who have seen both movie i and j . Ru, i is rating of a user u ϵ U for item i, and Ru is average rating of user u and Ru, j is rating of a user u ϵ U for item j.

Use of K-nearest neighbor concept of User-based Collaborative Filtering (CF) here, content-based approaches are built on items rated by neighbors of a target user. In order to predict rating of a target item for active user, proposed algorithm first searches the K-nearest users of a target user in the domain of D_ set. Adjusted cosine similarity between target user and all users in D_ set is computed using equation given below:

$$sin(i, j) = \frac{\sum_{u \epsilon U}(R_{u,i} - R_u)(R_{u,j} - R_u)}{\sqrt{\sum_{u \epsilon U}(R_{u,i} - R_u)^2}\sqrt{\sum_{u \epsilon U}(R_{u,j} - R_u)^2}}$$

where a set of items rated by both users i and j is denoted by I, Ri and Rj represent average rating for user i and j, respectively. After experiments, they found that it was not a good approach as the results they got were not better.

Building content-based approaches on the selected neighbours they have trained their content-based algorithm over the features of the neighbours of a target item (item-based version) or items rated by neighbours of the target user (user-based version) and built a classifier over these selected neighbours. So the basic aim here was to train classifiers over K-nearest neighbours. They have combined item-based and user-based CF with SVM, naive Bayes, Decision tree and Bayesian classifier, respectively [14].

2.3 Proposed Model

Architecture-1. In this approach, we modelled our architecture using state-of-art methods. First, after preprocessing the dataset, we implemented Matrix Factorization using SVD for model-based Collaborative Filtering (CF) approach [10].

For the Content-Based approach, we extracted the major features using the TF-IDF method.

Let us assume N the total number of documents that can be recommended, in our case movie titles, ki is the keyword that is present in ni of the titles. Now, the number of times the keyword ki is in the document dj is defined as fij. Then, $TF_{i,j} = \frac{f_{i,j}}{max_z f_{z,i}}$. where TFi, j is the term frequency or normalized frequency of the keyword ki in document dj, and the maximum is calculated over the frequencies fz, j of all keywords kz that appear in the document dj.

Nevertheless, the more popular words do not give us extra information, and are not useful if they appear in all documents, then recognizing a relevant document between others will not be possible. This is when the measure of the inverse document frequency (IDFi) is combined with the term frequency (TFi, j), then the inverse document frequency for keyword ki is defined as: $IDF_i = \log \frac{N}{n_i}$ where the TF-IDF weight for keyword ki in the document dj is as Eq. 2.8, and the content of the document dj is Content (dj) = (w1j, . . . ,wkj). $w_{i,j} = TF_{i,j} \times IDF_i$. After extracting, we implemented a Cosine-similarity method that gives us the angle between two users' vectors. Then we finally hybridized these two models based on the threshold value system.

In, threshold value system, we considered the total number of books the user has already read till now. From this, we can know how much the new user is to the system. Once we get to know the newness of the user from the system, we can reduce the cold start problem by taking major recommendations from the content-based filtering (CB) method and fewer recommendations from the collaborative based method. And, when the user is familiar with the system, we recommend the user majorly from the collaborative method and less from the content-based method. The threshold values for the system are decided by the brute force approach and it is standardized as, If the number of books read by the user is less than 5 then, the user must be new or inactive and for that scenario, the cold start problem will be the highest so we recommend 70% from the content-based model and 30% from the Collaborative based model. If the number of books read by the user is less than equal to 10 then, the user must be somewhat old to the system so the cold start problem will be less than the first scenario, so we recommend 50% from the content-based Model and 50% from the Collaborative based model. If the number of books read by the user is more than 10 then, the user must be properly familiarized with the system and the database is fairly populated by the semantic behaviour of this user, so the cold start problem will be least, so we recommend 40% from the content-based model and 60% from the Collaborative based model.

The above architecture can be shown mathematically as:

α1 = SVD ("Ratings.csv"), α2 = TF-IDFVectorizer ("Books.csv"), α3 = CosineSimilarity (2), α4 = HybridAlgo (1, 3), α5 = "New Data" , δ = γ (β).

Where α1 and α2 are the output sequence from the SVD and TF-IDF vectorization algorithm.

α3 is then obtained by passing α2 as an argument to the Cosine similarity algorithm. The above two outputs are then passed into the hybrid algorithm and

γ is produced as the output to the algorithm. The new data i.e. β is used for prediction purposes when passed as an argument to δ. Now finally, if the user has read more than 50 books, he is a consistent reader and must have already gotten a definitive taste concerning the system and reading, hence we recommend 30% from the content-based model and 70% from the collaborative model. We still recommend a content-based model to take care of the uncertain cold start problem in the scenario. Moreover, the user will find some new context that he might get interested in.

Architecture-2. Here, in this, we used the results obtained from architecture 1 and treated it as a training dataset for this architecture. We jointly learnt the compatibility relationships among items to facilitate effective recommendation. We employ a Bi-LSTM model to learn the compatibility relationships among the items by modelling an outfit as a sequence. Bi-LSTMs are proven especially helpful in the occasions where the context of the input is needed. In unidirectional LSTM information flows from the backward to forward. On the contrary in Bi-directional LSTM information not only flows backwards to forward but also forward to backwards using two hidden states. Hence Bi-LSTMs understand the context better. Bi-LSTMs was used to escalate the chunk of input information usable to the network. Structure of RNN with LSTM and RNN with BiLSTM [13]. BRNN follows such a process where the neurons of a normal RNN are broken into bi-directional ways. One is for backward states or negative time direction, and another is for forwarding states or positive time direction. The inputs of the reverse direction states are not connected to these two states' results. The structure of BiLSTM is shown in the diagram below. By utilizing two-time directions, input data from the past and future of the current time frame can be used. Whereas standard RNN requires delays for including future data [13].

According to the above flow chart, we have expressed the diagram mathematically as:

$\alpha 1$ = SVD ("Ratings.csv"), $\alpha 2$ = TF-IDF Vectorizer ("Books.csv"), $\alpha 3$ = CosineSimilarity ($\alpha 2$), $\alpha 4$ = HybridAlgo ($\alpha 1$, $\alpha 3$), $\alpha 5$ = "New Data", $\delta = \gamma (\beta)$.

From the above formula, we can get that $\alpha 1$ and $\alpha 2$ are derived from the output of SVD and Cosine similarity algorithms respectively. The two output sequences are then passed in a Bi-LSTM model for hybridizing both sequences. The model is trained and obtained for prediction purposes.

Architecture-3. In this architecture, we took the SVD results from the first architecture and trained the results on GRU. And for the content-based model, we used the Pearson correlation formula along with cosine similarity methods to reduce the chances of a cold-start problem. And finally, after implementing these two methods independently, we used the association rule mining method to hybridize the results for getting top-N recommendations of the items. The GRU's main objective is to solve the vanishing gradient problem which comes

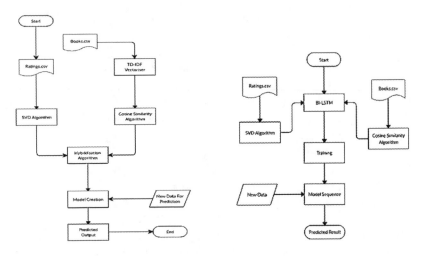

Fig. 1. The flow diagram of architecture-1

Fig. 2. The flow diagram of architecture-2

with a standard recurrent neural network. GRUs is the improved version of standard recurrent neural networks. GRU is a variant of LSTM with a gated recurrent neural network structure, and comparing with LSTM, there are two gates (update gate and reset gate) in GRU and three gates (forgetting gate, input gate, and output gate) in LSTM; meanwhile, GRU has fewer training parameters than LSTM, so GRU converges quicker than LSTM during training [7].

To solve the vanishing gradient problem of a standard RNN, GRU uses, so-called, update gate and reset gate. Basically, these are two vectors that decide what information should be passed to the output. The special thing about them is that they can be trained to keep information from long ago, without washing it through time or removing information that is irrelevant to the prediction.

Cold Start Problem: Content-based methods suffer far less from the cold start problem than collaborative approaches: new users or items can be described by their characteristics (content) and so relevant suggestions can be done for these new entities. Only new users or items with previously unseen features will logically suffer from this drawback, but once the system is old enough, this has little to no chance to happen.

Here, in the above flow chart the basic flow is given, we have expressed this flow mathematically by,

$\alpha 1$ = SVD ("Ratings.csv"), $\alpha 2$ = GRU ($\alpha 1$), $\alpha 3$ = Pearson Correlation ("Books.csv"), $\alpha 4$ = Cosine Similarity ("Books.csv"), $\alpha 5$ = Hybrid Content-Based ($\alpha 3$, $\alpha 4$), $\alpha 6$ = Hybrid Algorithm ($\alpha 2$, $\alpha 5$), $\alpha 7$ = "New Data", $\delta = \gamma$ (β).

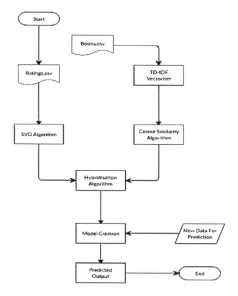

Fig. 3. The flow diagram of architecture-3

Where, α1 is the output sequence generated by the SVD algorithm when we passed the ratings.csv data file into it.

The α1 is then passed as an argument into the GRU interface where a sequence of outcomes is generated mimicking the output sequence of the SVD algorithm.

Simultaneously, on another thread, α3 is generated as an output to the Books.csv file when passed into the Pearson correlation algorithm.

Similarly, α4 is the product from training the Books.csv file under cosine similarity algorithm. Finally, after retrieving α 3 and α 4, these two outcomes are passed into the defined hybridized algorithm for hybridization and are produced as the output to the algorithm. The new data i.e. is used for prediction purposes when passed as an argument to.

3   Integration and Development

As mentioned previously about the tools and techniques used to integrate our Machine Learning model with the Android application (Fabula), we are using the Flask Restful API, We have used a python specific module named flask as a framework that is used to request and receive responses via HTTP protocols. In our case, we have the REST API that requests and receives responses to the OKHTTP client on the android end. SAP HANA is a cloud platform, mainly Platform as a Service (PaaS) that enables us to run, build and operate the applications on the cloud. OKHTTP is the library that will handle the HTTP responses and requests on the side of the android client sent by the Flask

Restful API. It is an open-source library that is used to send and receive HTTP responses, and it is used on the android platform in the project. We have created a Restful API in python to load our Machine learning models for a recommendation (Collaborative Filtering (CF) and Content-Based recommender models)[2], and deployed this to the cloud platform named "SAP HANA". This API will enable us to send and receive HTTP requests to the android client. On the Android side, we have used the OkHTTP library, to receive and request responses from the Rest API that is deployed on the cloud platform. So, the application (Fabula) will make requests for the recommendations from the deployed model via rest API and will get the recommendations. In the recommender system, we used a platform that comprises the following specifications: RAM of 8 GB, PROCESSOR of Intel(R) Core(TM) i5-7200UCPU - 2.50 GHz PLATFORM as 64-bit Operating System. Implementation of machine learning model is done in Python language, version 3.7.0+, and to implement the recommender system we used two third party libraries such as Scikit-Learn, it is an open-source and commercially usable library for simple and efficient predictive data analysis, mainly based on Numpy, Scipy and Matplotlib. Surprise Library. Surprise is a Python scikit building library for analyzing the recommender systems that specifically deals with the explicit rating data. On the Android part, ANDROID STUDIO has been employed which is the building tool for Android-based applications for handsets. This application has been targeted to the mobiles with minimum API level 21 (Lollipop 5.0.0). For the FRONT-END part of an ANDROID application, XML files have been used and all the principles for developing interactive, appealing and user-friendly design schemes, Material Design Concepts has been referenced. For the BACK-END part, Java with JRE (Java Runtime Environment) of 1.8 has been utilized for a smooth transaction between user inputs and application processing. Looking at the development part, we have exhaustively used many commercial third-party libraries and API services such as Google Book API for fetching Book details, OKHTTP of SquareUp, Glide for smooth image loading, Mobile Vision MLKit by Google for QR/BARCODE scanning and JSOUP for easy webpage parsing. For secured authentication of users, Firebase Cloud Authentication has been availed and the same is used as our Cloud Database. Websites like BookDepository and Library Genesis have been included for application capability enrichment. Phase wise, our application consists of basic three activities. Our first activity is for the authentication and registration of the user. We have used email passwords for the same. The next activity is the core of our application. It is the homepage of our application where the actual recommendation system is visible in action. On the top, we have provided an option to view their library where all books downloaded are visible, which can be read using our PDF viewer i.e. now the user need not be dependent on the system installed PDF viewer application. Also, to make the application more closed to the view level, different sections have been provided based on Genres, thus provisioning a well set of options for users to select books. Moreover, a Latest Section has been provided where users can see upcoming books that they can consider to be in their library. On the same activity, we have empowered one more ML tool for image processing i.e. QR/BARCODE Scanner which is used to scan QR/BARCODE printed on the book. The last stage consists of displaying the details of the interested book with free e-book download capability. We are using Library Genesis for downloading books. After downloading the books, it is available with the user for further reading and improvement of the recommendation system.

4   Results Analysis

Recommender systems are growing progressively more popular in online retail because of their ability to offer personalized experiences to unique users. Root Mean Square Error (RMSE) is typically the metric of choice for evaluating the performance of a recommender system. The less the RMSE, the more efficient the model is.

$$\sqrt{\frac{1}{n}\sum_{i=1}^{n}(f_i - o_i)^2}$$

Along with RMSE, We are using F-measure or F1 Score and Mean absolute error (MAE) for evaluating the performance of the models. The reason for taking F-measure as a metric is since this single metric will balance all the concerns regarding the precision and recall metrics that are commonly used in performance testing procedures. The traditional F measure is calculated as follows: F-Measure = (2 * Precision * Recall)/(Precision + Recall) For comparing the performances of our model concerning the state-of-the-art recommenders on our dataset, we divided our evaluation into three phases.

In the first phase, we measured all the three metrics for the Collaborative Filtering (CF) models as shown in the table below. We found out that due to the use of the SVD approach, the RMSE of our model is a little better than the other two models. And the same goes for the other two metrics. In the second

Table 4. Collaborative Filtering (CF) recommender systems

Name of the model	Root mean squared error value	F-measure	Mean absolute error
FABULA Recommendation System	0.67	0.72	0.53
Netflix Recommendation System	0.70	0.73	0.55
Hybrid Book Recommendation System Using TOC and Association Rule Mining	0.52	0.67	0.55

phase, we measured the performances of the content-based models with respect to the same metrics and these are the results below. In this, our model surely outperformed the Toc and association rule mining method but didn't perform well with respect to the Netflix recommendation system.

Table 5. Results for content-based recommender systems

Name of the model	Root mean squared error value	F-measure	Mean absolute error
FABULA Recommendation System	0.58	0.81	0.59
Netflix Recommendation System	0.87	0.80	0.43
Hybrid Book Recommendation System Using TOC and Association Rule Mining	0.60	0.78	0.51

Table 6. Hybrid recommenders

Name of the model	Root mean squared error value	F-measure	Mean absolute error
FABULA Recommendation System	0.62	0.78	0.51
Netflix Recommendation System	0.67	0.72	0.50
Hybrid Book Recommendation System Using TOC and Association Rule Mining	0.72	0.71	0.53

In the below table, the results show the performance of the hybrid model architectures. And from the result, it is clear that our model performed quite meticulously among the other two models. As the above tables clearly showed that the FABULA recommender system works quite well in recommending the books for the users so, we incorporated this hybrid model in our android tool.

5   Comparison Analysis

In this section, we did an Output Comparison Analysis as well as Error Analysis on the output of our model with the above-discussed models. In the comparison analysis, we tried to have the best recommendation from our architecture along with the other two state-of-the-art architecture and the final result was evaluated by a human who is also an avid reader. There were 4 human evaluators among which one of the evaluators was in our team.

We picked three commonly read books from the dataset and told our evaluators to take one of the recommended books that stand as the best-recommended book for that user. The books we chose are: "Harry Potter and the Sorcerer's Stone" by J.K Rowling, "Romeo and Juliet" by William Shakespeare and "Angels and Demons" by Dan Brown. For our model, 4 out of 4 users picked "Harry Potter and the Chamber of Secrets" by J.K Rowling as the best-recommended book from all the recommended books. For the second book, 3 out of 4 users picked "Othello" by William Shakespeare as their next book for reading and finally for the third book, 4 out of 4 users picked "Digital Fortress" by Dan Brown as their next book. For the Netflix recommender model, all the evaluators picked "Harry Potter and the Chamber of Secrets" by J.K Rowling as the best-recommended book by the system and for the second book, 3 evaluators chose "Julius Caesar" as their next book as "Othello" was not recommended for those users. For the third book, 3 users chose "Catcher in the Rye" by J.D

Salinger for their next read.For the last architecture, 3 evaluators picked "Harry Potter and the Prisoner of Azkaban" as the next read and simultaneously 4 of the users picked "The mad man" and "Da Vinci Code" for the second and third book.All the users were quite satisfied with the system as the relevance was much greater as compared to the other two models.

For the Error Analysis part, we asked our evaluators to test for some books where the model is performing poorly from their standpoint.From the above experiment, we collected that "Twilight" and "The Innocent Man" are the books where they found one such book that was worst recommended. For all the users, "Othello", which was recommended for "Twilight" was a very poor match, similarly, for "The Innocent Man", three users added "Divergent" as a poorly recommended book from the recommended list. The reason for such a match is the fact that the descriptive knowledge based on these books is limited only to the type of author and title along with the global ratings. So, we can improve its recommendation power by training the model based on more descriptive data that is present inside the book's pages.

6   Conclusion

By going through the works and analysis of the daily usage of different social feeds and platforms for Music, Books, News and others we conclude that Recommendation is Human Perspective analysis which may differ from peer to peer, person to person and generation to generation and thus we have made a practical implementation of a recommendation system which is an improvised version of the state of the art in terms of its actual usage by a user. The recommendations are more generalized to be a probable better match for a user; it also solves the cold start problem to a very good extent. The practical implementation is a user book recommendation android application named Fabula. As the android platform is the world's most used Operating System it gives a stage to the maximum users and their different perspectives on the usage with time.

References

1. Aggarwal, C.C., et al.: Recommender Systems. vol. 1. Springer, Cham (2016)
2. Alyari, F., Navimipour, N.J.: Recommender Systems. Kybernetes (2018)
3. Amatriain, X., Jaimes, A., Oliver, N., Pujol, J.M.: Data mining methods for recommender systems. In: Ricci, F., Rokach, L., Shapira, B., Kantor, P.B. (eds.) Recommender Systems Handbook, pp. 39–71. Springer, Boston (2011). https://doi.org/10.1007/978-0-387-85820-3_2
4. Cheng, H.T., et al.: Wide and deep learning for recommender systems. In: Proceedings of the 1st Workshop on Deep Learning for Recommender Systems, pp. 7–10 (2016)
5. Covington, P., Adams, J. Sargin, E.: Deep neural networks for youtube recommendations. In: Proceedings of the 10th ACM conference on recommender systems, pp. 191–198 (2016)

6. Davidson, J., et al.: The youtube video recommendation system. In: Proceedings of the fourth ACM conference on Recommender systems, pp. 293–296 (2010)

7. Gao, X., Li, X., Zhao, B., Ji, W., Jing, X., He, Y.: Short-term electricity load forecasting model based on EMD-GRU with feature selection. Energies **12**(6), 1140 (2019)

8. Gomez-Uribe, C.A., Hunt, N.: The netflix recommender system: algorithms business value and innovation. ACM Trans. Manag. Inf. Syst. (TMIS) **6**(4), 1–19 (2016)

9. Jomsri, P.: FUCL mining technique for book recommender system in library service. Proc. Manuf. **22**, 550–557 (2018)

10. Ng, Y.-K.: CBREC: a book recommendation system for children using the matrix factorisation and content-based filtering approaches. Int. J. Bus. Intell. Data Min. **16**(2), 129–149 (2020)

11. Okura, S., Tagami, Y., Ono, S., Tajima, A.: Embedding-based news recommendation for millions of users. In: Proceedings of the 23rd ACM SIGKDD International Conference on Knowledge Discovery and Data Mining, pp. 1933–1942 (2017)

12. Ramakrishnan, G., Saicharan, V., Chandrasekaran, K., Rathnamma, M.V., Ramana, V.V.: Collaborative filtering for book recommendation system. In: Das, K.N., Bansal, J.C., Deep, K., Nagar, A.K., Pathipooranam, P., Naidu, R.C. (eds.) Soft Computing for Problem Solving. AISC, vol. 1057, pp. 325–338. Springer, Singapore (2020). https://doi.org/10.1007/978-981-15-0184-5_29

13. Sarwar, B., Karypis, G., Konstan, J., Riedl, J.: Item-based collaborative filtering recommendation algorithms. In: Proceedings of the 10th international conference on World Wide Web, pp. 285–295, (2001)

14. Sattar, A., Ghazanfar, M., Iqbal, M.: Building accurate and practical recommender system algorithms using machine learning classifier and collaborative filtering. Arab. J. Sci. Eng. **42**, 3229–3247 (2017)

15. Schaffer, J., Hollerer, T., O'Donovan, J.: Hypothetical recommendation: a study of interactive profile manipulation behavior for recommender systems. In: The Twenty-Eighth International Flairs Conference. Citeseer (2015)

16. Wan, M., McAuley, J.: Item recommendation on monotonic behavior chains. In: Pera, S., Ekstrand, M.D., Amatriain, X., O'Donovan, J., (eds.) Proceedings of the 12th ACM Conference on Recommender Systems, RecSys 2018, Vancouver, BC, Canada, October 2–7, pp. 86–94. ACM (2018)

17. Wan, M., Misra, R., Nakashole, N., McAuley, J.: Fine-grained spoiler detection from large-scale review corpora. In: Korhonen, A., Traum, D.R., Màrquez, L., (eds.) Proceedings of the 57th Conference of the Association for Computational Linguistics, ACL 2019, Florence, Italy, July 28- August 2, vol. 1, Long Papers, pp. 2605–2610. Association for Computational Linguistics (2019)

18. Wu, L., Kong, C., Hao, X., Chen, W.: A short-term load forecasting method based on GRU-CNN hybrid neural network model. Mathematical Problems in Engineering (2020)

19. Xin, L., Haihong, E., Junde, S., Meina, S., Junjie, T.: Collaborative book recommendation based on readers' borrowing records. In: 2013 International Conference on Advanced Cloud and Big Data, pp. 159–163. IEEE (2013)

An Enhanced Personal Profile Ontology for Software Requirements Engineering Tasks Allocation

P. U. Usip[✉], E. N. Udo, and I. J. Umoeka

Computer Science Department, University of Uyo, Uyo, Nigeria
{patienceusip,edwardudo,iniumoeka}@uniuyo.edu.ng

Abstract. The availability of a web application for allocating software requirements engineering tasks to qualify personnel requires personal profile ontology (PPO) which includes both static and dynamic features. Several personal profile ontologies have been developed and deployed, but the personnel information represented is static, leaving out fundamental and dynamic properties of the personal data suitable for task handling in applications such as allocating tasks during the software requirement engineering processes. Personal profile is often modified for several purposes, calling for augmentation and annotation when needs arise. The resume is one resulting extract from personal profile and often contain slightly different information based on needs. The urgent preparation of a resume may introduce bias and incorrect information for the sole aim of projecting the personnel as being qualified for the available job. This work is aimed at providing an enhanced personal profile ontology for software requirements engineering task allocation that captures both static and dynamic properties of personal data. A mixed approach of existing ontologies like Methontology and Neon have been followed in the creation of this ontology. The enhanced personal profile ontology (e-PPO) is a constraint-based semantic data model tested using Protégé inbuilt reasoner with its updated plugins. Upon application of e-PPO, an abridged resumes otherwise referred to the smart resumes will be obtained from the populated ontology with instances, and this will aid in the decision and selection of the most qualified personnel for any queried software requirements engineering task.

Keywords: Intelligent system · Personnel selection · Semantic web · Smart resume

1 Introduction

In our day-to-day transactions, we are faced with situations where we need to take decision and make choice among several alternatives. Decision making process is about selecting the most suitable alternative(s) according to certain criteria. This process is considered to be tough for decision makers because of its

© Springer Nature Switzerland AG 2021
B. Villazón-Terrazas et al. (Eds.): KGSWC 2021, CCIS 1459, pp. 197–208, 2021.
https://doi.org/10.1007/978-3-030-91305-2_15

uncertainty and subjectivity [1,2]. This process therefore requires a systematic and logical approach in order to make the correct choice. Several works pointing to ontology-based decision support system capable of automatically suggesting the best suited human resources for specific task have been done [3] but for quick access to the needed resources for enhanced and effective decision, these decision support systems should be Semantic Web driven.

Semantic Web came with its essential objective to provide Web information with a well-defined meaning that makes it understandable to both humans, and computers [3]. Ontologies are the fundamental technology for modeling the domain information [4]. Ontology, a formal and explicit specification of a shared conceptualization [5,6], provides reusable and sharable knowledge with a proper and structured representation. Ontologies used for user profiling are mostly limited to taxonomies of user interests. Other domain knowledge such as software requirement engineering and development requires such technology for explicit specification.

Required guidelines are specified in the software requirements (SR) phase of the Software Development Life Cycle (SDLC) for any software product development. The requirements for a system are the descriptions of what the system should do, which reflect customers' needs for a system that serves a specific purpose. The process of finding out, analyzing, documenting, and checking these services as well as their constraints is called requirements engineering (RE) [7]. Generally, requirements are specified at the beginning of the development process, and these requirements specifications are used as guidelines for the software development [8]. IEEE Std 1233 (1998) defines requirement as a condition or capability that a system must meet or possess to satisfy a contract, standard, specification, or other formally imposed documents.

Software Requirements Engineering (SRE) provides the appropriate mechanism for understanding what the customer wants, analyzing needs, assessing feasibility, negotiating a reasonable solution, specifying the key unambiguously, validating the specification, and managing the requirements as they are transformed into an operational system [7]. Software requirement engineering is a well-defined process to identify stakeholders and their needs and also documents such requirements for proper system implementation [9]. SRE is a sub-category of (RE) that deals with the elicitation, specification and validation of requirements for software [10] and it is critical for successful software development. SRE processes and activities areas outlined in Table 1.

Selecting appropriate personnel with the requisite qualification and skills for SRE tasks becomes a significant challenge considering the various components of the SR tasks, the diverse computing skills, and the numerous entries in the e-PPO. Decision-making plays a vital role in real-time applications where there are many decision criteria [11]. For modeling uncertainties in industrial, natural, and human systems, fuzzy sets and fuzzy logic are powerful mathematical tools to adopt to facilitate decision-making as they use approximate reasoning and linguistic terms [12]. However, a piece of abridged information that is handy can go a long way to help in decision-making without using these mathematical

Table 1. Software requirement engineering processes and activities [7,13]

S/N	Process	Sub-process	Description/Activites
1	Feasibility Study	Problem Analysis	Assessing if the system is useful to the client Stating the problem, problem domain and environment Understanding the system behaviour and constraints in the system Knowing the system inputs and outputs (from output of existing system)
2	Elicitation and Analysis	Requirement Discovery Requirement Classification and organization Requirement prioritization and negotiation	Meeting with clients and stakeholders – those that will interact with the system and be affected by the system Users and customers ask questions about the system (scope, what they need, evolution etc.) Finding out about the application domain, services to be provided, required performance, hardware constraints etc. From documents describing the organization and work) Discovering all requirements Organizing and describing the requirements Ranking requirements (by stakeholders, customers and users) Resolving priority conflict Identification and analysis of risk associated with each requirement
3	Specification	Elaboration	Address issues such as representation, specification language, tools to use, etc. Produce Software Requirements Specification (SRS) Documents – should include natural language description, graphical models, scenarios Developing a refined technical model of software functions and features together with their constraints using UML diagrams, Use Cases, Data Flow Diagrams, Entity Relationship Diagrams, analysis models etc.
4	Requirement Management	Planning	Requirement identification Management of changes in requirement Tracing the relationship between each requirement and the system design (Traceability policies) Knowing the tools for processing of requirement information Managing relevant information and knowledge
5	Validation	Review and Inspection	Checking that the requirements define the system the stakeholders want by reviewing the SRS document and examines the specification Checking for errors (omission, inconsistency, incorrect fact, ambiguity) in requirement specification and other factors affecting quality Ensuring that work conforms to standards established for the process, project and product Carry out validation, consistency, completeness, realism checks as well as verifiability Adoption of some validation techniques such as requirement review, prototyping and test case generation

tools with its numerous and rigorous computations. Hence, there is a need for semantic web-driven curriculum vitae that can be referred to as the intelligent resume in this work.

The selection process is focused on personnel whose profiling has already been captured in the enhanced Personal Profile Ontology (e-PPO). The e-PPO is a variation of the existing Personal Profile Ontologies (PPO) which intends to capture the static and dynamic properties of the user.

2   Related Literature

Several approaches have been employed in resume parsing aimed at producing a smart resume. Some approaches include the Two-Step Resume Information Extraction Algorithm involving text block identification and named entity recognition. [14]; Statistical and rule-based [2] entity linking paradigm [15], named entity clustering algorithm [11], Combination of neural networks and conditional random fields [16] and NLP [17,18] approaches.

Ontologies have been deployed as efficient and intelligent knowledge management tools for timetabling [6] and as a secure semantic smart healthcare [19,20]. The use of ontologies for user profile creation can be traced back to [21], with methodologies (Methontology, Neon) [22,23] and applications carefully outlined. Requirements and knowledge engineering processes adopt the personal profile ontology in their reasoning [24] towards ontology-based persona-driven requirements and knowledge engineering.

Suarez-Figueroa [25] built ontology requirements specification, a reference ontology, to provide a consensual knowledge model of the employment domain to be used by public e-employment services. The application of ontologies has also been made in identifying requirements patterns in use cases [8]. An ontology-based approach was adopted in assigning human resources to software projects [3], but their work took into consideration only the static personnel profile properties. This work enhances personal profile ontology that captures the dynamic properties of personal data and the static ones to allocate tasks in the software requirements engineering domain.

3   Materials and Methods

The personnel selection process for SRE tasks requires explicit representation of the domain knowledge and documentation for appropriate and corresponding personnel selection. This involves modeling the personal profile with both static and dynamic properties, obtaining the criteria required to select any SRE task and its relative importance (weight).

3.1   The Enhanced Personal Profile Ontology (e-PPO)

Properties of the ontology, such as name, gender, date of birth, etc., are static in nature and may not change. Other static properties such as educational qualification and skills acquired can be updated while others, including specialization and profession, are dynamic and can be changed. Also, specializations cannot be out of the scope of one's profession; although one person can have multiple professions and skills, more than one profession can share things in common, such as the same professional qualification may be required, and so on. Hence, Fig. 1. shows the class hierarchy of the e-PPO with both static and dynamic properties of the personal profile, while Fig. 2 gives an ontograf that shows excerpts from the e-PPO.

The proposed e-PPO has a total of 54 classes being concepts and sub-concepts, 3 object properties. At the moment, the ontology is at the testing phase and has not been populated with established personnel data as instances for the task selection process. Only sample individuals were populated for testing. This ontology can formalize the software requirements, engineering documents, and the most qualified personnel. Educational Qualification, Profession, Area of Specialization, and Skills Acquired are the most sensitive properties of the PPO. Formalizing the ontology and the competencies of suitable personnel with

Fig. 1. Class hierarchies in enhanced personal profile ontology

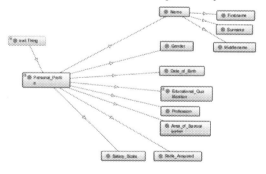

Fig. 2. Excerpts from enhanced personal profile ontology

varying properties for the SRE task is based on the relative importance of the well-labeled criteria and sub-criteria given in Sect. 3.2.

3.2 Formalizing the SRE Task Allocation for the Most Qualified Personnel

Before the formal representation, several weights have been assigned based on experts' views. The criteria have been weighted via linguistic expressions of relative importance. The consequences of the requirements for the personnel selection are determined by the decision-maker using the following linguistic variables: Important (A.I.), Strongly Important (S.I.), Fairly Important (F.I.), Weakly Important (W.I.), and Rarely Important (R.I.). The criteria used in

Table 2. Relative importance of criteria and the sub-criteria

Criteria	Criteria label	Rel* Imp*	Sub-criteria	Criteria label	Rel* Imp*
EDUCATIONAL QUALIFICATION	EDQ	A.I.	Ph.D M.Sc PGD B.Sc/HND ND/NCE	Ph.D M.Sc PGD B.Sc/HND ND/NCE	F.I. S.I. R.I. A.I. W.I.
PROFESSION	PRO	S.I.	Comp Science Business Management Info Technology	CS BM IT	A.I. F.I. S.I.
AREA OF SPECIALIZATION	AOS	A.I.	Software Engineering	SE	A.I.
			Project Management	PM	F.I.
			Management Information System	MIS	S.I.
			Business/Data Analytics	BDA	F.I.
			System Analysis	SA	A.I.
			Information Technology Management/ Entrepreneurship	ITME	F.I.
			Operations Management	OM	W.I.
SKILL ACQUIRED	SKA	S.I.	Knowledge Management	KM	A.I.
			Quality Assurance/ Engineering	QAE	F.I.
			Data/Information Analysis	DIA	A.I.
			Technical Writing	TW	S.I.
			System Development/Testing	SDT	S.I.
			Soft Productivity Tools Usage	SPT	S.I.
			Information Technology Risk Management	IRM	F.I.

Rel* Imp* - Relative Importance

the personnel selection process and the relative importance of each criteria and sub-criteria are shown in Table 2.

From Table 1, it is evident that any person must possess necessary educational qualifications in the required profession before being considered for task allocation. The consideration must be based on specific areas of specialization, and applicants must have acquired sufficient skills in a related area.

Formal rules representing the combinations of the criteria A to D (where A represents EDQ; B represents PRO; C represents AOS; D represents SKA) and sub-criteria of concern by the human resource agent in charge of software requirements engineering task allocation given in Table 1 are stated in rules AR1–AR12; BR –BR7; CR1–CR44; DR1-DR35, where $\Rightarrow$ stands for implication; $\wedge$ for logical AND; $\vee$ for logical OR.

Some rules guiding the evaluation of applicant's Educational Qualification (EDQ), Profession (PRO), Area of Specialization (AOS), and Skills Acquired (SKA) using the possible combinations of the sub-criteria in Table 2 are written down thus:

For EDQ:

AR1:	$EDQ \Rightarrow PhD \wedge MSc \wedge BSc$
AR2:	$EDQ \Rightarrow PhD \wedge MSc \wedge BSc \wedge NCE$
AR3:	$EDQ \Rightarrow PhD \wedge MSc \wedge HND \wedge ND$
AR4:	$EDQ \Rightarrow PhD \wedge MSc \wedge HND \wedge ND \wedge NCE$
AR5:	$EDQ \Rightarrow PhD \wedge MSc \wedge BSc \wedge HND \wedge ND$
AR6:	$EDQ \Rightarrow PhD \wedge MSc \wedge BSc \wedge HND \wedge ND \wedge NCE$
AR7:	$EDQ \Rightarrow PhD \wedge MSc \wedge PGD \wedge BSc$
AR8:	$EDQ \Rightarrow PhD \wedge MSc \wedge PGD \wedge BSc \wedge NCE$
AR9:	$EDQ \Rightarrow PhD \wedge MSc \wedge PGD \wedge HND \wedge ND$
AR10:	$EDQ \Rightarrow PhD \wedge MSc \wedge PGD \wedge HND \wedge ND \wedge NCE$
AR11:	$EDQ \Rightarrow PhD \wedge MSc \wedge PGD \wedge BSc \wedge HND \wedge ND$
AR12:	$EDQ \Rightarrow PhD \wedge MSc \wedge PGD \wedge BSc \wedge HND \wedge ND \wedge NCE$

For PRO:

BR1:	$PRO \Rightarrow CS$
BR2:	$PRO \Rightarrow BM$
BR3:	$PRO \Rightarrow IT$
BR4:	$PRO \Rightarrow CS \wedge BM$
BR5:	$PRO \Rightarrow CS \wedge IT$
BR6:	$PRO \Rightarrow BM \wedge IT$
BR7:	$PRO \Rightarrow CS \wedge BM \wedge IT$

Considering an instance where three personnel, P1, P2, and P3, have scaled through the different recruitment process stages, the human resource officer is now faced with the decision of whom to employ as the SRE analyst among the three personnel. Assuming the set of rules that fired to shortlist the three personnel were:

P1 (AR1, BR1, CR2, DR8)
P2 (AR3, BR4, CR40, DR2)
P3 (AR4, BR2, CR4, DR10)

Deciding the best personnel out of the three will require a smart resume of the three personnel. The model will then lookup for the components of the criteria and sub-criteria from the rules for each personnel as depicted by the architecture in Fig. 3.

For AOS:

$CR1$:	$AOS \Rightarrow SE$		$CR21$:	$AOS \Rightarrow SE \wedge ITME \wedge OM$
$CR2$:	$AOS \Rightarrow SA$		$CR22$:	$AOS \Rightarrow SE \wedge MIS \wedge OM$
$CR3$:	$AOS \Rightarrow SE \wedge SA$		$CR23$:	$AOS \Rightarrow SE \wedge OM$
$CR4$:	$AOS \Rightarrow SE \wedge SA \wedge MIS$		$CR24$:	$AOS \Rightarrow SE \wedge MIS \wedge PM \vee BDA \vee ITME$
$CR5$:	$AOS \Rightarrow SE \wedge SA \wedge MIS \vee BDA$		$CR25$:	$AOS \Rightarrow SE \wedge MIS \wedge PM \vee BDA \vee ITME \wedge OM$
$CR6$:	$AOS \Rightarrow SE \wedge SA \wedge MIS \vee PM$		$CR26$:	$AOS \Rightarrow SE \wedge MIS \wedge PM \wedge BDA \wedge ITME \wedge OM$
$CR7$:	$AOS \Rightarrow SE \wedge SA \wedge MIS \vee ITME$		$CR27$:	$AOS \Rightarrow SA \wedge MIS$
$CR8$:	$AOS \Rightarrow SE \wedge SA \wedge MIS \vee ITME \vee OM$		$CR28$:	$AOS \Rightarrow SA \wedge MIS \wedge BDA$
$CR9$:	$AOS \Rightarrow SE \wedge MIS$		$CR29$:	$AOS \Rightarrow SA \wedge MIS \wedge PM$
$CR10$:	$AOS \Rightarrow SE \wedge MIS \wedge BDA$		$CR30$:	$AOS \Rightarrow SA \wedge MIS \wedge ITME$
$CR11$:	$AOS \Rightarrow SE \wedge MIS \wedge PM$		$CR31$:	$AOS \Rightarrow SA \wedge BDA$
$CR12$:	$AOS \Rightarrow SE \wedge MIS \wedge ITME$		$CR32$:	$AOS \Rightarrow SA \wedge PM$
$CR13$:	$AOS \Rightarrow SE \wedge MIS \wedge BDA \wedge OM$		$CR33$:	$AOS \Rightarrow SA \wedge ITME$
$CR14$:	$AOS \Rightarrow SE \wedge MIS \wedge PM \wedge OM$		$CR34$:	$AOS \Rightarrow SA \wedge BDA \wedge OM$
$CR15$:	$AOS \Rightarrow SE \wedge MIS \wedge ITME \wedge OM$		$CR35$:	$AOS \Rightarrow SA \wedge PM \wedge OM$
$CR16$:	$AOS \Rightarrow SE \wedge BDA$		$CR36$:	$AOS \Rightarrow SA \wedge ITME \wedge OM$
$CR17$:	$AOS \Rightarrow SE \wedge PM$		$CR37$:	$AOS \Rightarrow SA \wedge OM$
$CR18$:	$AOS \Rightarrow SE \wedge ITME$		$CR38$:	$AOS \Rightarrow SA \wedge MIS \wedge OM$
$CR19$:	$AOS \Rightarrow SE \wedge BDA \wedge OM$		$CR39$:	$AOS \Rightarrow SA \wedge MIS \wedge BDA \wedge OM$
$CR20$:	$AOS \Rightarrow SE \wedge PM \wedge OM$		$CR40$:	$AOS \Rightarrow SA \wedge MIS \wedge PM \wedge OM$
			$CR41$:	$AOS \Rightarrow SA \wedge MIS \wedge ITME \wedge OM$
			$CR42$:	$AOS \Rightarrow SA \wedge MIS \wedge PM \vee BDA \vee ITME$
			$CR43$:	$AOS \Rightarrow SA \wedge MIS \wedge PM \vee BDA \vee ITME \wedge OM$
			$CR44$:	$AOS \Rightarrow SA \wedge MIS \wedge PM \wedge BDA \wedge ITME \wedge OM$

For SKA:

$DR1$:	$SKA \Rightarrow KM$		$DR18$:	$SKA \Rightarrow DIA \wedge TW \vee SDT \vee SPT$
$DR2$:	$SKA \Rightarrow DIA$		$DR19$:	$SKA \Rightarrow DIA \wedge TW \wedge SDT \wedge SPT$
$DR3$:	$SKA \Rightarrow KM \wedge DIA$		$DR20$:	$SKA \Rightarrow DIA \wedge SDT$
$DR4$:	$SKA \Rightarrow TW$		$DR21$:	$SKA \Rightarrow DIA \wedge TW$
$DR5$:	$SKA \Rightarrow SDT$		$DR22$:	$SKA \Rightarrow DIA \wedge SPT$
$DR6$:	$SKA \Rightarrow SPT$		$DR23$:	$SKA \Rightarrow KM \wedge QAE \vee IRM$
$DR7$:	$SKA \Rightarrow QAE$		$DR24$:	$SKA \Rightarrow DIA \wedge QAE \vee IRM$
$DR8$:	$SKA \Rightarrow IRM$		$DR25$:	$SKA \Rightarrow DIA \vee TW \vee SDT \vee SPT \vee QAE \vee IRM$
$DR9$:	$SKA \Rightarrow KM \wedge SDT$		$DR26$:	$SKA \Rightarrow DIA \wedge TW \wedge SDT \wedge SPT \wedge QAE \wedge IRM$
$DR10$:	$SKA \Rightarrow KM \wedge TW$		$DR27$:	$SKA \Rightarrow DIA \wedge TW \wedge QAE \wedge IRM$
$DR11$:	$SKA \Rightarrow KM \wedge SPT$		$DR28$:	$SKA \Rightarrow KM \wedge TW \wedge SDT \wedge SPT \wedge QAE \wedge IRM$
$DR12$:	$SKA \Rightarrow TW \wedge SDT$		$DR29$:	$SKA \Rightarrow KM \vee TW \vee SDT \vee SPT \vee QAE \vee IRM$
$DR13$:	$SKA \Rightarrow TW \wedge SPT$		$DR30$:	$SKA \Rightarrow KM \wedge DIA \wedge TW \wedge SDT \wedge SPT \wedge QAE \wedge IRM$
$DR14$:	$SKA \Rightarrow TW \wedge SDT \vee SPT$		$DR31$:	$SKA \Rightarrow KM \wedge DIA \wedge TW \wedge SDT \wedge SPT \wedge QAE \vee IRM$
$DR15$:	$SKA \Rightarrow TW \wedge SDT \wedge SPT$		$DR32$:	$SKA \Rightarrow KM \wedge DIA \wedge TW \vee SDT \vee SPT \wedge QAE \vee IRM$
$DR16$:	$SKA \Rightarrow KM \wedge TW \vee SDT \vee SPT$		$DR33$:	$SKA \Rightarrow KM \vee DIA \wedge TW \vee SDT \vee SPT \wedge QAE \vee IRM$
$DR17$:	$SKA \Rightarrow KM \wedge TW \wedge SDT \wedge SPT$		$DR34$:	$SKA \Rightarrow KM \wedge SDT \vee SPT$
			$DR35$:	$SKA \Rightarrow KM \wedge SDT \wedge SPT$

3.3   The Ontology-Based Personnel Selection System Architecture

Figure 3 shows the architecture of the ontology-based intelligent system, where the formalized rules are built into the e-PPO and used during the selection process to eliminate bias due to conflicting interests and select intelligently most competent personnel for the SRE tasks using the resulting smart resume.

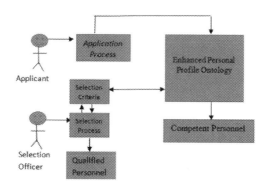

Fig. 3. The ontology based personnel selection system architecture

The applicant completes the application process as input to the e-PPO model from the architecture, and the enhanced personal profile ontology is used to generate competent personnel. The selection officer views the skilled personnel in the light of the organization's selection criteria to develop the most qualified personnel.

4   Results

The resulting sample smart resume from the illustration with personnel P1, P2 and P3 in section 3.2 is as given in Table 3, where the numbers 5, 4, 3, 2, 1 are equivalent to the linguistic variables: Absolutely Important (A.I.), Strongly Important (S.I.), Fairly Important (F.I.), Weakly Important (W.I.) and Rarely Important (R.I.) respectively.

From the sample smart resume, P1 has 12 points for EDQ; 5 points for PRO; 5 points for AOS and 3 points for SKA, giving him a total of 25 points. P2 has

Table 3. A sample smart resume

PERSONNEL_ID	RULES	EDQ	PRO	AOS	SKA	Computed relative importance	Total points
P1	AR1, BR1, CR2, DR8	PhD, MSc, BSc	CS	SA	IRM	3+4+5, 5, 5,3	25
P2	AR3, BR4, CR40, DR2	PhD, MSc, HND, ND	CS, BM	SA, MIS, PM, OM	DIA	3+4+5+2, 5+3, 5+4+3+2, 5	41
P3	AR4, BR2, CR4, DR10	PhD, MSc, HND, ND, NCE	BM	SE, SA, MIS	KM, TW	3+4+5+2+2, 3, 5+5+4, 5+4	42

14 points for EDQ; 8 points for PRO; 14 points for AOS and 5 points for SKA, giving him a total of 41 points. P3 has 16 points for EDQ; 3 points for PRO; 14 points for AOS and 9 points for SKA, giving him a total of 42 points.

Personnel P3 with total points of 42 is the most competence for the software requirements engineering process task followed by P2 with total points of 41. Personnel P1 is the least qualified with total points of 25. Therefore, P3 is qualified for the SRE analyst position. The designed ontology is available on bioportal that can be accessed with the link: https://bioportal.bioontology.org/ontologies/E-PPO.

5 Conclusions

Decision making process is about selecting the most suitable alternative(s) according to certain criteria. The enhanced personal profile ontology was created. Information represented in the ontology include static and dynamic properties of the personal profile suitable for task handling in applications such as promotion appraisal, and allocation of task during the software requirement engineering process. Selecting the most suitable alternative(s) according to certain criteria is sometimes considered to be a tough task for decision makers because of its complexity and subjectivity. The suitability of personnel's properties in this ontology for the software requirements engineering task allocation is returned based on the formal rules that fires. With these formal rules built into the ePPO, the static and dynamic features of personal profile can be analysed given the smart resume. As it is difficult to clarify the theoretical highlights that are liable for recognizing hostile content, the incorporation of additionally preparing information will push us to get it. For the programmed assessment of an image, we need a message as a diverse methodology. This content is frequently implanted on the image. Subsequently, to catch the inserted content, we can use OCR procedures.

References

1. Bai, S.-M., Chen, S.-M.: Automatically constructing grade membership functions of fuzzy rules for students' evaluation. Expert Syst. Appl. **35**(3), 1408–1414 (2008)
2. Jiang, Z., Zhang, C., Xiao, B., Lin, Z.: Research and implementation of intelligent chinese resume parsing. In: 2009 WRI International Conference on Communications and Mobile Computing, vol. 3, pp. 588–593. IEEE (2009)
3. Paredes-Valverde, A.M., del Pilar Salas-Zárate, M., Colomo-Palacios, R., Gómez-Berbís, J.M., Valencia-García, R.: An ontology-based approach with which to assign human resources to software projects. Sci. Comput. Program. **156**, 90–103 (2018)
4. Panchal, R., Swaminarayan, P., Tiwari, S., Ortiz-Rodriguez, F.: AISHE-Onto: a semantic model for public higher education universities. In: DG. O2021: The 22nd Annual International Conference on Digital Government Research, pp. 545–547 (2021)
5. Studer, R., Benjamins, V.R., Fensel, D.: Knowledge engineering: principles and methods. Data Knowl. Eng. **25**(1–2), 161–197 (1998)

6. Usip, P.U., Ntekop, M.M.: The use of ontologies as efficient and intelligent knowl-edge management tool. In: 2016 Future Technologies Conference (FTC), pp. 626–631. IEEE (2016)
7. Sommerville, I.: Software engineering. America (2011)
8. Couto, R., Ribeiro, A.N., Campos, J.C.: Application of ontologies in identifying requirements patterns in use cases. arXiv preprint arXiv:1404.0850 (2014)
9. Mustafa, A., Wan-Kadir, W.M., Ibrahim, N., Shah, M.A., Younas, M.: Integration of heterogeneous requirements using ontologies. Integration **9**(5) (2018)
10. Bourque, P., Dupuis, R., Abran, A., Moore, J.W., Tripp, L.: The guide to the software engineering body of knowledge. IEEE Softw. **16**(6), 35–44 (1999)
11. Sonar, S., Bankar, B.: Resume parsing with named entity clustering algorithm. paper, SVPM College of Engineering Baramati, Maharashtra, India (2012)
12. Tavana, M., Azizi, F., Azizi, F., Behzadian, M.: A fuzzy inference system with application to player selection and team formation in multi-player sports. Sport Manag. Rev. **16**(1), 97–110 (2013)
13. Pressman, R.S.: Software Engineering: A Practitioner's Approach. Palgrave Macmillan, London (2005)
14. Chen, J., Zhang, C., Niu, Z.: A two-step resume information extraction algorithm. Math. Probl. Eng. 2018 (2018)
15. Deepak, G., Teja, V., Santhanavijayan, A.: A novel firefly driven scheme for resume parsing and matching based on entity linking paradigm. J. Discret. Math. Sci. Cryptogr. **23**(1), 157–165 (2020)
16. Ayishathahira, C.H., Sreejith, C., Raseek, C.: Combination of neural networks and conditional random fields for efficient resume parsing. In: 2018 International CET Conference on Control, Communication, and Computing (IC4), pp. 388–393. IEEE (2018)
17. Sanyal, S., Hazra, S., Adhikary, S., Ghosh, N.: Resume parser with natural language processing. Int. J. Eng. Sci. **4484** (2017)
18. Sadiq, S.Z.A.M., Ayub, J.A., Narsayya, G.R., Ayyas, M.A., Tahir, K.T.M.: Intel-ligent hiring with resume parser and ranking using natural language processing and machine learning. Int. J. Innov. Res. Comput. Commun. Eng. 4(4), 7437–7444 (2016)
19. Tiwari, S.M., Jain, S., Abraham, A., Shandilya, S.: Secure semantic smart health-care (s3hc). J. Web Eng. **17**(8), 617–646 (2018)
20. Mishra, S., Jain, S.: Towards a semantic knowledge treasure for military intel-ligence. In: Abraham, A., Dutta, P., Mandal, J.K., Bhattacharya, A., Dutta, S. (eds.) Emerging Technologies in Data Mining and Information Security. AISC, vol. 755, pp. 835–845. Springer, Singapore (2019). https://doi.org/10.1007/978-981-13-1951-8_74
21. Maria, G., Akrivi, K., Costas, V., George, L., Constantin, H.: Creating an ontology for the user profile: method and applications. In: Proceedings AI* AI Workshop RCIS (2007)
22. Fernández-López, M., Gómez-Pérez, A., Juristo, N.: Methontology: from ontolog-ical art towards ontological engineering (1997)
23. Suárez-Figueroa, M.C., Gómez-Pérez, A., Fernández-López, M.: The NeOn methodology for ontology engineering. In: Suárez-Figueroa, M.C., Gómez-Pérez, A., Motta, E., Gangemi, A. (eds.) Ontology Engineering in a Networked World, pp. 9–34. Springer, Heidelberg (2012). https://doi.org/10.1007/978-3-642-24794-1_2
24. Sim, W.W., Brouse, P.: Towards an ontology-based persona-driven requirements and knowledge engineering. Procedia Comput. Sci. **36**, 314–321 (2014)

25. Suárez-Figueroa, M.C., Gómez-Pérez, A.: Ontology requirements specification. In: Suárez-Figueroa, M.C., Gómez-Pérez, A., Motta, E., Gangemi, A. (eds.) Ontology Engineering in a Networked World, pp. 93–106. Springer, Heidelberg (2012). https://doi.org/10.1007/978-3-642-24794-1_5

Leveraging Enterprise Knowledge Graphs for Efficient Bridging Between Business Data with Large-Scale Web Data

Samir Sellami[1(✉)], Taoufiq Dkaki[2], Nacer Eddine Zarour[1],
and Pierre-Jean Charrel[2]

[1] LIRE Laboratory, University of Constantine 2 - Abdelhamid Mehri,
Constantine, Algeria
{samir.sellami,nasro.zarour}@univ-constantine2.dz
[2] IRIT Laboratory, University of Toulouse 2 - Jean Jaurès, Toulouse, France
{dkaki,charrel}@univ-tlse2.fr

Abstract. The diversification of the web into social media and the Web of Data means that companies need to collect the necessary data to make the best-informed market decisions. To deal with this, the new concept of Enterprise Knowledge Graphs (EKGs) is emerging as a backbone for federating valuable open information on the web together with the information contained in internal enterprise documents and databases. This paper examines the current challenges in this area, discusses the limitations of some existing integration systems, and addresses them by proposing a set of tools for virtually integrating enterprise data with social and linked data at scale. The proposed framework's implementation is a configurable middleware and user-friendly keyword faceted search web interface that retrieves its input data from internal enterprise data combined with popular SPARQL endpoints and social network web APIs. We conducted an evaluation study to test our approach's effectiveness using various metrics and compare it to state-of-the-art systems. The evaluation results show a competitive accuracy and usability of the proposed approach, facilitating the integration of data into a knowledge graph.

Keywords: Knowledge graph · Semantic data integration · Schemas mapping · Linked data · Social data · Sources heterogeneity

1 Introduction

Data is rapidly becoming a key business asset in today's digital world. Companies need access to valuable web-based data to drive the most informed business decisions. The solid support that web-based technologies have received from researchers, developers, and practitioners has entirely changed the procedure for sharing information on the web [1]. As a result, many data sources in almost every field are now accessible through the Linked Open Data Cloud (LOD)[1]. In several cases, we can use these complementary data sources; in other words, the scattered data from these sources can be linked to find the desired result. However, despite the widespread adoption of the RDF (Resource Description Framework) by leading media and government sector organizations aiming to be the universal abstract data model for publishing their structured data, several web-based information services still expose and consume non-RDF data. Examples of these services include social media networks that continue to deliver their data via web APIs in a semi-structured format, such as XML or JSON. Companies' challenge is to integrate the entities from this rich social data with the information contained in their internal documents and databases. This combination of information can open up meaningful business opportunities for those who can understand the value of newly aggregated data supported by recent AI-powered applications.

The new concept of EKG appears to be a remarkable solution that can mediate between various data models and effectively support enterprise decision-making. An EKG represents a semantic graph of concepts, attributes, individuals, and links that refer to fundamental and domain knowledge pertinent to a company [2]. The idea is to link the knowledge graph schema to data entities of a given set of heterogeneous data sources to facilitate information discovery. The demand for knowledge graphs in enterprises has increased significantly in recent years. Although the business domain may differ, from marketing to manufacturing, knowledge graphs can increase performance, reduce costs, and deliver additional values to the company's services [3,4]. For example, Google acquired Freebase and turned it into its proprietary EKG[2], while DBpedia[3] gained a comparable position for the overall Web of Data.

In this paper, we tackle these challenges by proposing a set of complementary tools. First, we suggest MidSemI, a middleware for semantic integration that resolves interoperability conflicts among heterogeneous sources. MidSemI defines a knowledge graph as a global schema and a metadata model that allows us to describe source metadata in a flexible way. Second, we propose KGMap, a new entity matching approach that exploits the knowledge graph schema and the different sources' metadata elements to bridge heterogeneous data. KGMap relies on similarity measures that identify semantically equivalent entities. Finally, based on our MidSemI middleware and the KGMap semantic mapping approach, we propose KeyFS, a keyword-based semantic search engine. KeyFS is a reactive multi-faceted navigation interface designed to facilitate exploring the entities embedded behind the knowledge graph.

We implemented our approach through a data integration use case for a commercial enterprise in which entries are retrieved on the fly from its internal text documents and CRM database, combined with the DBpedia dataset and

---

[1] https://lod-cloud.net/.

[2] https://googleblog.blogspot.com/2012/05/introducing-knowledge-graph-things-not.html.

[3] http://wiki.dbpedia.org/.

Facebook web API. We conducted an empirical study to evaluate the effectiveness of our approach using different metrics. The observed results show that using a semantic-based similarity measure improves the efficiency of our approach in terms of accuracy and recall. This paper's remainder is structured as follows: Sect. 2 summarizes and discusses relevant related works. In Sect. 3, a motivating enterprise integration scenario is described. Section 4 presents an overview of the solution and the proposed tools. The results of the empirical evaluation are reported in Sect. 5. Finally, Sect. 6 wraps up and outlines future work.

2   Related Work

The problem of integrating heterogeneous data using semantic technologies has been the subject of research for years; in this section, we give a review of the most relevant works. **LDIF**: Linked Data Integration Framework by Schultz et al. [5] is an ETL (Extract-Transform-Load) based system oriented towards the integration of RDF datasets from the Web of Data and provides a set of independent components to support the interconnection task. The LDIF components include: (1) an expressive mapping language to transform data from various vocabularies into a coherent ontology; and (2) a Linked Data Analysis component to query SPARQL access points and remote RDF dumps. LDIF solves the identity resolution problem by specifying binding rules using the SILK tool [6]. Based on the established rules, SILK recognizes the links between entities in two datasets. **UnifiedViews** [7] is another example of an ETL framework for RDF data integration. UnifiedViews relies on SILK to carry out instance matching and provides custom data fusion modules to combine data from the discovered matches. Based on ODCleanStore [8], UnifiedViews provides support for a variety of processing tasks, including instance, linking, and data merging.

In the category of virtual-based systems, two primary methods are used (1) *GaV (Global-as-View)*, (2) LaV *(Local-as-View)*. **Ultrawrap** by Sequeda et al. [9] is an influential effort of the OBDA (Ontology-Based Data Access) using the LaV method. Ultrawrap leverages the algorithms and optimizations already provided by relational DBMS (database management systems) to efficiently execute SPARQL queries. Ultrawrap uses SQL views to encode a logical representation of RDF graphs. SPARQL queries are then translated into these views. Finally, the executions of these queries in the views are automatically optimized by the DBMS, allowing fast responses to complex SPARQL queries. Many other systems have attempted to integrate not only relational or RDF data but also semi-structured data. Fuentes-Lorenzo et al. [10] describe **SWIS**, a web-oriented system based on RESTful coding and ontologies to handle data aggregation from telecommunication companies. The system uses query mediation and provides tools for visualizing data. The middleware renders XML and RDBs (relational databases) in RDF form. RQL (Resource Query Language) queries are then compiled and optimized according to RDF views, and mappings are created. **SDM-RDFizer**, proposed by Iglesias et al. [11], is a novel interpreter of RDF Mapping Language (RML) that enables the transformation of raw data in several formats into an RDF-based knowledge graph. SDM-RDFizer implements new algorithms to perform logical operators between mappings in RML, which allows them to move to complex scenarios where the data is large and has a high duplication rate. Collarana et al. [12] describe **MINTE+**, a keyword search platform integrating heterogeneous data sources. MINTE+ is based on COMET [13], an entity matching technique that uses both context-based similarity metrics and the knowledge stated in RDF vocabularies to map contextually similar entities. MINTE+ is a usable and flexible solution in its field of interest, namely crime-related information. As part of the integration workflow, the application uses numerous components, including an appropriate vocabulary ontology called "OntoFuhSen." Wrappers are one of the vocabulary-related components designed to retrieve data from source outputs. The MINTE+ system associates for each data source a collection of wrappers. In its current state, it is designed to contain information about the targeted data. Even though this system allows for vocabulary expansion, its position suggests that users will have to undergo many further adjustments. Table 1 presents a comparison of the previously mentioned semantic integration systems.

Table 1. Comparison of the different semantic integration systems.

Name	Approach	Mapping	Ontology	Matching	Data models
LDIF [5]	Materialized	LaV	Yes	Manual *owl:sameAs*	Structured (RDF)
UnifiedViews [7]	Materialized	LaV	Yes	Manual *owl:sameAs*	Structured (RDF)
Ultrawrap [9]	Virtual	LaV	Yes	Manual *R2RML*	Structured (RDB)
SWIS [10]	Virtual	GaV	Yes	Manual	Structured, Semi-Structured (RDB, XML)
SDM-RDFizer [11]	Virtual	GaV	Yes	Semi-automatic *RML*	Structured, Semi-structured (RDF, XML)
MINTE+ [12]	Virtual	LaV	Yes	Semi-automatic	Structured,semi-structured (RDF, JSON)

Discussion: The main problem with using materialized ETL systems is the freshness of the information and the possible involvement of hardware resources for many datasets. Although ETL approaches effectively integrate heterogeneous data, they require considerable manual effort to configure their integration pipelines. Our work aims to define a universal integration approach that requires only a small number of high-level parameters while leaving room for minor adjustments. In comparison, the novelty of the approaches proposed in our work lies in creating a non-materialized knowledge graph that allows the integration of data distributed across internal enterprise data combined with different web segments. On the other hand, despite the success of the OBDA paradigm, it has been mainly studied on the integration of relational databases.

We argue that more research is needed on scenarios for integrating heterogeneous web sources. Most of the approaches that apply a virtual approach for data integration use RDF and SPARQL, where datasets must be completely transformed and published in advance in RDF so that they can be queried later with SPARQL engines. This transformation is costly, as it requires an additional step in the integration process and sometimes impossible given the confidentiality of some of the company's sensitive data. Besides, we argue that SPARQL is not an appropriate approach for all web data sources and hard to use by regular users. The goal of the proposed approach is to integrate data without transforming them. The sensitive business data will remain hidden behind the enterprise local network firewall, which will ensure data security and privacy. In contrast, social data and linked data will be accessed remotely by the mediator. In this work, we propose a keyword-based semantic search platform capable of integrating heterogeneous data models, from internal data provided by SQL databases and text documents; to social web APIs that provide a local view of the data in JSON objects or RDF data published in the linked open data cloud.

3   Motivating Scenario

The proposed approach is driven by an integration scenario for commercial enterprises. In this context, we study how knowledge graphs and semantic web techniques can help this category of companies better meet customer needs by identifying new opportunities. The knowledge about relevant business entities is dispersed over different data sources in the organizations' intranets or even on the web. For example, information about customers can be found in social networks or a CRM (customer relationship management) system. Similarly, product-related information can be found on e-commerce sites, private technical documents, or public repositories of product data published on the LOD. Figure 1(a) depicts that the manual process of collecting such diverse items of information is time-consuming and highly tedious for the end-user. The user needs access to a large number of different data sources and then tries to manually connect the individual search results. Figure 1(b) illustrates our concept of an automated integration platform that semantically links information from distributed sources. The user only needs to interact with the platform to access, search data on entities from a variety of information sources, and then apply analytic using AI-BI-driven applications. In terms of data sources, our objective is to gather and integrate relevant information from the Web of Data, the social web, and internal company data sources.

- **The Social Web** includes profiles and user-generated content; Twitter and Facebook are examples of these social networks. These social networks are equipped with a web API to query the data.

- **The Web of Data** is another precious source of information where we can find machine-understandable data sources that include billions of facts.

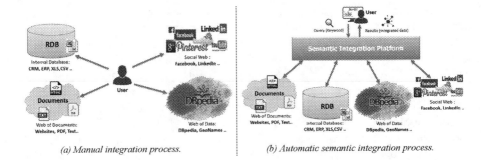

(a) Manual integration process.   (b) Automatic semantic integration process.

Fig. 1. Overview of semantic integration - adapted from [14]. (a) Manual integration process over various internal data, plus open web data. (b) Semantic integration platform that automatically integrates data from internal and distributed web sources.

This data space provides relevant background knowledge for aggregating information; it includes datasets such as DBpedia and Wikidata[4]

- **Internal Data.** Finally, the main objective of the platform is to integrate all this open web information with the company's internal data sources such as a CRM relational database, Excel spreadsheets, and text documents. These information sources can be unstructured, semi-structured, or structured data.

4   Overview of the Solution

This work makes theoretical and practical contributions to the field of integrating data from relational databases and text documents with semi-structured social and structured linked entities. Figure 2 shows a workflow of the three main contributions of the approach:

MidSemI (Middleware for Semantic Integration). To resolve interoperability conflicts between heterogeneous sources at the integration time, we propose the MidSemI approach [15], which allows: (1) the creation of the knowledge graph; (2) the adding of data sources and the metadata extraction; (3) the establishment of semantic mappings between the knowledge graph schema and the sources metadata elements; and (4) the rewriting of user queries and the visualization of the integrated results. From an abstract point of view, the architecture of MidSemI is based on a mediator. It is composed of the following layers: *(a) Presentation Layer* - includes a user interface and navigational logic that allows easy access to the integrated information. *(b) Metadata Layer and Schema* - includes ontologies and vocabularies that provide a formal, machine-understandable description of the accumulated knowledge graph and metadata about data sources to facilitate data discovery. *(c) Instance Layer* - contains a

---

[4] https://www.wikidata.org.

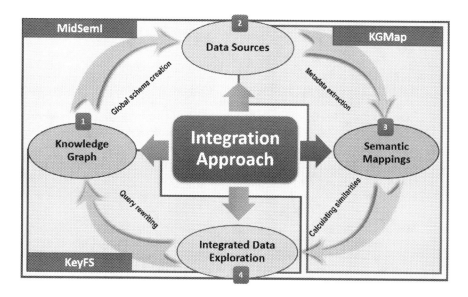

Fig. 2. The workflow of the main contributions of the approach.

specific set of local databases and sets of open web-based data sources related to the business.

KGMap (Knowledge Graph Mapping Model). A mapping approach to exploit a knowledge graph and similarity measures to bridge heterogeneous text, relational, social, and linked data. KGMap [16] consists of three sub-models: (1) the knowledge graph representation model, (2) the source metadata description model, and (3) the mapping model. The KGMap approach manages these models and defines different mapping cases for concepts and attributes. The algorithm in KGMap automatically detects pairs of direct correspondences between elements of knowledge graph schema and source metadata. A similarity measure is an essential component of our approach. That is why we are conducting an experimental study to test the efficiency of the KGMap using different similarity measures.

KeyFS (Keyword-Based Faceted Search over Integrated Data). Based on our MidSemI middleware and our KGMap semantic mapping model for information integration, KeyFS enables a semantic search engine for integrated data. KeyFS is a keyword-based search interface for searching entities over integrated data. By exploiting Natural Language Processing (NLP) techniques, sources metadata, and mapping information, KeyFS is able to rewrite user queries expressed as keywords into different queries in the native query languages of heterogeneous data sources. KeyFS executes the queries, merges the data, and visualizes the final responses to the user in a responsive multi-faceted navigation interface. An evaluation of the usability of the interface suggests that KeyFS offers advantages over traditional keyword-based searching.

5 Empirical Evaluation

5.1 Implementation

In this section, we present an implementation of the proposed framework. Mid-SemI is a mediator-based integration system that integrates information. It searches for entities about people, organizations, and products in the CRM database of the local enterprise then links them to semi-structured Facebook social network profiles and structured DBPedia linked data. We devise our platform by building two complementary prototype modules: *(a) a middleware application* and *(b) a faceted browsing web application.* The implementation of the KGMap approach is a part of MidSemI middleware. Figure 3 shows the main user interface of the MidSemI middleware application. To ensure proper configuration, we divided the middleware component into three modular parts: the first for curating knowledge graph, the second for adding data sources and extracting their metadata, and the last for establishing semantic mappings with the knowledge graph. Figure 4 illustrates the graphical user interface of the "Mapping Information" module, which maintains identified mapping correspondences. Figure 5 shows the faceted navigation web interface of the platform. The main features of the faceted browsing web interface are receiving keyword-based queries from users, rewriting the query for underlined connected data sources, and visualizing the results through a multi-faceted navigation user interface. To demonstrate the feasibility of the prototype components, we tested them on the public SQL database Adventure Works LT[5], which is a typical database used in Microsoft CRM. For querying Facebook, we coded an instance of the API

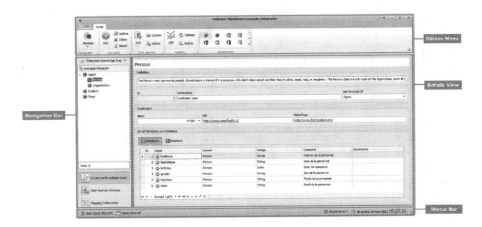

Fig. 3. The main interface of the middleware component - selected module "Enterprise Knowledge Graph" displays the example of a business knowledge graph in the Navigation Bar. The Details View displays the information about the selected concept *"Person."*

---

[5] https://github.com/Microsoft/sql-server-samples.

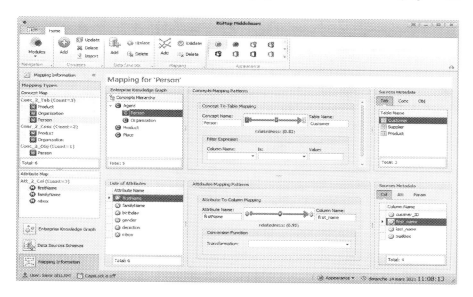

Fig. 4. Mapping information graphical interface – Navigation Bar shows the mapping information. Details View displays the mapping patterns, i.e., the relatedness measure for the concept *"Person"* of the knowledge graph to the *"Customer"* Table of the SQL CRM DB and the attribute *"firstName"* to the column *"first_name."*

wrapper component using its web API[6]. For querying DBpedia, we developed an RDF wrapper component that runs a SPARQL query against a local Fuseki server[7], i.e., a SPARQL endpoint for an RDF dump file of the DBpedia dataset. The experiments were performed on a computer machine with the Windows 10 system equipped with an Intel i5 2.8 GHz processor and 8 GB of RAM. We coded the three modules of the middleware prototype in Visual Studio IDE using C# language and Microsoft SQL Server database to implement the Mapping Schema model. The faceted navigation engine was fluently coded following the MVC paradigm in the ReactJS and ASP.Net frameworks. The source code of the MidSemI platform is available publicly on GitHub repository[8].

5.2   Evaluation

We evaluated the effectiveness of our mapping technique implemented in KGMap by observing the impact of applying two distinct similarity measures to identify the relatedness between terms:

- **The Jaro-Winkler similarity measure** [17]: is a string similarity algorithm. This algorithm employs a combination of string and set similarity, meaning that the compared values of terms are tokenized before the regular Jaro-Winkler algorithm is applied and the maximum overall score is picked.

---

[6] https://developers.facebook.com/docs/graph-api/.
[7] https://jena.apache.org/documentation/fuseki2.
[8] https://github.com/SamRepository/.

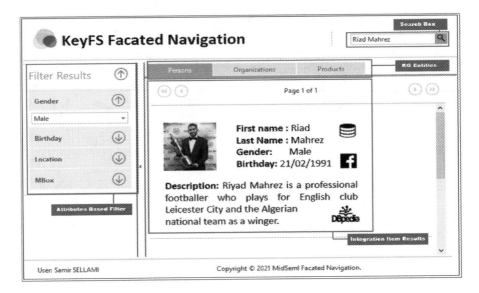

Fig. 5. KeyFS faceted navigation screen – visualizes the results of integration for the keyword *"Riad Mehrez."* The output item is shown in the *"Persons"* tab of the knowledge graph. *"Male"* was applied to the attribute *"Gender"* as a filter criterion.

- **The UMBC similarity measure** [18]: is a tool constructed by mixing LSA (Latent Semantic Analysis) word similarity and WorldNet knowledge. It focuses on the semantics of the word rather than its lexical category. Table 2 provides additional statistics on the experimental configuration for the assessment.

Table 2. Gold standard/data sources description. Data sources are described regarding the number of their metadata and the number of necessary mappings to the Gold Standard KG.

Sources	Adventure Works (RDB)		DBpedia (RDF)		Facebook (JSON)		Knowledge graph (GS)	
Metadata Elements	Tables	Columns	Concepts	Attributes	Objects	Params	Concepts	Attributes
	3	14	2	11	2	11	4	18
Concept_Map	3		2		2		7	
Attribute_Map	9		11		6		26	

Gold Standard (GS): We created a ground truth KG schema as described in Sect. 3. It contains four (04) concepts and eighteen (18) attributes extracted from three different vocabularies. For this, the KGMap component connects to the linked open data vocabularies portal[9], then curates and maintains knowledge graph schema elements in the knowledge graph model. We manually generate both mappings for concepts *(Concept_Map)* and mapping for attributes *(Attribut_Map)* for the three heterogeneous data sources. We maintained mapping pairs in the mapping model. This Gold Standard is used in the evaluation to calculate the Precision and Recall of the KGMap approach.

Test Datasets: We used three heterogeneous data sources:

- Adventure Works LT DB: Microsoft CRM relational DB[10] used for test proposes. We used a portion of this database: three (03) tables and fourteen (14) columns populated with sample data.
- DBpedia Products & Organizations: an RDF-based dataset. We extracted a dump file from the live release of the English DBpedia (July-2016)[11], containing instances of two concepts (product, organization) and their attributes.

Table 3. Effectiveness of KGMap. Comparison between Jaro-Winkler and UMBC similarity measures been applied to KGMap with a variable threshold (T). The highest values of obtained metrics are highlighted in bold.

KGMap approach (Jaro-Winkler similarity)						
Threshold	T0.2	T0.3	T0.4	T 0.5	T0.6	T0.7
Precision	0.4	0.45	0.45	0.47	0.55	**0.84**
Recall	0.5	0.1	0.06	0.03	0.01	0.004
F-Measure	0.44	0.17	0.11	0.06	0.02	0.01
KGMap approach (UMBC semantic similarity)						
Threshold	T0.2	T0.3	T0.4	T 0.5	T0.6	T0.7
Precision	1.0	1.0	1.0	1.0	1.0	**1.0**
Recall	**1.0**	0.99	0.98	0.77	0.59	0.07
F-Measure	**1.0**	0.99	0.99	0.87	0.74	0.13

- Facebook Users: a JSON file extracted using Facebook API contains some public information about Facebook user-profiles and page objects. The file describes the user, the page objects, and their parameters.

The reason behind choosing such popular and accessible datasets is that they cover diverse data models spread over the enterprise's intranet and various web segments (i.e., the Web of Data and social web). KGMap maintains metadata about these datasets in the metadata description model.

Metrics: We measured KGMap's behavior using the following metrics:

---

[9] https://lov.linkeddata.es/dataset/lov.
[10] https://github.com/Microsoft/sql-server-samples/releases/tag/adventureworks.
[11] https://wiki.dbpedia.org/downloads-2016-10.

- Precision: is the fraction of true mappings (M) for concepts and attributes that have been identified by KGMap and overlap with the mappings in the Gold Standard (GS). $Precision = |M \cap GS|/|M|$.
- Recall: is the intersection cardinality of identified mappings by KGMap (M) and Gold Standard (GS), divided by that of Gold Standard (GS). $Recall = |M \cap GS|/|GS|$.
- F-measure: is the harmonic mean for both Recall and Precision.

Discussion: Precision, Recall, and F-measure are calculated according to the Gold Standard. Table 3 shows the values of these metrics for the two similarity measures Jaro-Winkler and UMBC. Jaro-Winkler demonstrates lower performance because its algorithm is based only on the syntax of the string. It does not use the semantics and synonyms embedded in the knowledge graph to determine the degree of relatedness between terms. On the other hand, UMBC shows better performance because it focuses on the semantics of terms rather than on its lexical category. Nevertheless, the performance is affected by the threshold parameter. The performance with Jaro-Winkler similarity decreases rapidly with higher thresholds. How-ever, UMBC similarity can maintain stable performance and quality for thresholds up to 0.6. UMBC is a typical similarity measurement means for data mapping approaches where sources use different names and structures but with the same semantics.

Table 4. Comparison of KGMap with LDIF and MINTE+.

LDIF Triple-based approach (Silk)					
Threshold	T0.2	T0.3	T0.4	T 0.5	T0.6	T0.7
Precision	1.0	1.0	1.0	1.0	1.0	**1.0**
Recall	0.55	0.55	0.55	0.55	0.55	**0.55**
F-Measure	0.71	0.71	0.71	0.71	0.71	**0.71**
MINTE + Molecule-based approach (Jaccard)					
Precision	1.0	1.0	1.0	1.0	1.0	**1.0**
Recall	**0,81**	0,81	0,81	0,77	0,55	0,07
F-Measure	**0,90**	0,90	0,90	0,87	0,71	0,13
KGMap approach (UMBC semantic similarity)					
Precision	1.0	1.0	1.0	1.0	1.0	**1.0**
Recall	**1.0**	0.99	0.98	0.77	0.59	0.07
F-Measure	1.0	0.99	0.99	0.87	0.74	0.13

We empirically evaluated the KGMap on test sets to measure its accuracy using UMBC semantic similarity against LDIF with a triple-based technique implemented by Silk tool and MINTE+ with a molecule-based approach using embedded Jaccard similarity.

Discussion: The Precision, Recall, and F-measure values were calculated according to the Gold Standard described in Table 2. Table 4 shows these measures for KGMap in comparison to LDIF and MINTE+. The highest values are highlighted in bold. The results indicate high precision, i.e., only true positives were identified. The recall of LDIF remains stable as it is configured using the Silk tool to generate only *owl:sameAs* matches based on exact equivalence for the DBpedia RDF dataset. For MINTE+ and KGMap, recall decreases with a higher threshold for the Jaccard or UMBC semantic similarity measures. Higher thresholds increase the number of common entities in the metadata needed to classify them as similar in the knowledge graph elements, i.e., with low thresholds, only common entities in the metadata of the sources related to the knowledge graph terms are enough to mark the pairs as semantically similar. KGMap has slightly higher accuracy than MINTE+. This is due to the ability of our KGMap model to cover not only web datasets (DBpedia and Facebook) but also relational data models from the CRM database.

6   Conclusion

A considerable amount of valuable data is distributed over the web that companies can leverage to create enterprise-wide knowledge graphs if combined effectively with internal databases and text documents. These datasets are semantically and syntactically heterogeneous since they use different data models and schemas. In this paper, we have provided a summary of existing data integration systems and discuss their limitations. To bridge the gap between internal enterprise data and new web-based data models, we proposed a set of tools to leverage enterprise knowledge graphs by linking between these diverse heterogeneous data models. The approach will contribute to building semantic virtual integration systems that will provide uniform access to heterogeneous and large-scale sources. Finally, our work can have an impact on semantic aggregated search and serve as bases for fields like web query optimization, data quality, and even the Internet of things (IoT).

References

1. Hogan, A.: Web of data. In: The Web of Data, pp. 15–57. Springer International Publishing, Cham 2020). https://doi.org/10.1007/978-3-030-51580-5_2
2. Galkin, M., Auer, S., Vidal, M.E., Scerri, S.: Enterprise knowledge graphs: a semantic approach for knowledge management in the next generation of enterprise information systems. In: ICEIS 2017 - Proceedings of the 19th International Conference on Enterprise Information Systems, vol. 2, SciTe Press. pp. 88–98, April 2017. ISBN: 9789897582486. http://www.scitepress.org/documents/2017/63252, https://doi.org/10.5220/0006325200880098

3. Hislop, D., Bosua, R., Helms, R.: Knowledge Management in Organizations: A Critical Introduction. Oxford University Press, Oxford (2018). ISBN: 9780198724018

4. Villazón-Terrazas, B., Ortiz-Rodríguez, F., Tiwari, S.M., Shandilya, S.K.: Knowledge graphs and semantic web. In: Proceeding of the Second Iberoamerican Conference and First Indo-American Conference, KGSWC 2020, Mexico, November 26–27. Springer, Cham (2020). https://doi.org/10.1007/978-3-030-65384-2

5. Schultz, A., Matteini, A., Isele, R., Mendes, P.N.C., Becker, B.C.: LDIF-a framework for large-scale linked data integration. In: 21st International World Wide Web Conference, vol. 10. WWW: Developers Track. Lyon, France (2012)

6. Isele, R., Bizer, C.: Active learning of expressive linkage rules using genetic programming. J. Web Seman. **23**, 215 (2013). ISBN: 15708268, https://doi.org/10.1016/j.websem.2013.06.001

7. Knap, T., Skoda, P., Klımek, J., Necask, M.: Unifiedviews: towards ETI tool for simple yet powerfull RDF data management. In: DATESO, pp. 111–120 (2015)

8. Michelfeit, J., Knap, T.: Linked data fusion in odcleanstore. In: 11th International Semantic Web Conference, Boston, MA, USA, 11–15 November 2012, vol. 45 (2012)

9. Sequeda, J.F., Miranker, D.P.: Ultrawrap mapper: a semi-automatic relational database to RDF (RDB2RDF) mapping tool. In: International Semantic Web Conference (posters & demos) (2015)

10. Fuentes-Lorenzo, D., Sánchez, L., Cuadra, A., Cutanda, M.: A restful and semantic framework for data integration. Softw. Pract. Exp. **45**(9), 11611188 (2015)

11. Iglesias, E., Jozashoori, S., Chaves-Fraga, D., Collarana, D., Vidal, M.-E.:SDMRDFizer: An RML interpreter for the efficient creation of RDF knowledge graphs. In: Proceedings of the 29th ACM International Conference on Information & Knowledge Management, p. 30393046 (2020)

12. Collarana, D., Galkin, M., Lange, C., Scerri, S., Auer, S., Vidal, M.-E.: Synthesizing knowledge graphs from web sources with the MINTE$^+$ framework. In: Vrandečić, D., et al. (eds.) ISWC 2018. LNCS, vol. 11137, pp. 359–375. Springer, Cham (2018). https://doi.org/10.1007/978-3-030-00668-6_22

13. Tasnim, M., Collarana, D., Graux, D., Galkin, M., Vidal, M.-E.: COMET: a contextualized molecule-based matching technique. In: Hartmann, S., Küng, J., Chakravarthy, S., Anderst-Kotsis, G., Tjoa, A.M., Khalil, I. (eds.) DEXA 2019. LNCS, vol. 11706, pp. 175–185. Springer, Cham (2019). https://doi.org/10.1007/978-3-030-27615-7_13

14. Collarana, D., Lange, C., Auer, S.: FuhSen: a platform for federated, RDF-based hybrid search. In: Proceedings of the 25th International Conference Companion on World Wide Web, pp. 171–174 (2016)

15. Sellami, S., Dkaki, T., Zarour, N.E., Charrel, P.-J.: MidSemI a middleware for semantic integration of business data with large-scale social and linked data. Int. J. Inf. Syst. Model. Des. **10**(2), 1–25 (2019)

16. Sellami, D., Dkaki, T., Zarour, N.E., Charrel, P.-J.: KGMap: leveraging enterprise knowledge graphs by bridging between relational, social and linked web data. In: Proceedings of the 2019 3rd International Conference on Advances in Artificial Intelligence, pp. 90–96 (2019)

17. Cahyono, S.: Comparison of document similarity measurements in scientific writing using jaro-winkler distance method and paragraph vector method. IOP Conf. Ser. Mater. Sci. Eng. **662**, 052 016 (2019)

18. Han, L., Kashyap, A.L., Finin, T., Mayfield, J., Weese, J.: UMBC EBIQUITY-CORE: semantic textual similarity systems. In: Second Joint Conference on Lexical and Computational Semantics (* SEM), vol. 1: Proceedings of the Main Conference and the Shared Task: Semantic Textual Similarity, pp. 44–52 (2013)

Metadata Driven Semantically Aware Medical Query Expansion

Rituraj Ojha[1][(✉)] and Gerard Deepak[2]

[1] Department of Metallurgical and Materials Engineering, National Institute
of Technology, Tiruchirappalli, Tiruchirappalli, Tamil Nadu, India
[2] Department of Computer Science and Engineering, National Institute
of Technology, Tiruchirappalli, Tiruchirappalli, Tamil Nadu, India

Abstract. The query used to retrieve information related to the medical domain may not contain the technical terms which are used in the medical industry. The user query should include more relevant terms and therefore, query expansion technique is required in the medical domain for their Information Retrieval Systems. In this paper, a metadata driven semantically aware medical query expansion methodology is proposed. The proposed approach takes a query as an input which is preprocessed and then Latent Semantic Indexing is used to generate new topics for each query word. A set of ontologies of PubMed keywords are semantically aligned using Lesk similarity and Normalized Pointwise Mutual Information. A Knowledge Tree is formed which is used to classify the metadata generated from Google Books using Recurrent Neural Networks. Finally, the terms from the Knowledge Tree are enriched using Wikidata, CASNET, and Hepatitis Knowledge Base, and are semantically integrated with 25% of the classified metadata using Normalized Pointwise Mutual Information under the Social Spider algorithm. The proposed MDSA-MQE methodology achieves the Precision of 90.12%, Recall of 93.87%, Accuracy of 92.08%, F-Measure of 91.95%, and Normalized Discounted Cumulative Gain value of 0.94 making it a better approach than the baseline approaches.

Keywords: Entity enrichment · Information retrieval · Medical query expansion · Metadata

1 Introduction

The Information Retrieval Systems are software programs used for finding the relevant information or documents that the user needs. A web search engine is an excellent example of the Information Retrieval System. Information on the internet in the medical field is increasing at a fast rate. A proper Information Retrieval System is required which fetches relevant medical documents as per the user's query.

However, it is very tough to access this large amount of increasing data. Furthermore, the user query lacks the essential technical terms that are contained

© Springer Nature Switzerland AG 2021
B. Villazón-Terrazas et al. (Eds.): KGSWC 2021, CCIS 1459, pp. 223–233, 2021.
https://doi.org/10.1007/978-3-030-91305-2_17

in the relevant document set. As a result, the user might not receive the required medical information that he needs. Hence, a proper Information Retrieval System is required, which uses a query expansion methodology to enhance the user query with more technical and essential terms for fetching the relevant document set that is most suitable.

Motivation: Medical terms are highly technical, and their technical interpretation is very challenging for Information Systems, and therefore there is a necessity for a better understanding of medical terminology. When a system is queried with medical terminologies, a better query understanding or better query expansion recommendation system is required. Also, there are very few systems in this domain that return results with high accuracy. Therefore, building this system having higher accuracy than the existing approaches was a major motivating factor.

Contribution: A metadata driven semantically aware medical query expansion system is proposed. The input queries by users related to the medical domain drives the proposed framework. The query is preprocessed and Latent Semantic Indexing is used to generate new topics for each query word. A set of ontologies of PubMed keywords are semantically aligned using Lesk Similarity and Normalized Pointwise Mutual Information (NPMI). A Knowledge Tree is formed which is used to classify the metadata generated from Google Books using Recurrent Neural Networks (RNN). Finally, the terms from the Knowledge Tree are enriched using Wikidata, CASNET, and Hepatitis Knowledge Base and semantically integrated with 25% of the classified metadata using NPMI under the Social Spider algorithm. The values of metrics like, Precision, Accuracy, Recall, nDCG, and F-Measure of the proposed methodology are improved.

Organization: The flow of the remaining paper is as follows. A condensed summary of the related works is provided in Sect. 2. Section 3 depicts the architecture of the proposed system. Section 4 describes the architecture implementation. Section 5 presents the evaluation of results and performance. The conclusion of the paper is presented in Sect. 6.

2   Related Works

Arbabi et al. [1] have proposed a machine learning model which automatically recognizes medical concepts in a large unstructured text. They have proposed a neural dictionary model, called Neural Concept Recognizer (NCR), which can identify the synonyms which were unobserved previously, by using biomedical ontology. Kim et al. [2] have proposed a healthcare context information system based on ontology. The proposed model helps in providing the customized service environments by extracting and classifying the contextual information.

Yunzhi et al. [3] have presented a technique for the expansion of medical query which is based on Hepatitis ontology. Their methodology uses the semantic approach to retrieve better results by expanding the query with synonyms, hypernym and similar query related technical words. Gao et al. [4] have proposed a methodology for automatic expansion of query which will be used for retrieving relevant BIM resources from web. They have proposed a search engine using IFC IR ontology.

Kuzi et al. [5] have presented an approach for expanding query using word embeddings. Their approach expands the given query with the words which are semantically related using Word2Vec's CBOW embedding technique. Oh and Jung [6] have proposed a query expansion technique using several collections from external sources. Their approach uses pseudo-relevance feedback technique.

Keikha et al. [7] have proposed a supervised and unsupervised query expansion technique which uses pseudo-relevance feedback approach. In this approach, Wikipedia articles are extracted which are highly related to the user query. Dahir et al. [8] have proposed a methodology for the extraction of candidate terms for query expansion. Their methodology is based on DBpedia and WordNet.

Jain et al. [9] have proposed an approach to retrieve medical records using semantic query expansion technique for helping patient with their current symptoms. The proposed Electronic Medical Record (EMR) retrieval system uses domain ontologies, automatic sematic relationship learning, information retrieval, and domain knowledge from professionals. Raza et al. [10] have surveyed and presented the recent approaches and models for semantic query expansion. They have discussed strength and weakness of each model and organized them into a taxonomy. The papers [11] and [12] have proposed several approaches based on ontologies and machine learning models.

Mourao et al. [13] have proposed a medical IR system which supports image and text queries. The system can retrieve relevant PubMed articles and can expand the query using MeSH thesaurus. Hanauer et al. [14] reports about an IR system, namely EMERSE, which helps in retrieving information stored in clinical notes in EHRs.

From the literature analysis, it is inferable that either the models are based on traditional machine learning paradigm with static Ontologies or they use standard knowledge sources, like DBPedia and WordNet. Certain approaches have used semantic techniques alone. Word2Vec with clustering mechanisms are also incorporated along with a learning of relations. However, some of the models extract features from the dataset alone and do not focus on the standard knowledge stores. In some of the approaches, either a medical database which is highly domain specific or secondary modeled thesaurus has been used. It is to be noted that a combination of machine learning with semantics is quite rare in query expansion. However, encompassment of standard knowledge stores and specialized medical extracts infused with the highly stringent semantics with learning and inferencing is the need of the hour in medical query expansion which has been targeted in the proposed model.

3   Proposed System Architecture

The architecture for query expansion is depicted in Fig. 1. The proposed approach takes place in several steps. Initially, the query is taken as an input and is preprocessed using Tokenization, Lemmatization, stop word removal, and Named Entity Recognition (NER). Tokenization is the process of breaking the texts into small pieces called tokens. Byte Pair Encoding (BPE) is used for the tokenization process. Lemmatization involves grouping together several inflected kinds of the same word so that they are analyzed as one term. During stop word removal, the common ubiquitous words are removed as they add no value for the analysis and only increase the dimension of the feature set. The NLTK python library is used for stop word removal. NER is the process of finding and categorizing the data or entity into predefined categories. After the preprocessing stage, a Query word set is obtained. In the next step, Latent Semantic Indexing is used to generate new topics for each term in the query word set. Latent Semantic Indexing is the method for analyzing documents and producing a set of topics related to that document.

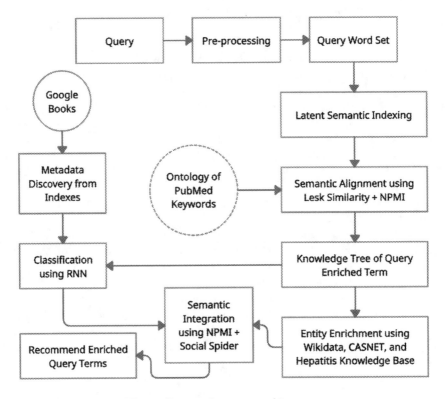

Fig. 1. Proposed system architecture

Now, the ontology of PubMed keywords which has been modeled and generated is used for further decision making and knowledge inclusion into the framework. PubMed is used for accessing the MEDLINE database containing data on life sciences and biomedical. For every word in the query word set coming from

Latent Semantic Indexing, a set of ontologies of PubMed keywords are aligned. The Semantic alignment is achieved by computing the semantic similarity using Lesk Similarity [15] and NPMI measure. The Lesk Similarity measure assumes that words in the same neighborhood will share a common topic. It is mainly used for word sense disambiguation. The NPMI is the normalized form of PMI (Pointwise mutual information) measure. The value for NPMI ranges between the bounds -1 and 1 that assists the process of selective filtering and separates the items relevant to query from irrelevant items [16].

$$pmi(x; y) = J(x) + J(y) - J(x, y) \tag{1}$$

$$npmi(x; y) = \frac{pmi(x; y)}{J(x, y)} \tag{2}$$

Equation (1) represents the Pointwise Mutual Information. The $J(x)$ represents the self-information, or $-\log_2 p(X = x)$. Equation (2) represents Normalized Pointwise Mutual Information. The $J(x, y)$ represents joint self-information, which is equal to $-\log_2 p(X = x, Y = y)$.

Furthermore, the Knowledge Tree of the query enriched terms is formulated by computing the semantic similarity using Lesk and NPMI measures between the instances in the Ontology and the Latent Semantic Indexing enriched initial query words. Now, taking the tree as the input, we will classify using the RNN. From Google Books, the metadata is generated from indexes using OpenCalais and RDF Distiller. The top 25% of the classified results are retained for Semantic Integration. For terms coming from Knowledge Tree, entity enrichment is performed using Wikidata, CASNET, and Hepatitis Knowledge Base. The two medical knowledge bases, namely the CASNET and Hepatitis Knowledge Base are accessed using Python APIs. Wikidata will be queried using SPARQL endpoints. A CASNET is a semantic net, a knowledge structure consisting of nodes representing the concepts, characteristics, events, and branches specifying the relationships between nodes. It helps in treatment of Glaucoma.

Now, all the enriched entities along with the Knowledge Tree have been integrated with the 25% of the classified contents from the medical books from Google Books. The Semantic Integration is done using NPMI under Social Spider algorithm, which is a heuristic algorithm. It was created by imitating the behavior of spiders in nature. After all these steps, the enriched query terms are recommended by the system.

4   Implementation

The algorithm for the proposed technique is depicted in Table 1. The dataset used for this approach is the STS Benchmark dataset (https://ixa2.si.ehu.eus/stswiki/index.php/STSbenchmark). It contains a collection of the English datasets and there are about 8628 sentence pairs contained in the benchmark. The input taken is the query along with google books and ontology of PubMed keywords. The algorithm returns the recommended enriched query words as output.

Algorithm 1. Proposed System Architecture

Input: Query, Google Books, Ontology of PubMed Keywords
Output: Enriched Query Terms
Begin
Step 1: The Query Q is subjected to query pre-processing. Q is tokenized, lemmatized, and NER and stop word removal is performed to obtain query word set Qw.

Step 2: while (Qw.next()!=NULL)
for each Qw as label
Qw ← Latent Semantic Indexing Generated Topics
end for
end while

Step 3: for each Qw Semantic alignment of set of ontologies of PubMed Keywords end for
Step 4: Knowledge Tree will be formed
Step 5: 5.1: Metadata generation using Google Books 5.2: Classifying metadata taking knowledge tree as input using RNN
Step 6: Qw ← entity enrichment using Wikidata, CASNET, and Hepatitis knowledge base
Step 7: SemanticIntegration(Top 25% of classified contents from Google Books, Enriched entities from Knowledge Tree)
Step 8: Recommend enriched Query Terms
End

5 Results and Performance Evaluation

The performance of the proposed MDSA-MQE (Metadata Driven Semantically Aware Medical Query Expansion) approach is measured by considering Precision, Recall and Accuracy. Other measures including F-Measure and Normalized-Discounted Cumulative Gain (nDCG) are also used. The performance is evaluated for 6871 queries and the ground truth has been collected.

$$Precision = \frac{Retrieved \cap Relevant}{Retrieved} \tag{3}$$

$$Recall = \frac{Retrieved \cap Relevant}{Relevant} \tag{4}$$

$$Accuracy = \frac{ProportionCorrectsofeachQueryPassedtheGroundTruthTest}{TotalNumberofQueries} \tag{5}$$

$$F - Measure = \frac{2 \times (Precision \times Recall)}{Precision + Recall} \tag{6}$$

$$nDCG = \frac{DCG_\alpha}{IDCG_\alpha} \tag{7}$$

$$DCG = \sum_{i=1}^{\infty} \frac{rel_i}{\log_2(i+1)} \tag{8}$$

Equations (3), (4), and (5) represent Precision, Recall and Accuracy, respectively. Furthermore, the Eqs. (6), (7), and (8) represent F-Measure, nDCG and Discounted cumulative gain, respectively. The reason for considering these above metrics for evaluation is because they measure the relevance of the results. The Knowledge Base is extensively vast and, in this case, it is primarily used for entity population and increasing the density of the incoming auxiliary knowledge into the framework. The Recall computation is carried out with respect to the dataset and not with respect to the Knowledge Base. The number of relevant documents in the dataset is already known for each query which has been tested, as the ground truth collection was carried out by a simple voting mechanism by 714 candidates who were domain experts and top 25 relevant documents for each query was taken. However, 20 coherent relevant documents, based on the maximum voting, were shortlisted and considered as relevant for each subsequent query. The queries were distributed such that each candidate had to answer 20 queries and top 20 relevant documents from the dataset had to be recommended by them. Instead of using a query tool, a human-in-the-middle approach was followed for the collection of ground truth based on the documents in the dataset. For the query expansion, the keywords in the documents based on the frequency of occurrences and the uniqueness of terms were considered to be relevant.

Table 1. Performance comparison of the proposed MDSA-MQE with other approaches

Search technique	Average precision %	Average recall %	Average accuracy %	Average F-measure %	nDCG
MQES [19]	78.32	81.79	79.44	80.02	0.75
CRDESLM-QET [17]	74.36	77.12	75.69	75.71	0.74
QEMO [18]	83.78	87.92	85.56	85.80	0.91
Proposed MDSA-MQE	90.12	93.87	92.08	91.95	0.94

Table 1 represents the performance comparison of the proposed MDSA-MQE with other approaches. It is evident from the table that the proposed approach achieves the highest average accuracy with the Precision of 90.12%, Recall of 93.87%, Accuracy of 92.08%, F-Measure of 91.95%, and nDCG value of 0.94.

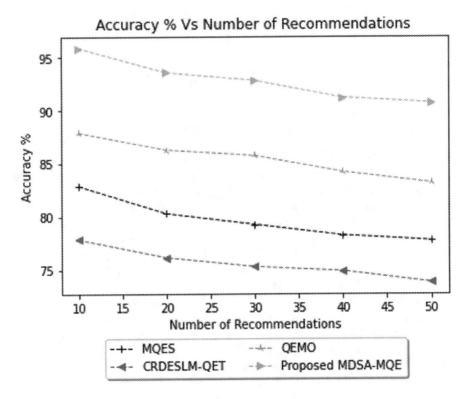

Fig. 2. Accuracy % vs number of recommendations

Figure 2 represents the Accuracy % vs Number of Recommendations of the proposed approach. The proposed MDSA-MQE approach is better than the other approaches because of several reasons. MQES [19] uses DBPedia and Wikidata as standard knowledge sources but for computing the relevance, it only uses Kullback–Leibler Divergence. As a result, MQES [19] achieves less accuracy than the proposed MDSA-MQE model. Generally, the greater the number of relevant knowledge bases, greater is the probability of relevant knowledge fed into the approach, thereby increasing the density of auxiliary knowledge and improving the overall accuracy of the approach. The CRDESLM-QET [17] uses a clustering method which is not as good as the proposed approach. In the QEMO [18] approach, they have used MeSH medical ontology to enrich the query with medical terms. Modelling ontology is highly complicated and depending on only modelled ontology at every instance of time is not the right strategy since every time ontology cannot be modelled. Also, a bag of terms has been used which is unsuitable when a lot of external knowledge sources are to be integrated into the model. Therefore, the density of enriched entities will be quite low in this approach. The proposed MDSA-MQE approach achieves a high density of entities because there are many knowledge sources. New topics are generated using Latent Semantic Indexing and metadata coming from Google Books is classified and semantically integrated with the query set. Also, ontology of PubMed keywords is used for better accuracy. Enrichment of the Knowledge Tree takes place using Wikidata, CASNET, and Hepatitis Knowledge Base. Hence, because of these reasons, the proposed MDSA-MQE approach is much better than the existing models.

Table 2 presents two examples from several of the expanded queries produced by the proposed model. Only the top 8 expanded queries results are displayed here.

Table 2. Examples of query expansion by proposed model

Model medical queries	Query expansion by proposed MDSA-MQE
Vitamin D status	1. Vitamin D status during gestation
	2. VItamin D status during infancy
	3. Vitamin D status of children
	4. Vitamin D status of adults
	5. Vitamin D status in geriatric patients
	6. Vitamin D status in men
	7. Vitamin D status in women after menopause
	8. Vitamin D status in first trimester pregnancy
Oral Ciprofloxacin is the first line of antibiotic	1. Oral Ciprofloxacin is the first line of antibiotic for urinary tract infection
	2. Oral Ciprofloxacin is the first line of antibiotic for gonorrhea
	3. Oral Ciprofloxacin is the first line of antibiotic for chancroid
	4. Oral Ciprofloxacin is the first line of antibiotic for skin
	5. Oral Ciprofloxacin is the first line of antibiotic for bone
	6. Oral Ciprofloxacin is the first line of antibiotic for joint infections
	7. Oral Ciprofloxacin is the first line of antibiotic for typhoid fever
	8. Oral Ciprofloxacin is the first line of antibiotic for plague

6   Conclusion

There is much necessity for satisfying the users by providing relevant information pertaining to medical areas. There is no medical query expansion technique which can enrich the user query with high accuracy. Therefore, the MDSA-MQE is proposed which takes queries as input. The query is preprocessed and Latent Semantic Indexing is used to generate new topics for each query word. A set of ontologies of PubMed keywords are semantically aligned using Lesk similarity and NPMI. A Knowledge Tree is formed which is used to classify the metadata generated from Google Books using RNN. Finally, the terms from the Knowledge Tree are enriched using Wikidata, CASNET, and Hepatitis Knowledge Base and semantically integrated with 25% of the classified metadata using NPMI under the Social Spider algorithm. The proposed methodology achieves the Precision of 90.12%, Recall of 93.87%, Accuracy of 92.08%, F-Measure of 91.95%, and nDCG value of 0.94. The overall accuracy of the proposed methodology is much better than the existing approaches.

References

1. Arbabi, A., Adams, D.R., Fidler, S., Brudno, M.: Identifying clinical terms in medical text using ontology-guided machine learning. JMIR Med. Inf. **7**(2), e12596 (2019)
2. Kim, J., Chung, K.-Y.: Ontology-based healthcare context information model to implement ubiquitous environment. Multimed. Tools Appl. **71**(2), 873–888 (2011). https://doi.org/10.1007/s11042-011-0919-6
3. Yunzhi, C., Huijuan, L., Shapiro, L., Travillian, R.S., Lanjuan, L.: An approach to semantic query expansion system based on Hepatitis ontology. J. Biol. Res.-Thessaloniki **23**(1), 11–22 (2016)
4. Gao, G., Liu, Y.S., Wang, M., Gu, M., Yong, J.H.: A query expansion method for retrieving online BIM resources based on industry foundation classes. Autom. Constr. **56**, 14–25 (2015)
5. Kuzi, S., Shtok, A., Kurland, O.: Query expansion using word embeddings. In: Proceedings of the 25th ACM international on Conference on Information and Knowledge Management, pp. 1929–1932, October 2016
6. Oh, H.S., Jung, Y.: Cluster-based query expansion using external collections in medical information retrieval. J. Biomed. Inform. **58**, 70–79 (2015)
7. Keikha, A., Ensan, F., Bagheri, E.: Query expansion using pseudo relevance feedback on Wikipedia. J. Intell. Inf. Syst. **50**(3), 455–478 (2017). https://doi.org/10.1007/s10844-017-0466-3
8. Dahir, S., Khalifi, H., El Qadi, A.: Query expansion using DBpedia and WordNet. In: Proceedings of the ArabWIC 6th Annual International Conference Research Track, pp. 1–6, March 2019
9. Jain, H., Thao, C., Zhao, H.: Enhancing electronic medical record retrieval through semantic query expansion. Inf. Syst. e-Bus. Manag. **10**(2), 165–181 (2012)
10. Raza, M.A., Mokhtar, R., Ahmad, N., Pasha, M., Pasha, U.: A taxonomy and survey of semantic approaches for query expansion. IEEE Access **7**, 17823–17833 (2019)
11. Panchal, R., Swaminarayan, P., Tiwari, S., Ortiz-Rodriguez, F.: AISHE-onto: a semantic model for public higher education universities. In DG. O2021: The 22nd Annual International Conference on Digital Government Research, pp. 545–547, June 2021
12. Gaurav, D., Rodriguez, F.O., Tiwari, S., Jabbar, M.A.: Review of machine learning approach for drug development process. In: Deep Learning in Biomedical and Health Informatics, pp. 53–77. CRC Press (2021)

13. Mourão, A., Martins, F., Magalhaes, J.: Multimodal medical information retrieval with unsupervised rank fusion. Comput. Med. Imaging Graph. **39**, 35–45 (2015)
14. Hanauer, D.A., Mei, Q., Law, J., Khanna, R., Zheng, K.: Supporting information retrieval from electronic health records: a report of university of Michigan's nine-year experience in developing and using the electronic medical record search engine (EMERSE). J. Biomed. Inform. **55**, 290–300 (2015)
15. Lesk, M.: Automatic sense disambiguation using machine readable dictionaries: how to tell a pine cone from an ice cream cone. In: Proceedings of the 5th Annual International Conference on Systems Documentation, pp. 24–26 (SIGDOC 1986). Association for Computing Machinery, New York (1986). https://doi.org/10.1145/318723.318728
16. Bouma, G.: Normalized (pointwise) mutual information in collocation extraction. In: Proceedings of GSCL, pp. 31–40 (2009)
17. Keyvanpour, M., Serpush, F.: ESLMT: a new clustering method for biomedical document retrieval. Biomed. Eng./Biomedizinische Tech. **64**(6), 729–741 (2019)
18. Díaz-Galiano, M.C., Martín-Valdivia, M.T., Ureña-López, L.A.: Query expansion with a medical ontology to improve a multimodal information retrieval system. Comput. Biol. Med. **39**(4), 396–403 (2009)
19. Dahir, S., El Qadi, A., ElHassouni, J., Bennis, H.: Medical query expansion using semantic sources DBpedia and Wikidata. In: ISIC 2021: International Semantic Intelligence Conference, ISIC 2021, 2019 (2021)

Property Assertion Constraints for an Informed, Error-Preventing Expansion of Knowledge Graphs

Henrik Dibowski[(✉)] [iD]

Robert Bosch GmbH, Corporate Research, 71272 Renningen, Germany
henrik.dibowski@de.bosch.com

Abstract. The expansion of knowledge graphs (KGs) by new triples is an elementary process, which is needed for enriching and extending the represented knowledge. In order to function correctly and reliably, it is of utmost importance for many knowledge-driven applications that the expansion only adds semantically correct statements to the KG. Existing validation methods however, including description logic reasoning, SHACL and ShEx, can only detect wrong statements after they have materialized in the KG. They are of no or limited value for preventing errors when expanding KGs. To solve that problem, Property Assertion Constraints (PAC) are introduced as main contribution of this paper. For the context of a given instance and property, a PAC can identify all valid instances, which result in semantically correct property value assertions. By only offering them to users as options to choose from, the creation of semantically wrong statements is prevented and users can greatly benefit from this informed preselection. The main principle of PAC consists in the restriction of a property's range definition by additional logic, which needs to be fulfilled additionally to the range. Similar to SHACL, PAC utilize SPARQL for defining the constraints, which can comprise almost arbitrarily complex conditions or business logic. The fundamental difference to SHACL and other integrity constraint approaches however is that PAC quasi negate the principle of formalizing constraints from constraints that detect erroneous (already materialized) facts into constraints that do the complete opposite, namely finding all semantically correct assertions (before materializing them).

Keywords: Knowledge graph expansion · Property value assertion · Error prevention · Constraint validation · Ontology · SHACL · SPARQL

1 Introduction

Knowledge Graphs (KGs) are on the rise and are spreading into more and more domains and use cases. It is obvious that their graph-structured data model much better reflects real world knowledge, which is highly unstructured and does not fit well into classical, structured data models such as relational databases. KGs are hence not only widely used for the Semantic Web, but also play an increasing role in industrial use cases, for example.

© Springer Nature Switzerland AG 2021
B. Villazón-Terrazas et al. (Eds.): KGSWC 2021, CCIS 1459, pp. 234–248, 2021.
https://doi.org/10.1007/978-3-030-91305-2_18

Whereas KGs for the Semantic Web may be incomplete and contain incorrect statements, industrial use cases often require the opposite: a sound and complete representation of the real world. In industrial use cases, KGs are often used for modeling products, systems, factories, processes or data, and the interactions and interoperability between them. Here, KGs replace conventional structured data models such as relational databases, XML or structured text, and surpass them by size and complexity of the contained information. Many KG-driven applications require the defined information to be comprehensive and free-of-errors to function accurately.

This however imposes an even bigger challenge on the curation and expansion of KGs. Automatically extracting and adding information from text corpora, data, human-readable documents etc., which is known under the synonym terms automatic KG *expansion* and *completion*, is usually not an option here, as it results in too many errors or misses relevant information. Instead, information is typically human-curated by experts of that field.

For a human-curated expansion of KGs, however, no adequate means exist that can reasonably support it. Indeed, mature KG validation methods are available, such as reasoning or constraint checking methods like SHACL [1] or ShEx [2]. They however can detect errors only after they have materialized in the KG, but are of no or limited value for guiding human-curated expansions and for preventing errors.

For closing that gap, this paper presents *Property Assertion Constraints (PAC)*. Instead of detecting (already materialized) errors, PAC can prevent errors by guiding humans (but also machines) during the expansion of KGs. They do so by determining all valid property value assertion upfront, which result in semantically correct statements. By only offering them as options to choose from, PAC can prevent the creation of semantically wrong statements. Altogether, PAC enable an informed, error-preventing expansion of KGs.

The paper is structured as follows: Sect. 2 describes work related to the validation and completion of KGs, and Sect. 3 criticizes major drawbacks and explains the problem statement. Section 4 is the main part of the paper and describes the PAC approach in detail. Section 5 finally concludes the paper.

2 Related Work

This section presents work related to the validation and completion of KGs. As the primary focus of KGs and the proposed approach is about the A-box, this section concentrates on A-box approaches.

Knowledge validation is a critical task, and measures whether statements from KGs are *semantically correct* and correspond to the so-called "real" world [3]. Semantically wrong statements can be referred to as error. Via validation, errors in a KG can be detected (*error detection*), and via specific strategies they can be resolved (*error correction*). Various KG validation methods can be found in literature [3].

Besides, multiple methods exist that can facilitate an automatic KG completion [4]. Whereas error detection is about ensuring that a KG is *free-of-errors*, automatic completion aims at the *completeness* of a KG. However, both go hand in hand when curating a KG, as the expanded KG should ideally be both error-free and (more) complete.

It has been noted in [5] that methods for KG completion can be employed for error detection as well, but their performance has not yet been extensively evaluated there.

Methods for error detection and completion of KGs can be distinguished by different criteria. The first criterion is the *target*, which can be either *instance assertions, property value assertions,* or *equality assertions* [3]. A second criterion is the data used, i.e. only the KG itself (*internal methods*), or further external sources (*external methods*), such as text corpora or other KGs [4]. The proposed *PAC approach targets property value assertions* and uses *internal data* only. In this context, a property value assertion is referred to as wrong or erroneous, when the property value assertion is semantically wrong [3].

In some KGs, logical reasoning is applied for validating the consistency of statements in the graph and removing the inconsistent statements. For real-world KGs, however, reasoning can be difficult due to the presence of errors and noise in the data [6, 7], or because the KGs come with ontologies not rich enough to detect inconsistencies via reasoning [4].

Constraint checking languages and methods are much better suited for real-world KGs, as they are more expressive and work under the closed world assumption. The most prevalent constraint languages are SHACL [1] and ShEx [2], but others exist as well, such as SPIN [8], Stardog ICV [9], IBM's Resource Shapes [10], and RDD [11]. All fall into the same category as the PAC approach, and can also cover the validation of property value assertions.

Further methods for identifying wrong property value assertions and correcting them are mentioned in [3]. They apply knowledge streams [12], outlier detection [13–15], and property mining [16] techniques. For KG completion, also paths in KGs have been proven to be valuable features [5]. [17] proposes an error detection method, which relies on path and type features used by a classifier for every relation in the graph exploiting local feature selection. It applies SHACL.

3   Criticism and Problem Statement

All methods mentioned in Sect. 2 have one thing in common: they can only detect errors, which have already materialized in a KG. This however is very inconvenient and insufficient especially for a human-curated expansion of KGs. Users, who are responsible for providing and adding information to a KG, typically use a specific tool and user interface, which supports the viewing and editing of information. A typical view of such tools, as known from Protégé, TopBraid and others, is an instance-centric view, where for a selected instance all property value assertions are shown on one page, grouped by the different properties. There, a user can remove property value assertions, or add new ones. For adding new property assertions, a user typically sees a list of all possible values he or she can choose from. For an object property, such a list contains (a possibly very large number of) all the instances of the defined range class(es) of the property (and its subclasses), as the range is the only available means today for filtering the possible values BEFORE altering the KG. A more advanced validation, whether property assertions are semantically correct, is only possible with the available methods (Sect. 2) AFTER expanding the KG. This badly impacts the user experience, as many choices that a user makes can turn out to be semantically incorrect after running a validation, and the user needs to revert the changes and start over again and select other property values, that then hopefully are semantically correct. Seeing a list of values to choose from, that just a moment later can turn out to be invalid options, is very inefficient and user-unfriendly. The currently available methods (Sect. 2) only allow for an incremental validation, where a KG is validated before and after an expansion, in order to see whether the changes caused any new violations or not. If so, the changes have to be reverted, and a new attempt can start. This however is the opposite of an informed, error-preventing expansion. Tools that utilize this approach cannot adequately support users in the expansion of KGs. They instead require the users to be experts, who know the KG, domain and respective laws in order to determine upfront, which property value assertions are semantically correct ones, in order to select valid instances only. Without such knowledge, the expansion of KGs equates to a blind, uninformed trial and error, and is nearly impossible.

Also the potential workaround to apply incremental validation on a mirroring backup in order to determine all valid property assertions before showing them to a user, equals a blind trial and error, as ALL values need to be tested one by one, each requiring an expansion, validation and then rollback of the mirrored KG. Especially with large numbers of possible values and in large KGs this approach becomes resource- and performance-wise expensive or infeasible and highly questionable.

The PAC approach introduced in this paper can close this gap. Its main goal is the prevention of errors, instead of their detection and correction. It supports a curated expansion of KGs by determining upfront, which values result in valid property value assertions. Thus, it can prevent wrong property value assertions without the need to materialize and check them first. PAC enable an informed, error-preventing expansion of KGs by humans or machines. The PAC approach can relieve humans from the burden of applying or even knowing this expertise. The approach is explained in detail in the following section.

4   Property Assertion Constraints

PAC are the main contribution of this paper and are explained in detail in this section. PAC constitute an approach, which offers a fundamental support for the creation and (especially human-curated) expansion of KGs. PAC can prevent a KG from changing from a semantically correct into a semantically incorrect state. They do so by preventing the creation of semantically wrong property value assertions and hence models, which violate constraints and laws expressed and in place for a KG and the domain it represents. Thus, the correctness of the represented knowledge can be ensured, and a transition into an erroneous state can be avoided.

At each moment in time, PAC can help to determine those instances, which lead to semantically correct property value assertion for a given instance, i.e. which do not introduce errors to the KG when assigning them to the instance. By allowing a human or machine to choose only from those values, the approach can ensure that the expansion of a KG is semantically correct.

PAC offer a significant advantage over other existing validation methods (see Sect. 2 and Sect. 3), as they allow for an informed, error-preventing expansion of KGs.

Ensuring the correctness of KGs at any point in time is essential for many kinds of knowledge-driven applications, which base their operation, decisions and actions on the underlying knowledge.

The following subsections explain the various aspects of PAC in more detail.

4.1 The Main Principle

PAC are a mechanism that allows to specify, given a class C, and an OWL object property P, which instances y make it legal to expand the KG with a triple x P y, if x is an instance of class C. In other words, for a given instance and object property, the method delivers a list of instances to choose from, such that any of these instances will lead to a valid KG extension, when assigned to the instance via the property.

PAC start from the defined range of a property and extend it by additional logic, which needs to be fulfilled additionally to the property range definition. Only *instances matching* both, *the range definition AND the PAC*, are considered as *valid* values.

The logic of PAC is expressed with SPARQL and can range from simple to almost arbitrarily complex conditions or business logic. Due to its high expressiveness, SPARQL is an ideal query language candidate. Its closed world semantics overcomes typical issues with OWL, and opposite to rule languages, such as SWRL, it also supports negation and other important features. SPARQL has proven to be an expressive constraint language also by its utilization in SHACL [1].

The main principle of the PAC approach consists in the dynamic generation of SPARQL queries for the context of a given instance and property, for which all valid instances should be determined that result in correct property value assertions. The SPARQL query is composed from two pieces:

1. The *PAC core query*: A parameterizable and reusable SPARQL SELECT query able to retrieve all instances that comply with the range of the property.
2. A *PAC pattern*: A SPARQL query fragment specific for a given class-property or instance-property pair. It consists of one or more SPARQL graph patterns, and defines the additional conditions or business logic that the values need to fulfill, additionally to the range. In general, PAC patterns can use all keywords, functions and operators that are permitted within WHERE clauses of SPARQL SELECT queries.

The PAC pattern is dynamically injected into the PAC core query at query generation time. The resulting composed *PAC query* is a SPARQL SELECT query that can be executed on the KG. As result it returns all valid instances for the given instance-property pair.

The next section explains how PAC can be defined in RDF, followed by a section, which shows a PAC core query and the query composition on an example.

4.2 Definition of Property Assertion Constraints in RDF

While the previous section outlined the main idea behind the PAC approach, this section describes how PAC can be defined syntactically in RDF.

From all existing state of the art approaches (see Sect. 2) SHACL is the closest to the proposed PAC approach. Both SHACL and PAC are about the validation of triples and work under the closed world assumption. RDFS and OWL on the contrary function under the open world assumption and are about the logical consequence. SPARQL is utilized by both SHACL and PAC and allows the definition of even complex constraints. The fundamental difference between the two, however, is that PAC quasi negate the principle of SHACL (and also ShEx) from formalizing constraints that detect erroneous (already materialized) facts into constraints that can find all semantically correct assertions upfront, as will be shown in the following.

For defining and serializing PAC, we chose SHACL as suitable language. In particular, we identified and propose SHACL property shapes as suitable place for attaching the definitions of PAC. We argue that this is reasonable, as a PAC is yet another constraint imposed on the property of a class, and could hence reside next to the other SHACL property shape constraints.

Figure 1 shows a class definition example with SHACL constraints in turtle syntax. In this figure, `sc:ControllingDevice` is declared as both an OWL class and SHACL node shape. The SHACL property `sh:property` attaches a property shape definition to the node shape, which defines several constraints on the object property `sc:hasHardware`. In particular, it uses the value type constraint component `sh:class` for defining the range of the object property. For all instances of `sc:ControllingDevice`, the constraint specifies that only instances of the class `sc:Hardware` (and implicitly its subclasses) are valid objects for the object property. Besides, it also defines a minimum (`sh:minCount`) and maximum cardinality (`sh:maxCount`) of 1, which requires each `sc:ControllingDevice` instance to be associated with exactly one `sc:Hardware`.

In the lower part, Fig. 1 shows an example of a PAC definition for the same object property `sc:hasHardware`. The respective lines appear in bold type. Two new OWL annotation properties are introduced and used for defining a PAC:

1. `pac:pattern`: For attaching a PAC pattern (see Sect. 4.1) to a property shape. The value is of type string. PAC patterns can optionally contain an `%%instanceIRI%%` placeholder to be replaced by the IRI of the given instance.
2. `pac:comment`: For attaching a human readable comment of a PAC to a property shape. Values have to be of type string and can be language-tagged, i.e. specify the used language. Several values, one per language, can be attached to the same property shape. The comment is intended to be shown to the users of an application, and it should make them aware of a PAC and help to understand or resolve it.

Just like SHACL property shapes are inherited to subclasses down the class tree, we intend and define the same behavior for PAC. This means that PAC apply to instances of the respective class of a property shape and all its subclasses (*inheritance of PAC*).

```
sc:ControllingDevice
  a owl:Class ;
  a sh:NodeShape ;
  sh:property [
    a sh:PropertyShape ;
    sh:path sc:hasHardware ;
    sh:class sc:Hardware ;
    sh:nodeKind sh:IRI ;
    sh:name "Hardware" ;
    sh:minCount 1 ;
    sh:maxCount 1 ;
    pac:pattern
      """BIND (%%instanceIRI%% as ?subjectInstance).
         ?subjectInstance sc:belongsTo ?productFamily.
         ?instance sc:releasedFor ?productFamily.""" ;
    pac:comment "A product can only use hardware components
      released for the corresponding product family"@en ;
    pac:comment "Ein Produkt kann nur Hardwarebausteine
      verwenden, die für die entsprechende Produktfamilie
      freigegeben wurden"@de ;
  ] ;
  ...
```

Fig. 1. RDF definition of a SHACL property shape (black lines, prefix "sh:"), comprehended by a Property Assertion Constraint (bold blue lines, prefix "pac:").

4.3 PAC Core Query and Query Composition

As explained in Sect. 4.1, the main principle of the PAC approach consists in the dynamic generation of SPARQL queries for the context of a given instance and property, which can determine all instances that result in semantically correct property value assertions when being assigned. The SPARQL query is composed from two pieces: The PAC core query, and a PAC pattern.

As also introduced in Sect. 4.1, a *PAC core query* is a parameterizable and reusable SPARQL SELECT query, which is able to retrieve all instances that comply with the range of the property. Figure 2 shows the PAC core query that we use in our implementation. It needs to be parameterized with the range class of the property in line 6. The range class can be taken from the sh:class property of the corresponding SHACL property shape. For now, let's ignore the placeholder in line 5, it will be explained later.

Parameterized with a valid range class IRI and executed on the KG, the PAC core query can retrieve all instances that comply with the range of the property. The core query implements the following steps: It determines all subclasses of the range class (line 7) and retrieves all instances of the range class and its subclasses (line 8)[1]. If a rdfs:label exists for an instance, it is bound to the ?label variable (line 9).

---

[1] Remark: When reasoning is enabled for the KG, line 7 is obsolete and line 8 can use the ?superClass variable directly, as the reasoner can then take care of the class membership checking.

As result of its execution, the query returns all instances that are compliant with the range of the object property. The result contains the IRIs of the instances, along with their class IRI and optionally the human readable label of the instances to be shown to a user. This is the minimum required amount of information for choosing an instance.

```
01  PREFIX rdfs: <http://www.w3.org/2000/01/rdf-schema#>
02  PREFIX owl: <http://www.w3.org/2002/07/owl#>
03  SELECT DISTINCT ?instance ?class ?label
04  WHERE {
05    # %%PACPatternPlaceholder%%
06    BIND (%%rangeClassIRI%% AS ?superClass).
07    ?class rdfs:subClassOf* ?superClass.
08    ?instance a ?class.
09    OPTIONAL {?instance rdfs:label ?label.}
10  }
```

Fig. 2. Property Assertion Constraint core query.

Line 5 of the PAC core query represents an additional placeholder, which needs to be replaced by the corresponding *PAC pattern*, whenever a PAC exists for a property. Otherwise the line is omitted and the core query retrieves instances complying with the range definition only. This is the fallback to the current state of practice. As the previous Sect. 4.2 showed, the PAC pattern is attached to the corresponding SHACL property shape and can be retrieved from there, similarly to the IRI of the range class (sh:class property).

The combination of the PAC core query and the inserted PAC pattern forms the *final PAC query*. By executing it on the KG, it can retrieve all instances, which are compliant with the property's range definition AND with the PAC. These instances are the valid ones from which finally a human or machine can choose from. The resulting property value assertions lead to semantically correct expansions of the KG.

Coming back to the PAC example from Fig. 1 (see Sect. 4.2), the parameterization of the PAC core query results in the PAC query shown in Fig. 3. Here, the PAC pattern was inserted for the pattern placeholder in line 5 of the query, and the %%rangeClas-sIRI%% placeholder was replaced by the class IRI sc:Hardware. Additionally, the %%instanceIRI%% placeholder inside the PAC pattern was replaced by the IRI of the instance of interest. A more detailed explanation of this example PAC and resulting PAC query follows in the next section.

The PAC core query shown in Fig. 2 is applicable to object properties with one defined range class. This typically covers most of the cases in an ontology. In some rare cases, however, several alternative range classes could be defined for an object property, for example with SHACL's logical constraint component sh:or. In such cases, the PAC core query needs to be extended by one or more UNION clauses with an additional BIND statement, one for each additional range class. Each UNION clause can take care of one range class and retrieve all its instances.

```
PREFIX rdfs: <http://www.w3.org/2000/01/rdf-schema#>
PREFIX owl: <http://www.w3.org/2002/07/owl#>
SELECT DISTINCT ?instance ?class ?label
WHERE {
  BIND (d:Room_Temp_Controller_A as ?subjectInstance).
  ?subjectInstance sc:belongsTo ?productFamily.
  ?instance sc:releasedFor ?productFamily.

  BIND (sc:Hardware AS ?superClass).
  ?class rdfs:subClassOf* ?superClass.
  ?instance a ?class.
  OPTIONAL {?instance rdfs:label ?label.}
}
```

Fig. 3. Property Assertion Constraint Query – Example.

4.4   Examples of Property Assertion Constraints

After explaining the main principle of PAC in the previous sections, a few examples are demonstrated in this section.

PAC Example 1: Compatible Hardware for Controlling Devices. The previous two sections already showed a first PAC, which has not been explained yet. It is the PAC from Fig. 1 and its resulting PAC query shown in Fig. 3. The PAC is defined for the class sc:ControllingDevice and its object property sc:hasHardware. For a given instance of sc:ControllingDevice (the subject), it can determine all valid instances that can be in the object position of the relationship. Valid instances can only be instances of class sc:Hardware (defined as range), which comply to the following conditions: The hardware needs to be released for the same product family that the controlling device belongs to.

The constellation for a given instance d:Room_Temp_Controller_A is illustrated in Fig. 4. On the right hand side, it shows four instances of sc:Hardware, which fulfill the PAC, i.e. which are released for the product family of the given controlling device. The PAC query shown in Fig. 3 can find and return them. It is then up to a user or machine to choose one out of these four and assign it to the given instance via sc:hasHardware relationship.

PAC Example 2: Nonrecurring Instance Assertion. Another PAC example is about the integrity of aggregation and composition relationships. Both are specific types of associations that represent a part-of relationship. Whereas instances with an aggregation relationship can also exist independently, instances with a composition relationship cannot.

A relevant PAC pattern for aggregation and composition relationships is shown in Fig. 5. It can prevent the recurring assertion of instances to multiple instances via a given object property. It can for example avoid that the same physical device is installed at multiple locations (which is physically impossible). Or that the same birth certificate is assigned to multiple persons.

The PAC pattern needs to be customized to a specific object property by replacing the `#objectPropertyIRI#` placeholder by its IRI. Then the PAC can be attached to the respective property shape and used. At runtime, the instance in the subject position of the property needs to be inserted for the `%%instanceIRI%%` placeholder. Inserted into the parameterized PAC core query (Fig. 2), the resulting PAC query can find all instances of the desired range class, which are not yet assigned to any other instance via the given object property. The given instance itself is excluded by the `FILTER` statement in line 3, so that instances already assigned to it are also amongst the valid instances, if this is their only assignment.

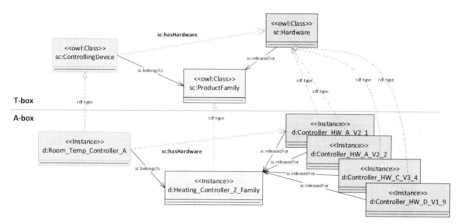

Fig. 4. Property Assertion Constraint example for class `sc:ControllingDevice` and object property `sc:hasHardware` - Constraining the configuration of controlling devices to use compatible hardware only.

```
01    FILTER NOT EXISTS {
02        ?subject #objectPropertyIRI# ?instance.
03        FILTER (?subject != %%instanceIRI%%)
04    }
```

Fig. 5. Property Assertion Constraint example: prevention of recurring instance assertions.

Further PAC Examples. The previous examples are rather simple, descriptive PAC consisting of a few SPARQL patterns. One can easily add here multiple other, more complex examples that demonstrate the strength of the PAC approach even better. Due to the limited space, however, a short remark is given in the following instead.

In principle, PAC can formalize any kind of conditions that can be expressed with SPARQL. This includes also very comprehensive SPARQL patterns with many lines, matching multiple conditions, possibly traversing long paths and exploring large parts of a KG. Even complex business logic can be formalized in this way. Hence the use cases for PAC are basically numberless.

4.5 Types of Property Assertion Constraints

According to their scope, PAC can be classified into class-specific and instance-specific PAC. *Class-specific PAC* are defined for a specific class and one of its properties. They apply to all instances of the class for the given property. This is the kind of PAC that was shown in the previous subsections. As explained in Sect. 4.2, we propose to attach the PAC definition to the corresponding SHACL property shape of the class (see Fig. 1).

In rare cases it can also make sense to define *instance-specific PAC*. Such PAC are not defined on class level, but on instance level, i.e. they apply to a particular instance only. With RDF, this can be accomplished by assigning the PAC definition directly to an instance, instead of a property shape. Therefore, as in the case of class-specific PAC, the annotation properties `sh:pattern` and `sh:comment` can be used (cf. Fig. 1). Instance-specific PAC are an option for instances of a unique kind, which only exist once. Consider, for example, an instance that represents a prototype of a machine or vehicle, or a living being, with very specific characteristics and hence constraints beyond the scope of its most specific class defined in the KG.

4.6 Workflow of Applying Property Assertion Constraints

The previous sections already outlined various steps of utilizing PAC on a KG, from their definition and retrieval over the PAC query generation and execution. In this section, the overall workflow of utilizing PAC is described in detail. The workflow can be the basis for implementing a software algorithm that realizes the PAC approach. It is shown in Fig. 6 as flow chart.

The KG expansion starts with a given instance and property. As a first step, relevant PAC for the given instance-property pair are retrieved from the KG with SPARQL. Instance-specific PAC are retrieved from the instance itself with a simple SPARQL SELECT query. Class-specific PAC are retrieved from the corresponding property shape of the instance's class, or its superclasses. If an instance-specific PAC exists, it is selected. Else, if a class-specific PAC of the direct class of the instance exists, that one is selected. Else, the class-specific PAC of the closest superclass is selected (inheritance of PAC, see Sect. 4.2). If no PAC exists, the PAC core query alone is taken and parameterized (see Sect. 4.3). This case is the fallback to the state of practice, where only instances compliant with the defined range are retrieved.

As next step, the PAC query is composed from the PAC core query and the selected PAC pattern (see Sect. 4.3). Then, the resulting SPARQL query is executed on the KG. The instances it returns are the valid values, from which a user or machine can finally choose one or more. They can be asserted to the given instance via the given property (KG expansion). The whole workflow can then start again for a new instance-property pair.

4.7 Implementation of Property Assertion Constraints

The workflow from Fig. 6 can be implemented on a computer in a programming language of choice. We implemented the PAC approach as a REST endpoint (API) in TypeScript and have applied it to several industrial use cases already. The KG itself is stored on a

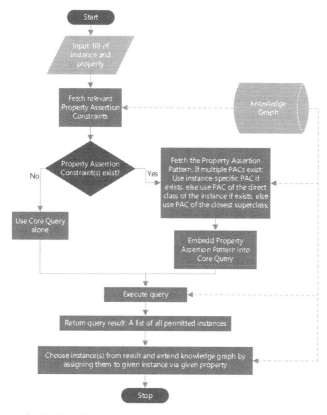

Fig. 6. Workflow of applying Property Assertion Constraints.

Stardog triple store. The endpoint can be reached remotely and requires the following input parameters: KG name, instance IRI, property IRI. Via its name, the endpoint can find the respective KG in Stardog and connect with it via the SPARQL Protocol [18]. The algorithm performs the steps shown in Fig. 6, i.e. it fetches and selects the respective PAC from the KG, composes and parameterizes the PAC query, runs it on the given KG, and finally returns the query result.

The implementation proved to be performant and scalable. On average, the endpoint responds within milliseconds, even for large amounts of data or complex PAC patterns. It proved to be totally sufficient for human-curated KG expansions.

Furthermore, the PAC approach has been filed as patent and is in status "pending".

4.8 Application of Property Assertion Constraints

The PAC approach can support both human- and machine-curated expansions of KGs. A convenient way of allowing users to expand a KG is via a user interface, e.g. in the form of a web frontend. For a selected instance, the user interface can list all available properties and currently assigned values. When the user chooses a particular property, the PAC implementation is automatically triggered in the background and can retrieve and provide a list of all valid instances, which can be assigned via the property. The user can inspect the list and, depending on the maximum cardinality of the property, choose and assign one or more values.

Also machines can use PAC for expanding KGs (semi-)automatically: Software algorithms can use PAC (e.g. via a REST endpoint, see Sect. 4.7) to retrieve the valid values of a property, from which they can choose values according to specific criteria, algorithms or heuristics that they implement.

PAC formalize the expertise that is required for determining the valid, semantically correct values for a property. The expertise can range from rather simple to even complex business logic, capturing the knowledge of human experts or laws of a domain. The PAC approach relieves the user or machines from applying or even knowing this expertise, but lets a computer handle it instead. User can benefit greatly from that, and can curate KGs easier, faster and better.

By embedding the PAC as RDF statements in a KG (see Sect. 4.2), this expertise is a part of the KG itself. Instead of implementing expertise via business logic inside the applications' code in the traditional way of coding, applications can be decoupled from business logic, which can now reside mainly or exclusively on the KG. PAC constitute a knowledge-driven approach. Adding or changing PAC can be done entirely on the KG, without the need of changing the applications' code.

It is important to mention here also that PAC can be used with reasoning. By using a triple store that supports reasoning, the PAC can incorporate facts computed by a reasoner. This can allow a simplification of the PAC logic (i.e. PAC pattern), as pieces of the logic can be shifted from the PAC to the reasoner.

4.9 Correlation to SHACL and ShEx

Even though the primary purpose of PAC is to provide humans or machines an informed, error-preventing support in the expansion of KGs, they can be used also for validating KGs, in particular property value assertions. This can be done in the following way: For a given instance from the KG (e.g. an instance that a user is currently inspecting in a user interface), iterate over all asserted properties. For each asserted property, get all assigned values and check whether they all are amongst the valid values that the corresponding PAC determines. Assigned values not being amongst the valid ones violate the PAC, they constitute errors in the KG to be resolved. This validation capability means a certain overlap with other constraint checking methods, such as SHACL and ShEx, which is briefly discussed in the following.

PAC function by determining a positive list of valid values that can be assigned to an instance. SHACL and ShEx work the opposite way and try to detect negative cases, i.e. invalid statements that violate constraints. Whereas PAC can be applied before making a change, SHACL and ShEx can only detect errors that already materialized.

The scope of SHACL and ShEx is however broader than the one of PAC, as they can also express and check other types of constraints, such as cardinalities. Also for avoiding the need of utilizing two different kinds of constraint checking methods simultaneously, it would be desirable to use PAC for the expansion of KGs, and SHACL or ShEx for their validation. In order to avoid specifying the same constraints twice, one time as PAC, and a second time with SHACL or ShEx, it would be worthwhile to have an automatic transformation between them. SHACL is the more suitable candidate than ShEx, as it supports SPARQL. Also, the forward direction from the positive case expressed by a PAC to the negative cases expressed as SPARQL-based SHACL constraint, appears to be more promising. Additional research needs to be done to further investigate and develop this idea.

5 Conclusion

This paper presents Property Assertion Constraints (PAC) as its main contribution. PAC can guide humans and machines during the expansion of KGs by determining and providing all semantically correct property value assertions as options. By only choosing from them, PAC can prevent the creation of semantically wrong statements. PAC thus enable an informed, error-preventing expansion of KGs. This differentiates PAC from other existing integrity constraint validation methods, such as SHACL and ShEx, which can only detect errors that already materialized as statements. Rather than focusing on error detection and correction, PAC can prevent errors. Not only the approach, but also the way how the constraints work, is fundamentally different: Instead of having constraints that detect erroneous (already materialized) facts, PAC function in the complete opposite way via constraints that can find all semantically correct assertions upfront (before materializing them).

Although we propose to use SPARQL as constraint expression language, and to attach PAC to SHACL property shapes, the PAC approach can be generalized for graph databases as such, using a different query language and syntactical representation.

PAC formalize the expertise that is required for determining semantically correct property value assertions with SPARQL. The expertise can range from rather simple to even complex business logic, capturing the knowledge of human experts or laws of a domain. The PAC approach relieves humans or machines from applying or even knowing this expertise, but lets a computer handle it instead. By embedding the PAC as RDF statements in a KG, this expertise is a part of the KG itself. Applications can be decoupled from business logic, which can now reside mainly or only on the KG.

The PAC approach leaves space for further research. A promising direction is an automatic transformation of PAC to SHACL, which would allow the utilization of the formally expressed expertise for both the expansion and validation of KGs.

References

1. Knublauch, H., Kontokostas, D.: Shapes Constraint Language (SHACL). W3C Recommendation (2017). https://www.w3.org/TR/shacl/. Accessed 16 Apr 2021
2. Prud'hommeaux, E., Boneva, I., Gayo, J.E.L., Kellogg, G.: Shape Expressions Language 2.1 (ShEx). Final Community Group Report 8 (2019). http://shex.io/shex-semantics/. Accessed 16 Apr 2021
3. Huaman, E., Kärle, E., Fensel, D.: Knowledge Graph Validation (2020). https://arxiv.org/abs/2005.01389. Accessed 16 Apr 2021
4. Paulheim, H.: Knowledge graph refinement: a survey of approaches and evaluation methods. Semant. Web **8**(3), 489–508 (2016)

5. Melo, A., Paulheim, P.: Detection of relation assertion errors in knowledge graphs. In: Proceedings of the Knowledge Capture Conference (K-CAP 2017), Austin, Texas, US, pp. 1–8 (2017)
6. Polleres, A., Hogan, A., Harth, A., Decker, S.: Can we ever catch up with the Web? Semant. Web 1(1), 45–52 (2010)
7. Ji, Q., Gao, Z., Huang, Z.: Reasoning with noisy semantic data. In: Antoniou, G., et al. (eds.) ESWC 2011. LNCS, vol. 6644, pp. 497–502. Springer, Heidelberg (2011). https://doi.org/10.1007/978-3-642-21064-8_42
8. Knublauch, H., Hendler, J.A., Idehen, K.: SPIN – Overview and Motivation. W3C Member Submission (2011). https://www.w3.org/Submission/spin-overview/. Accessed 16 Apr 2021
9. Clark & Parsia LLC: Validation Constraints. The Stardog Manual. http://stage.docs.stardog.com.s3-website-us-east-1.amazonaws.com/2.2.4/#_validating_constraints. Accessed 16 Apr 2021
10. Ryman, A., Hors, A.L., Speicher, S.: OSLC resource shape: a language for defining constraints on linked data. In: Proceedings of the 8th Workshop on Linked Data on the Web (LDOW 2013), Florence, Italy, pp. 1549–1550 (2013)
11. Fischer, P.M., Lausen, G., Schätzle, A.: RDF constraint checking. In: Proceedings of the EDBT/ICDT 2015 Joint Conference, Brussels, Belgium (2015)
12. Shiralkar, P., Flammini, A., Menczer, F., Ciampaglia. G.L.: Finding streams in knowledge graphs to support fact checking. In: Proceedings of the 2017 International Conference on Data Mining (ICDM2017), New Orleans, USA, pp. 859–864 (2017)
13. Syed, Z.H., Röder, M., Ngomo, A.-C.: Unsupervised discovery of corroborative paths for fact validation. In: Ghidini, C., et al. (eds.) ISWC 2019. LNCS, vol. 11778, pp. 630–646. Springer, Cham (2019). https://doi.org/10.1007/978-3-030-30793-6_36
14. Thorne, J., Vlachos, A.: An extensible framework for verification of numerical claims. In: Proceedings of the 15th Conference of the European Chapter of the Association for Computational Linguistics (EACL2017), Valencia, Spain, pp. 37–40 (2017)
15. Wienand, D., Paulheim, H.: Detecting incorrect numerical data in DBpedia. In: Presutti, V., d'Amato, C., Gandon, F., d'Aquin, M., Staab, S., Tordai, A. (eds.) ESWC 2014. LNCS, vol. 8465, pp. 504–518. Springer, Cham (2014). https://doi.org/10.1007/978-3-319-07443-6_34
16. Shi, B., Weninger, T.: Discriminative predicate path mining for fact checking in knowledge graphs. Knowl. Based Syst. **104**(2016), 123–133 (2016)
17. Melo, A., Paulheim, H.: Automatic detection of relation assertion errors and induction of relation constraints. Semant. Web **11**(5), 801–830 (2020)
18. Feigenbaum, L., Williams, G.T., Clark, K.G., Torres, E.: SPARQL 1.1 Protocol. W3C Recommendation (2013). https://www.w3.org/TR/sparql11-protocol/. Accessed 16 Apr 2021

Fake News Detection Using Deep Learning

Srishti Sharma[1](✉), Mala Saraswat[2], and Anil Kumar Dubey[2]

[1] The NorthCap University, Gurugram, India
srishti@ncuindia.edu
[2] ABES Engineering College, Ghaziabad 201009, India

Abstract. Owing to the rapid explosion of social networking portals in the past decade, we spread and consume information via the internet at an expeditious rate. It has caused an alarming proliferation of fake news on social networks. The global nature of social networks has facilitated international blowout of fake news. Fake news has proven to increase political polarization and partisan conflict. Fake news is also found to be more rampant on social media than mainstream media. The evil of fake news is garnering a lot of attention and research effort. In this work, we have tried to handle the spread of fake news via tweets. We have performed fake news classification by employing user characteristics as well as tweet text. Thus, trying to provide a holistic solution for fake news detection. For classifying user characteristics, we have used the XGBoost algorithm which is a collaboration of decision trees utilizing the boosting method. Further to correctly classify the tweet text we used various natural language processing techniques to preprocess the tweets and then applied a sequential neural network and state-of-the-art BERT transformer to classify the tweets. The models have then been evaluated and compared with various baseline models to show that our approach effectively tackles this problem.

Keywords: Fake news · Transfer learning · Classification · Transformers · Gradient boosting · Text classification · Twitter

1 Introduction

The rising proliferation of social networking portals is considered to be the key reason behind the dissemination of fake news at an unprecedented scale. This computerized data age has produced new outlets for content makers to fabricate imaginary articles to build readership or as part of psychological warfare, financial and political gain. News of questionable credibility breaks the genuineness equilibrium of the news network. The developing use of algorithms in robotized news circulation and creation has made it easy and inexpensive to provide news online at a fast pace. Gartner analysis predicts that "By 2022, the overwhelming majority of individuals in developed economies will devour more false knowledge than real information [1]". Social media is a perilous weapon when mishandled, abused or invaded. One of the biggest challenges is that in social networks, the influence of spread and impact of content sharing happens so quickly that contorted, incorrect or misleading information obtains a colossal probability of causing

B. Villazón-Terrazas et al. (Eds.): KGSWC 2021, CCIS 1459, pp. 249–259, 2021.
https://doi.org/10.1007/978-3-030-91305-2_19

significant negative societal effects, in practically no time, for millions of users. It is palpable that one of the utmost well-known fake news was considerably more rapidly diffused on a popular social networking giant than the most renowned credible standard newsflash at the time of ballots in USA in 2016 [2]. Social media platforms enable sharing, commenting and talking about news in seconds. For instance, 62% people in the United States admitted to getting newscasts via social networks in 2016, whereas in 2012, only 49% testified to obtaining updates via social media. It has also been revealed that social networking sites on the internet now outflank TV as the significant news source [3].

The issue of tackling and controlling the explosion of fake news needs immediate attention. Any endeavors to mislead or troll in the cyberspace through fake news or misleading content sources are now considered grave matters with supreme adequacy and warrants genuine efforts from security scientists. As such, there is a dire need to come up with a fake news detection and filtering system. This is of utmost importance that such systems are built, as they can help both news readers and tech companies alike. Since, the dynamic nature and varying styles of fake news are a great hurdle, the objective is to propose a Fake News Detection scheme that comprehensively considers the user characteristics, content and social context. This hybrid approach should yield us a robust and effective system to combat the fake news epidemic efficiently at early stages of its propagation.

Through this work, we outline a system for fake news detection that makes use of a tool to detect and eliminate counterfeit sites amongst the results returned by search giants or news applications. This tool can be downloaded by the user and, then, be supplemented to the user's browser or any application that the user is making use of to acquire news feeds. Section 2 presents the Survey of Literature followed by Proposed Approach in Sect. 3. Section 4 present analysis of the Result and Sect. 5 presents Conclusion and Future Work.

2   Survey of Literature

Internet is what aids the fast spread of fake news in a short time. There exist some significant examples that can be used for Fake News Detection (FND) in social media. Fake news has 4 significant segments: fake news creator, target victim, fake news content, and fake news social context. Supported by the examination of various elements, FND approaches are often divided as: originator and user examination, news content examination and social context examination.

Castillo et al. 2011 proposed methods for automatically assessing the credibility of tweets and microblog postings based on features from the text of posts, from public references citations, from users' posting and re-tweeting behavior [4]. Among a few different highlights, the authors also proclaimed that reliable news is spread through writers that have recently composed an enormous number of messages, have numerous re-posts, deep propagation trees, tend to include URLs and start at a solitary or a couple of users in the network. Qazvinian et al. addressed the issue of rumor detection and recognizing disinformers by investigating content-based features, network-based features, and microblog-explicit images for effective rumor identification [5]. In 2012, Balmas assessed the impact of the interaction between different kinds of media use on political sensibilities of an individual in fostering the sentiments of incapability, estrangement, and negativity toward government officials [6].

Afroz et al. proposed methods for detecting stylistic deception in written documents using stylometry with 96.6% accuracy [7]. They argued that stylistic deception can be recognized by identifying linguistic features in writing style that is content-independent and determined that function words are the most effective of all features. Chu et al. designed a classification system that identifies a Twitter user as a humanoid, bot or cyborg [8]. This was done considering the entropy measures to check for periodic or regular tweet timing patterns, tweets text to check for junk, and certain Twitter related properties to check for irregular standards of external URL proportion and tweeting device makeup. Takahashi et al. proposed a sequence of processes to develop and evaluate a rumor detection system from Twitter [9]. They first applied named entity extraction techniques to generate a target list, then used retweet ratio to capture spreading topics and lastly identified negative rumors from spreading topics. In 2013, Kwon et al. analyzed the rumor spreading pattern on Twitter by discovering three aspects of diffusion: time-based, organizational, and etymological [10].

A novel episodic time series fitting archetypal was proposed to extract time-based characteristics which exhibited that rumors are likely to have variations over time. This was combined with structural and linguistic features to give a 92% recall on the proposed model. Cheng et al. designed a detection technique to distinguish legitimate users from online paid posters, in China, using semantic and non-semantic investigation using everyday trace figures [11]. In 2014, Mayu et al. applied feature learning using autoencoders for anomaly detection and compared the results with linear and kernel PCA to elucidate the characteristics of autoencoders [12].

TargetVue was applied in a community bot recognition test using Twitter and the evaluation showed promising results. Rubin et al. proposed an SVM-based algorithm to identify satirical news [14]. This algorithm was enhanced with 5 predictive features (Absurdity, Humour, Grammar, Negative Affect, and Punctuation) and a blend of these features was tested on 360 news articles. Hardalov et al. proposed a language-independent methodology for automatically recognizing credible from counterfeit news, considering a rich feature set [15].

In 2019, Vicario et al. presented a framework for timely identification of polarizing content on social media considering users' polarization and confirmation bias, to determine future potential targets that are susceptible to misinformation with 77% accuracy [16]. User behavior and related characteristics on social media were took into consideration to build a FND classifier. Zhang et al. presented a survey characterizing the negative effect of online fake news, and the top tier recognition strategies [17]. It was observed that most of these methods relied on recognizing features of the users, content, and context that demonstrate deception. Fernandez and Devaraj reaped online credible and fake news samples in the Philippines to capacitate the disparity in writing style between genuine news and fake news and recommended that news can be distinguished just by their headline or content at a precision of 87% and 88%, respectively [18]. Gaurav et al. [19] proposed an approach for a similar task of spam mail detection using classifiers like Naïve Bayes, Decision Tree and Random Forest. Yang et al. investigated on identifying fake news in an unsupervised way [20]. News authenticity and user's credibility were treated as latent random factors and a probabilistic graphical model was worked to capture the total generative range. An efficient collapsed Gibb's sampling approach was proposed to gauge the news legitimacy and the users' credibility simultaneously without any labelled data. Users' engagements on social media were exploited to recognize their sentiments towards the legitimacy of news.

Further, we understand the challenges of combating fake news. We require training datasets without any inconsistencies, incompleteness and missing data. So, we investigated the web for appropriate datasets and catalogued the results in Table 1. Besides this, there are still other fake news datasets which are available online and can be used to train the prediction models. An exploration of datasets that have been built for FND was also carried out and the findings are listed in Table 1.

In the recent past, deep learning models have been applied and have shown remarkable performance improvement in a variety of tasks like depression detection [21], in self-driving cars [22], etc. Hence, we proposed a model for fake news detection using Deep Learning.

Table 1. Appropriate dataset details for fake news

S. no	Dataset name	No. of rows	Sources
1	LIAR dataset	12,800	Politifact API
2	Getting real about fake news – Kaggle	12,999	Text and metadata from 244 websites, webhose.io API, BSDetector
3	Buzzfeed dataset	2000	News samples from Facebook
4	CREDBANK	60 Million	Twitter
5	PHEME	5802	Twitter
6	FEVER	185,445	Wikipedia
7	Twitter 15	1497	Twitter
8	Twitter 16	892	Twitter
9	Emergent	2595	News articles
10	FakeNewsNet	422	Politifact API and Buzzfeed
11	Fake news challenge dataset	50,000	News headlines
12	Benjamin political news dataset	75	News articles
13	Burfoot Satire news dataset	4233	News samples

3   Proposed Work

The proposed model for Fake News Detection works in three phases as outlined in Fig. 1.

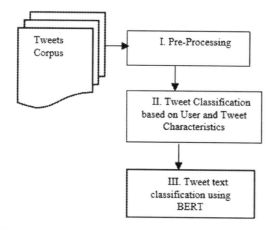

Fig. 1. Block diagram of the proposed architecture for Fake News Detection

3.1 Phase I: Dataset Used and Pre-processing

In this work, we utilize the dataset provided by Shu et al. in FakeNewsNet. They've created a repository of news content from fact-checking websites like PolitiFact and GossipCop, that assign rating to news bulletins on a scale of 0 (fake) to 10 (real) to categorize news bulletins. We amass from this news bulletins having ratings of less than 5 as fake news stories. The dataset provided had tweet ids and their corresponding labels of either True or False. We used the python library tweepy to extract tweet features by utilizing the tweet ids. We collected a total of 27,910 tweets out of which 14,854 tweets had the label 'True' while 13,056 had the label 'False'. Since we are using tweets the data was highly unstructured and noisy. We performed the following pre-processing steps:

1. Converted emojis to a textual description. This was done using the emoji library in python. For e.g. The emoticon 😂was converted to face_with_tears_of_joy. All occurrences of emojis were replaced in this manner.
2. Any mentions of the following were normalized using the ekphrasis python library: 'url', 'percent', 'email', 'money', 'user', 'phone', 'time', 'date', 'number'.
3. All occurrences of the following were annotated: 'hashtag', elongated', 'allcaps', 'emphasis',,'repeated', 'censored'.
4. All hashtags were unpacked. For e.g. #BreakingNews was unpacked to 'breaking news'. 5. All contractions were unpacked. For e.g. 'can't' unpacked to 'can not'.
5. Word Segmentation was carried out using the Viterbi algorithm which in turn is adapted from [23]. For e.g. "smallandinsignificant" segmented to "small and insignificant".
6. Spell correction was also performed using Peter Norvig's spell-corrector [24]. Lemmatization is not executed and punctuation marks are not eliminated as pre-trained embeddings are always used. No stop-word is removed for fluency.

3.2   Phase II: Classification of Tweets Based on User and Tweet Characteristics

For the classification of tweets, the two most popular XGBoost and BERT deep learning models are implemented. The equation for the XGBoost model, in which model learns from the weak model is:

$$Y_m = Y_{m-1} + b \tag{1}$$

Where, Ym is the output of the model based on the previous step Y_{m-1} and the base learner b which is known as a weak learner which is fit on basis of the taken training set.

$$b = \alpha\theta(m) \tag{2}$$

The base learner can be found using Eq. 3.

$$\theta m = \text{argmin} i = 1n21h(x) - gxhx - \theta(x)2 \tag{3}$$

Where g(x) and h(x) are gradient decent, and second derivative of gradient known as hessian respectively.

3.3   Phase III: BERT Text Classification

Language typical pre-training has been shown to be effective in learning extensive language representations. As a result, we will employ transformers to classify tweets. Bidirectional Encoder Representations from Transformers (BERT) has achieved remarkable effectively in a variety of receptive language tasks for language pre-training. BERT uses the following steps for the text classification:

1. Tokenization at sentence level.
2. Adding [CLS] token at the beginning of the first sentence and a [SEP] token at the end of each sentence.
3. Padding is added to make all sequence of text of same size 512.
4. Adding positional embedding to each token to indicate its position in the sequence. The concept and implementation of positional embedding is represented in Fig. 2.
5. Encoder output is added with a classification layer on top.
6. Embedding matrix is multiplied with output vectors so as to transform them into the vocabulary dimension.
7. Softmax is used for calculating the probability of each word in the vocabulary.

Implementation
For the tweet classification, the following attributes are selected:

1. 'No. of Favourites',
2. 'No. of Followers',
3. 'No. of Friends/Following',
4. 'No. of Tweets Posted',

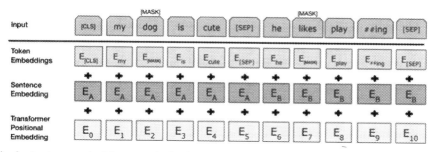

Fig. 2. Sentence embeddings are similar in concept to token embeddings with a vocabulary of 2.

5. 'No. of Retweets',
6. 'Length of Username',
7. 'Account Age',
8. 'Verified Account',
9. 'Length of User Description',
10. 'Total Tweets
11. 'Liked By Account',
12. 'Public List Mentions',
13. 'URL Provided',
14. 'Using Default Profile Image',
15. 'Using Default Profile Theme'.

Firstly, for giving the input to the selected models for classification, the preprocessing of the text is done using the nltk package. The text is cleaned by removing the hashtags, URLs, @symbols, emoticons re replaced with text and beautiful soup is used to identify and to remove the other http symbols. To implement XGBOOST classifier the grid-search cross-validation is used for the hyperparameter tuning and Accuracy, confusion matrix and ROC-AUC curve were used as metrics for measuring and the classification accuracy of the model. Similarly, for the tuning of the Bert model 12 encoder and decoder layers were used with 786 feed-forward networks and 12 attention heads. The bath size for the model selected is 32 and the maximum length of each sentence taken is 152 which is maximum length in the downloaded tweets. The data preprocessing was done for the tweet texts using various natural language processing techniques.

For transformers, Pytorch's implementation is utilized. To train the model, use the Colab platform's Compute Engine to create a virtual machine (VM) instance. This VM included virtual CPUs, 30 GB of RAM, and one NVIDIA Tesla T4 GPU. It takes about 5 h to train. The dataset used included 27910 rows, of which 2791 were used as the test set, 2512 as the validation set, and 22607 as the training set. As evaluation measures, accuracy, confusion matrix, and ROC-AUC curve were used. The model's scores are compared to those of other baseline models. The learning rate was determined by plotting the loss vs. the log learning rate with the lr_find() function. The learning rate was chosen by picking a number in the midpoint of the dropping loss 1e−5. The autofit approach, which employs a triangle learning rate policy, was then utilized to train 5 epochs.

4 Analysis and Result

The results of the classification of tweets based on user and tweet characteristics using XGBoost classifier are listed in Table 2. For the purpose of evaluation, we compare our proposed model with seven prominent models used by researchers in the field listed below and the comparative result of these models and our proposed fake news detection model using XGBoost classifier is outlined in Table 3. It can be concluded that the proposed model is better than all the other models in terms of accuracy as well as F1 score.

Table 2. XGBoost classification results

	Precision	Recall	F1-score	Support
False	0.78	0.81	0.80	2583
True	0.83	0.81	0.82	2999
Accuracy	0.81	0.81	0.81	5582
Macro avg	0.81	0.81	0.81	5582
Weighted avg	0.81	0.81	0.81	5582

BERT model for classification of tweets based on tweet text was trained for five epochs with a maximum learning rate of $0.1e-05$. The model was trained on 22607 samples and validated on 2512 samples. The results obtained are listed in Table 3.

Table 3. Comparison of proposed XGBoost model with other models for classification of tweets based on twitter user characteristics

Method	Description	Accuracy	Real (F1)	Fake (F1)
DTC [4]	Decision Tree	0.454	0.733	0.355
SVM-RBF [25]	SVM (RBF Kernel)	0.318	0.455	0.037
SVM-TS [26]	SVM (Time Series)	0.544	0.796	0.472
DTR [13]	Decision Tree Ranking	0.409	0.501	0.311
GRU [27]	RNN	0.646	0.792	0.574
RFC [28]	Random Forest	0.565	0.810	0.422
PTK [29]	SVM (Propagation Tree Kernel)	0.75	0.804	0.698
Proposed	XGBoost	0.81	0.82	0.8

Accuracy achieved by BERT is 98.53% and Matthews Correlation Coefficient (MCC) is 0.9706. BERT's performance is compared with other baseline models in Table 4. The baselines models considered are from work done by Ajao et al. [30]. The models compared are LSTM: vanilla model trained to detect fake tweets without preceding field

Table 4. Comparison of BERT and other models

Method	Accuracy	Precision	Recall	F1-score
LSTM	82.29	44.35	40.55	40.59
LSTMDrop	73.78	39.67	29.71	30.93
LSTM-CNN	80.38	43.94	39.53	39.70
Our approach (BERT)	98.53	98.20	98.51	98.57

knowledge of the subjects being deliberated, LSTMDrop: LSTM method with dropout regularization and LSTM-CNN: LSTM-CNN hybrid model. It can be clearly seen that the proposed BERT model for Classification of tweets based on tweet text far outperforms all other models.

5   Conclusions and Future Work

Through this study, we outlined a fake news detection model. We performed tweet classification based on user and tweet characteristics and achieved an accuracy of 81% using the XGBoost classifier. Further, we did tweet text classification using the BERT transformer which gave us an accuracy of 98%. The accuracies achieved by our models are superior to those attained by other baseline models. In the future, these models can also be extended for early detection of fake news taking the temporal features in consideration. These models can also be extended to news articles in the future. Future research work could also include enhancing the accuracy of a fake news detector model by making a hybrid of XGBoost and BERT classifiers using any ensembling technique such as bagging, boosting and stacking.

Acknowledgments. The authors would like to thank Kai Shu, Deepak Mahudeswaran, Suhang Wang, Dongwon Lee, Huan Liu from FakeNewsNet for making their data available, enabling our research.

References

1. Gartner reveals Top Predictions for IT organizations and users in 2018 and and beyond, https://www.gartner.com/en/newsroom/press-releases/2017-10-03-gartner-reveals-top-predictions-for-it-organizations-and-users-in-2018-and-beyond, Accessed 20 Jan 2021
2. Allcott, H., Gentzkow, M.: Social media and fake news in the 2016 election. J. Econ. Perspect. **31**(2), 211–236 (2017)
3. News Use across Social Media Platforms 2016. https://www.journalism.org/2016/05/26/news-use-across-social-media-platforms-2016/
4. Castillo, C., Mendoza, M., Poblete, B.: Information credibility on twitter. In: Proceedings of the 20th International Conference on World Wide Web, pp. 675–684, March 2011
5. Qazvinian, V., Rosengren, E., Radev, D., Mei, Q.: Rumor has it: identifying misinformation in microblogs. In: Proceedings of the 2011 Conference on Empirical Methods in Natural Language Processing, pp. 1589–1599, July 2011

6. Balmas, M.: When fake news becomes real: combined exposure to multiple news sources and political attitudes of inefficacy, alienation, and cynicism. Commun. Res. **41**(3), 430–454 (2014)

7. Afroz, S., Brennan, M., Greenstadt, R.: Detecting hoaxes, frauds, and deception in writing style online. In: 2012 IEEE Symposium on Security and Privacy, pp. 461–475, IEEE May 2012

8. Chu, Z., Gianvecchio, S., Wang, H., Jajodia, S.: Detecting automation of twitter accounts: are you a human, bot, or cyborg? IEEE Trans. Dependable Secure Comput. **9**(6), 811–824 (2012)

9. Takahashi, T., Igata, N.: Rumor detection on twitter. In: The 6th International Conference on Soft Computing and Intelligent Systems, and the 13th International Symposium on Advanced Intelligence Systems, pp. 452–457. IEEE November 2012

10. Kwon, S., Cha, M., Jung, K., Chen, W., Wang, Y.: Prominent features of rumor propagation in online social media. In 2013 IEEE 13th International Conference on Data Mining, pp. 1103–1108. IEEE, December 2013

11. Chen, C., Wu, K., Srinivasan, V., Zhang, X.: Battling the internet water army: detection of hidden paid posters. In: 2013 IEEE/ACM International Conference on Advances in Social Networks Analysis and Mining (ASONAM 2013), pp. 116–120. IEEE, August 2013

12. Sakurada, M., Yairi, T.: Anomaly detection using autoencoders with nonlinear dimensionality reduction. In Proceedings of the MLSDA 2014 2nd Workshop on Machine Learning for Sensory Data Analysis, pp. 4–11, December 2014

13. Zhao, Z., Resnick, P., Mei, Q.: Enquiring minds: early detection of rumors in social media from enquiry posts. In: Proceedings of the 24th International Conference on World Wide Web, pp. 1395–1405, May 2015

14. Rubin, V.L., Conroy, N., Chen, Y., Cornwell, S.: Fake news or truth? using satirical cues to detect potentially misleading news. In: Proceedings of the Second Workshop on Computational Approaches to Deception Detection, pp. 7–17, June 2016

15. Hardalov, M., Koychev, I., Nakov, P.: In search of credible news. In: Dichev, C., Agre, G. (eds.) AIMSA 2016. LNCS (LNAI), vol. 9883, pp. 172–180. Springer, Cham (2016). https://doi.org/10.1007/978-3-319-44748-3_17

16. Vicario, M.D., Quattrociocchi, W., Scala, A., Zollo, F.: Polarization and fake news: early warning of potential misinformation targets. ACM Trans. Web (TWEB) **13**(2), 1–22 (2019)

17. Zhang, X., Ghorbani, A.A.: An overview of online fake news: characterization, detection, and discussion. Inf. Process. Manag. **57**(2), 102025 (2020)

18. Fernandez, A.C.T., Devaraj, M.: Computing the linguistic-based cues of fake news in the philippines towards its detection. In: Proceedings of the 9th International Conference on Web Intelligence, Mining and Semantics, pp. 1–9, June 2019

19. Gaurav, D., Tiwari, S.M., Goyal, A., Gandhi, N., Abraham, A.: Machine intelligence-based algorithms for spam filtering on document labeling. Soft. Comput. **24**(13), 9625–9638 (2019). https://doi.org/10.1007/s00500-019-04473-7

20. Yang, S., Shu, K., Wang, S., Gu, R., Wu, F., Liu, H.: Unsupervised fake news detection on social media: a generative approach. In: Proceedings of the AAAI Conference on Artificial Intelligence, vol. 33, pp. 5644–5651, July 2019

21. Sharma, S., Kalra, V., Agrawal, R.: Depression discovery in cancer communities using deep learning. In: Handbook of Deep Learning in Biomedical Engineering, pp. 123–154. Academic Press, Boca Raton (2021)

22. Kanagaraj, N., Hicks, D., Goyal, A., et al.: Deep learning using computer vision in self driving cars for lane and traffic sign detection. Int. J. Syst. Assur. Eng. Manag. **12**, 1011–1025 (2021). https://doi.org/10.1007/s13198-021-01127-6

23. Segaran, T., Hammerbacher, J.: Beautiful Data: The Stories Behind Elegant Data Solutions, O'Reilly Media Inc., Beijing (2009)

24. Norwig, P.: How to write a spelling corrector. norvig.com
25. Yang, F., Liu, Y., Yu, X., Yang, M.: Automatic detection of rumor on Sina Weibo. In: MDS 2012 (2012)
26. Ma, J., Gao, W., Wei, Z., Lu, Y., Wong, K.-F.: Detect rumors using time series of social context information on microblogging websites. In: Proceedings of the 24th ACM International on Conference on Information and Knowledge Management (CIKM 2015). Association for Computing Machinery, New York, NY, USA, pp. 1751–1754 (2015). https://doi.org/10.1145/2806416.2806607
27. Ma, J., et al.: Detecting rumors from microblogs with recurrent neural networks. In: IJCAI, pp. 3818–3824 (2016)
28. Kwon, S., Cha, M., Jung, K.: Rumor detection over varying time windows. Plos One **12**, e0168344 (2017). https://doi.org/10.1371/journal.pone.0168344
29. Ma, J., Gao, W., Wong, K.-F.: Detect Rumors in Microblog Posts Using Propagation Structure via Kernel Learning (2017). https://doi.org/10.18653/v1/P17-1066
30. Ajao, O., Bhowmik, D., Zargari, S.: Fake news identification on twitter with hybrid cnn and rnn models. In: Proceedings of the 9th International Conference on Social Media and Society, pp. 226–230, July 2018

Efficient Visual Sentiment Prediction Approaches Using Deep Learning Models

Ganesh Chandrasekaran and D. Jude Hemanth[✉]

Department of ECE, Karunya Institute of Technology and Sciences, Coimbatore, Tamilnadu,
India
judehemanth@karunya.edu

Abstract. Sentiment analysis of images is becoming very important with the increase in the use of social media by people. Many existing works in the literature focus on textual sentiment analysis with the text being extracted from the social media sites like Twitter, Facebook, Amazon and Movie reviews, etc. But sharing of images and videos through social media is increasing compared to text. Images reflect the sentiment in a much better way compared to the text and thus are preferred in analyzing the sentiment. So, there is a need to develop a robust model to carry out image sentiment prediction. In this paper, we employ a transfer learning model based on VGG-16 architecture to carry out the image sentiment analysis. The dataset employed is the Crowdflower database that has more than 15,000 images (Twitter) URLs with its polarity label (Positive, Negative). The proposed model can handle a large set of data as it is based on deep learning and there is no need for explicit feature extraction. The results show the effectiveness of our proposed model in performing sentiment prediction on images.

Keywords: Natural Language Processing (NLP) · Image sentiment prediction · Transfer learning and deep learning

1 Introduction

The field of Natural Language Processing (NLP) is getting popular among researchers and sentiment analysis, which is an important branch of NLP, is essential in predicting sentiments [1]. Sentiment analysis of the text has been successfully used in the applications like stock market prediction, human-computer interaction and Election result prediction [2–4]. Social media are preferred by people to share their views and expressions by posting Text, Images and Video, etc. [5, 6]. Most of the data available in social media are in the form of text which is in very short form. Sometimes text cannot reflect the actual sentiment as it contains many informal words with sarcastic remarks. In addition to text, people prefer images to convey their opinions on various events (political and social, etc.), share information about important events of their life, exhibit their love and friendship through social media. This sharing of images with the people helps researchers to have a huge collection of images that can be used in a better manner.

Analyzing the visual sentiment is a tedious task and there are only a few works found in the existing literature to determine the image sentiment compared to the text-based

© Springer Nature Switzerland AG 2021
B. Villazón-Terrazas et al. (Eds.): KGSWC 2021, CCIS 1459, pp. 260–272, 2021.
https://doi.org/10.1007/978-3-030-91305-2_20

analysis. We also need a large collection of images with their labels to carry out the supervised machine learning which involves much time and personnel help. Sometimes, the techniques for sentiment classification may become domain-dependent and may not work in a different domain. Our research work aims to make use of the transfer learning concept which is pre-trained on a large collection of images for the task of predicting the image sentiments. The advantage of the transfer learning approach over other approaches is that it does not need expert knowledge regarding psychology to carry out the image sentiment analysis. We have used the existing architecture of the VGG-16 model which has been successfully used in carrying out image classification by the researchers [7]. We have included some additional layers to improve the system performance for image sentiment prediction. We have included some techniques like weight regularization and batch normalization to overcome the over-fitting problem.

The rest of this research article is organized as follows: In Sect. 2, we present the existing related works that are carried out in predicting the visual/image sentiments from different social media sites. The block diagram of the proposed work has been shown in Sect. 3 which gives a detailed explanation of the overall flow of the process. Section 4 explains the basics of the transfer learning concept and the architecture details of the pre-trained model. In Sect. 5, the details about the collected dataset are given. In Sect. 6, the experimental results were discussed briefly with the help of performance metrics. The last section, i.e. Sect. 7 deals with the conclusion and the future scope of this research work.

2   Related Work

In this section, we present the review of existing literature on visual or image sentiment analysis using different approaches like Low-level features, Mid-level or semantic features and deep learning-based models. In the conventional approach for visual sentiment prediction, Low-level features like color histogram, color and texture, etc. are used. The researchers [8] have used local image statistics for sentiment classification and the fuzzy histograms are employed by the authors [9] in their work regarding emotions. The low-level features are used in video-based sentiment analysis by the researchers [10] in which they have done the performance comparison of these features in emotion analysis. The mid-level features which are based on the concept Visual Sentiment Ontology (VSO) and SentiBank with Adjective Noun Pairs (ANP) such as "beautiful sky" and "dull eyes" are used in the work [11]. Following the similar approach of VSO, the authors [12] have used 102 scene-based attributes with facial expressions that convey the people's sentiments in a better way. These mid-level or semantic approaches are based on psychological theories and the Plutchik Wheel of Emotions [13]. The mid-level techniques for sentiment prediction have yielded better results compared to the low-level features like Color histogram, GIST, SIFT and other related approaches. But the drawback of using mid-level features is that training requires knowledge about psychology and human intervention.

The development of deep learning techniques like Convolutional Neural Network (CNN), Long Short Term Memory Networks (LSTM) and Recurrent Neural Networks (RNN) has helped to improve the performance of sentiment classification. The authors [14] have developed a progressive training model for CNN, which performed sentiment analysis on a large set of Flickr images. The results obtained show that the designed progressive CNN has obtained better performance metrics compared to the other machine learning techniques for sentiment classification. An image sentiment prediction framework based on domain-specific tuning was developed by the researchers [15] that have improved the performance of the CNN models. The drawback of this approach is that it is trained on lesser data compared to the other existing models involving CNN. An image sentiment analysis model was built by the researchers of [16] using Deep Neural Network (DNN) and Convolutional Neural Network (CNN) to determine the image sentiments. This proposed model overcomes the drawbacks of the Adjective Noun Paris (ANP) in dealing with unlabeled images in sentiment prediction. The authors in [17] have used the combination of Conventional Neural Networks (CNN) with handcrafted features like Color Histogram and Bag of Visual Words (BoVW) to carry out image sentiment prediction on the Twitter dataset. The authors of [18] have built a model to discover the affective regions present in the image that convey sentiment and CNN to find the sentiment scores. They have applied this model on eight benchmark datasets and it could outperform the other existing techniques. Visual cues have been used by the authors [19] in their work based on Convolutional Neural Networks (CNN) to determine the sarcasm in the Flickr images. Their model has obtained an accuracy of 84% and outperformed the other related works regarding sarcasm detection. The researchers [20] have built different models based on the deep Convolutional Neural Network for training a large amount (3 million tweets) of user-generated and unlabeled data. They have proven that their approach is very effective in training a large set of images for sentiment classification.

3   Proposed Work-Overview

This section presents a block diagram to explain the steps involved in classifying the image sentiments by making use of the VGG-16 model with additional layers for sentiment prediction. The process starts with the loading of images collected using the crowdflower image sentiment analysis dataset (https://data.world/crowdflower/image-sentiment-polarity). This dataset contains image URL's with their sentiment polarity in an excel file and we have downloaded the images from the given URL and prepared a dataset of 1000 images. The sentiment labels (positive and negative) are saved in a separate text file and the images are assigned with the corresponding labels in the next step. The pre-processing of images like converting the images in other formats to RGB is followed by the resizing the images into the dimensions of 224 * 224 * 3 as required by the pre-trained model (VGG-16). The normalization of the image pixel intensity is also done so that the normalized pixels are in the range of 0 to 1. The separation of the dataset into training and testing samples is done in the next step. We have separated the total images of 1000 into training samples of 795 images and testing samples of 205 images from the dataset. The training process is started by building a pre-trained model architecture and the evaluation of the test samples is done after the training. The overall process flow of our work is depicted in the following figure (Fig. 1).

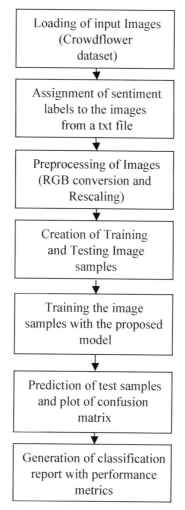

Fig. 1. Overall process - flow diagram of the proposed model for image sentiment prediction based on VGG-16 architecture.

4   Methodology

This section brings out details about the concept of transfer learning, layers present in the existing VGG-16 model and the architectural details of the proposed network.

4.1   Transfer Learning

It involves the usage of knowledge gained from solving a previous problem to solve a new problem of a similar kind. It is preferred if we have only less training data and it allows us to make use of many pre-trained models that are trained on a huge dataset. To use these models we need to import them and train them on our dataset. The VGG-16,

VGG-19 and other models like DenseNet121 have been pre-trained on a million images from the ImageNet dataset. Using such pre-trained models helps us to reduce the task of constructing a huge network and saves time also.

4.2 Layers of VGG-16

Visual Geometric Group (VGG-16) model is a 16 layer Convolutional Neural Network (CNN) architecture that has won the ILSVR – Image net competition in 2014 and it has fewer number of hyper-parameters. It loads the weights that are pre-trained on ImageNet containing over 15 million images and it has achieved top-5 accuracy of 90.1% with 138,357,544 parameters.

The VGG group has developed a group of Convolutional Neural Network (CNN) modelers. The VGG-16 model has been designed with the following layers:

1. Input Layer
2. Convolutional Layer
3. Max pooling layer
4. Fully connected (Dense Layers)

The input layer accepts the images of size 224×224 with 3 channels. The convolutional layers follow the input layer and the filters in these layers have the size of 3×3 and a stride of 1. Filters in these layers can capture edge-related information from the image pixels. It has 5 blocks of convolutional layers with their corresponding max-pooling layers. The row and column padding (zero paddings) is added after convolution so that the size of the feature maps obtained before and after the convolution process remains the same. The width of the first convolutional layer is 64 which increases by a factor of 2 as we proceed to the successive layers. The final block (block 5) has a convolutional layer of width 512.

4.3 Architecture of the Proposed Model

There is a need for fine-tuning the model as our training dataset is small (1000 images) and it is not similar to the ImageNet dataset on which the VGG-16 model has been pre-trained. We have freezed the first three convolutional blocks (block 1, block 2 and block 3) and un-freezed the remaining layers in the VGG-16 model. These un-freezed layers are trained with our crowdflower image sentiment analysis dataset. The reason behind un-freezing and training the higher layers is that the lower layers learn the general features and the higher layers could learn the features related to the problem domain. We have also included the following additional layers that are added after the 5 convolutional blocks.

1. Flatten Layer – Converts the 2D output that is obtained from the last max-pooling layer of the VGG-16 model (Block 5) to a one-dimensional vector
2. Batch Normalization Layer – It helps in reducing the overfitting and it is used in normalizing the outputs of the previous layers. It also helps in reducing the Internal Covariate Shift that will speed up the learning process.

3. Dropout Layer – It facilitates reducing the overfitting of the model during the training. It makes some of the input neurons to be disabled randomly by setting it to '0'.
4. Dense Layers – Neurons are fully connected (512 units) with the 'ReLU' activation function.
5. Output dense layer with 'softmax' activation function for 2 classes (Positive and Negative).

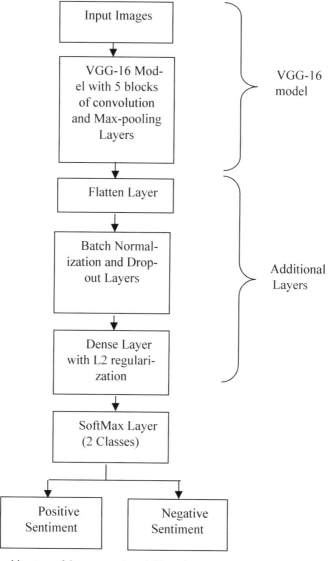

Fig. 2. The architecture of the proposed model based on VGG-16 for image sentiment prediction

The above figure (Fig. 2) shows the architecture of the proposed network which is based on VGG-16 architecture that extracts the low, mid and high-level features of image pixels using different blocks of convolutional layers (Block 1 to Block 5). We have fully connected layers at the end, which also helps in obtaining the feature representation of the input images. We have applied the 'L2' kernel regularization on the dense layer with '512' units that will overcome the problem of overfitting by penalizing the weights. The addition of the regularization layer improves the accuracy of the proposed model. The cost function is calculated by adding the loss term with the regularization term. The cost function is calculated as,

$$\text{Cost function} = \text{Loss} + \frac{\lambda}{2m} * \sum \left\| w^2 \right\| \tag{1}$$

Where,

w-Represents the weight parameter

λ-Regularization parameter and its value is chosen between $1 * e-1$ to $1 * e-6$.

The final output dense layer with the 'Softmax' function gives the result of sentiment classification i.e. either 'Positive' or 'Negative' class.

5   Dataset

The proposed model is evaluated on the images obtained from the Crowd Flower – Image sentiment Polarity dataset (https://data.world/crowdflower/image-sentiment-pol arity). This dataset has 15,000 images URL with their sentiment polarity scores. It was labeled by several contributors and they have labeled the images into classes like highly positive, highly negative, neutral, positive and negative classes. We have collected the images belonging to the classes 'Positive' and 'Negative' by downloading them from their respective URLs. We have collected 1000 images in which the training set has 795 images and the testing set contains 205 images. The data about the collected images are shown in the table (Table 1) below.

Table 1.   Input image database details

Sentiment class	Number of images
Positive	642
Negative	358
Total	1000

6   Experimental Results and Discussion

To carry out the image-based sentiment analysis, we have employed the Google Collaboratory, which is a tool developed by Google to write and execute python codes. To run our model we have used Tesla P100-PCIE GPU @ 2.30 GHz with 16 GB of RAM. The program coding is implemented with the Python3.5 language. The Keras - a high-level neural network library is used to build and implement the transfer learning model. The confusion matrix and classification report are generated using the Scikit-learn library. For plotting the results the MatPlotLib library is used. The source code of our work is available online at https://github.com/GaneshC86/Image-sentiment-analysis.

The total images (1000) available in the collected dataset have been divided into testing and training samples. The training sample contains 795 images and the testing samples contain 205 images. The input images are extracted from a folder and they have been assigned with corresponding labels stored in a separate.txt file. The input images are resized to the dimension (224, 224, 3) as required by the VGG-16 model. The pre-processed images are divided into training (795 images) and testing samples (205 images). The existing VGG-16 model has been imported from the python Keras library and it is pre-trained on the "ImageNet" weights. The output from the final max-pooling layer is converted into a 1D array of feature vectors by using the Keras flatten class. It creates a long feature vector that is suitable to be fed to the following layers. The output of the flatten layer is normalized using the batch normalization layer and a drop out layer is also added to avoid the over-fitting problem. The dense layer that follows the dropout layer has 512 units with a 'relu' activation function that passes only the positive values to the next layer. The 'L2' regularization technique is applied to the dense layer which helps in reducing the over-fitting by penalizing the network weights. Finally, a dense layer with '2' units is used with the 'softmax' function that helps in predicting the sentiment classes (Positive and Negative).

6.1 Generation of Confusion Matrix

This proposed model is compiled with the 'Adam' optimizer and the 'Categorical cross-entropy' loss function is applied. The Adam optimizer is preferred over the popular Stochastic Gradient Descent (SGD) as the former one has an adaptive learning rate and works well with large datasets. It has also got an easy implementation and works well on inputs with noisy gradients. The model is then trained on a training set of images with a batch size of '20' and for '50' epochs. After training the model it is evaluated by applying the test set of images and its confusion matrix is obtained. The following figure (Fig. 3) shows the confusion matrix generated after evaluating the testing samples with the proposed model.

6.2 Generation of Classification Report

The classification report of the proposed model is generated using SciKit learn library which gives the values of various performance metrics that are defined below.

$$\text{Accuracy} = \frac{TP + TN}{TP + TN + FP + FN} \tag{2}$$

$$\text{Precision} = \frac{TP}{TP + FP} \tag{3}$$

$$\text{Recall Recall} = \frac{TP}{TP + FN} \tag{4}$$

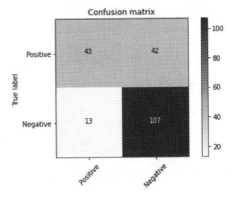

Fig. 3. Confusion matrix generated by the proposed model

$$F1 \text{ Score } = 2 * \frac{(\text{Precision} * \text{Recall})}{(\text{Precision} + \text{Recall})} \tag{5}$$

$$\text{Sensitivity } = \frac{TP}{TP + FN} \tag{6}$$

$$\text{Specificity } = \frac{TN}{TN + FP} \tag{7}$$

Where,
True Positive (TP) is the number of positive sentiments predicted as positive
True Negative (TN) is the number of negative sentiments predicted as negative
False Positive (TN) is the number of positive sentiments predicted as negative
False Negative (FN) is the number of negative sentiments predicted as positive

Table 2. Performance metrics of the VGG-16 model for image sentiment prediction

VGG-16 model			
Sentiment class	Precision	Recall	F1-score
Positive	0.77	0.51	0.61
Negative	0.72	0.89	0.80
Accuracy	7416%		

From the performance metrics which are summarized in the above table (Table 2), we can conclude that for the given input visual dataset, the proposed model which based on VGG-16 architecture yields good accuracy (74.16%) with precision over 70%.

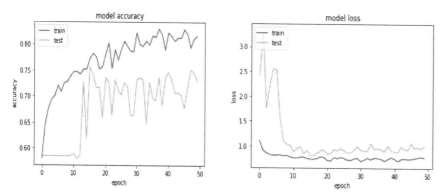

Fig. 4. Model accuracy and model loss plots of the proposed model for image sentiment prediction

The above plot (Fig. 4) shows the model accuracy and model loss over the epoch. It indicates that the proposed model which is based on the pre-trained VGG-16 model has a testing accuracy of 74.16. The model loss is maximum at the beginning of the epoch and continues to decrease as we reach beyond '10' epochs and settles to a lower value while nearing 10 epochs.

7   Comparison with the Existing Works on Image Sentiment Analysis

Many existing research works have employed various machine and deep learning models to carry out sentiment analysis on images. We have compared our work with the other related works that are mentioned in the section Related works (Sect. 2) of our paper. Even though the comparison is not fair as the other works used different datasets but it gives an idea about the features used and the classification approach employed with their results. The following table (Table 3) presents the comparison of other existing works with our approach for image sentiment analysis.

Table 3. Comparison of existing works with our image sentiment analysis model

S. No	Author name	Dataset employed	Classification Approach	Accuracy
1	Yuan, J et al. (2013) [11]	SUN database with 660 positive and 140 negative image samples	Linear SVM Logistic Regression (LR)	61.4% (SVM) 61.2% (LR)
2	Quanzeng You et al. [14]	Flickr	Convolutional Neural Network (CNN) & Progressive CNN (PCNN)	72.3% (PCNN) 71.2% (CNN)
3	Jindal, S. and Singh, S [15]	Flickr	CNN with domain specific tuning	53.5%
4	Fengjiao, W., and Aono, M. [17]	Twitter dataset with 1269 images with Positive and Negative polarity	CNN with BoVW features	72.2%
5	Our model (Fine-tuned VGG-16)	Crowdflower sentiment polarity dataset with 1000 images	Fine-Tuned version of pre-trained VGG-16 model	74.16%

The table (Table 3) above summarizes and compares the different existing methods for image sentiment analysis on different datasets. We could conclude that the pre-trained model when fine-tuned can be effective in analyzing the image sentiments and its performance can be improved by using a large sample of images for training.

8   Conclusion and Future Work

The objective of this research work is to determine the visual sentiment of social media images (1000 images) taken from the Crowdflower database using the concept of transfer learning. We have used the existing VGG-16 model and added some additional layers to its architecture to avoid over-fitting during the training process. The system performance is improved by adding a dropout layer, batch normalization layer and performing weight regularization in the additional dense layer. In predicting the image sentiments, the proposed framework which is based on the VGG-16 architecture gives an accuracy of 74.16% on the collected data set. The Keras library has been used to implement the transfer learning concept and Matplotlib is used in the visualization of the important parameters like model accuracy and loss, etc. The limitation of this work is, it has less collection of images for training which has to be increased. The future work is to build a large dataset of images to improve the overall performance of this model and to present a comparative study of different pre-trained models on our dataset.

References

1. Pang, B., Lee, L.: Opinion mining and sentiment analysis. Foundations and Trends® Inf. Retri. **2**(1–2), 1–135 (2008)
2. Wu, H., Harris, W., Gongjun, Y., Akula, V., Shen, I.: A novel social media competitive analytics framework with sentiment benchmarks. Inf. Manag. **52**(7), 801–812 (2015)
3. Rajput, P., Sapkal, P., Sinha, S.: Box office revenue prediction using dual sentiment analysis. Int. J. Mach. Learn. Comput. **7**(4), 72–75 (2017)
4. Bansal, B., Srivatsava, S.: On predicting elections with hybrid topic based sentiment analysis of tweets. Sci. Dir. Procedia Comput. Sci. **135**, 346–353 (2018)
5. Tyagi, P., Tripathi, R.: A review towards the sentiment analysis techniques for the analysis of twitter data. In: Proceedings of 2nd International Conference on Advanced Computing and Software Engineering (ICACSE-2019), https://papers.ssrn.com/sol3/papers.cfm?abstract_id=3349569
6. Chandrasekaran, G., Nguyen, T.N., Jude Hemanth. D.: Multimodal sentimental analysis for social media applications: a comprehensive review, Wiley Interdiscip. Rev. Data Min. Knowl. Discov. **11**, e1415 (2021). https://doi.org/10.1002/widm.1415
7. Vadicamo, L., et.al.: Cross-media learning for image sentiment analysis in the wild. In: IEEE International Conference of Computer Vision Workshops (ICCVW), (2017)
8. Yanulevskaya, V., Van Gemert, J.C., Roth, K., Herbold, A.K., Sebe, N., Geusebroek, J.M.: Emotional valence categorization using holistic image features. In: 15th IEEE International Conference on Image Processing, San Diego, pp. 101–104 (2008). https://doi.org/10.1109/ICIP.2008.4711701
9. Wei-Ning, W., Ying-Lin, Y., Sheng-Ming, J.: image retrieval by emotional semantics: a study of emotional space and feature extraction. In: IEEE International Conference on Systems, Man and Cybernetics, Taipei, pp. 3534–3539 (2006). https://doi.org/10.1109/ICSMC.2006.384667
10. Jiang, Y., Xu, G.B., Xue, X.: Predicting emotions in user-generated videos. In: AAAI Conference on Artificial Intelligence, pp.73–79 (2014)
11. Borth, B., Chen, T., Ji, R., Chang, S.: SentiBank: large-scale ontology and classifiers for detecting sentiment and emotions in visual content. In: ACM International Conference on Multimedia, pp.459–460 (2013)
12. Yuan, J., Mcdonough, S., You, Q., Luo, J.: Sentribute: image sentiment analysis from a mid-level perspective. In: ACM International Workshop on Issues Of Sentiment Discovery and Opinion Mining, p. 10 (2013)
13. Plutchik, R.: Emotions: a general psycho evolutionary theory: approaches to emotion, pp.197–219 (1984)
14. Ji, R., Chen, F., Cao, L., Gao, Y.: Cross-modality microblog sentiment prediction via bi-layer multimodal hypergraph learning. IEEE Trans. Multimedia **21**(4), 1062–1075 (2019). https://doi.org/10.1109/TMM.2018.2867718
15. You, O., Luo, J., Jin, H., Yang, J.: Robust image sentiment analysis using progressively trained and domain transferred deep networks. In: Proceedings of the Twenty-Ninth AAAI Conference on Artificial Intelligence, AAAI 2015, pp. 381–388. AAAI Press, Austin (2015)
16. Jindal, S., Singh, S.: Image sentiment analysis using deep convolutional neural networks with domain specific fine tuning. In: International Conference on Information Processing (ICIP), Pune, pp. 447–451 (2015). https://doi.org/10.1109/INFOP.2015.7489424
17. Mittal, N., Sharma, D., Joshi, M.L.: Image sentiment analysis using deep learning. In: IEEE/WIC/ACM International Conference on Web Intelligence (WI), Santiago, pp. 684–687 (2018). https://doi.org/10.1109/WI.2018.00-11

18. Fengjiao, W., Aono, M.: Visual sentiment prediction by merging handcraft and CNN features. In: 5th International Conference on Advanced Informatics: Concept Theory and Applications (ICAICTA), Krabi, pp. 66–71 (2018). https://doi.org/10.1109/ICAICTA.2018.8541312

19. Yang, J., She, D., Sun, M., Cheng, M., Rosin, P., L., Wang, L.: Visual sentiment prediction based on automatic discovery of affective regions. IEEE Trans. Multimedia **20**(9), 2513–2525 (2018). https://doi.org/10.1109/TMM.2018.2803520

20. Das, D., Clark, A.J.: Sarcasm detection of Flickr using a CNN. In: Proceedings of the 2018 International Conference on Computing and Big Data, pp. 56–61 (2018). https://doi.org/10.1145/3277104.3277118

Uniform Textual Feedback Analysis for Effective Sentiment Analysis

Alok Kumar[✉] and Renu Jain

Department of Computer Science and Engineering, University Institute of Engineering and Technology, CSJM University, Kanpur, Kanpur, India

Abstract. In this paper, a machine learning-based methodology is proposed to measure the users' sentiments expressed in textual feedback. The methodology uses collaborative filtering to evaluate the degree of positivity or negativity for every important aspect from each user's perspective participating in the feedback analysis, hence proposing a uniform feedback analysis. Key aspects of a particular item or an issue are identified through topic modeling and taking into account the syntactic and semantic properties of words after processing the merged document obtained from all the feedbacks. Aggregate sentiment of an item is evaluated by considering the importance and sentiments of key aspects. This methodology can be used to analyze textual feedbacks of any domain with very little domain-dependent information. In this paper, feedbacks of two different domains have been analyzed and presented. Results show that the performances of the same items of different brands can be compared easily.

Keywords: Natural language processing · Text mining · Aspect identification · Uniform sentiment analysis · Sentiment aggregation · Topic modeling

1 Introduction

Opinions help human beings make the right decisions in every aspect of their life, like purchasing an expensive item, deciding a college for admission, joining an organization, and availing any service like medical, entertainment, repair work, etc. (B. Liu [1]). Progressive service providers and product manufacturers continuously try to improve the qualities of their services/products based on feedback given by their customers. Nowadays, feedbacks are mostly provided online in the textual form by customers in place of word of mouth or by filling the question-answer format (Sasikala et al. [2]).

A questionnaire-based feedback system (Kumar and Jain [3]) is still a formal method used for opinion analysis in the organization. In this system, the questionnaire is decided by the senior members based on their experience and knowledge. Such systems tend to become restrictive and static (S. Debois [4]). Text-based feedback systems allow the users to express their feelings and emotions freely in the form of running text. There are many online platforms like e-commerce websites, blogs, social networking sites, etc., where users share their views on any issue or item. Sentiment analysis is about capturing and consolidating users' feelings from textual feedback (Sasikala et al. [2]).

© Springer Nature Switzerland AG 2021
B. Villazón-Terrazas et al. (Eds.): KGSWC 2021, CCIS 1459, pp. 273–289, 2021.
https://doi.org/10.1007/978-3-030-91305-2_21

Text-based feedback evaluation systems provide flexibility to users to express their opinions on every aspect of the item. The sentiment analysis of feedback texts can be done in three levels (B. Liu [1]), i.e., 1. Document-level sentiment analysis: where each feedback is classified simply as "positive" or "negative" or "neutral", 2. Sentence level sentiment analysis: where each sentence is processed to know whether the sentence is objective or subjective, further subjective sentence is classified as "positive" or "negative" or "neutral" and then overall sentiment score of the feedback is evaluated, and 3. Aspect based sentiment analysis: a more in-depth level sentiment analysis, each feedback is processed to estimate sentiments of different aspects/features of an item. Aspect-based sentiment analysis tries to estimate the user likes or dislikes on essential aspects of an item instead of just measuring the product's overall quality. It has few limitations, as mentioned below (Kumar and Jain [5]).

Comparing different brands of a product: Comparison between two or more brands of the same product is only possible when the same aspects are mentioned in each feedback. However, the list of important aspects for every user may be very different because a user may write only about those aspects in his/her feedback, which is essential to him/her. Therefore, different feedback of an item may have sentiments expressed about different aspects, making it difficult to compare the different brands in aspect-based sentiment analysis.

1. Uniform aspect sentiment aggregation: It is a known fact that some customers only want to know the overall rating of a product without going into the details of each aspect. Sentiment aggregation gives us an overall picture of a product's performance or service by averaging all aspects' sentiment scores. Still, textual feedbacks do not have a uniform structure. Due to this, it becomes challenging to find the overall sentiment of the item.

2. Evaluating the overall goodness of any product/service: There are many aspects/features associated with each item. All aspects may not have the same significance or importance; some aspects may be more valuable than other aspects. The overall effectiveness of an item should be computed by the weighted average of sentiment scores of aspects. There is a need to estimate the importance (weightage) of different aspects in aspect-based sentiment analysis.

In this paper, an integrated methodology to perform uniform analysis of textual feedback is proposed. The first step is to identify all the important (essential) aspects of an item from the combined document of feedbacks using linguistic and statistical text knowledge. In the next steps, the sentiment score of each aspect is calculated uniformly. Sentiments of mentioned aspects are computed using the statistical knowledge and linguistic properties of sentiment-bearing words present in the feedback, and collaborative filtering is applied to estimate the sentiment scores of those aspects which are not explicitly mentioned in some feedbacks. This paper is divided into six sections. Work done by other researchers in this area is discussed in Sect. 2. The proposed methodology is explained in Sect. 3. Section 4 of this paper describes the performance of the proposed methodology. Discussion about the work done is given in the next section, and research work is concluded in Sect. 6 with future work.

2   Literature Review

Sentiment analysis is the extraction of authors' sentiments described in a natural language text about an item/issue. This is one of the emerging areas of research in natural language processing, text mining, machine learning, etc. Much work has been done in this area (Dave et al. [6]; Esuli and Sebastiani [7]; Waila et al. [8]; Balage Filho and Pardo [9]; Ghiassi et al. [10]), still more work needs to be done to achieve the performance closer to the level of human understanding. Sentiment analysis is categorized into three levels; document, sentence, and aspect level. Document-level and sentence-level sentiment analysis is applied when the requirement is to find a product/item's overall sentiments. Aspect-based sentiment analysis is used to get the users' opinions on important features of a product. Researchers have used different algorithms and techniques to implement aspect-based sentiment analysis. The processing of aspect-level sentiment analysis can be divided into three subproblems (B. Liu [1]), i.e., aspect identification, sentiment evaluation of identified aspects, and aggregation of sentiment score.

Hu and Liu [11] identified aspect terms based on the words' syntactic categories removing meaningless aspects using association-based filters. They formed rules and used syntactic information to assign the sentiment values to aspects. Zhuang et al. [12] used a dependency parser to check the validity of feature-opinion pairs and sentiments evaluated based on related opinion words. Shi et al. [13] augmented the frequency-based extraction method with pointwise mutual information to extract the important aspect terms from online reviews. Jin et al. [14] used lexicalized Hidden Markov Model (HMM) based method to extract the aspects and their sentiment terms. Shariaty and Moghaddam [15] used a Conditional Random Field (CRF) to enhance the HMM-based model's performance. Li et al. [16] proposed a skip-tree CRF model to identify significant aspect and sentiment terms to incorporate more language-dependent features. Nandal et al. [17] used a support vector machine to classify the sentiment words attached to aspect words. They also classified the bipolar words as positive or negative on the basis of nearby words. Chuhan et al. [18] proposed a hybrid unsupervised approach for fine-grained sentiment analysis. They extracted phrases from text using chunk-level linguistics. They then used these chunks as pseudo-labeled data to train Gated Recurrent Unit (GRU) neural network architecture for extracting aspect and opinion terms. Poria et al. [19] used a deep learning approach combined with linguistic patterns to extract the aspects for opinion mining for products. D. Hussein [20] did a comprehensive study to identify the sentiment analysis's major challenges. Some of the common challenges are negation words, bipolar words, abbreviations, sarcasm, spam, fake detection, etc. Maharani et al. [21] suggested some new syntactic patterns to identify the explicit aspects from textual reviews.

Da'u and Salim [22] used a multi-channel convolutional neural network for aspect extraction. The first channel encoded semantic information of the words and the second channel encoded sequential syntactic tagging. Barnaghi et al. [23] used a Convolutional Neural Network (CNN) to extract aspects of products using two types of word embedding. They used SemEval datasets [24, 25] to test their system. Dragoni et al. [26] proposed a domain-independent unsupervised aspect extraction strategy for monitoring real-time reviews. They used parsing structure and morphological characteristics to find the aspect-opinion pairs. Valdivia et al. [27] implemented the methodologies used by

M. Thelwall [28], Hu and Liu [10], and F.N Ribeiro [29] for feedback of three popular monuments collected from TripAdvisor [30] and observed that the distributions of polarities are quite different from the actual ratings given by users. James Lappeman et al. [31] analyzed online conversations using human validation techniques to know the combined impact of qualitative and quantitative analysis of reviews. It concluded that a combination of qualitative and quantitative analysis is more suitable to detect the sentiments.

Ghallab et al. [32] reviewed 108 Arabic sentiment analyzer research papers and found that Arabic sentiment analyzers' performance can be enhanced using language-specific features and lexicons. Muthukumaran and Suresh [33] used a mixture language model to extract relevant features of products, and a pattern-based technique is used to estimate the sentiments of identified aspects. Alsaeedi and Khan [34] conducted a detailed study on sentiment analysis for Twitter data and found that ensemble and hybrid approaches are more suitable than other approaches.

Cambria et al. [35] have briefly discussed different methodologies used for sentiment analysis and highlighted that a sentiment analyzer's performance could be enhanced by using broader and deeper common sense knowledge. Cambria et al. [36] discussed that though sentiment analyzers' performances can be enhanced using deep learning machine learning techniques. Significant bottlenecks are dependency, consistency, and transparency, which can be resolved/enhanced by core natural language processing techniques only. Poria et al. [37] performed multimodal sentiment analysis with three different deep learning architectures. They used CNN to extract textual aspects while 3-D-CNN and openSMILE7 were used to find visual and acoustic features. Wladislav et al. [38] developed a tool 'Sentilyzer' to analyze product reviews. In this research, two category-specific dictionaries (sentiment and aspect) are created by crawling product reviews, and created dictionaries are further used to perform aspect-oriented sentiment analysis.

Cambria et al. [39] has divided affective computing into two tasks, i.e., emotion recognition and polarity detection. In this study, the author concluded that hybrid approaches are more suitable for affective computing and sentiment analysis, which exploit the power of both knowledge-based techniques and statistical methods. Cambria and Hussuain [40] concluded in their book that common sense knowledge representation and natural language understanding are necessary for accurate sentiment evaluation. Authors have explained "sentic computing" using the SenticNet tool [41], a new framework to do the concept-level sentiment analysis. Sentic Net [41] is a freely available semantic resource in the public domain for concept-level sentiment analysis that exploits an ensemble of graph mining and multidimensional scaling to fill the gap between word and concept-level language processing. Ma et al. [42] proposed an extended Long Short Term Memory (LSTM) network to integrate implicit and explicit knowledge of the text. Performance of knowledge-embedded LSTM is enhanced due to the inclusion of common sense knowledge. Md Akhtar et al. [43] suggested a stacked ensemble method for estimating the intensity of emotion and sentiment. In this method, outputs of several deep learning and feature-based models are combined using a multi-layer perceptron network to predict the degree of intensity of emotion and sentiment.

After studying various researchers' work, it is found that hybrid methods can give better results because they exploit the power of both rule-based methods and statistical methods. The performance of sentiment analyzers can be enhanced by incorporating some domain-dependent and commonsense knowledge in the system. Aspect-based sentiment analysis is the most suitable approach to estimate the correct opinion about a product, but due to the uneven structure of feedbacks, sentiment aggregation and comparison of two or more products becomes difficult.

3 Proposed Methodology

This research includes the positive characteristics of existing feedback systems and removes the shortcomings of other systems. Uniformity is one of the key characteristics of the proposed methodology. In this methodology, essential aspects of an item are identified from feedback with an integer value representing the weight of the aspect. For every individual feedback, essential aspects are divided into two types, i.e., cited aspects and non-cited aspects. Cited aspects are the essential aspects mentioned by the customer explicitly in the feedback, and non-cited aspects are those essential aspects that are not mentioned in the feedback explicitly. Each feedback is processed uniformly to estimate sentiments of all essential aspects (cited and non-cited). The proposed methodology works based on the intuition that each user likes to give feedback on those aspects of an item which he/she feels vital and for which user has a firm opinion, either positive or negative, and leaving out other important aspects of the item. In this method, the sentiments of mentioned (cited) aspects are decided on the basis of sentiment orientations of contextual words, and sentiments of not mentioned aspects are decided based on sentiments of these aspects in similar feedbacks. An item's overall effectiveness is estimated by considering aspect importance and users' sentiments on all essential aspects. The salient characteristics of the proposed methodology are:

1. **Flexibility:** It is flexible and can be used to analyze textual feedbacks of any domain with very little domain-dependent information. It allows the users to write the feedbacks without any restriction.
2. **Automatic Identification of Essential Aspects:** Essential aspects of any item are not pre-decided by the customers or manufacturers. They are automatically identified from the collection of all feedback based on statistical knowledge of the text.
3. **Flexible Evaluation Scale:** The proposed approach allows us to decide the sentiment evaluation measurement scale based on sentiment-bearing words' sentiment scores. The scale is decided on the basis of retrieved sentiment-bearing words.
4. **Uniform Analysis:** After selecting essential aspects and evaluation scale, each feedback is evaluated to estimate all essential aspects' sentiments. Sentiments of mentioned aspects are estimated based on contextual sentiment bearing and sentiment shifter words. Sentiments of all non-mentioned aspects are decided based on sentiments of similar aspects in similar feedback. This way, the system can evaluate the sentiment score of each identified aspect for every user. The proposed approach allows the users to compare different brands of the same item.
5. **Automatic Aspect Weight Estimation:** For each item, some aspects are more important in comparison to others. Therefore, a weight representing the dominance of an aspect is assigned to each aspect. The weight of each essential aspect is dynamically estimated with the help of statistical information. These weights of aspects play an important role in the evaluation of the overall usefulness of an item.

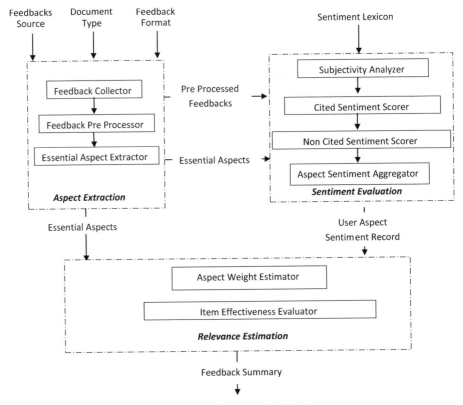

Fig. 1. Architecture of proposed evaluation system

The complete processing is divided into three modules, i.**e.,** *'Aspect Extraction'*, *'Sentiment Evaluation'*, **and** *'Relevance Estimation'*. Basic architecture of the proposed methodology is shown in Fig. 1. The functionality and details of all the modules are given below.

3.1 Aspect Extraction

This module's major responsibilities are feedback collection, pre-processing of collected textual feedback, and identifying essential aspects from pre-processed feedback. This module is implemented using three sub-modules, i.e., *'Feedback Collector'*, *'Feedback Pre Processor'*, and *'Essential Aspect Extractor'*. *Feedback Collector* module collects textual feedbacks of an item from specified remote locations. For each location, it takes three inputs. The first input is the address of the remote location where feedback of an item is stored, second input is the template used to store the feedback at that location, and third is the type of the source document, i.e., pdf, doc, docx, html or xml. The raw opinions/feedback contain various unwanted characters, symbols, tags, images, links, etc., and it is cleaned by *Feedback Pre Processor* module.

Essential Aspect Extractor module extracts the important aspects of the product using topic modeling and linguistic knowledge. Important aspects represent mostly features of the product, parts of product, properties or qualities of product or attributes of the product. In this research, Latent Dirichlet Allocation (LDA) technique (Blei et al. [44]) is used with the assumption that all feedback sentences are generated from K different topics. LDA is a more robust and efficient topic modeling method than other topic modeling methods (George and Birla [45]).

Initially, K clusters are formed using LDA, and then from each cluster, high probability terms are selected to build the first list of probable aspects. In LDA, K different topics, i.e. $\{\beta_1, \beta_2...... \beta_k\}$ are identified where $\{\beta_1, \beta_2...... \beta_k\}$ are the probabilistic distributions of all vocabulary words in different topics. The optimum value of K is decided based on the topic coherence score (C_v score). It also finds the coverage of each sentence by every topic, i.e. $\{\Theta_{i1}, \Theta_{i2}.... \Theta_{ij}....\Theta_{ik},\}$, where Θ_{ij} is the coverage of a jth topic in the ith sentence. The probability of a particular word 'w' (P(w)) in a sentence is computed by taking into account its probability in K clusters and coverage of different topics in the sentence. The high probability words from each cluster are selected as tentative aspects in a list L1. Further syntactic and semantic-based filters are used to get the final list of valid aspects. The complete process to identify valid aspects is explained below.

a) ***Removal of terms from the tentative list of aspects/features based on syntactic knowledge:***
   It is known that ordinarily syntactic categories of aspects are noun, adjective or adverb. Therefore, as a first step, all those words whose syntactic category is not noun or adjective, or adverb are removed from the list L1. Having a syntactic category of either adjective or adverb is analyzed using the tool SentiWordNet [46]. The words that represent only sentiments like 'good', 'awesome', 'bad', 'best' etc., are also removed from list L1.

b) ***Removal of least significant terms on the basis of contextual knowledge:***
   It is observed that valid aspects are paradigmatic (similar context) words. The relation between two words is called paradigmatic if one word can be used in place of another word without violating the sentence syntactic structure or acceptability. The degree of paradigmatic reflects an agreement between lexical neighborhoods. Each tentative term's contextual similarity is compared with the seed list's actual terms to get the most relevant aspects. As tiny domain-specific seed aspect list L2 is chosen, it is used to compute the context similarities between words in the tentative aspect list L1 and L2. The contextual similarity between terms is defined by cosine similarity between contextual vectors. Term frequency and inverse document frequency (TF-IDF) weighting scheme is used for vector representation of contexts. Terms in list L2 and terms of tentative list L1 having higher contextual similarities are added in list L2. This is an iterative process, and it is continued till new terms keep getting added to the list L2.

c) ***Removal of less significant terms on the basis of association with sentiment words:***
   In this step, the terms that are weakly associated with general sentiment words are removed from the list L2. To measure the association, Pointwise Mutual Information (PMI) is computed between the terms of L2 list and the words in the sentiment list.

d) *Removal of terms having a similar sense:*
   In this step, redundant aspects are removed by using sense similarities among words of list L2. Sense similarities between words are computed using the WordNet lexicon [47].

e) *Removal of terms having the same root:*
   Words having the same root word (like knowledge and knowledgeable) are checked, and duplicate words are removed from L2.

f) *Identification of multi-term aspects:*
   In this step, two or more terms are joined to form a new aspect if those terms occur together in the text frequently. Words are joined on the basis of their co-occurrences. Highly co-occurring words are considered as a single valid aspect. Pointwise mutual information gain is used to estimate co-occurrences between the terms present in the list L2.

g) *Identification of missing aspects:*
   In this last step, the original feedback text is processed one more time to check any left out aspects. Missing aspects are identified based on syntactic and semantic relationships between terms in the aspect list L2 and sentiment words. Those words of the text which possess very close relations with the words in L2 are treated as relevant aspects and added in the final aspect list. Syntactic and semantic relationships between aspect and sentiment terms are identified with Stanford Dependency Parser [48].

3.2   Sentiment Evaluation

In the existing aspect-based sentiment evaluation systems (B. Liu [1], Madhoushi et al. [49]), only sentiments of aspects are explicitly present in the feedback are evaluated using sentiment bearing terms, while in the proposed system, Sentiment Evaluation module estimates sentiments for every essential aspect identified by Aspect Extraction module for each feedback. Sentiment Evaluation module uses four modules i.e., 'Subjectivity Analyzer', 'Cited Sentiment Scorer', 'Non-Cited Sentiment Scorer', and 'Sentiment Aggregator', to calculate the sentiments of aspects.

The Subjectivity Analyzer module uses Naive Bayes based approach to decide whether a sentence in the feedback is subjective or objective. It is assumed that subjectivity analysis is a 2-class classification problem. Naïve Bayes algorithm generates a probabilistic distribution of words for every class and prior probabilities of each class based on the training set's examples. Objective sentences of feedbacks are ignored, and subjective sentences are kept for further processing. Cited Sentiment Scorer processes all feedbacks one by one to estimate sentiment scores of all mentioned aspects in every feedback. The sentiments of mentioned aspects are computed with sentiment bearing words and sentiment shifter words present in the sentence. Unknown sentiment score, i.e., '?' is assigned to all non-mentioned aspects by the Cited Sentiment Scorer. The Non-Cited Sentiment Scorer module computes the sentiment score of non-mentioned aspects. The complete algorithm of Cited Sentiment Scorer is given below as Algorithm 1.

Sentiment scores of non-mentioned aspects are estimated with the help of sentiments of mentioned aspects in similar feedbacks. The collaborative filtering based method

(Kumar and Jain [5]) estimates non-mentioned aspects' sentiments. User-to-User collaborative filtering first finds similar users. Then, sentiment scores of non-mentioned aspects are projected using the similarity matrix and similar users' sentiment scores of that aspect. Cosine similarity is used to calculate the degree of similarity between the users. Each user is represented as an N-dimensional vector, where N is the number of essential aspects of an item. The cosine similarity between two users, 'U1' and 'U2' is evaluated using Eq. 1.

$$\text{Sim}(U_1, \ U_2) = \frac{U_1.U_2}{|U_1||U_2|} = \frac{\sum_{i=1}^{m} S_{1i}.S_{2i}}{\sqrt{\sum_{i=1}^{m}(S_{1i})^2}\sqrt{\sum_{i=1}^{m}(S_{2i})^2}} \tag{1}$$

In this equation, U1 and U2 are user vectors for user1 and user2, and S1i and S2i are the sentiments on ith aspect given by user 1 and user2, respectively.

Algorithm 1: Cited Sentiment Scorer	
Input:	Pre-processed feedbacks, a list of essential aspects identified by the Aspect Extraction module, and Sentiment Lexicon.
Output:	User Aspect Sentiment Record
Step 1:	Select a feedback.
Step 2:	Read the next sentence from the selected feedback and make entries in the User Aspect sentiment Record for every essential aspect for every user/ feedback using following steps.
Step 3:	Pass sentence to Subjectivity Analyzer module to determine whether the sentence is subjective or objective.
Step 4:	If the sentence is objective, then ignore it and go to step 2, otherwise go to step 5.
Step 5:	Look for the aspect in the sentence and match it with the list provided by the Aspect Extraction module. If the aspect match with the list provided by the Aspect Extraction module, then go to step 6 otherwise, go to step 2.
Step 6:	If the part of speech of the identified aspect is adjective or adverb, then sentiment 'positive', 'negative' or 'neutral' is assigned by looking at the sentiment lexicon. Sentiment is inverted if any sentiment shifter word is present in the context window.
Step 7:	If the part of speech of identified aspect is noun or noun phrase, nearby qualifiers are extracted to estimate the sentiment value. If the extracted qualifier is present in the positive lexicon, then sentiment 'positive' is assigned to aspect; otherwise, 'negative' sentiment assigned to identified aspect. If any sentiment shifter is present, invert sentiment..
Step 8:	Go to step 2 until all sentences of feedback are processed.
Step 9:	Unknown sentiment score '?' is assigned to all other aspects not mentioned in the feedback.
Step 10	Go to step 1 until all feedbacks are processed.
Step 11	Return User Aspect Sentiment Record with 'undefined' entries.

A particular non-mentioned aspect's sentiment score is estimated using a weighted average of K similar users' sentiment scores for that aspect.

$$S_{ij} = \sum_{x \in n} Sim(i, x) * S_{xj} / \sum_{x \in n} Sim(i, x) \tag{2}$$

In Eq. 2, S_{ij} is the sentiment score of jth aspect in the feedback of ith user and $Sim(i, x)$ denotes a similarity between i^{th} and x^{th} users. The complete algorithm for calculating the sentiment scores of non-mentioned aspects using User-to-User collaborative filtering used by the Non-Cited Sentiment Scorer module is given below in Algorithm 2.

Algorithm 2: Sentiment Evaluation using User-to-User Collaborative Filtering

Input :	User Aspect Sentiment Record with 'undefined' entries
Output:	User Aspect Sentiment Record without 'undefined' entries.
Step1:	Read the table to find an entry marked as 'undefined'.
Step2	Store the row and column location of that entry (Assume it is at (I, J) location in the table).
Step3:	Identify all the users similar to User I on the basis of the sentiment scores assigned for other aspects and who has cited aspect J.
Step4:	Store the locations of closest users that fall within a certain threshold.
Step5:	Evaluate the estimated value of (I,J) entry by taking the weighted average of sentiment scores given by the closest K users for the Jth aspect.
Step6:	Repeat steps 1 to 5 till all the 'undefined' entries of the table are processed.

The Sentiment Aggregator module computes the aggregate sentiment score of an essential aspect of an item by considering all sentiments for that aspect. The aggregate sentiment score of an essential aspect 'a' (aspect_aggregate_score (a)) is calculated using the formula given below in Eq. 3. In this aggregation, the sentiment score '+1' and '−1' sentiment score is assigned to each aspect with 'positive' and 'negative' sentiments. Sentiment score of 'neutral' feedback is computed by fractional biasness of positivity and negativity for a particular aspect 'a'. Let P, N and Neut are the numbers of positive, negative, and neutral sentiments of a particular aspect 'a'.

$$aspect\_aggregate\_score(a) = \frac{P * (+1) + N * (-1) + log\left(\frac{P+1}{N+1}\right) * Neut * (+1)}{P + N + \left|log\left(\frac{P+1}{N+1}\right)\right| * Neut} \tag{3}$$

Value of aspect_aggregate_score () is always between +1 and −1. This aggregation represents the overall sentiment score of an essential aspect.

3.3 Relevance Estimation

This module tries to find the relevance of the product by assigning a single numerical number. It first identifies the most worthy aspects which actually decide the goodness of the product. All the aspects are graded as per their importance. Weight is assigned to each aspect using the degree of inclusion in the feedback. In the estimation of aspect weight, it is assumed that important aspects are frequently mentioned in the feedbacks while less important aspects are ignored. The overall worth of the item is estimated by using the aspect weights and aspect aggregate sentiment scores. Relevance estimation of the product allows customers to compare two or more brands of the same product. An algorithm to compute the overall worth is given below as Algorithm 3.

Algorithm 3: Item Effectiveness Evaluation	
Input	VF: List of Essential Aspects, FW: Essential Aspects Weight Vector, FS: Essential Aspects' Aggregate Sentiment Score Vector.
Output	Overall Effectiveness of the Item
Step 1	Effective_score = 0
Step 2	Set pointer i at the beginning of list VF
Step 3	Effective_score= Effective_score + Weigth of aspect pointed by pointer i in list FW (FW[i]) * Aggregate sentiment score of aspect pointed by pointer i in list FS (FS[i]).
Step 4	If pointer i is not at the end of list VF then increment pointer i and go to step 3.
Step 5	Overall Effectiveness = Effective_score / total number of feedback in the list LF (Length of list LF).

4 Performance Evaluation of Proposed Methodology

Two different systems, i.e., Faculty Feedback Evaluation System (FFES) and Laptop Feedback Evaluation System (LFES), were implemented to measure the proposed methodology's effectiveness. FEES and LFES perform uniform aspect-based sentiment analysis of textual feedback for faculty members and laptops, respectively. Feedbacks of laptops were collected from a public platform released by SemEval [24, 25]. Feedbacks of faculty members were collected from three different sources, i.e., public platform for sharing feedback of faculty from United State of America [50], public platform for sharing feedbacks of faculty from India [51] and textual feedbacks of faculty members collected from one engineering institute [52].

The basic architecture of FFES and LFES are the same except the difference between domain-dependent information. The effectiveness of two major subsystems (Aspect Extraction, Sentiment Evaluation) is computed using three performance parameters, i.e., precision, recall, and accuracy. Performance parameters of Aspect Extraction and Cited Sentiment Scorer modules in FFES and LFES are shown in Table 1 and Table 2.

The proposed methodology is a novel method to estimate sentiments of all essential aspects (mentioned and non-mentioned) in every feedback. The proposed method's overall results cannot be directly compared with other existing aspect-based sentiment evaluation systems. Performance of Aspect Extraction and Cited Sentiment Scorer module of the proposed system is compared with some pioneer research is mentioned in Table 3.

Table 1. Performance parameters of *Aspect Extraction* module

Aspect extraction	FFES	LFES
Average precision	87.23	88.85
Average recall	87.10	85.12
Average accuracy	87.85	87.25

Table 2. Performance parameters of *Cited Sentiment Scorer* module

Cited sentiment scorer	FFES	LFES
Average precision	87.48	85.17
Average recall	88.43	85.65
Average accuracy	83.13	83.14

Table 3. Result comparison with some existing methods

Research	Dataset/Domain	Performance	
		Aspect extraction	Sentiment evaluation
Proposed method	*Faculty Feedback* [45–47]	*Precision: 87.23* *Recall: 87.10* *Accuracy: 87.85*	*Precision: 87.48* *Recall: 88.43* *Accuracy: 83.13*
	Laptop Feedback/SemEval [24, 25]	*Precision: 88.85* *Recall: 85.12* *Accuracy: 87.25*	*Precision: 85.17* *Recall: 85.65* *Accuracy: 83.14*
Zhang et al. [53]	Laptop Feedback/SemEval [24, 25]	F-score: 65.88	Precision: 65.26 Recall: 69.46 F-Score: 67.30
Wang et al. [54]	Laptop Feedback/SemEval [24, 25]	F- score: 78.42	F-score: 79.44
Kiritchenko et al. [55]	Laptop Feedback/SemEval [24, 25]	Precision: 78.77 Recall: 60.70 F-Score: 68.57	Accuracy: 80.16

Table 4 shows the performance of the Non-Cited Sentiment Scorer module. This table highlights how the performance depends upon the value of K (no of similar users). The table shows that the system gets optimum performance for K = 20.

Table 4. Performance parameters of *Non-Cited Sentiment Scorer* module

Hybrid Collaborative Filtering	Average Accuracy in LFES		Average Accuracy in FFES	
	Average of K Sentiment	Weighted Average of K Similar Sentiments	Average of K Sentiments	Weighted Average of K Similar Sentiments
K=5	54.43	57.72	55.03	55.78
K=10	74.13	75.27	75.35	76.12
K=15	81.54	83.32	80.83	83.00
K=20	89.92	91.16	86.71	93.26
K=25	88.79	88.99	89.12	88.32
K=30	86.48	87.69	84.11	86.80
K=35	79.87	81.92	80.42	82.56

5   Discussion

Existing textual feedback evaluation systems allow the users to write their opinions freely without any kind of restriction. In it, each feedback is evaluated to estimate the sentiment of only mentioned aspects. Due to non-uniformity in feedbacks, performance of different brands of an item cannot be compared based on users' feedback.

In this research, a new methodology is proposed to include uniformity in the feedback evaluation. This methodology works in three phases. In the first phase, important (essential) aspects of an item are identified using statistical and linguistic knowledge of the text; in the second phase, sentiments of all mentioned aspects in feedback are estimated on the basis of contextual information. Finally, in the third phase, non-mentioned aspects are estimated using collaborative filtering by considering similar aspects in similar feedback.

The proposed methodology helps in finalizing the overall effectiveness/usefulness of an item. An item's overall performance is computed by considering weights (importance) and aggregate sentiment scores of all essential aspects. With it, two or more brands of an item can be compared easily on the basis of users' feedback. This methodology will help the customers and manufacturers; customers can effectively select the appropriate brand of his/her requirement, and manufacture can quickly identify strong and weak aspects of their item to enhance the quality of their product/service.

6   Conclusion and Future Work

It can be concluded that the results obtained by FFES and LFES are quite encouraging. Table 5 shows the essential features of the existing and the proposed feedback evaluation systems. It can be seen that all systems require some domain-dependent information. Questionnaire-based systems have the flexibility of having any scale of evaluation, but they restrict the user. Aspect-based systems provide the flexibility to the user to give his/her opinion on any aspect using any scale of evaluation through textual feedback. This system adds the feature of uniformity by finding the sentiments of missing aspects.

Researchers would like to mention that this system has a major limitation of skipping tiny messages like "good product", "very noisy" etc. Because such feedback does not have aspects, they cannot contribute any significant knowledge to an aspect-based sentiment evaluation system. The second limitation is that it requires some domain-dependent knowledge to identify important aspects using few seed aspects. However, the number of required seed aspects are very few (in the range of 4–7), which are necessary and common.

Researchers are trying to extract more meaningful relevant aspects through advanced machine learning approaches. Researchers are also working towards adding more semantic knowledge of sentiment-bearing words and understanding every sentence's meaning through natural language processing (NLP) approaches to estimate the correct sentiment values. In the future, researchers have a plan to include short messages and experiment with feedbacks from other domains.

Table 5. Summary of comparison between existing and proposed feedback evaluation system

Characteristics	Questionnaire Based Feedback Evaluation System	Existing Aspect Based Textual Feedback Evaluation System	Proposed Uniform Textual Feedback Evaluation System
Domain-Independent	✖	✖	✖
Allows users to evaluate any aspect	✖	✓	✓
Allows a wider range of scale	✓	Partial	Partial
User flexibility to select the scale of evaluation	✖	✓	✓
Uniform feedback evaluation	Partial	✖	✓
Allows to evaluate missing aspects	✖	✖	✓
Allows to compare two brands of the same item	✓	✖	✓
Assign a weight to aspects	✖	✖	✓
Estimation of the overall usefulness of an item	✓	✖	✓
Weighted sentiment evaluation	Partial	✖	✓

References

1. Liu, B.: Sentiment Analysis and Opinion Mining. Morgan & Claypool Publishers, San Francisco (2012)
2. Sasikala, P., Mary Immaculate Sheela, L.: Sentiment analysis of online product reviews using DLMNN and future prediction of online product using IANFIS. J. Big Data **7**, 33 (2020)
3. Kumar, A., Jain, R.: Opinion sentiment analysis. Int. J. Adv. Appl. Sci. **5**(3), 128–136 (2016)
4. Debois, S.: Ten Advantages and Disadvantages of Questionnaires, SurveyAnyplace, March 2019. https://surveyanyplace.com/questionnaire-pros-and-cons
5. Kumar, A., Jain, R.: A Collaborative filtering based sentiment analyzer to evaluate textual user feedbacks/opinions. Int. J. Appl. Eng. Res. **12**, 6670–6677 (2017)
6. Dave, K., Lawrence, S., Pennock, D.: Mining the peanut gallery: opinion extraction and semantic classification of product reviews. In: Proceedings of WWW, pp. 519–528 (2003)
7. Esuli, A., Sebastiani, F.: Determining the semantic orientation of terms through gloss classification. In: Proceedings of the 14th ACM International Conference on Information and Knowledge Management, Bremen, Germany (2005)
8. Waila, P., Singh, V.K., Singh, M.K.: Evaluating machine learning and unsupervised semantic orientation approaches for sentiment analysis of textual reviews. In: Computational Intelligence & Computing Research (ICCIC), pp. 1–6 (2012)
9. Balage Filho, P.P., Pardo, T.A.: NILC USP: a hybrid system for sentiment analysis in twitter messages. In: Second Joint Conference on Lexical and Computational Semantics, vol. 2, pp. 568–572 (2013)
10. Ghiassi, M., Skinner, J., Zimbra, D.: Twitter brand sentiment analysis: a hybrid system using n-gram analysis and dynamic artificial neural network. Expert Syst. Appl. **40**(16), 6266–6282 (2013)
11. Hu, M., Liu, B.: Mining and summarizing customer reviews. In: Proceedings of the Tenth ACM SIGKDD International Conference on Knowledge Discovery and Data Mining (KDD 2004), pp.168–177. ACM, New York (2004)
12. Zhuang, L., Jing, F., Zhu, X.-Y.: Movie review mining and summarization. In: Proceedings of the 15th ACM International Conference on Information and Knowledge Management, CIKM 2006, pp. 43–50. ACM, New York (2006)
13. Shi, L., Lina, Z., Yijun, L.: Improving aspect extraction by augmenting a frequency-based method with web-based similarity measures. Inf. Process. Manage. **51**(1), 58–67 (2015)
14. Jin, W., Ho, H.H., Srihari, R.K.: OpinionMiner: a novel machine learning system for web opinion mining and extraction. In: Proceedings of the 15th ACM SIGKDD International Conference on Knowledge Discovery and Data Mining (KDD 2009) , pp. 1195–1204. ACM, New York (2009)
15. Shariaty, S., Moghaddam, S.: Fine-grained opinion mining using conditional random fields. In: Data Mining Workshops (ICDMW), IEEE 11th International Conference, pp. 109–114 (2011)
16. Li, F., Han, C., Huang, M., Zhu, X., Xia, Y.-J., Zhang, S., Yu, H.: Structure-aware review mining and summarization. In: Proceedings of the 23rd International Conference on Computational Linguistics, pp. 653–661 (2010)
17. Nandal, N., Tanwar, R., Pruthi, J.: Machine learning based aspect level sentiment analysis for Amazon products. Spatial Inf. Res. **28**(5), 601–607 (2020). https://doi.org/10.1007/s41324-020-00320-2
18. Chuhan, W., Fangzhao, W., Sixing, W., Yuan, Z., Huang, Y.: A hybrid unsupervised method for aspect term and opinion target extraction. Knowl.-Based Syst. **148**, 66–73 (2018)
19. Poria, S., Cambria, E., Gelbukh, A.: Aspect extraction for opinion mining with a deep convolutional neural network. Knowl.-Based Syst. **108**, 42–49 (2016)

20. Hussein, D.: A survey on sentiment analysis challenges. J. King Saud Univ. Eng. Sci. **30**(4), 330–338 (2018)
21. Maharani, W., Widyantoro, D., Khodra, M.: Aspect extraction in customer reviews using syntactic pattern. Procedia Comput. Sci. **59**, 244–253 (2015)
22. Da'u, A., Salim, N.: Aspect extraction on user textual reviews using multi-channel convolutional neural network. PeerJ Comput. Sci. **5**, e191 (2019)
23. Barnaghi, P., Kontonatsios, G., Bessis, N., Korkontzelos, Y.: Aspect extraction from reviews using convolutional neural networks and embeddings. In: Métais, E., Meziane, F., Vadera, S., Sugumaran, V., Saraee, M. (eds.) NLDB 2019. LNCS, vol. 11608, pp. 409–415. Springer, Cham (2019). https://doi.org/10.1007/978-3-030-23281-8_37
24. SemEval Trial Data. http://alt.qcri.org/semeval2014/task4/data/uploads/laptops-trial.xml
25. SemEval Train Data. http://metashare.ilsp.gr:8080/repository/browse/semeval-2014-absa-laptop-reviews-train-data
26. Dragoni, M., Federici, M., Rexha, A.: An unsupervised aspect extraction strategy for monitoring real-time reviews stream. Inf. Process. Manage. **56**(3), 1103–1118 (2019)
27. Valdivia, A., Luzón, M.V., Herrera, F.: Sentiment analysis in TripAdvisor. IEEE Intell. Syst. **32**(4), 72–77 (2017)
28. Thelwall, M.: Heart and soul: sentiment strength detection in the social web with sentistrength. In: Holyst, J.A. (ed.) Cyberemotions: Collective Emotions in Cyberspace, pp. 119–134. Springer, Cham (2017). https://doi.org/10.1007/978-3-319-43639-5
29. Ribeiro, F.N.: SentiBench: a benchmark comparison of state-of-the-practice sentiment analysis methods. EPJ Data Sci. **5**(1), 1–29 (2016)
30. TripAdvisor. http://times.cs.uiuc.edu/~wang296/Data
31. Lappemana, J., Clark, R., Evans, J, Rubia, L.S., Gordon, P.: Studying social media sentiment using human validated analysis. MethodsX **7**, 100867 (2020)
32. Ghallab, A., Mohsen, A., Ali, Y.: Arabic sentiment analysis: a systematic literature review. Appl. Comput. Intell. Soft Comput., 1–21 (2020)
33. Muthukumaran, S., Suresh, P.: Text analysis for product reviews for sentiment analysis using NLP methods. Int. J. Eng. Trends Technol. **47**(8), 474–480 (2017)
34. Alsaeedi, A., Khan, M.Z.: A study on sentiment analysis techniques of twitter data. Int. J. Adv. Comput. Sci. Appl. **10**(2), 361–374 (2019)
35. Cambria, E., Schuller, B., Xia, Y., Havasi, C.: New avenues in opinion mining and sentiment analysis. IEEE Intell. Syst. **28**(2), 15–21 (2013)
36. Cambria, E., Poria, S., Gelbukh, A., Thelwall, M.: Sentiment analysis is a big suitcase. IEEE Intell. Syst. **32**(6), 74–80 (2017)
37. Poria, S., Majumder, N., Hazarika, D., Cambria, E., Gelbukh, A., Hussain, A.: Multimodal sentiment analysis: addressing key issues and setting up the baselines. IEEE Intell. Syst. **33**(6), 17–25 (2018)
38. Wladislav, S., Johannes, Z., Christian, W., André, K., Madjid, F.: Sentilyzer: aspect-oriented sentiment analysis of product reviews. In: International Conference on Computational Science and Computational Intelligence (CSCI), Las Vegas, NV, USA, pp. 270–273 (2018)
39. Cambria, E.: Affective computing and sentiment analysis. IEEE Intell. Syst. **31**(2), 102–107 (2016)
40. Cambria, E., Hussuain, A.: Sentic computing: a common-sense-based framework for concept-level sentiment analysis (socio-affective computing). Cogn. Comput. **7**, 183–185 (2015)
41. SenticNet. https://sentic.net/
42. Ma, Y., Peng, H., Khan, T., Cambria, E., Hussain, A.: Sentic LSTM: a hybrid network for targeted aspect-based sentiment analysis. Cogn. Comput. **10**(4), 639–650 (2018). https://doi.org/10.1007/s12559-018-9549-x

43. Md Akhtar, S., Ekbal, A., Cambria, E.: How intense are you? Predicting intensities of emotions and sentiments using stacked ensemble [application notes]. IEEE Comput. Intell. Mag. **15**(1), 64–75 (2020)
44. Blei, D.M., Ng, A.Y., Jordan, M.I.: Latent Dirichlet allocation. J. Mach. Learn. Res. **3**, 993–1022 (2003)
45. George, L.E., Birla, L.: A study of topic modeling methods. In: Second International Conference on Intelligent Computing and Control Systems (ICICCS), Madurai, India, pp. 109–113 (2018)
46. SentiWordNet. https://github.com/aesuli/SentiWordNet
47. WordNet. https://wordnet.princeton.edu
48. Stanford Dependency Parser. http://nlp.stanford.edu:8080/parser/index.jsp
49. Madhoushi, Z., Hamdan, A.R., Zainudin, S.: Aspect-based sentiment analysis methods in recent years. Asia-Pac. J. Inf. Technol. Multimedia **7**(2), 79–96 (2019)
50. Online American platform for teachers' feedback. www.ratemyprofessor.com
51. Online Indian platform for teachers' feedback. www.myfaveteacher.com
52. Textual feedbacks collected from 120 engineering students for 20 teachers of the University Institute of Engineering and Technology, CSJM University, Kanpur
53. Zhang, F., Zhang, Z., Lan, M.:. ECNU: a combination method and multiple features for aspect extraction and sentiment polarity classification. In: Proceedings of the 8th International Workshop on Semantic Evaluation (SemEval 2014), pp. 252–258 (2014)
54. Wang, W., Pan, S.J., Dahlmeier, D., Xiao, X.: Recursive neural conditional random fields for aspect-based sentiment analysis. arXiv preprint arXiv, pp. 616–626 (2016)
55. Kiritchenko, S., Zhu, X., Cherry, C., Mohammad, S.: Detecting aspects and sentiment in customer reviews. In: Proceedings of the 8th International Workshop on Semantic Evaluation (SemEval 2014), pp. 437–442 (2014)

Towards Development of Knowledge Graph for Narrative Information in Medicine

Udaya Varadarajan[1,2(✉)] and Biswanath Dutta[1]

[1] Documentation Research and Training Centre, Indian Statistical Institute, Bangalore, India
{udayav,bisu}@drtc.isibang.ac.in
[2] Department of Library and Information Science, Calcutta University, Kolkata, India

Abstract. The purpose of this work is to provide a framework for patient-doctor narration. The framework was designed as a step-by-step approach in two phases. The initial phase was to construct a base model for the narration supported by the narrative models and theory. To represent the composite model with actual information, ontology development methodology was followed. This was phase two. State of the art study revealed that there are ontology-based models for narration in various domains. But none exists in the medical domain. This is overcome by providing a framework to capture the narration in medical field. The study resulted in the initial development of a composite model for patient-doctor narration. Hence this study contributes in capturing of patient-doctor narration. The framework reuses the existing vocabularies, schemas etc. to build the model.

Keywords: Ontology development · Narrative ontology · Clinical narration · Framework · Reuse · Methodology · Medicine

1 Introduction

Narrative medicine emerged as a "challenge to the reductionist, fragmented medicine that currently holds little regard patient's life". Medical practitioners, academicians, literary scholars believe that "narrative knowledge and skills" are the way to improve healthcare [11]. Chad Hiner [10], a medical practitioner highlights the importance of narrative information as, "the overall symptom assessment and treatment plan can be dramatically improved by listening to the patient and adequately documenting their story". He stresses that "selecting and check-marking items" from a pull-down list cannot capture adequate information to treat a patient. Acquiring the skill can help in increasing the efficiency of clinicians. This will also assist them in gaining a wider knowledge of their patients. This in effect deepens the "therapeutic, personal and social elements of patient's and doctor's lives" [11].

© Springer Nature Switzerland AG 2021
B. Villazón-Terrazas et al. (Eds.): KGSWC 2021, CCIS 1459, pp. 290–307, 2021.
https://doi.org/10.1007/978-3-030-91305-2_22

The current patient - doctor conversation is mostly one sided, where the doctor asks and the patient answers. There are various electronic health systems that capture data such as GNU Health[1], GNU med[2], OpenEMR[3], and Open-MRS[4]. There are various data types present in a patient record. Structured data types are, for example, case report forms etc. Digital types include images such as Xray, MRI etc. These data are mostly generated by machines. Unstructured data types, such as subject interviews, observations, mostly exist in the form of videotaping, audio recording or in the form of note taking [26]. Patient record contains narrative. Whatever is left out of the EHR model for e.g.: the ethnicity, social history, causes of discontinuation of medication, initial state the patient was found (covered in sweat, covered in urine, or found bloody). Putting this together is in the approach of medicine to story approach. But the work, currently under process, is in the approach of story to medicine where the patient if narrates anything, can be of medical significance.

The data in the last category are important because they contain medically significant data. While with the other two types of data, they are recorded in a structured format or already contain some result or inferencing, the unstructured data doesn't have any of these [26]. But unfortunately, these data are not exploited beyond the immediate use i.e., for treating the patient. The collected data, either through videotaping or audio recording or through note taking can be used to infer better result. A system can be developed to capture these data and used in a community information system or can help in developing a guideline for data management in hospitals. This will help in providing a holistic approach in treating the patients. Capture and representation through ontologies are one route through which the unstructured data can be utilised. According to [24] and [32] "an ontology is a set of representational primitives" (which are classes, attributes or properties, and relationships) which models a domain of knowledge or discourse, including their meaning and constraints). In general, ontologies are useful as they help in identifying implicit relations, allow navigation, supporting reasoning ability, representing a formal computable model for machine-understandability, querying from a graph structure, and so on [17]. Specifically, the ontologies are used in the [6,14,29,44] for its ability to extract genres, and media types, support narrative reasoning, as an initial step in the development of Artificial Intelligence (AI) based system for reproducing human-like narrative behaviour, express, comprehend and reason the event sequence in the models [41]. In the current work, the authors, represent the initial work undertaken in building a framework for capturing the real-world patient narration [40,42].

The aim of the study has been to develop (a) a simple logical framework for capturing patient narration and (b) enable inferencing new insights of medical significance from the stories. The work contributes a framework to capture patient narration which is a first step towards building ontology model for patient stories. Real-life use cases have been collected by interviewing a sample. Based

---

[1] https://www.gnuhealth.org/.
[2] https://www.gnumed.de/documentation/.
[3] https://www.open-emr.org/.
[4] https://openmrs.org/.

on the cases, a generic framework was developed. Apart from the fact that such a framework contributes to the vast collection of existing semantic artefact, OntoPaN (Ontology for Patient Narration), is based on the norms of narrative theories and ontology. Besides these, the guiding norms for the framework are derived from top-level ontology such as BFO and theories of mereology. Thus, this framework is a theoretically enhanced one.

The sections following this are state of the art study that discusses the relevant work, followed by a study on the narrative theory. Methodology section describes the steps followed for achieving the objective. This section also discusses the framework. The paper settles with discussion and future work.

2   Research Background

2.1   State of the Art

The authors encountered significantly fewer studies that reviewed ontologies created for capturing and reasoning narrative information. However, it is important to conduct a formal examination of the previously published works. Some of the works that have developed ontologies in domains such as literature, mythology, transmedia and so on are detailed in this section. Table 1 summaries the literature studied.

The Archetype Ontology [14], is built to explore the digital archive via narrative relations among the resources. Major philosophies of the work are based on iconological classification, imitation, and remediation [7] and Propp's theory of functional roles [38]. Constructed on the basis that the narrative situation [30] needs characters and objects which forms a larger story once connected. Specific ontologies are reused to develop this ontology, namely - Ontology for media resources [31], FRBR ontology [35] and Drammar ontology [33]. For example, the property, *evokes* connects the classes *Artifact* and *Archetype*. The property, *displays* connect *Artifact* to *Entity*. The class *Artifact* links the *Dynamics* with the relation *describeAction*. A Story recall Archetype and Story hascharacter Entity. Note that the classes of archetype ontology are created under the owl: Thing.

To represent narration in a literary text, The ODY-Onto [29] was constructed. The ontology developed is part of a system constructed for querying information from the literary texts. The vocabularies TIMEPLUS and OWLTIME [13] along with the upper-level ontology, Proton[5] was used to model the ontology. The ODY-Onto structure given in Fig. 1 depicts the major classes. The linking between them occurs through the classes Ody Event, via a subclass of Event class, Temporal Event, via a subclass of Event class, and temporalPartOf property, Simple Event, via hasParticipant property, and both Fantastic Character, and Animal class by being the subclass of Agent.

Transmedia ontology [8] allow users to explore and retrieve the information limited to the transmedia worlds. There is lacuna for depicting elements found

---

[5] http://proton.semanticweb.org/.

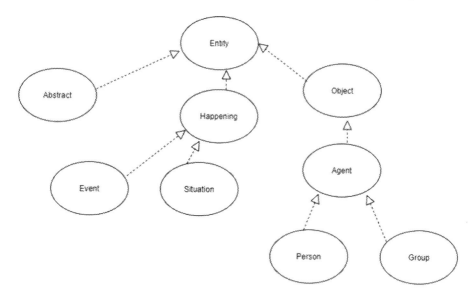

Fig. 1. ODY Onto top level

within the fictional worlds, but a model such as this will help in bringing about a standard. The ontology will help in inferring connections between transmedia elements such as *characters, elements of power* associated with characters, *items, places,* and *events.* The ontology contains a staggering 72 classes and 239 properties. The Transmedia Creative Work connects the works to *Transmedia Properties, Story Worlds,* and *Storylines. Story Worlds* is a "single consistent canon of work". *Storylines* are "works connected within a single narrative" that can be in more than one canon. The classes are connected to Transmedia Property through a hierarchical web of relationships. This web of relations allows reasoning and the AI system to identify *Story Worlds* and the narrative belonging to them explicitly. The properties and classes of this model are borrowed from the other vocabularies such as Schema.org[6], The Comic Book Ontology [36], Ontology of Astronomical Object Types Version 1.3 [16], and SKOS[7]. Such reuse of the ontologies allows interoperability. Biographical Knowledge Ontology (BK onto) [45] was created to capture the biographical information. The ontology was deployed in the *Mackay Digital Collection Project Platform*[8] for linking "the event units with the contents of external digital library and/or archive systems for more assorted digital collections to be offered in StoryTeller system". There are four major ontologies deployed - storyline ontology, event ontology, historical ontology, and timeline ontology. The diagram, Fig. 2, represents the instance layer with the major classes - StoryLine related via contains to the Event class,

---

[6] https://schema.org/.
[7] https://www.w3.org/TR/skos-reference/skos-xl.html#.
[8] http://dlm.csie.au.edu.tw/.

which is linked to the class LocationStamp by PlaceAt and by TimeStart and TimeEnd to the TimeStamp class.

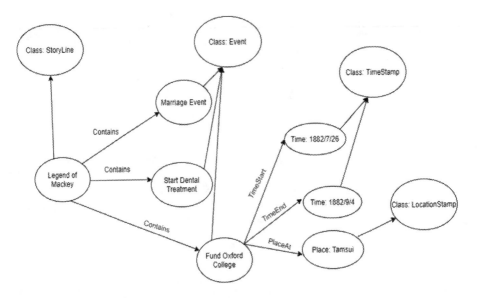

Fig. 2. Instance layer of BK Onto

The Drammar ontology was developed to represent the elements of drama independent of the media and task. It is a theoretical model of drama which unambiguously describes the elements. Drama, as a domain is evolving, but there is a concrete manifestation of drama such as in scripts, dramatic performances, radio plays, movies, etc. The users of this model benefit from the formal encoding of drama and the realizations of drama (such as text and authorship) as defined by the drama studies. The model benefits the user community by providing an automatic reasoning tool and a formal specification for these tools. Top four classes of the dramatic entities are (1) Drama Entity is the class of the dramatic entities, i.e. the entities that are peculiar to drama, (2) Data Structure is the class that organizes the elements of the ontology into common structures (3) Description Template contains the patterns for the representation of drama according to role-based templates (4) External Reference is the class that bridges the description of drama to common sense and linguistic concepts situated in external resources [15].

There are few works in the medical domain that have used ontologies for better performance of the electronic health record. The Obstetric and Neonatal Ontology (OntoNeo Ontology) [20], a semantic artefact that was developed as an all-inclusive infrastructure that provides access to information applicable to scientific research and to healthcare professionals. The main goal of OntoNeo, as the name suggests, is provide a representation of the medical information present

Table 1. Summary of the relevant literature

Ref	Title	Year of publication	Subject/domain	Purpose
[14]	Ontological Representations of Narratives: A Case Study on Stories and Actions	2013	Cultural History	To link the various cultural artifact by their narrative relations
[29]	Leveraging a Narrative Ontology to Query a Literary Text	2016	Literature	To describe the actors, locations, situations, and explicit formal representation of the timeline of the story found in any text
[45]	StoryTeller: An Event-based Story Ontology Composition System for Biographical History	2017	Literature	To model the biography of any person
[8]	Representing Transmedia Fictional Worlds Through Ontology	2017	Literature	To allow users to search and retrieve transmedia information
[15]	The ontology of drama	2019	Literature	Formalize drama independent of media and task
[20]	OntONeo: The Obstetric and Neonatal Ontology	2016	Obstetric and Neonatal	To represent the obstetric and neonatal information in electronic health record

in electronic health records and medical information systems related to obstetric and neonatal domain. Accordingly, OntoNeo aims to mitigate the lack of interoperability among the myriad computational medical resources available nowadays. Electronic health record (EHR) contains complex, multiple and domain specific data. They handle concepts such as spatial-temporal data, documents, digital images, and financial transactions. A large base, with efficient data models is required and is hard to maintain. These complexity increases (a) the cost of developing EHR systems, and (b) chance of high failure rate of implementation. An EHR solution is proposed by [39] where the ontology plays a supporting role in the whole architecture. Ontology is used in code reuse, extension, and customization of the system. Software factory techniques are adopted to build tools that automatically handles data persistence, access, and exchange. Business logic is expressed using an ontology-based process flows and rules. This makes sure of the data quality. But this paper discusses mainly the requirements for an effective EHR solution, in which ontology is one of the techniques employed. EHR semantic interoperability is one of things that medical field is trying to achieve, in order to improve healthcare quality. The approach adopted in the [3] was to conduct a literature search among the existing works that details various aspects of semantic interoperability, including, the descriptions, standards, schematics, prototypes, and vocabularies. The survey resulted in identifying the most intuitive EHR semantic interoperability approach. To achieve global interoperability, fuzzy ontology development is the way. This is since the terms in medical domain are vaguely defined and that the stakeholders of the domain use these terms vaguely, according to Adel et al. According to Yehia, 2019, [46] an Ontology-Based Clinical Information Extraction System (OB-CIE), was developed to extract (named entities recognition) clinical notions from free-text transcripts of the medical practitioner and convert the unstructured datatypes to structured information. This was achieved by developing a dictionary of semantic categories and using a rule-based approach to classify clinical sentences to their predefined categories. The motivation of the work was to allow easier access to electronic health records. OB-CIE system helps in the continual workflow for physicians.

3 Methodology

With the literature studied, a methodology was adopted for the current work. The methodology is in two phases. Phase I is a base model development involving the identifying, extracting, and formulating the elements of narration. Phase II presents a composite model construction where the actual information is modelled. The steps are detailed below. In order to achieve the objective of the work, i.e., in order to produce a simple logical framework for capturing patient narration, systematic steps were followed [9]. The Fig. 3 below illustrates the workflow.

Phase I: Identifying elements of narration
Step 1: **Definition of research question**
This step derives the relevant research question based on your objectives. This set of questions is the major starting point in the methodology. For our work, the framed research questions are listed below (Q1–Q4).

> *Q1 What are the models for narrative information?*
> *Q2 What are the elements of a story?*
> *Q3 What are the terms used for narrative information?*
> *Q4 What are the elements of literature (creative product of artistic value)?*

Step 2: **Formulating keywords**
From the questions developed in the above step, prepare a set of keywords. In this work the keywords derived from the questions are listed below (K1–K5):

> *K1 narrative information*
> *K2 narrative model*
> *K3 elements of narration*
> *K4 elements of story*
> *K5 terms of literature*

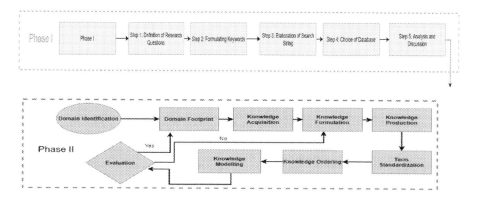

Fig. 3. Phase I & II of OntoPaN framework

Step 3: **Elaboration of search string**

Formulate search strings by using various combinations of the keyword from Step 2. From the derived keywords, the authors formulated the following search strings.

> *S1* *"narrative models"*
> *S2* *"narrative terms"*
> *S3* *"narrative information" AND "elements"*
> *S4* *"narrative" AND "terms"*
> *S5* *"elements of literature"*
> *S6* *"parts of narrative"*
> *S7* *"model for storytelling"*
> *S8* *"parts of story"*

Step 4: **Choice of databases**

Choose databases for searching the resources. While choosing databases, keep in mind features such as availability (or subscription by institution or organisation), reputation and subject covered. Databases searched for this work are Google Scholar[9], Scopus[10], Web of Science[11], Gale Literature[12], The Science Fiction and Fantasy Research Database[13]. They were selected because of their reputation and the availability provided by the institute.

---

[9] https://scholar.google.com/.
[10] https://www.scopus.com/home.uri.
[11] https://clarivate.com/webofsciencegroup/solutions/web-of-science/.
[12] https://www.gale.com/intl/databases/gale-literature.
[13] https://sffrd.library.tamu.edu/site/.

Step 5: **Analysis and Discussion**

The search across various platform yielded the models relevant for the study. The models are described as below and summarised in Table 2.

Starting from Aristotle's elements, exposition (initial situation in a narrative), crisis (disturbances in the initial situation), and denouement (resolution of the crisis leading to new exposition) [30] and [27]. Another model mainly relevant for the fairytale representation was Propp's 31 functions and roles. According to him, there is an initial situation (introduction of the hero) followed by the absence of the family members and a strict command from them not to do certain things. The hero disobeys and the villain gets the opportunity to manipulate and hurt the family, causing the hero into action. The hero emerges victorious and is recognized. The villain is defeated and punished [38]. Greimas's contribution to the narrative model has been to propose six actants (the actantial model). They are paired as binary units and often assist the characters. The six actants are-subject/object, sender/receiver, helper/opponent. In addition, they also perform the task such as search, aim, desire (by subject/object), communication (by sender/receiver), support or hindrance (by helper/opponent) [5,28] and [23]. Canonically, there are the traditional notions of plot (what happens), characters (figure presented in a literary text), narrative situation (who speaks (speaker), who sees (audience) and setting (where and when an event takes place) [1,2,5,22,30]. The plot can be of three types: linear (event as it unfolds), flashback (a telling of an earlier event or scene that interrupts the normal chronology of a story), and foreshadowing (the telling of the future event that interrupts the normal chronology of the story) [31]. There can be three major types of speakers or narrators: authorial (unspecified narrator with a God-like presence), first person (specific narrator who participates in the actions of the story and is a protagonist), and figural (narrator who participates in the action but is the third person) [30]. Similarly, there are three types of audience for the story (i.e., who sees), namely - zero focalization (sees the whole story), internal focalization (character sees what is happening at the point of time), and external focalization (character sees what is happening at the point of time in the third person) [30].

These theories, beginning from the classical to the modern, have split narrative into its various components. The current work comprehends the theories and components of narratology relevant to the research in modelling the elements in a narrative ontology. "stories have shapes which can be drawn on graph paper, and that the shape of a given society's stories is at least as interesting as the shape of its pots or spearheads" [43]. There exist shapes of stories. By shape what is meant is that the story has an 'emotional arc'. An emotional arc corresponds to the fall and the rise, not necessarily in this order, of the protagonist's journey. Another theory comes from Kurt Vonnegut. He plots a line like the mathematical x axis y axis concept. The 'Beginning-End' (BE axis) represents the beginning and end of the story. This is equivalent to the mathematical x-axis. The 'Ill Fortune-Great Fortune' (GI axis), mathematically like the y-axis, places Ill Fortune, at the bottom and Good Fortune, at the top. Ill fortune is defined by Vonnegut as "sickness and poverty" and good fortune as "wealth and boisterous good health". All stories fall in between these points [43]. There are three arcs and their inverses totalling to six emotional arcs. Freytag's Pyramid or Freytag's analysis [1,21] is another narrative theory that explains the plot structure of the story. The elements of the Pyramid are:

a) Exposition
b) Rising action
c) Climax
d) Falling action
e) Catastrophe

Table 2. Summary of the yielded models

Reference	Model Name	Domain	Elements of the model
[30]	Aristotle's Analysis	Epics	exposition—crisis—denouement
[19]	Morphology of the Tale	Folklore	an initial situation (introduction of the hero)—absence of the family members—strict command not to do certain things—hero disobeys—villain manipulates—family hurt—hero acts—hero victorious—villain defeated and punished
[23]	The actantial model	Action that takes place in a story	subject/object—sender/receiver—helper/opponent—tasks such as search—aim—desire (by subject/object)—communication (by sender/receiver)—support or hindrance (by helper/opponent)
[43]	Shapes of Stories	Domain independent	The 'Beginning-End' (BE axis) represents the beginning and end of the story (mathematical equivalent of x-axis). The 'Ill Fortune-Great Fortune' (GI axis), (mathematically equivalent to y-axis). All stories trace a path through this graph
[1,21]	Freytag's Pyramid		Exposition—Rising action—Climax—Falling action—Catastrophe

The study on the narrative models throws light on the elements of narration. The major elements identified from the study are listed in the Table 3 below.

Phase II: Composite model construction
For development of a semantic artefact (an umbrella term covering ontologies, controlled vocabularies, subject headings, thesauri, a model (i.e., elements and mutual relationships [12] and classifications with functions such as organizing and retrieving information, navigation, and orientation through concepts, finding information, and inferring it.) there are multiple development methodologies [34].

Table 3. Elements of Narration

Elements	Definition
Story or storyline or plot	that discusses the whole story
Actors/character/agent/author	person present in the story
Events and event properties	something that happens at a given place and time
Spatial factors	space or location where an event occurs
Temporal factors	the time in which event occurs
Theme or the key terms in a story	the subject matter
Act or actions or scenes	the series of events that form a plot

One of the ontology development methodologies is METHONTOLOGY methodology by FĂŠrnandez et al. It is one of the initial development methods specifically for ontology engineering progressions. The work suggests, an ontology lifecycle consisting of six phases or stages: *Specification, Conceptualisation, Formalisation, Integration, Implementation,* and *Maintenance.* Another methodology is The On-To-Knowledge Methodology (OTKM) [39]. It is a methodology for ontology engineering, like that of METHONTOLOGY. OTKM covers ontology engineering, knowledge management and knowledge processes. OTKM underlines collaboration between domain specialists and ontology engineers in the initial phases. DILIGENT (Distributed, Loosely-Controlled and Evolving Engineering of Ontologies), by Pinto et al., [37] is a method for ontology engineering in a distributed semantic web environment. Decentralised processes flow, ontology usage and evolution management, involvement of domain expert are the primary focus of the model. Yet Another Methodology for Ontology or YAMO [18] is a theoretically enhanced methodology. The principles of analytico-synthesis approach (complex concepts are broken into their fundamental concepts then analysed by their characteristics, grouped together and relationship is established between concepts) and a combination of top-down and bottom-up approaches (making it flexible). Phase II was inspired by the latter methodology due to the advantages such as theoretical enhancement, detailed step by step explanation and the ease in building a multi-faceted framework. There has been alteration in the steps and is because, this framework is only an initial step. Once the model matures, it will be formalised and represented as a knowledge graph. The steps below describe the Phase II of the methodology.

Step 0: Domain Identification - As is the case with any methodology, the primary step includes identification of a domain (field of study) or a problem that requires solution. Domain for the construction of the semantic artefact is chosen from the problem at hand or the user requirement [18]. For the present work, the chosen field of study is the patient - doctor narration.

Step 1: Domain Footprint - This step explores the motivation behind the construction of the framework. The framework is constructed to model narration that occurs among the doctors and their patient. Such a framework will capture the data from subject interviews, observations, videotaping data, audio recording or the note taking that seldom finds any place in the patient record and carries significant medical importance. In our work, we came across multiple real-world scenarios of friends, family and acquaintances and their encounter with their doctors through conversations. For example, one such motivational case was:

Case 1: A woman visits a doctor complaining of cough and cold. As part of the treatment, she is prescribed medicines for the cold and cough. Even after the course of medicines are over, the complaint does not stop. A follow up with the doctor, alerts him, who enquires the lifestyle. The patient narrates her daily routine. In this, they notice a change in the environment of her work environment. The only change was that of a new 3D printer in her workspace. Suspicious of this, the doctor advises her to move the printer to a more open space. The actual cause for the cough and cold was the micro particles that come out of the machine, when printing happens. Once the change was made, the patient recovered.

Steps 2: Knowledge Acquisition - This step involves the process of acquiring terms related to the domain of study. This is acquired from different resources. People, online videos were referred to collect stories, anonymised patient records, electronic health systems such as GNU Health, GNU med, OpenEMR, Open-MRS that capture data, medical vocabularies, and thesaurus such as the Unified Medical Language System[14], SNOMED[15] and so on. Besides these there are vocabularies such as StoryLine Ontology[16], Schema.org[17] or Wikidata[18].

Some of the collected terms are listed below:

actor, character, story, event, action, medicine, treated, mouth ulcer, no effect, not reduce, patient, complain, paediatrician, distressed, facial features, coarsening

Step 3: Knowledge Formulation and Production - Once the terms were identified, they were analysed. Terms that have similar characteristics were grouped together as shown in the figure below. For example, in our model, the terms *patient* and *doctor* were collectively understood as *Role* (Fig. 4) that a character has[19]. For the framework, using [4, 25] an understanding of the whole-part relation was developed. This helped in modelling the Event and Action classes with appropriate relations, as in the Fig. 5 given below. Once the analysis and grouping are done, the terms are mapped further higher general terms.

Step 4: Term Standardization and ordering - Standardization is an important step. Each concept can be expressed in different terms. When such terms exist, there is a need to choose a standard term. This fosters the best practice of re-using the existing vocabularies, leading towards standardisation. The literature review has enabled us in choosing the appropriate terms in modelling. There are multiple terms used for a doctor such as physician and medical practitioner. But the term "physician" from the UMLS was used. Similarly, *Drammatic Structure* was used instead of *Plot Structure*. This process was followed throughout the

---

[14] https://www.nlm.nih.gov/research/umls/index.html.
[15] https://www.snomed.org/.
[16] https://www.bbc.co.uk/ontologies/storyline.
[17] https://schema.org/.
[18] https://www.wikidata.org/wiki/Wikidata:Main_Page.
[19] https://www.hl7.org/fhir/v3/RoleClass/cs.html#4.4.2.110.

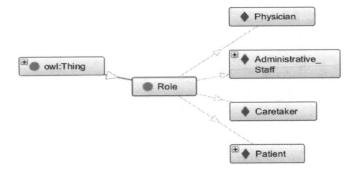

Fig. 4. Class *Role* and the instances

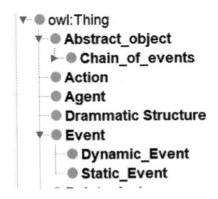

Fig. 5. Glimpse of the Class hierarchy

whole framework. The term ordering was done in no particular order. The practice of reusing the vocabularies enables interoperability. The reuse of the terms from other vocabularies such as UMLS, Wikidata taxonomy, SNOMED etc. were reused.

Step 5: Knowledge Modelling- This step establishes entity, entity relationships and their properties. This "allows preservation of knowledge and reapplication" of the framework. The entities of the model are also called classes. For example, *Event* and *Action* are two classes with instances or individuals such as *Encounter with physician* and *express complain of cough and cold*. Entity relation *includesAction* establishes the relationship between *Event* and *Action*. A glimpse of the model is represented in Fig. 6 below. A partial modelling of case 1 is depicted in Fig. 7. This figure is the instance layer of the OntoPaN schema.

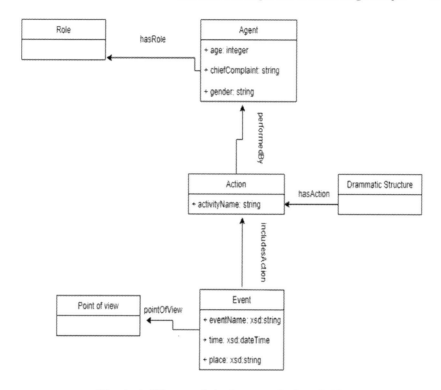

Fig. 6. A Glimpse of the framework, OntoPaN

Step 6: Evaluation - This step involves the appraisal of the value of something regarding "quality, standard and specification" of the framework. The framework can be evaluated by taking another use case and modelling it in the framework developed. This will help in identifying the flaws and improve the model. Another approach is to collect competency questions and evaluate the number of questions the framework tries to answer. The former was use to evaluate the model. The second use case used for evaluation is given below.

Case 2: An old woman suffers from breathing difficulty. She arrives to the hospital complaining of the same. Her medical records show a history of asthma. She is questioned regarding her previous medicines. Her routine is asked and any change in it. The woman says about a switch from her usual fertiliser. Her previous medicines are tested. The chemical composition of the new fertiliser is countering the effect of her medications.

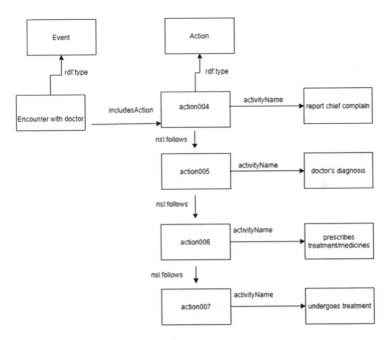

Fig. 7. An example of the instance layer of OntoPaN

4   Discussion and Conclusion

The elements of narrative act as a framework for modelling narrative across various domains. They differ due to the domain specificity. From the state of the art, it was found that the classes and properties used to model a literary domain, act as the basic framework and as the domain changes, alters to suit the storytelling in various domains. For example, the domain independent have a generic model, the classes include 'Concept' which is a generic class to associate the theme of the story. The model rooted in the cultural heritage domain focuses on representing the artifact and the type of objects in the domain. It is interesting to note that the application of narrative information has a great significance in the medicine domain. But from the literature, it is observed that, so far there exists no narrative ontology model. The concepts from Table 3 have helped in modelling the concepts of the framework (Fig. 6).

Once the initial framework was constructed, it was evaluated. Post evaluation, it was found that there is a set of standard clinical workflow that follows for every patient. Each process was now recorded as Event. This made the model simpler by allowing us to connect the activity associated with each process to that individual event. For example, the pre-evaluation model had class *Event* and blank nodes such as event 001, event002 and so on. Each event was associated with multiple Agents (like doctors, caretaker, patient etc.). This complex modelling was reduced by creating instances for the class *Event* such as *"Encounter with doctor"*, *"Visit clinic/hospital/doctor"* and so on. The class *Chain of events* is used to capture the story of each patient. This not only reduced complexity, but also made the processes associated, more explicit. Once the framework matures to a graph, the evaluation can be conducted by running the appropriate methods such as SPARQL. This takes us back to the domain footprint, indicating that the semantic artefact construction is iterative and constantly improved.

The work was started with the motivation to capture the unstructured data types, such as subject interviews, observations, mostly exist in the form of video-taping, audio recording or in the form of note taking. This type of data is important because they contain medically significant data. The unstructured data doesn't contain result or inferencing [26]. Such data are under-exploited and most often not beyond the immediate use i.e., for treating the patient. The collected data, either through videotaping or audio recording or through note taking can be used to infer better result. In future, a system will be envisioned to capture these data and used in a community information system. An end-user application will also be developed to exploit the valuable narrative data. The framework developed can be deployed in such systems. With the emerging importance to data and its management, such system or framework can assist in developing a guideline for data management in hospitals. This will help in providing a holistic approach in treating the patients.

The primary aim of the paper has been to develop a simple logical framework for capturing patient narration. This was achieved by following a two-phase methodology for ontology development. Phase I involved the identifying, extracting, and formulating the elements of narration. Phase II was composite model construction, where the actual information is modelled. This is an initial step towards the capturing, processing, and managing the narration that occurs within the four walls of the medicine. As mentioned throughout the document, data of medical significance will help the patient for better treatment and doctor for better treatment plans.

References

1. Abbott, H.P.: The Cambridge Introduction to Narrative. Cambridge Introductions to Literature, 2 edn. Cambridge University Press (2008). https://doi.org/10.1017/CBO9780511816932
2. Abrams, M.H.M.H., Harpham, G.G.: A glossary of literary terms, p. 430 (2012)
3. Adel, E., El-Sappagh, S., Barakat, S., Elmogy, M.: Ontology-based electronic health record semantic interoperability: a survey. In: U-Healthcare Monitoring Systems, pp. 315–352. Elsevier (2019)
4. Artale, A., Franconi, E., Guarino, N., Pazzi, L.: Part-whole relations in object-centered systems: an overview. Data Knowl. Eng. **20**(3), 347–383 (1996)
5. Barry, P.: Beginning Theory: An Introduction to Literary and Cultural Theory. Manchester University Press, Manchester (2020)
6. Bartalesi, V., Meghini, C., Metilli, D.: Steps towards a formal ontology of narratives based on narratology. In: 7th Workshop on Computational Models of Narrative (CMN 2016). Schloss Dagstuhl-Leibniz-Zentrum fuer Informatik (2016)
7. Bolter, J.D., Grusin, R.: Remediation. Competizione e integrazione tra media vecchi e nuovi, p. 228 (2003)

8. Branch, F., Arias, T., Kennah, J., Phillips, R.: Knowledge organization in transmedia fictional worlds: a study of harry potter, lord of the rings, marvel universe, and star wars (2016)
9. Camacho, L.A.G., Alves-Souza, S.N.: Social network data to alleviate cold-start in recommender system: a systematic review. Inf. Process. Manag. **54**(4), 529–544 (2018)
10. Chad, H.: Capturing patient stories—nvoq, May 2016. https://sayit.nvoq.com/capturing-patient-stories/
11. Charon, R., et al.: The Principles and Practice of Narrative Medicine. Oxford University Press, Oxford (2016)
12. Coen, G.: Introduction to semantic artefacts (2019)
13. Cox, S., Little, C., Hobbs, J.R., Pan, F.: Time Ontology in OWL. W3C Recommendation (October), pp. 1–47, July 2017. https://www.w3.org/TR/2016/WD-owl-time-20160712/www.w3.org/TR/2017/REC-owl-time-20171019/
14. Damiano, R., Lieto, A.: Ontological representations of narratives: a case study on stories and actions. In: 2013 Workshop on Computational Models of Narrative, pp. 76–93. Schloss Dagstuhl Leibniz-Zentrum für Informatik (2013)
15. Damiano, R., Lombardo, V., Pizzo, A.: The ontology of drama. Appl. Ontol. **14**(1), 79–118 (2019)
16. Derriere, S., Preite-Martinez, A., Richard, A., Cambrésy, L., Padovani, P.: Ontology of astronomical object types version 1.3. IVOA Note 03 March 2010, p. 303 (2010)
17. Dutta, B.: Examining the interrelatedness between ontologies and linked data. Library Hi Tech (2017)
18. Dutta, B., Chatterjee, U., Madalli, D.P.: YAMO: yet another methodology for large-scale faceted ontology construction. J. Knowl. Manag. **19**(1), 6–24 (2015)
19. El-Atawy, S.S., Khalefa, M.E.: Building an ontology-based electronic health record system. In: Proceedings of the 2nd Africa and Middle East Conference on Software Engineering, pp. 40–45 (2016)
20. Farinelli, F., Almeida, M., Elkin, P., Smith, B.: OntONeo: the obstetric and neonatal ontology (2016)
21. Freytag, G.: Freytag's Technique of the Drama: An Exposition of Dramatic Composition and Art. Scott, Foresman and Company, Northbrook (1908)
22. Genette, G.: Frontiers of narrative. In: Figures of Literary Discourse, pp. 127, 144 (1982)
23. Greimas, A.J.: On meaning : selected writings in semiotic theory/Algirdas Julien Greimas; translation by Paul J. Perron and Frank H. Collins; foreword by Fredric Jameson; introduction by Paul J. Perron. University of Minnesota Press, Minneapolis (1987)
24. Guarino, N., Oberle, D., Staab, S.: What is an ontology? In: Staab, S., Studer, R. (eds.) Handbook on Ontologies. IHIS, pp. 1–17. Springer, Heidelberg (2009). https://doi.org/10.1007/978-3-540-92673-3_0
25. Guarino, N., Welty, C.: A formal ontology of properties. In: Dieng, R., Corby, O. (eds.) EKAW 2000. LNCS (LNAI), vol. 1937, pp. 97–112. Springer, Heidelberg (2000). https://doi.org/10.1007/3-540-39967-4_8
26. Harris, P.: Data management for clinical research—coursera. https://www.coursera.org/learn/clinical-data-management
27. Herman, D., Herman, R.D.: The Cambridge Companion to Narrative. Cambridge University Press, Cambridge (2007)

28. HÅŠbert, L., Tabler, J.: An introduction to applied semiotics: tools for text and image analysis. Taylor and Francis (2019). https://doi.org/10.4324/9780429329807/INTRODUCTION-APPLIED-SEMIOTICS-LOUIS-H

29. Khan, A.F., Bellandi, A., Benotto, G., Frontini, F., Giovannetti, E., Reboul, M.: Leveraging a narrative ontology to query a literary text. Open Access Series in Informatics (2016)

30. Klarer, M.: An Introduction to Literary Studies. Routledge, Abingdon (2013)

31. Lee, W., et al.: Ontology for media resources 1.0. W3C recommendation 9 (2012)

32. Liu, L., ÉOzsu, M.T.: Encyclopedia of Database Systems, p. 3749 (2009)

33. Lombardo, V., Damiano, R., Pizzo, A., Lieto, A., Battaglino, C.: Drammar ontology (2014)

34. Mamat, A., Rahman, A.A.: Designing a conceptual model for herbal research domain using ontology technique. In: 2009 Ninth International Conference on Intelligent Systems Design and Applications, pp. 1167–1172. IEEE (2009)

35. Newman, R., Davis, I.: Expression of core FRBR concepts in RDF (2005)

36. Petiya, S.: Comic Book Ontology (2020). https://comicmeta.org/cbo/

37. Pinto, H.S., Staab, S., Tempich, C.: Diligent: towards a fine-grained methodology for distributed, loosely-controlled and evolving engineering of ontologies. In: Proceedings of the 16th European Conference on Artificial Intelligence (ECAI), pp. 393–397. IOS Press (2004)

38. Propp, V.: Morphology of the Folktale, 20 edn. (2009)

39. Sure, Y., Staab, S., Studer, R.: On-to-knowledge methodology (OTKM). In: Staab, S., Studer, R. (eds.) Handbook on Ontologies. International Handbooks on Information Systems, pp. 117–132. Springer, Berlin (2004). https://doi.org/10.1007/978-3-540-24750-0_6

40. Tiwari, S., Al-Aswadi, F.N., Gaurav, D.: Recent trends in knowledge graphs: theory and practice. Soft. Comput. **25**(13), 8337–8355 (2021). https://doi.org/10.1007/s00500-021-05756-8

41. Varadarajan, U., Dutta, B.: Models for narrative information: a study. arXiv preprint arXiv:2110.02084 (2021)

42. Villazón-Terrazas, B., Ortiz-Rodríguez, F., Tiwari, S.M., Shandilya, S.K.: Knowledge graphs and semantic web. Commun. Comput. Inf. Sci. **1232**, 1–225 (2020)

43. Vonnegut, K.: Kurt Vonnegut Lecture - YouTube (2004). https://www.youtube.com/watch?v=4_RUgnC1lm8

44. Winer, D.: Review of ontology based storytelling devices. In: Dershowitz, N., Nissan, E. (eds.) Language, Culture, Computation. *Computing of the Humanities, Law, and Narratives.* LNCS, vol. 8002, pp. 394–405. Springer, Heidelberg (2014). https://doi.org/10.1007/978-3-642-45324-3_12

45. Yeh, J.H.: Storyteller: an event-based story ontology composition system for biographical history. In: 2017 International Conference on Applied System Innovation (ICASI), pp. 1934–1937. IEEE (2017)

46. Yehia, E., Boshnak, H., AbdelGaber, S., Abdo, A., Elzanfaly, D.S.: Ontology-based clinical information extraction from physicianâs free-text notes. J. Biomed. Inform. **98**, 103276 (2019)

Automatic Text Summarization Using Transformers

Siwar Abbes, Sarra Ben Abbès$^{(\boxtimes)}$, Rim Hantach, and Philippe Calvez

CSAI Lab ENGIE, Paris, France
{Sarra.Ben-Abbes,Rim.Hantach}@external.engie.com,
Philippe.Calvez1@engie.com

Abstract. Nowadays, we are facing to huge amount of data that makes the task of information analysis quite complex. In this context, automatic text summarization has gained a great deal of success where it is able to extract an efficient short version of documents covering the most important information. In this paper, we propose a new extractive approach for automatic text summarization based on deep learning techniques. This extractive approach can be easily applied on any document independently of its language. Furthermore, by selecting sentences from the document, we guarantee the grammatical and linguistic correctness of summaries. Some experimental results were conducted in order to improve the performance of the proposed approach.

Keywords: Text summarization · Deep learning · Natural language processing

1 Introduction

With the growth of textual information on the web, we are facing to huge amount of data that makes the task of information analysis quite complex. Therefore, natural language processing methods are required to deal with problems related to the tremendous volume of textual data. In this context, text summarization domain is becoming important in the information retrieval domain. In fact, it is very difficult for human beings to manually extract the summaries of a large amount of documents. It has gained a great deal of success where it is able to extract an efficient short version of documents covering the most important information. It has been emerged in different application domains such as news headline generation [15], scientific document abstract generation [23], product review summary [8]. Three types of approaches are proposed [5]: (1) the extractive summarization, aims to select the most important sentences, paragraphs etc., of the original document and concatenates them into a shorther form, (2) the abstractive summarization, aims to create new sentences based on the most useful information from the source document. It is an understanding of the main concepts in a document and then express those concepts in clear natural language, and (3) the hybrid summarization, aims to combine the two models (1) and (2) in order to address its problems and weakness.

© Springer Nature Switzerland AG 2021
B. Villazón-Terrazas et al. (Eds.): KGSWC 2021, CCIS 1459, pp. 308–320, 2021.
https://doi.org/10.1007/978-3-030-91305-2_23

Several efforts have been made to perform text summarization results. However, such methods suffer from defects related to the reliability and the performance of models.

The goal of this work is to propose a new automatic text summarization approach that represents the relevant information of the original document without changing the document intent. In the following paper, we present firstly recent related works. The second section details our proposed approach. In the last section, we highlight some experiments done so far.

2   Related Works

In recent years, text summarization has been widely studied. There are two basic approaches of how to create summaries from document; abstraction and extraction. The main difference between them is how information is extracted from the document and how the summary is generated. Another recent hybrid approaches are proposed.

2.1   Extractive Text Summarization (ETS)

The extractive method is characterized by estimating the relevance of sentences or paragraphs in a document to generate a summary by concatenating the most relevant parts. A single document consists of n sentences $D = \{s_1, s_2, ..., s_n\}$. The ith sentence is denoted as: $s_i = \{w_{i1}, w_{i2}, ..., w_{im}\}$ where w_{ij} is the jth word in s_i. The extractive module learns to pick up a subset of D denoted as

$$\widehat{D} = \{\widehat{s}_1, \widehat{s}_2..., \widehat{s}_k, |\widehat{s}_i \in D\}$$

where k sentences are selected. Kageback *et al.* [10] use neural networks to map sentences into vectors and select sentences based on those vectors. Cheng and Lapata [4] select sentences based on an LSTM classifier that predicts a binary label for each sentence. Nallapati et al. [16] adopt a similar approach, SummaRuNNer, a RNN-based model for extractive summarization of documents. It is essentially a two-layer RNN based on sequence classifier.

The drawback here is that it is difficult to optimize the learning due to vanishing gradient problem and that's why, the RNN approach as described does not work particularly well for longer sentences. The other problem plaguing RNNs is the fact that the computation is, by definition, sequential. What does this property entail? A sequential computation cannot be parallelized, since we have to wait for the previous step to finish before we move on to the next one and this lengthens the training time. A common addition to the standard RNN model is to use bidirectional encoders [21], meaning that the input, as well as the input in reverse are encoded into hidden states. Both the forward and the backwards hidden states are then concatenated and fed to the decoder. Bidirectional encoders have been shown to improve performance when encoding longer sequences.

Recently, there has been an attempt at redesigning the RNN-based model by relying more on the attention mechanism introduced by Vaswani et al. [20]. The reason for introducing the attention mechanism was to improve interpretation and enable better generation of longer sequences of text. In [7], the authors introduced a bidirectional attentive encoder-based summarization, where the document encoder has two layers of RNNs; the first layer is based on a self-attentive structure [13] in order to represent a document as a vector and in the second layer, each sentence is concatenated with the document representation returned by the first layer. We can also mention the approach HIBERT (HIerachical Bidirectional Encoder Representations from Transformers) [25] which uses two BERT encoders; a sentence encoder to transform each sentence to a vector and a document encoder to learn sentence representations given their surrounding sentences as context. The main advantage of this approach is the importance of bidirectional language representations: not a shallow concatenation of independently trained left-to-right and right-to-left models. Added to that, the multi-head attention in transformers allows the model to jointly attend to the information from different representation sub-spaces at different positions.

2.2   Abstractive Text Summarization (ATS)

Abstraction is a way of creating summary by rewriting original sentences into shorter ones with preservation of the most important information. This type of summarization builds internal semantic structures and uses NLP techniques to re-phrase the document. Although abstractive summary that is very similar to human produced summary, lack of advancements in NLP and NLU, has hindered its research. Due to the difficulty of automatically generating coherent text, ATS has been considered more complex than the extractive counterpart. In [17], Ramesh Nallapati *et al.* proposed a framework of sequence-to-sequence models based on the attentional Gated Recurrent Unit (GRU) encoder-decoder model. The encoder consists of a bidirectional GRU, while the decoder consists of a uni-directional GRU with the same hidden-state size as that of the encoder, and an attention mechanism over the source-hidden states.

Asli Celikyilmaz *et al.* [2] presented deep communicating agents in an encoder-decoder architecture to address the challenges of representing a long document for abstractive summarization. With deep communicating agents, the task of encoding a long text is divided across multiple collaborating agents, each in charge of a subsection of the input text. These encoders are connected to a single decoder, trained end-to-end using reinforcement learning (RL) to generate a focused and coherent summary.

Similar to this approach, another research [26] was done based on RL for ATS. The authors investigate the effectiveness of another metric of evaluation called BERTScore which is a recently proposed evaluation metric based on n-gram soft-match, as a novel reward function for RL on the abstractive summarization task. They demonstrate its advantage over the most widely-used metric, ROUGE score, via both quantitative evaluation and human evaluation.

The main disadvantage of these approach is that the model describes a sequence of possible events in which the probability of each event depends only on the state attained in the previous event. However, in text summarization, it is preferable to take into consideration not only the left context of the word but also the right one in order to get a better encoding of the input sequence. RŁ can also lead to an overload of states, which can impact the results.

2.3 Hybrid Methods

Various extractive and abstractive summarization techniques have been investigated but existing approaches are rarely proposed the combination of these two techniques.

In [19], the goal is to generate summaries with varying amounts of reused text by fixing a copy rate as the percentage of summary n-grams appearing in the source text. It uses a Transformer-based architecture to both encode the source text and decode the summary.

In [9] Hsu *et al.* also proposed a unified model where the extractive model consists of a hierarchical bidirectional GRU which selects sentence representations and a classification layer for predicting the relevance of each sentence. The abstractor is based on a bidirectional LSTM to encode the input words and a unidirectional LSTM to decode the summary. In [22], the authors introduced a new approach based on sharing pre-trained BERT decoder: the model first selects sentences by an extractive decoder and then generates summary according to each selected sentence by an abstractive decoder. The main advantage of hybrid methods is the combination of ETS and ATS strengths. However, this type of methods can be time-consuming and costly to create summaries.

Based on the analysis of existing approaches, we decided to conceive two architectures, one based on RNN and another based on Transformers. We choose to work on ETS because by selecting sentences from the summaries, we guarantee the grammatical and linguistic correctness. Moreover, it is easier to apply extractive models on any text document independently of its language. In addition to that, abstractive systems require natural language generation and semantic representation, which are complex and can hardly meet the demands of generating correct facts with proper word relations.

In the next section, we will present the proposed approaches we have worked on which are based on LSTM and Transformer based models.

3   Our Proposed Approaches

The goal of the proposed approaches is to select the most informative sentences, which cover necessary information that is belonged to the gold summary.

Our solutions are based on three modules (see Fig. 1): (i) the first one based on BERT which is designed to learn a contextualized embedding of each sentence in an unsupervised way, (ii) the second one is developed to extract document-level features from the sentence representations. In the first proposition, this

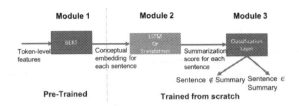

Fig. 1. Proposed architecture.

second module is based on an LSTM model and in the second approach, this module uses Transformers, and (iii) the third module is a classification-layer which, based on the output of the second module, will calculate the probability that a sentence should appear in the final summary or not. In the following sections, we will describe the data preprocessing then we will detail each module in the proposed architecture and justify the choice of models that we have applied.

3.1 Data Preprocessing

To preprocess our data, we tokenized our text documents. Tokenization is the process of converting sentences into separate tokens. In this paper, we used the BERT Word-Piece tokenizer. It means that a word can be broken down into more than one sub-words. This type of tokenization is useful because it deals with out-of-vocabulary words issue. To adapt BERT for text summarization task, we applied some modifications to the original input format of BERT. In the original BERT's configuration [6], the input embeddings are the sum of three kinds of embedding:(i) Token embeddings which represents the meaning of each token, (ii) Segmentation embeddings which are used to differentiate between two sequences, and (iii) Position embeddings which indicates the position of each token in the input. Moreover, special tokens are added to the input sequence. A [CLS] token is used to get features from one sentence or a pair of sentences. The final hidden state corresponding to this token is used as the aggregate sequence representation. To get the representation vector of each sentence, we adopted similar modifications, used in [22], to the input format of BERT. Since we need a symbol for each sentence representation, we should insert the [CLS] token before each sentence. Added to that, we add an interval segment embedding to distinguish multiple sentences within a document. Furthermore, for each sentence we assign a segment embedding SE_0 or SE_1 conditioned on the position of the sentence in the document, is odd or even. As described in [22], our first module is based on 12-layer BERT which will be detailed in the following section.

3.2 First Module: BERT

The first module of our proposed architecture uses BERT model [6] as an embedding module to extract a rich context-based representation of each sentence. BERT stands for Bidirectional Encoder Representations from Transformers.

It is a language model designed to pre-train deep bidirectional representations from unlabeled text by jointly conditioning on both left and right context in all layers. As detailed in [6], the transformers in BERT's architecture are linked to capture the bidirectionality. Moreover, BERT is pre-trained on a large corpus of unlabelled text consisting in 33000 million words including the entire Wikipedia and Book Corpus. This pre-training step plays an important role in BERT's success. This can be explained by the fact that training a model on a large text corpus helps to pick up the deeper understandings of how the language works. Furthermore, the BERT model is mostly used in the transfer learning approaches, which consists in adapting the pre-trained model to a specific task which is in our case automatic text summarization. We believe that thanks to its powerful architecture for learning complex features and its pre-training on a large datasets, BERT model can be exploited to build a promising architecture. The output of this first module is a contextualized representation of each sentence which is the [CLS] symbol representation T_i from the top BERT encoder. These sentence-level features will be used as an input to our second module.

3.3 Second Module

The second module describes the two proposed approaches: (1) LSTM-based model, and (2) Transformer-based model. LSTM-based model Long Short-Term Memory (LSTM) networks are a modified version of recurrent neural networks (RNN), which makes it easier to remember past data in memory. We choose LSTM model because it solves the vanishing gradient issue of RNN. In fact, it preserves gradients over time using dynamic gates that are called memory cells. The hidden state plays an important role in the neural networks memory. It holds information on previous data that the model has seen before. LSTM model [11] contains three gates:

- **Input gate** identifies the values that should be updated and decides what information is relevant to add from the current step.
- **Forget gate** decides what information from the previous hidden state and from the current input should be thrown away or kept.
- **Ouput gate** determines what the next hidden state should be based on the input and the memory of the block.

In order to improve the performance of LSTM-based model, we opt for the Bidirectional LSTM (BiLSTM). BiLSTM [1] has two separate states for forward and backward inputs that are generated by two different LSTMs. In the forward layer, the input is a regular sequence that starts from the beginning of the sentence, while in the backward layer, the input sequence is fed in the opposite order. The idea behind bi-directional network is to capture information of surrounding inputs.

Transformer-Based Model. Our alternative choice for the second module is Transformer-based model. As a second proposed architecture, we applied a

Transformer's encoder instead of an LSTM-based model over the BERT outputs in order to learn summarization-specific features. Recently, there has been an attempt at redesigning the RNN-based model by relying more on the attention mechanism in the context of text summarization. The Transformer, proposed in [20], removed the need of the RNN part by combining the attention mechanism and feedforward layers. Therefore, models based on Transformers reach state-of-the-art results, improving their performance especially on longer sequences of text. The Transformer also proved to train faster than RNN-based models because it allows for more operations running in parallel during training. Moreover, the Transformer was initially applied for the task of machine translation where it outperformed state-of-the art solutions by decreasing training time and increasing translation quality. Thanks to the similarity of the two problems of machine translation and automatic text summarization, it would be reasonable to expect that the Transformer would perform well on. The Transformer's encoder layer [14] has two sub-layers:

1. the first one is a multi-head self-attention mechanism which allows the model to jointly attend to information from different representation sub-spaces at different positions
2. the second one is a fully connected feed-forward network with a single hidden layer which is applied to each position separately and identically. This layer is used to project the attention outputs potentially giving it a richer representation

We employ a residual connection around each of the two sub-layers, followed by layer normalization. The residual connections help the network train, by allowing gradients to flow through the networks directly. The layer normalizations are used to stabilize the network which results in substantially reducing the training time necessary.

We add a positional encoding to the inputs since the Transformer model does not contain recurrence nor convolution. In our case, the positional encoding indicated the position of each sentence in the document.

Multi-Head attention consists of several attention layers running in parallel. Each of these attention layer is a linear transformation of the input representation. It allows the model to associate each input sentence in the document, to other sentences. This helps the model to capture several different aspects of the input and improve its expressive ability. Therefore, the model will be able to generate document-level features which be used as input to the final classification layer.

We will stack the Transformer's encoder several times to further encode the information, where each layer has the opportunity to learn different attention representations therefore potentially boosting the summarization power of the transformer network.

3.4   Third Module: Classification-Layer

This module takes as input the second module's output, denoted by Z_i and adds a linear layer into the outputs of the second module. Then, we compute the probability of action $a_i \in \{0, 1\}$ to sentence s_i as:

$$p(a_i|Z_i) = \sigma(W_0 Z_i + b_0)$$

where W_0 and b_0 are the model parameters, σ is the sigmoid function. To optimize the extractive module, we use a Binary Cross Entropy Loss:

$$L = -\frac{1}{N} \sum_{i=1}^{N} (y_i \log p(a_i = 1|Z_i) + (1 - y_i) \log(1 - p(a_i = 0|Z_i))$$

where $y_i \in \{0, 1\}$ is the ground-truth label for sentence s_i and N is the number of sentences. When $y_i = 1$, it indicates that sentence s_i should be extracted and be in the summary.

In order to improve the performance of our classification task, we adopted the repetition avoidance technique that was used in [18]. In fact, as illustrated in Fig. 2, while generating the predicted summary, we opt to reduce redundancy as follows: if a candidate sentence, selected to be in the generated summary, has a trigram already existed in the partial summary then it will be skipped. This technique ensures that the predicted summary has not two or more identical set of three successive words. Therefore, we avoid repetition in the produced summaries (based on LSTM or Transformers).

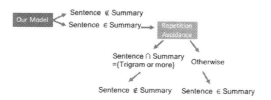

Fig. 2. Repetition avoidance

3.5   Example

An example of the summary generated by our proposed approach. Figure 3 shows that our summary reports the important information of the article and it is close to what is in the gold summary.

The next section will be devoted to the different experiments and the results we got.

4   Experimental Results

Experiments are performed on the CNN/DailyMail dataset [3] that contains news stories in CNN and Daily Mail websites. They are advantageous because

Article

Matthew Kenney smoked flakka and then ran naked. A florida man who was high on a designer drug called flakka stripped and ran naked through traffic in fort lauderdale to escape from imaginary killers who he believed stole his clothes and wanted to murder him. Matthew Kenney, 34, told police he smoked flakka before he streaked though traffic early on saturday evening while only wearing a pair of sneakers, Flakka, which can be injected, snorted, smoked, swallowed or taken with other substances, has been nicknamed '$5 insanity' for its mind-bending effects and cheap cost. after he was arrested, kenney told police he would 'rather die than be caught by these unknown people', the sun sentinel reported. he added that 'if i got hit by a car they would stop chasing me' according to a fort lauderdale police reported. kenney has previous arrests for disorderly conduct, making a riot and possession of a controlled substance. he was hospitalized for a psychiatric evaluation. Flakka is usually made from the chemical alpha-pvp, a synthetic version of the stimulant cathinone, that is the same type of chemical that is used to make bath salts. scroll down for video . Kenney, 34, ran through traffic early on saturday evening while only wearing sneakers in fort lauderdale, florida . The suspect said he was escaping imaginary killers who he believed stole his clothes and wanted to murder him . The use of flakka a designer drug that can be even stronger than crystal meth or bath salts, is up in florida . flakka resembles a mix of crack cocaine and meth and it has a a strong odor 'like a sweaty sock', 25 news reported. once ingested, the drug causes a feeling of euphoria, hallucinations and sometimes psychosis or even superhuman strength.

Gold Summary

Matthew Kenney, 34, said he smoked flakka before he went streaking . He was arrested on saturday after run through fort lauderdale, florida. Drug is made from same version of stimulant used to produce bath salts. It causes euphoria, hallucinations, psychosis and superhuman strength .

Our Generated Summary

Matthew Kenney, 34 , told police he smoked flakka before he streaked though traffic early on Saturday evening while only wearing a pair of sneakers. Flakka is usually made from the chemical alpha-pvp, a synthetic version of the stimulant cathinone. Matthew kenney smoked flakka and then ran naked.

Fig. 3. Example of the summary generated by our proposed approach

each article comes, is paired with a short set of summarized bullet points that represent meaningful highlights. The unique characteristics of this dataset such as long documents, and ordered multi-sentence summaries present interesting challenges. In order to make a fair comparison with recent text summarization approaches, we used the standard splits of [3] for training (287,113 samples), validation (13,368 samples), and testing (11,490 samples).

4.1 Evaluation Measures

As evaluation measures, we opt for the same metrics used to evaluate the state-of-the-art solutions. The most common evaluation metric is ROUGE score. In addition to that, BERTscore is also used to assess the performance of a summarizer model.

ROUGE Scores. One of the automatic evaluation metrics is ROUGE score [12], which is a measure of overlapping n-grams in the generated summary and one or several reference summaries constructed by humans. The most commonly used versions in previous studies are:

- ROUGE-1 (R1) refers to the overlap of uni-gram(each word) between the system and reference summaries
- ROUGE-2 (R2) refers to the overlap of bi-grams between the system and reference summaries
- ROUGE-L (RL): refers to the Longest Common Sub-sequence. It takes into account sentence level structure similarity naturally and identifies longest co-occurring in sequence n-grams automatically.

For each metric we computed three scores [12]; Precision, Recall and F1-score. ROUGE scores have a major limitation as an evaluation metric. In fact, as ROUGE scores only measure token hard-match, in some cases they will penalize two sentences conveying exactly the same semantic information, but highly reward sentences with completely different semantics yet in similar surface forms.

BERTscore (BT). It is a recently proposed evaluation metric in [24]. Similar to ROUGE score, BERTscore computes a cosine similarity score for each token in the generated summaries with each token in the reference summaries. By computing token similarity using contextualized word embeddings provided by BERT [6], BERTScore successfully incorporates semantic information behind sentences, thus can provide better evaluations for cases where ROUGE score fails to account for meaning-preserving lexical and semantic diversity.

Correlation Between BT and ROUGE. A case study was done in [26] on 2000 cases randomly sampled from the test set of CNN dataset to compare between BERTScore and ROUGE score. The correlation between the two metrics can be explained by the fact that when ROUGE score is maximized, the number of overlapping tokens in reference summaries and predicted summaries are high. In this case, BERTscore is also high as BERTscore between two identical sets of words is 100%. However, having a high BERTscore does not lead to obtain good ROUGE scores as reference and predicted summaries can have the semantic information with completely different words.

4.2 Results

In order to compare our approaches to the existing state-of-the-art, we will take into consideration only the F1-score of each evaluation metric as it is the weighted average of Precision and Recall. The setting used for evaluation was structured as the following: in the first approach, we tested the LSTM then the BiLSTM as a second module. While in the second approach, we stacked the Transformer several times. As mentioned in the previous section, the first and the third modules in both approaches are the same. As we notice in Table 1, the BiLSTM-based model performs better than the LSTM as it takes into consideration both the left and the right context for each input sequence. However, while analyzing the obtained results, we noticed that the Transformer-based approach yields great results compared to the LSTM-based models. This can be explained by the fact

Table 1. Best results of our proposed approaches using F1-score of each evaluation metric.

	R1	R2	RL	BT
First approach				
LSTM	34,24	13,93	30,12	61,85
BiLSTM	36,71	14,62	33,24	**62,34**
Second approach				
1 Transformer	39,72	17,12	36,13	74,14
2 Transformers	40,37	17,51	37,41	86,83
3 Transformers	41,08	18,23	38,92	**86,92**

Table 2. Testing results on the CNN/DailyMail dataset using ROUGE F1.

Model	R1	R2	RL	BT
Extractive models				
Our model	41,08	18,23	**38,92**	**86,92**
Attentive Encoder-based	38.80	12.61	33.85	–
SummaRuNNer	39.60	16.20	35.30	–
HIBERT	42.37	19.95	38.83	–
Abstractive models				–
RNNabs	35.46	13.30	32.65	–
RL	41.69	19.47	37.92	–
RLbertscore	**43.28**	18.69	36.58	62.77
Hybrid models				
Unified model	40.68	17.97	37.13	–
Sharing BERT	41.76	19.31	38.86	–

that, unlike RNNs models, Transformers can handle long sequences with long range of dependencies. In addition, to achieve a higher evaluation scores, the Transformer trains faster and can learn on longer input and output sequences before running out of memory. As illustrated in Table 2, the approach with 3 stacked Transformers shows the best performance so we will compare its scores with the proposed systems mentioned in the second chapter state-of-the-art solutions. Note that our best model is based on 3 Transformers. As illustrated in Table 2, not all systems are evaluated with BERTscore and unfortunately, we did not find an extractive approach that was evaluated with BERTscore because it is a very recent evaluation metric. From the obtained results, our second approach based on three stacks of Transformers outperforms the state-of-the-art result in ROUGE-L and BERTscore. On the one hand, the good score of ROUGE-L shows that our model can generate informative and coherent summaries.

In addition, the highest BERTscore obtained by our approach, can be explained by using an extractive approach as the system summaries, which are semantically very close to the reference summaries. Moreover, we can also notice that pre-trained based summarization approaches [25] and [22] using BERT, have the best performances. We can then conclude that the powerful architecture of BERT helps automatic summarization systems to achieve the highest scores. Furthermore, based on the ROUGE-1 and ROUGE-2 scores, our model is also comparable with most mentioned approaches. In fact, compared to the models [7,16,17] which use RNN-based models, our model achieves better performance. This can be explained by the use of Transformers and its advantages against RNNs models. We can add to that our second approach achieves almost the similar performance of hybrid models [9] and [22] knowing that these systems combine the pros of extractive and abstractive models. However, our model has an advantage against hybrid approaches considering its fast training without forgetting that these methods are costly to create summaries.

5 Conclusion

In this paper, we propose a new automatic text summarization method. This work focus on extractive model because it will be easier to apply it on any document independently of its language. Different modules have been done: (i) Bert module, (ii) LSTM or Transformer models, and (iii) classification layer. Experimental results shows the ability of our models to extract informative contents and proves that the Transformer-based models outperform LSTM-based models. As future works, our proposed approach can be improved by carrying out more hyper parameter tuning for better performance, which has not been exhaustively performed due to limited time. It is also possible to use a reward function as a linear combination of ROUGE and BERTScore that better approximates human evaluation. Experimentations on different real world datasets will be tested.

References

1. Cai, L., Zhou, S., Yan, X., Yuan, R.: A stacked bilstm neural network based on coattention mechanism for question answering. Comput. Intell. Neurosci. 1–12 (2019)
2. Celikyilmaz, A., Bosselut, A., He, X., Choi, Y.: Deep communicating agents for abstractive summarization. In: Conference of the North American Chapter of the Association for Computational Linguistics, pp. 1662–1675. Louisiana (2018)
3. Chen, D., Bolton, J., Manning, C.D.: A thorough examination of the CNN/Daily Mail reading comprehension task. In: Computational Linguistics Association, pp. 2358–2367. Germany (2016)
4. Cheng, J., Lapata, M.: Neural summarization by extracting sentences and words, pp. 484–494 (2016)
5. Dalal, V., Malik, L.: A survey of extractive and abstractive text summarization techniques. In: International Conference on Emerging Trends in Engineering and Technology, pp. 109–110. USA (2013)
6. Devlin, J., Chang, M.W., Lee, K., Toutanova, K.: Bert: pre-training of deep bidirectional transformers for language understanding (2018)
7. Feng, C., Cai, F., Chen, H., de Rijke, M.: Attentive encoder-based extractive text summarization. In: International Conference on Information and Knowledge Management, pp. 1499–1502. USA (2018)
8. Gong, Y., Luo, X., Zhu, K., Ou, W., Li, Z., Duan, L.: Automatic generation of Chinese short product titles for mobile display. In: Proceedings of the AAAI Conference on Artificial Intelligence, pp. 9460–9465 (2019)
9. Hsu, W.T., Lin, C.K., Lee, M.Y., Min, K., Tang, J., Sun, M.: A unified model for extractive and abstractive summarization using inconsistency loss. In: Computational Linguistics Association, pp. 132–141. Australia (2018)
10. Kågebäck, M., Mogren, O., Tahmasebi, N., Dubhashi, D.: Extractive summarization using continuous vector space models. In: Workshop on Continuous Vector Space Models and their Compositionality, pp. 31–39. Sweden (2014)

11. KNIME: Once Upon A Time ... by LSTM Network (2019). https://www.knime.com/blog/text-generation-with-lstm
12. Lin, C.Y.: ROUGE: a package for automatic evaluation of summaries. In: Text Summarization Branches Out, pp. 74–81. Spain (2004)
13. Lin, Z., et al.: A structured self-attentive sentence embedding. In: International Conference on Learning Representations (2017)
14. Mozer, M.: BERT Does Business: Implementing the BERT Model for Natural Language Processing at Wayfair (2019)
15. Murao, K., et al.: A case study on neural headline generation for editing support. In: Computational Linguistics Association. Minnesota (2019)
16. Nallapati, R., Zhai, F., Zhou, B.: Summarunner: a recurrent neural network based sequence model for extractive summarization of documents. In: CoRR (2017)
17. Nallapati, R., Zhou, B., Dos Santos, C., Gulcehre, C., Xiang, B.: Abstractive text summarization using sequence-to-sequence RNNs and beyond. In: Conference on Computational Natural Language Learning, pp. 280–290 (2016)
18. Paulus, R., Xiong, C., Socher, R.: A deep reinforced model for abstractive summarization. In: International Conference on Learning Representations (2018)
19. Song, K., Wang, B., Feng, Z., Liu, R., Liu, F.: Controlling the amount of verbatim copying in abstractive summarization. In: Conference on Artificial Intelligence, pp. 8902–8909 (2020)
20. Vaswani, A., et al.: Attention is all you need. In: Advances in Neural Information Processing Systems, pp. 5998–6008 (2017)
21. Wang, W., Chang, B.: Graph-based dependency parsing with bidirectional LSTM. In: Computational Linguistics Association, pp. 2306–2315. Germany (2016)
22. Wei, R., Huang, H., Gao, Y.: Sharing pre-trained BERT decoder for a hybrid summarization. In: Chinese Computational Linguistics, pp. 169–180 (2019)
23. Yasunaga, M., et al.: ScisummNet: a large annotated corpus and content-impact models for scientific paper summarization with citation networks. In: Conference on Artificial Intelligence (2019)
24. Zhang, T., Kishore, V., Wu, F., Weinberger, K.Q., Artzi, Y.: Bertscore: evaluating text generation with BERT. In: International Conference on Learning Representations (2020)
25. Zhang, X., Wei, F., Zhou, M.: Hibert: document level pre-training of hierarchical bidirectional transformers for document summarization. In: Computational Linguistics Association, pp. 5059–5069. Italy (2019)
26. hui Zhang, Y., Wang, R., Zhou, Z.: Improving neural abstractive summarization via reinforcement learning with Bertscore. In: Conference on Empirical Methods in Natural Language Processing, pp. 4078–4087. Belgium (2019)

Soft Computational Techniques to Discover Unique and Precise Knowledge from Big Data

D. Basavesha[1(✉)], S. Bharathi[2], and Piyush Kumar Pareek[3]

[1] Sridevi Institute of Engineering and Technology, Tumakuru, India
[2] Dr. Ambedkar Institute of Technology, Bangalore, India
[3] East West College of Engineering, Bangalore, India

Abstract. Big Data is playing a key role in diverse areas worldwide as these contains vast amount of essential information. The security as well as privacy of the data has become an unfathomable provocation that requests more awareness so as to achieve provide well-organized way of transference with secrecy perspective as the information consists of huge amount of important data. From the past few years, Data achieved a lot of observation by investigation group. The data was developed in large scale in about each area which is unprocessed as well as unstructured. Discovering awareness on appropriate data through huge raw information is the vital confrontation, existing nowadays. Different soft computing techniques and computational intelligence have been suggested for systematic information examination. These are mostly used in Artificial Intelligence (AI) computing technique that take part in an essential part in present big information confrontation by pre-refining as well as restructuring data. The administration domains in which conventional fuzzy sets and higher order fuzzy sets have shown exceptional results. Even though, this investigation domain in "fuzzy techniques in Big Data" is getting a few observations, there is a powerful demand for an inspiration to uplift investigators to research a lot in this arena. This paper organized bibliometric learning on upcoming growth in this area of "fuzzy methods in big information". Dilatory, a juxtapose examination is done on the fuzzy methods in information after examining the majority of effective works in this area.

Keywords: Algorithm · Big Data · Fuzzification · Fuzzy techniques · MapReduce · Soft computational

1 Introduction

The digital transition has influenced about all outlooks of contemporary community. The former decade has shown immense development in the field of mobility, automation, IoT, internet, health and familiar fields. This development is leading to colossal data-capturing prerequisites, and data generation prerequisites [1].

© Springer Nature Switzerland AG 2021
B. Villazón-Terrazas et al. (Eds.): KGSWC 2021, CCIS 1459, pp. 321–329, 2021.
https://doi.org/10.1007/978-3-030-91305-2_24

As a result, Big Data has nowadays become a completely well-known scientific field. This paper allows an outline of the present research attempts in Big Data science, with specific significance on its request, as well as conceptual basis. Data driven outlook have become a pivotal part in most of the scientific areas, as well as in the humanities, social sciences, financial areas and the business [1]. The provided data is constantly designed via human activity, the ability to identify actionable insights, sensor information, financial transactions, and handed-down trends have become a concern for many institutions. The Centre of attention for Big Data research is basically on four different properties, though in a distinct way a huge number of these properties are contemplated:

- Velocity: Real-time data hike number of challenges as acceptable refinery power must be located to provide a systematic evaluation within particular time variants. Although, depending on the type and dynamics of distinct data, different techniques are required to be executed to give enough efficiency.
- Volume: The quantity of data developed daily is vast. The amalgamation of real-time and conventional data gives a wealth of data to identify the correct and best conclusion process.
- Veracity: Information is likely to contain counter information, which could jeopardize the complete process of acquisition, evaluation, and administration of information.
- Variety: Information division of different types, formats, and structures. For example, data is accumulated from video or audio sources, as well as from textual and sensual sources, to name but a few. This needs suitable tools and methods that can be used in properly dealing with the distinct data types.

The divisional element is the basic method in information extracting and broadly handed-down in different fields [3]. Data mining is a categorization basis which provides articles in gathering to decide categories. Normally, the main concept of categorization is to perfectly determine the conclusion category for each and every part in the big data by handling the structured prototype. The conventional data in categorization project is identically divided into two different data parts: first for constructing the prototype; and the second for testing the prototype. The decision tree algorithm is the mostly handed-down categorization algorithm. But today, the conventional decision tree algorithms have reached many provocations due to the increased development of information. Firstly, As the memory storing capability is bounded, various computations enhanced to external storing feature [4]. Secondly, information becomes enormously gigantic; the method of restructuring a decision tree model is very time-consuming. Hence, expand the input/output cost.

By this paper, a new perspective is conducted to divide the information, by the parts of Fuzzy Logic, the open-source software Hadoop and the C4.5 decision tree algorithm. The primary step is to fuzzily the information to divide it utilizing the fuzzification techniques and save it into HDFS. Subsequently, the information is saved into HDFS, we conclude that the set of instructions of the C4.5 algorithm have relevance on information by utilizing the MapReduce programming prototype. From this, it can be concluded that the aim of this enhanced technique is to fuzzify the algorithm so as to take care of the imprecision and uncertainty information, and so as to divide the complete big data utilizing the fuzzified algorithm in the absence of creating the difficulty at the running time [5]. Fuzzy Systems (FS) are those methods that utilize the fuzzy set concept created by different researchers. The fuzzy set concept provides the computing presentation as well as refining of uncertain as well as imprecise data, that are huge in the present scenario [6]. Actually, many provided computer outlook cannot directly refine data with uncertainty and imprecision, creating fuzzy systems a precious option to study with domains representing these values. Rule-based fuzzy systems, specific class of fuzzy system, utilizing a justification method based on estimate justification which is capable to represent the subjectivity as well as ambiguity existing in human justification.

The fuzzy systems secure awareness presented by basis of regulations. A fuzzy system divides an Inference Mechanism (IM) and a Knowledge Base (KB) [7]. The Knowledge Base consists of two parts basically. The first one is-Fuzzy Rule Base (FRB) and the second one is-Fuzzy Database (FDB). The Fuzzy Rule Base consists of the regulations that create the main structure. These regulations are structurally dependent on fuzzy sets delivering the quality of the structure, saved in the fuzzy database. The Fuzzy rule base and Fuzzy database are utilized to divide new instances [8]. Advances in data mining and machine learning methods for classification and regression open the door of identifying complex patterns from domain sensitive data [9]. There is direct relation between deep learning and diagnosis, Deep learning will help in diagnosis and the prediction of disease spread [10,11]. Artificial intelligence (AI) and machine learning (ML) methods for various purposes against the COVID-19 outbreak have increased because of their significant advantages [12]. Scalable database management systems (DBMS)—both for update intensive application workloads as well as decision support systems for descriptive and deep analytics—are a critical part of the cloud infrastructure and play an important role in ensuring the smooth transition of applications from the traditional enterprise infrastructures to next generation cloud infrastructures [13]. Omics facilities are restricted to affluent regions, and personalized medicine is likely to widen the growing gap in health systems between high and low-income countries. This is mirrored by an increasing lag between our ability to generate and analyze big data [14].

2   Literature Review

Fatima Es-sabery et al. [15] conducted a research on "A Map reduce C4.5 Decision Tree Algorithm based on Fuzzy Rule-Based system" where he focused on hybrid approach to suggest a trending C4.5 decision tree algorithm utilizing fuzzy set concept and logic to hold imprecision as well as undetermined information, and Hadoop in creating our work. Through this paper, he concluded that the normal reasoning technique is used to set the fuzzy regulations to divide the latest examples as well as examine the impact of the suggested prototype. The upcoming study is to combine the complication neural network, decision tree and fuzzy logic so as to find the wrong news, bringing up into consideration distinct variables connected to fruitful mining.

Fakhitah Ridzuan et al. [17] wrote a paper on 'A Review on Data Cleansing Methods for Big Data' The writer handed-down the data of cleansing refinery, the provided data cleansing techniques and the challenges of information cleansing for big data. The data mining refinery is complicated as well as timely process so as to assure the mining information gives good aspect of information. The essentiality of domain expertise in information mining refinery is unacceptable as validation as well as verification is the key points on the mined information. This paper focuses at viewing the provided data cleansing techniques particularly for big data. Hence, information mining platform provides to complete information feature standard and complete big data identification, hence this paper characterizes the information mining provocation in big data.

Mirza Golam Kibria et al. [16] conducted a research on the Big Data Analytics and Artificial Intelligence in Next-Generation Wireless Networks. A set of network optimization and design schemes are represented concerned data analytics. This paper gives a discussion of challenges and the profits of adapting big data analytics. A novel idea of self-aware, proactive, and predictive networking and self-adaptive is much required. The network operators have authorization to large amounts of information, especially from the subscribers and the networks. A set of network design and optimization schemes are represented in regards with the data analytics. This paper gives a discussion of challenges and the profits of adopting artificial intelligence, ML, and big data analytics in the upcoming peer group communication systems.

3   Methodology

3.1   Design

From a security standpoint, big data has been really important in today's world. Various techniques for discovering knowledge from big data have been studied. Big Data methods and necessary challenges must be hold by an essential research initiative. Various researchers have identified new approaches for Big Data and soft computational methods. As a result, it's critical to look at any new approaches or techniques to address the current data problems. Figure 1 illustrates the improved algorithm with the help of Fuzzy technique to discover data.

3.2   Instrument

This test was carried out with a desktop mounted on with a 64-bit operating system and 16 GB of RAM. For a variety of factors, this MATLAB has been recognized of the most valuable pieces of software throughout the last decade. Inside MATLAB, there are a number of interesting tools that provide especially for applications for solving a plethora of issues.

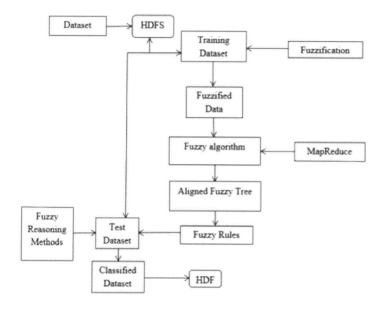

Fig. 1. Illustrates flow chart of optimized algorithm.

3.3   Data Analysis

– Save the dataset in the Hadoop disperse.
– Put in the fuzzification technique to fuzzify big data to fuzzy set, in this study we utilize the fuzzification technique known as triangular membership function (MFs).
– Subsequently, the fuzzification refinery is finished; the fuzzified information is secured in information set into HDFS.
– Put in the aligned fuzzy algorithm.
– Subsequently, the running as well as implementation of the aligned fuzzy C4.5, the aligned fuzzy tree is developed, and this outcome decision tree was utilized to reduce the fuzzy regulation.
– After the Inference regulation, the conventional and extensive reasoning techniques were utilized to divide the new instances. At last, secure the categorization outcome in the HDFS.

The below table illustrates the list of publicly provided diabetes datasets that have independent qualities such as several symptoms of diabetes, and a rely-on feature that depicts whether the individual is diabetic or not. In the Table 1, there are number of fields such as dataset titles, papers that are handed-down in this data collection and a proper description regarding the datasets are mentioned below.

Table 1. Illustrates the different databases name and their description

Sl no	Database name	Database description
1	Pima Indians Diabetes Database	The dataset contains 625 sample with 4 independent variables
2	Abel Vikas Diabetes Database	The dataset contains 537 samples with 3 independent variables
3	LARS Diabetes Database	The dataset contains 635 samples with 5 independent variables
4	Diabetes Database	The dataset contains 525 samples with 2 independent variables

4   Results and Discussion

This experiment has been carried out in order to effectively evaluate and examine the different techniques to discover more knowledge from Big Data. In this part, we are representing the practical outcomes of our initiatives (MapReduce + FuzzyLogic + C4.5). These practical outcomes are achieved by putting in our initiative and other initiatives like C4.5, ID3, Fuzzy + C4.5, MapReduce + C4.5. The categorization utilizing the initiative will end up in an aligned way with the help of MapReduce prototype and Hadoop structure with HDFS. This structure divides one master junction as well as four salve junction. Then we handed-down the fuzzification technique, basically to fuzzify the tutoring information set. Subsequently, we put in our evaluation method (aligned fuzzy decision tree) to fuzzify the information we get in a fuzzy decision tree. Although, we utilized the originated fuzzy tree to find out mounted regulations. At last, we put-in the different fuzzy reasoning techniques on the regulations to divide the test instructions as well as secure the divided information into the HDFS. Figure 2 illustrates accuracy between two different approaches i.e., Approach 1 and Approach 2 while fetching the data from datasets. Figure 3 illustrates the accuracy between two different approaches i.e., Approach 1 and C4.5 while fetching the data from datasets.

Other examination is done to juxtapose some conventional approaches like, approach1 and C4.5, to determine whether the administration of fuzzy affects the categorization outcome, for first examination, we put in two outlooks on the three selected information's. This illustrates the outcome of the accuracy rate utilizing two algorithms: classical and fuzzy. In Fuzzy + C4.5algorithm, the general reasoning technique is used. The Fuzzy + C4.5algorithm are used in the conventional reasoning technique. For this work, we will utilize the useful technique to divide the latest examples. We have also reduced the administration of fuzzy logic on C4.5 which provides us changing the categorization correctness of the conventional C4.5. Hence, in this study, we will put in the fuzzy algorithm. At last, we focus that the utilization of the MapReduce prototype lessens the used time acquired in C4.5 on a large scale of information. Consequently, with

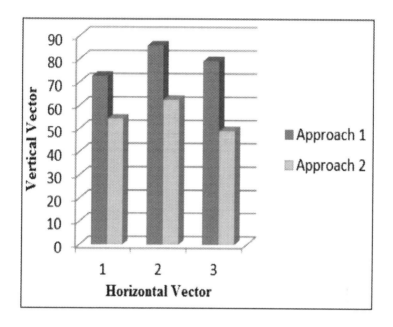

Fig. 2. Accuracy rate while using Approach 1 and Approach 2

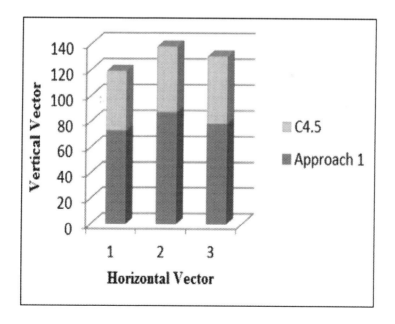

Fig. 3. Accuracy rate while using C4.5 and Approach 1

this paper, we have collaborated fuzzy logic, MapReduce and C4.5, so that, we can assess the representation of the outlook Fuzzy Logic + C4.5 + MapReduce.

5   Conclusion

Big Data is playing a main role in different areas worldwide as these contains vast amount of necessary information. This paper changed the decision tree algorithm at the point of using with constant-valued variables. Fuzzy logic is brought up for this change. This first phase is conducted to handle the imprecise and uncertainty information. For second step, aligned fuzzy algorithm is put in to make the decision tree, and after that mine the dataset of fuzzy regulation. At last, the extensive reasoning technique is put in to create the fuzzy regulation to divide the present examples and after that examine the impact of our presented prototype. Basically, the presented outlook gathers Hadoop framework, fuzzy logic and C4.5 decision tree. To determine the effect of the presented prototype (MapReduce+FuzzyLogic + C4.5), a few another outlooks such as ID3, FuzzyLogic + C4.5, C4.5, are used to distinguish with the presented one.

As we go through distinct methods that have been used so far and distinguish models that are made so far for diabetes diagnosis, we establish that they have demonstrated to give correctly high accuracies. With our core arenas of investigation that includes two methods namely data extracting and fuzzy logic we draw the different conclusions. Fuzzy logic methods have successfully presented accuracies as high as 96%. Through this study we show that Fuzzy Inference Systems are systematic with less complexity and high accuracies. Our upcoming study is to combine the intricacy fuzzy logic, neural network and decision tree so as to discover more and more data from Big Data. There is powerful proof that commerce presentation is enhanced efficiently through information-driven decision creating, information-science techniques, and dataset technologies based on big data.

References

1. Es-sabery, F.: A MapReduce C4.5 decision tree algorithm based on fuzzy rule-based system, 1–54 (2021)
2. Cheng, S., Zhang, Q., Qin, Q.: Big data analytics with swarm intelligence, 5–6 (2021). https://doi.org/10.1108/IMDS-06-2015-0222/full/html
3. Oussous, A., Benjelloun, F., Ait, A.: Big data technologies: a survey. J. King Saud Univ. Comput. Inf. Sci. **30**, 431–448 (2018)
4. African, S.: Big data, analytics and artificial intelligence for sustainability. Sci. African **9**, 1–14 (2021)
5. Thakkar, H., Shah, V., Yagnik, H., Shah, M.: Comparative anatomization of data mining and fuzzy logic techniques used in diabetes prognosis. Clin. eHealth **4**, 12–23 (2021)
6. Provost, F., Fawcett, T.: Data science and its relationship to big data and data-driven decision making. Big Data **1**(1), 1–12 (2021)

7. Access, O., Hariri, R.H., Fredericks, E.M., Bowers, K.M.: Uncertainty in big data analytics: survey, opportunities, and challenges. J. Big Data **6**(1), 1–16 (2019)
8. Yang, C., Huang, Q., Li, Z., Liu, K., Hu, F.: Big data and cloud computing: innovation opportunities and challenges. Int. J. Digit. Earth **10**(1), 13–53 (2017)
9. Reza, M.R., et al.: Automatic diabetes and liver disease diagnosis and prediction through SVM and KNN algorithms. In: Hassanien, A.E., Bhattacharyya, S., Chakrabati, S., Bhattacharya, A., Dutta, S. (eds.) Emerging Technologies in Data Mining and Information Security. AISC, vol. 1300, pp. 589–599. Springer, Singapore (2021). https://doi.org/10.1007/978-981-33-4367-2_56
10. Gaurav, D., Rodriguez, F.O., Tiwari, S., Jabbar, M.A.: Review of machine learning approach for drug development process. In: Deep Learning in Biomedical and Health Informatics, pp. 53–77. CRC Press (2021)
11. Raoof, S.S., Jabbar, M.A., Tiwari, S.: Foundations of deep learning and its applications to health informatics. In: Deep Learning in Biomedical and Health Informatics: Current Applications and Possibilities (2021)
12. Dogan, O., Tiwari, S., Jabbar, M.A., Guggari, S.: A systematic review on AI/ML approaches against COVID-19 outbreak. Complex Intell. Syst. **7**, 2655–2678 (2021)
13. Agrawal, D., Das, S., El Abbadi, A.: Big data and cloud computing: current state and future opportunities. In: Proceedings of the 14th International Conference on Extending Database Technology, pp. 530–533. ACM (2011)
14. Alyass, A., Turcotte, M., Meyre, D.: From big data analysis to personalized medicine for all: challenges and opportunities. BMC Med. Genomics **8**, 1–33 (2015)
15. Es-sabery, F., Hair, A.: A MapReduce C4.5 decision tree algorithm based on fuzzy rule-based system. Fuzzy Inf. Eng. **11**(4), 446–473 (2019). https://doi.org/10.1080/16168658.2020.1756099
16. Kibria, M.G., Nguyen, K., Villardi, G.P., Zhao, O., Ishizu, K., Kojima, F.: Big data analytics, machine learning, and artificial intelligence in next-generation wireless networks. IEEE Access **6**, 32328–32338 (2018). https://doi.org/10.1109/ACCESS.2018.2837692
17. Ridzuan, F., Zainon, W.M.N.W.: A review on data cleansing methods for big data. Procedia Comput. Sci. **161**, 731–738 (2019). https://doi.org/10.1016/j.procs.2019.11.177. ISSN 1877-0509

Correction to: An Enhanced Meta-model to Generate Web Forms for Ontology Population

Petko Rutesic, Mirjana Radonjic-Simic, and Dennis Pfisterer[iD]

Correction to:
Chapter "An Enhanced Meta-model to Generate
Web Forms for Ontology Population"
in: B. Villazón-Terrazas et al. (Eds.): *Knowledge Graphs*
***and Semantic Web*, CCIS 1459,**
https://doi.org/10.1007/978-3-030-91305-2_9

In the originally published version of chapter 9 the two references were incomplete. The references [5] and [9] have been extended in the revised version.

The updated version of this chapter can be found at
https://doi.org/10.1007/978-3-030-91305-2_9

Author Index

Printed in the United States
by Baker & Taylor Publisher Services